Researching Multilingualism

Researching Multilingualism explicitly engages with the new sociolinguistics of multilingualism, addressing contemporary diversities, the globalized communicative order and the particular social and cultural conditions of our times. It shows how research practice is being re-imagined and reshaped, critically and ethnographically. Sixteen chapters by leading authorities and key emerging researchers illustrate the range of current methodological innovation. The chapters are organized around five themes covering:

- Researching trajectories, multilingual repertoires and identities
- Researching discourses, policies and practices on different scales
- Researching multilingual communication and multisemioticity online
- Multilingualism in research practice: voices, identities and research reflexivity
- Ethnographic monitoring and critical collaborative analysis for social change

This state-of-the-art overview of the new research landscape and of new research approaches to the study of language and literacy practices in multilingual contexts will be of interest to all students and researchers working in a range of fields such as Linguistics, Applied Linguistics, Anthropology, Education, Social Policy, and Communication and Cultural Studies.

Marilyn Martin-Jones is an Emeritus Professor and founding Director of the MOSAIC Centre for Research on Multilingualism, School of Education, University of Birmingham. Her recent publications include: *Multilingualism, Discourse and Ethnography* (co-edited with Sheena Gardner, Routledge 2012) and the *Routledge Handbook of Multilingualism* (co-edited with Adrian Blackledge and Angela Creese, Routledge 2012). She is also editor of the Routledge book series: *Critical Studies in Multilingualism* (with Joan Pujolar).

Deirdre Martin, Professor and Head of the Centre for Language, Culture and Learning at Goldsmiths, University of London, 2014–2016, is the author of *Language Disabilities in Cultural and Linguistic Diversity* (2009), and editor of *Researching Dyslexia in Multilingual Settings* (2013).

Researching Multilingualism
Critical and ethnographic perspectives

**Edited by Marilyn Martin-Jones and
Deirdre Martin**

LONDON AND NEW YORK

First published 2017
by Routledge
2 Park Square, Milton Park, Abingdon, Oxon OX14 4RN

and by Routledge
711 Third Avenue, New York, NY 10017

Routledge is an imprint of the Taylor & Francis Group, an informa business

© 2017 Marilyn Martin-Jones and Deirdre Martin

The right of Marilyn Martin-Jones and Deirdre Martin to be identified as the authors of the editorial material, and of the authors for their individual chapters, has been asserted in accordance with sections 77 and 78 of the Copyright, Designs and Patents Act 1988.

All rights reserved. No part of this book may be reprinted or reproduced or utilised in any form or by any electronic, mechanical, or other means, now known or hereafter invented, including photocopying and recording, or in any information storage or retrieval system, without permission in writing from the publishers.

Trademark notice: Product or corporate names may be trademarks or registered trademarks, and are used only for identification and explanation without intent to infringe.

British Library Cataloguing-in-Publication Data
A catalogue record for this book is available from the British Library

Library of Congress Cataloguing-in-Publication Data
A catalog record for this book has been requested

ISBN: 978-0-415-74841-4 (hbk)
ISBN: 978-0-415-74842-1 (pbk)
ISBN: 978-1-3154-0534-6 (ebk)

Typeset in Times New Roman
by Out of House Publishing

Contents

List of figures	viii
List of contributors	ix
Acknowledgements	xiv

1	Introduction	1
	MARILYN MARTIN-JONES AND DEIRDRE MARTIN	

PART 1
Researching trajectories, multilingual repertoires and identities — 29

2	Narrative analysis in migrant and transnational contexts	31
	MIKE BAYNHAM AND ANNA DE FINA	
3	Biographical approaches to research in multilingual settings: Exploring linguistic repertoires	46
	BRIGITTA BUSCH	
4	The risks and gains of a single case study	60
	KAMRAN KHAN	
5	Researching student mobility in multilingual Switzerland: Reflections on multi-sited ethnography	73
	MARTINA ZIMMERMANN	

PART 2
Researching discourses, policies and practices on different scales — 87

6	Nexus analysis as scalar ethnography for educational linguistics	89
	FRANCIS M. HULT	

vi   *Contents*

7 Critical ethnography of language policy: A semi-confessional tale   105
DAVID CASSELS JOHNSON

8 Investigating visual practices in educational
settings: Schoolscapes, language ideologies and
organizational cultures   121
PETTERI LAIHONEN AND TAMÁS PÉTER SZABÓ

PART 3
Researching multilingual communication and
multisemioticity online   139

9 Methodologies for researching multilingual online texts and
practices   141
DAVID BARTON AND CARMEN LEE

10 Investigating multilingualism and multisemioticity as
communicative resources in social media   155
SIRPA LEPPÄNEN AND SAMU KYTÖLÄ

11 Virtual ethnographic approaches to researching
multilingualism online   172
AOIFE LENIHAN AND HELEN KELLY HOLMES

PART 4
Multilingualism in research practice: Voices, identities and
researcher reflexivity   187

12 Reflexive ethnographic research practice in
multilingual contexts   189
MARILYN MARTIN-JONES, JANE ANDREWS AND DEIRDRE MARTIN

13 Reflexivity in team ethnography: Using researcher
vignettes   203
ANGELA CREESE, JASPREET KAUR TAKHI AND
ADRIAN BLACKLEDGE

14 Researching children's literacy practices and identities in
faith settings: Multimodal text-making and talk about text as
resources for knowledge-building   215
VALLY LYTRA, EVE GREGORY AND ARANI ILANKUBERAN

Contents vii

15 Multilingual dynamics in the research process: Transcribing
   and interpreting interactional data   229
   SABINA VAKSER

PART 5
Ethnographic monitoring and critical collaborative
analysis for social change   245

16 Countering unequal multilingualism through ethnographic
   monitoring   247
   HALEY DE KORNE AND NANCY H. HORNBERGER

17 Ethnographic monitoring and the study of complexity   259
   JEF VAN DER AA AND JAN BLOMMAERT

   Name Index   272
   Subject Index   275

Figures

3.1	Participants are asked to map their 'languages' and 'ways of speaking' with regard to a body silhouette	54
6.1	Intersecting discourses in nexus analysis	93
8.1	Panopticon classroom (designed for teaching music)	128
8.2	Classroom for group and individual work (designed for teaching arts)	129
8.3	The dominance of 'British English'	130
8.4	Beyond 'British English'	131
8.5	Hidden Slovak national symbols in a Hungarian minority school	134
8.6	Hungarian national symbols displayed through alphabet cards in Slovakia	135
10.1	Mikael Forssell's Twitter	161
10.2	The PISS shred	165
14.1	The Tamil 'Om'	222
14.2	Why do Hindus consider 'Om' sacred?	223

Contributors

Jane Andrews works at the University of the West of England in Bristol, UK, as an Associate Professor of Education. She teaches and conducts research in a range of areas within the field of education and has a particular interest in multilingualism, learning and children's perspectives on being multilingual.

David Barton is Professor of Language and Literacy in the Department of Linguistics at Lancaster University, UK. His most recent books are *Language Online* (with Carmen Lee 2013) and *Researching Language and Social Media* (with others 2014), both published by Routledge.

Mike Baynham is Professor in TESOL at the University of Leeds, UK. His research interests include literacy studies, narrative and migration and adult ESOL. He is currently researching translanguaging and developing research on queer migrations. Recent books include The *Future of Literacy Studies* (edited with Mastin Prinsloo, Palgrave Macmillan 2009) and *Globalization and language in contact* (edited with Stef Slembrouck and Jim Collins, Continuum 2009).

Adrian Blackledge is Professor of Bilingualism and current Director of the MOSAIC Centre for Research on Multilingualism at University of Birmingham, UK. He is author of numerous articles and books based on his research on multilingualism in education and in society. His recent books include *Heteroglossia as Practice and Pedagogy* (2014); *The Routledge Handbook of Multilingualism* (2012); *Multilingualism: A Critical Perspective* (2010).

Jan Blommaert is Professor of Language, Culture and Globalization at Tilburg University, the Netherlands, where he directs the Babylon Center for the Study of Superdiversity. He also holds appointments at Ghent University (Belgium), University of the Western Cape (South Africa) and Beijing Language and Culture University (China). His work encompasses theoretical and empirical approaches to language and globalization. He has a special interest in old and new forms of inequality that emerge from globalization processes.

x   *Contributors*

Brigitta Busch holds a Berta Karlik professorship in Applied Linguistics at the University of Vienna, Austria. Her main areas of research interest are: the connections between migration, linguistic diversity, vulnerability and resilience as well as the development of biographical approaches to research on multilingualism and speaker-centred approaches to language rights (www.heteroglossia.net).

Angela Creese is Professor of Educational Linguistics at the School of Education, University of Birmingham, UK. Her research interests are in linguistic ethnography, language ecologies, multilingualism in society and multilingual classroom pedagogy. Her most recent books are *Heteroglossia as Practice and Pedagogy* (with Adrian Blackledge, Springer 2014) and *Linguistic Ethnography* (with Fiona Copland, Sage 2015).

Anna De Fina is Professor of Italian Language and Linguistics in the Italian Department at Georgetown University, USA. Her interests and publications focus on identity, narrative, migration and diversity. Her books include *Identity in Narrative: A Study of Immigrant Discourse* (John Benjamins 2003), *Analyzing Narratives* (with A. Georgakopoulou, Cambridge University Press 2012) and *Discourse and Identity* (edited with D. Schiffrin and M. Bamberg, Cambridge University Press 2006).

Eve Gregory is Emeritus Professor of Language and Culture in Education at Goldsmiths, University of London, UK. She has directed or co-directed five ESRC-funded projects. She has also led on a Leverhulme and a Paul Hamlyn funded project and gained EU funding for research into minority ethnic children in Luxembourg. Her latest book is *Navigating Languages, Literacies and Identities: Religion in Young Lives* (with Vally Lytra and Dinah Volk, Routledge 2016).

Nancy H. Hornberger is Professor of Education at the University of Pennsylvania, USA. A prolific author and editor, her research interests include anthropology of education, bilingualism and biliteracy, language policy and Indigenous language revitalization. With sustained commitment and work with Quechua speakers and bilingual intercultural education in the Andes, beginning in 1974, she has also taught, lectured, and consulted on multilingual language policy and education, in Indigenous contexts throughout the world, including Brazil, Paraguay, Mexico, New Zealand, South Africa and Scandinavia.

Francis M. Hult is an Associate Professor at the Lund University Centre for Languages and Literature, Sweden. He investigates the management of linguistic diversity in multilingual settings using ethnographic and discourse analytic methods. He has written and lectured widely in areas such as educational linguistics, educational language policy, and linguistic landscape analysis.

Contributors xi

Arani Ilankuberan is the South Indian language collections Curator at the British Library. She is also a PhD student at the Department of Educational Studies in Goldsmiths, University of London, UK. Her thesis explores the impact of Tamil Hindu religious film on the identity of second-generation British Tamil Hindu teenagers in London. From 2009–2013 Arani was part of the BeLiFS project, working, alongside Dr. Vally Lytra, with families from the Tamil Hindu community in London.

David Cassels Johnson is an Associate Professor at the University of Iowa, USA. His research focuses on the interaction between language policies and educational opportunity. He is the author of *Language Policy* (Palgrave Macmillan 2013) and co-editor (with Francis M. Hult) of *Research Methods in Language Policy and Planning: A Practical Guide* (Wiley-Blackwell 2015).

Helen Kelly-Holmes is Professor of Applied Languages at the University of Limerick, Ireland. She has published widely on economic aspects of multilingualism, and media and multilingualism. Her publications include: *Multilingualism and the Periphery* (edited with Sari Pietikäinen, Oxford 2013), *Thematising Multilingualism in the Media* (edited with Tommaso Milani, Benjamins 2013), *Language and the Market* (edited with Gerlinde Mautner, Palgrave 2010) and *Advertising as Multilingual Communication* (Palgrave 2005).

Kamran Khan is a researcher on the ESRC project: *The UK Citizenship Process: Exploring Immigrants' Experiences* at the University of Leicester, UK. He gained his PhD at the University of Birmingham and the University of Melbourne. His research interests include citizenship, ESOL and language testing.

Haley De Korne (PhD Educational Linguistics, University of Pennsylvania) conducts research and advocacy in relation to minoritized language communities, multilingual education, and language politics. She has participated in Indigenous language education projects in a variety of contexts, most recently in Oaxaca, Mexico, and is a member of the Center for Multilingualism in Society across the Lifespan, at the University of Oslo, Norway.

Samu Kytölä is a Senior Lecturer at the Department of Languages, University of Jyväskylä, Finland. His research interests include the transculturality and multilingualism of football (soccer) discourses, particularly ethnocultural diversity and sexual minorities in football texts, the sociolinguistics of inequalities, ethnographies of ways of writing (particularly digital writing), sociolinguistic diversity in Finland, and the metapragmatics of discourses about diversity.

xii *Contributors*

Petteri Laihonen is an Academy Research Fellow at the Centre for Applied Language Studies, University of Jyväskylä, Finland. His publications deal with sociolinguistics, multilingualism, regional linguistic minorities, language ideologies, linguistic landscapes and language policy in East-Central Europe.

Carmen Lee is Associate Professor in the Department of English at the Chinese University of Hong Kong. Her research interests include internet linguistics, digital discourse and literacies, and multilingual practices online. She is co-author of the book *Language Online* (with David Barton, Routledge 2013).

Aoife Lenihan is an associate member of the Centre for Applied Language Studies at the University of Limerick . She received her PhD in Applied Language Studies from the University of Limerick, Ireland. She specializes in multilingualism, minority languages and new media. Recent publications include contributions to two edited volumes: *Digital Discourse* (edited by C. Thurlow & K. Mroczek, Oxford 2011) and *The Language of Social Media* (edited by P. Seargeant & C. Tagg, Palgrave 2014).

Sirpa Leppänen is a Professor at the Department of Languages at the University of Jyväskylä, Finland. With her research team (www.socialmediadiscourses.fi/), she investigates the ways in which resources provided by languages, other forms of semiosis and discourses are used by individuals and groups in social media and the ways in which such resources are used for social action and cultural production.

Vally Lytra is Senior Lecturer in Languages in Education, in the Department of Educational Studies at Goldsmiths, University of London, UK. She has researched multilingualism in schools, homes and communities in the UK, Greece and Switzerland. She recently published *When Greeks and Turks Meet: Interdisciplinary Perspectives on the Relationship since 1923* (Ashgate 2014) and *Languages, Literacies and Identities: Religion in Young Lives* (with Dinah Volk and Eve Gregory, Routledge 2016).

Deirdre Martin was Professor and Head of the Centre for Language, Culture and Learning at Goldsmiths, University of London, UK, from 2014 to 2016. She has directed and co-directed five ESRC-funded projects. She has also received a Leverhulme Fellowship, and worked with local and national research bodies in the UK. Her research and publications focus on multilingualism and disability.

Marilyn Martin-Jones is an Emeritus Professor and former Director of the MOSAIC Centre for Research on Multilingualism, University of Birmingham, UK. Her research focuses on multilingual discourse practices and literacies, in classrooms and community contexts, and on the ways in which such discourse practices and literacies index local and global

Contributors xiii

relations of power. She is editor of the Routledge book series: *Critical Studies in Multilingualism* (with Joan Pujolar).

Tamás Péter Szabó is a postdoctoral researcher at the University of Jyväskylä, Finland. In his current project, he is investigating various forms of discourse, ideology and interaction in Hungarian and Finnish education. His research interests include the management of diversity in institutional settings, schoolscapes, and agency in interaction.

Jaspreet Kaur Takhi joined the University of Birmingham, UK, in June 2010 as a bilingual Research Fellow on the HERA project "Investigating discourses of inheritance and identity in four multilingual European settings", to work with Adrian Blackledge and Angela Creese. Her research interests include translanguaging, negotiating identity through language, popular culture and conflict between migrant generations.

Sabina Vakser has a PhD degree from the University of Melbourne. The theme of her doctoral research was the "superdiversity of Russianness" in family settings. She also hold an MA in French from the University of Arizona. Her research interests include the sociolinguistics of mobility, transnational identity, foreign language pedagogy, and semiotic landscapes.

Jef Van der Aa is a researcher at the Department of Culture Studies, Tilburg University, the Netherlands. His work focuses on immigrant and refugee families in the Belgian care system, with a specific focus on these families' on- and off-line epistemologies of survival.

Martina Zimmermann is a Lecturer in the field of foreign languages at the University of Teacher Education in Lucerne, Switzerland. She is also associated with the Institute of Multilingualism, University of Fribourg. In her thesis, submitted in July 2016, she analysed the discourses and practices of (im-)mobility in higher education and tracked the trajectories of students across linguistic borders in Switzerland.

Acknowledgements

This volume builds on research activities that were developed under the auspices of a research capacity-building project (May 2010 to April 2013) entitled: *Researching multilingualism, multilingualism in research practice.* The project was funded by the UK's Economic and Social Research Council (ESRC), under its Researcher Development Initiative (RDI) (Round 4). The members of the project team were: Deirdre Martin (principal investigator), Marilyn Martin-Jones, Adrian Blackledge, Angela Creese and Sheena Gardner. The final conference for this project was held on the 25th and 26th March 2013 at the MOSAIC Centre for Research on Multilingualism, School of Education, University of Birmingham, UK. The participation was international, with contributions to the programme being made by scholars from ten different countries. The overall theme of the conference was: *Responding to contemporary multilingual realities, recasting research methodologies.* Our heartfelt thanks to all those who took part in this conference, and to those who contributed to the overall success of the three-year project by organising one of the regional workshops and/or by participating in the research activities based at the MOSAIC Centre at the University of Birmingham. This volume is dedicated to you all.

We would also like to thank the members of the editorial staff at Routledge who have worked with us on this particular book project from the outset: Louisa Semlyen, Sophie Jacques and Laura Sandford. Their support and guidance have been greatly appreciated.

Marilyn Martin-Jones,
MOSAIC Centre for Research on Multilingualism, School of Education,
University of Birmingham
Deirdre Martin,
Centre for Language, Culture and Learning at Goldsmiths,
University of London, 2014–2016

1 Introduction

Marilyn Martin-Jones and Deirdre Martin

Over the last two decades, sociolinguistic research on multilingualism has been transformed. Two broad processes of change have been at work: first, there have been broad epistemological shifts in the field of sociolinguistics to ethnographic and critical approaches. These broad shifts have reflected the wider turn, across the social sciences, towards poststructuralist and postmodern perspectives on social life. Second, there has been increasing focus on the study of the social, cultural and linguistic changes ushered in by globalisation, including the intensification of transnational population flows, the advent of new communication technologies, and changes taking place in the political and economic landscape of different regions of the world. These changes have had major implications for the ways in which we conceptualise the relationship between language and society and the multilingual realities of the late modern era. They have also obliged us to adjust our research lenses and recast our research methodologies. A new sociolinguistics of multilingualism is now being forged: one that takes account of the new communicative order and the particular cultural conditions of our times, while retaining a central concern with the social and institutional processes involved in the construction of social difference and social inequality. The main aim of this volume is to provide a state-of-the-art overview of this distinct new research landscape and to illustrate the ways in which research methodologies are being reshaped in different strands of critical and ethnographic research in multilingual settings.

In the first part of our chapter, we trace the ways in which epistemological shifts in the broad field of sociolinguistics have contributed to the development and consolidation of ethnographic approaches and critical approaches to research in multilingual settings. We take a wide-angle, historical approach here, so as to fully contextualise the contributions to this volume. Our starting point is with the roots of ethnography in the seminal work of Dell Hymes and John Gumperz in the 1960s and 1970s and in their intense concern with "the interaction of language and social life" (Gumperz & Hymes, 1964, 1972). We then turn to the development of critical approaches to research on multilingualism in the late 1980s/early 1990s, foregrounding in particular the transdisciplinary influence of social theory and poststructuralist thought. We chart the specific ways in which critical approaches to research were developed in

2   M. Martin-Jones and D. Martin

the field of multilingualism and we show how ethnography gained further epistemological status in research that adopted a poststructuralist perspective.

In the second part of the chapter, we then focus in on the ways in which the sociolinguistic study of multilingualism has been recast in the wake of globalisation and the ways in which it is still evolving. We consider the specific nature of the social changes ushered in by globalisation and we illustrate some of the ways in which researchers, such as those contributing to this volume, are rethinking their research goals and methods. In the third part of the chapter, we turn to the role of research in contributing to social change. We point to different ways in which concern about this role has been voiced by sociolinguists over the decades and to the specific ways in which this concern is expressed in this volume. In the fourth and final section, we then introduce the contributions to the volume, linking them to five broad themes.

Shifting epistemologies in research on multilingualism

The foundations of contemporary ethnographic research on language in social life

The foundations of contemporary ethnographic approaches to language in social life were laid, from the 1960s onwards, by Dell Hymes (e.g. 1969, 1972, 1974, 1983, 1996) and by John Gumperz (e.g. 1972, 1982, 1996, 1999). Dell Hymes' particular legacy is evident in the fact that his contributions to theory-building are cited in half of the chapters in this volume. John Gumperz' influence is evident in the continued use, and refinement, in the sociolinguistics of multilingualism of key analytic concepts such as 'repertoire' and 'contextualisation' (Gumperz, 1982), which were first forged in his extensive empirical work in multilingual contexts.

Hymes and Gumperz were developing their distinctive yet complementary ethnographic approaches to language, culture and society in an era of intense intellectual exploration. Diverse strands of research into language in interaction were emerging due to the pervasive influence of social constructionism. Some strands of research, such as pragmatics, conversation analysis and early anthropological linguistics, privileged the study of the linguistic and/or organisational features of interaction, while other strands, such as the ethnography of communication (e.g. Gumperz & Hymes, 1964, 1972) and the ethnography of speaking (e.g. Bauman & Sherzer, 1974), were explicitly rooted in the longer tradition of linguistic anthropology and, thus, ethnography was seen as the key means of knowledge building related to language in social life.

In this period, the label 'sociolinguistics' came to be used to refer to a broad range of research on language, culture and society, from conversation analysis to the ethnography of speaking. However, as Bucholtz and Hall (2008) point out:

> The difference between anthropological and linguistic approaches to sociolinguistics was also becoming apparent, with the former seeking to

Introduction 3

explicate culture through the investigation of speech events (e.g. Hymes, 1974) and interactional practice (Gumperz, 1982) and the latter largely drawing on social information to illuminate issues of linguistic structure, variation, and change.

(Bucholtz & Hall, 2008: 402)

We see traces of a tension between these different approaches in the explicit assertion of the epistemological status of ethnography by Gumperz and Hymes in their early work: first, in the title of their jointly edited volume *Directions in Sociolinguistics: The Ethnography of Communication* (Gumperz & Hymes, 1972), and second, in the title of Hymes' volume *Foundations in Sociolinguistics: An Ethnographic Approach.* In the latter volume, Hymes (1974: 83) confirmed this way of defining sociolinguistics in the following terms: " 'Sociolinguistics' is the most recent and most common term for an area of research that links linguistics with anthropology". Hymes and Gumperz were the first to dislodge the view of the relationship between language and society that had guided earlier research, namely the view that local 'communities' were stable, homogeneous entities and that language use was governed by 'community-wide' norms. Instead, they argued that attention needed to be paid to the situated ways in which language practices contribute to the ongoing construction of social identities and relationships and to the ways in which social and cultural meanings are contextualised in and through interaction. As Gumperz (1982) put it, the aim of the analysis of discourse-in-interaction was to forge a "closer understanding of how linguistic signs interact with social knowledge in discourse" (1982: 29).

Over the two decades from the 1960s to the late 1980s, a considerable body of research was built on these early foundations, in the interlinked fields of ethnography of communication and interactional sociolinguistics. Researchers espousing these approaches had ample scope for investigating speaker agency and the dynamic and situated ways in which social identities, relationships and boundaries are constructed in and through interaction in different multilingual contexts.

The development of critical and poststructuralist perspectives

By the end of the 1980s, interest had shifted to the new epistemological spaces opened up by developments in social theory, notably the turn towards poststructuralism and critical theory. Within the field of multilingualism, three linguistic anthropologists – Gal (1989), Heller (1995, 1999) and Woolard (1985, 1989) – were the first to lay the foundations of a critical, ethnographic sociolinguistics. They did this by engaging with the new lines of theory-building within the social sciences, in the work of scholars such as Bourdieu (1977, 1991), Foucault (1971, 1972) and Giddens (1990). Gal, Heller and Woolard were doing extended fieldwork in multilingual sites in Austria, French Canada and Catalonia respectively, and they were seeking

4   *M. Martin-Jones and D. Martin*

ways of linking insights from ethnographic observation and analysis of interactional practices with their analyses of wider institutional and historical processes, wider discourses about language and identity, and specific political and economic conditions.

Following the ground-breaking work of these three linguistic anthropologists, a distinctive tradition of critical, ethnographic and discourse analytic research on multilingualism emerged from the 1990s onwards, and it is clearly reflected in this volume. Some of this research has been developed at the interface with related fields such as the study of multilingual classroom discourse (e.g. Lin, 1999; Heller & Martin-Jones, 2001); the study of complementary schools and heritage language classes (e.g. Blackledge & Creese, 2010; Creese et al., Chapter 13, this volume); the ethnography of multilingual literacy practices (e.g. Martin-Jones & Jones, 2000; Warriner, 2007; Lytra et al. 2016), the ethnography of language policy (e.g. Johnson, 2009; Ramanathan, 2005; McCarty, 2011), and, more recently, visual ethnography and the study of multimodal communication (e.g. Pietikäinen, 2012). Since the late 1980s, research has been carried out in diverse cultural and historical contexts and in different domains of social life – in schools, in heritage language classes, in workplaces, in bureaucratic encounters and in local life-world settings. This research has incorporated critical reflexivity (Pennycook, 2001), while aiming to reveal the links between local multilingual practices and wider social and ideological processes. These links have been investigated in different ways, for example by focusing on the ways in which linguistic and discursive practices are bound up with the processes of social categorisation and/or exclusion that are at work in particular contexts (e.g. Heller, 1999), or by focusing on the ways in which identities and social boundaries are constructed, negotiated or contested in different multilingual settings (e.g. Pavlenko & Blackledge, 2004).

The influence of poststructuralist thought was particularly evident in the writing on language ideology that flourished in the 1990s (e.g. Gal & Woolard, 1995; Schieffelin et al. 1998; Blommaert, 1999). The research addressed the central question of "how linguistic units came to be linked to social units" (Gal & Irvine, 1995: 970), how particular language resources and ways of speaking came to be associated with simplified and essentialised social categories (e.g. categories of ethnicity or gender) or how languages came to be tied to whole populations within a particular polity. This strand of work in sociolinguistics and linguistic anthropology provided a trenchant critique of grand narratives and modernist assumptions about the links between languages and particular social groups, or between whole populations and nation-states. In its critique of the language–nation-state nexus, it had a significant historical dimension and involved tracing the discursive threads involved in the construction of nationhood in primarily unitary and essentialised terms, in different historical contexts: for instance in nineteenth-century Europe (e.g. Grillo, 1989; Rindler Schjerve, 2003; Heller, 2007), in the language revitalisation and minority rights movements of the twentieth century (e.g. Urla, 1993;

Introduction 5

Jaffe, 1999; Pujolar, 2007) and in postcolonial contexts (e.g. Errington, 2008; Stroud, 2007).

The influence of poststructuralist thinking is also visible in recent writing about language (e.g. Makoni & Pennycook, 2007; Heller, 2007; Errington 2008). For example, Makoni and Pennycook (2007: 2) argue that the notion that languages are discrete, bounded entities and "countable institutions" is a social construct. They call for critical, historical research that unpacks the discursive processes involved in the classification, naming and invention of languages. They refer to this project as the "disinvention" of languages. Given the creativity and hybridity emerging today in urban popular culture, in minority group vernaculars and in mediated communication, there is growing consensus that it is more useful to talk about linguistic resources than 'languages' and to take account of the full range of human communicative activities, online and offline. This is the stance taken by several contributors to this volume. This shift in thinking echoes Hymes' (1996: 70) early call for a focus on ways of speaking and on "varieties, modalities, styles and genres, ways of using language as a resource".

Poststructuralist perspectives and the consolidation of ethnographic approaches

Ethnography is well suited to the challenges involved in developing sociolinguistic research from a poststructuralist perspective. It involves commitment to participant observation and engagement with participants over an extended period of time, so this enables researchers to track social and ideological processes as they unfold or change over time, and to build detailed accounts of particular social and linguistic practices as they occur. At the same time, the ethnographic goal of gaining insights into the emic perspectives, beliefs and values of research participants opens up the possibility of building an understanding of the significance of ongoing social and ideological processes for the participants themselves.

A further strength of ethnography lies in the long-established tradition of designing research projects so as to include different methods of data collection and analysis, and the triangulation of data sources. Working in these ways enables researchers to uncover the complexity of the social and linguistic practices of contemporary social life (Blommaert, 2007). We return to this point later.

In addition, there is now much greater reflexivity among researchers and greater awareness of the ways in which researchers' historically and socially situated subjectivity shapes the different stages of the research process. The turn to reflexivity has largely been due to the critique of the long-established practices of ethnographic writing and representation by scholars such as Marcus and Fischer (1986) and Clifford and Marcus (1986). The need for reflexivity in research – at all stages of the research process – is a theme that recurs across the chapters of this volume. There is also ample discussion of the plural and polyphonic nature of knowledge building (see, e.g. Chapters 12–15).

6   *M. Martin-Jones and D. Martin*

Researching multilingualism in a global age

As sociolinguistic research on multilingualism was being transformed through the incorporation of poststructuralist perspectives, from the late 1980s onwards, far-reaching changes were also taking place across the world. New social, cultural and ideological conditions were being created as a result of changes in the global political economy, the expansion of capitalism, the advent of the internet and new communication technologies, the rapid increase in transnational population flows and the ever-increasing and constantly diverging circulation of material and symbolic resources. In the sociological and anthropological literature, these changes have come to be viewed as different dimensions of globalisation and there is general agreement that the political, economic, social and cultural conditions of late modernity are markedly different from earlier periods of history (e.g. Harvey, 1989; Giddens, 1990; Appadurai, 1996; Castells, 2000).

Global changes in political economy: new discourses and practices

At the political and economic level, globalisation ushered in a broad shift from a world order in which nation-states regulated markets to one in which state control over capital has been eroded in the face of the rapid expansion of capitalism and the increasing globalisation of economic activity. Nation-states have now taken on the role of facilitating globalised markets of trade and finance. These major shifts in the world political and economic order have been accompanied by a decline in industrial capitalism in the countries of the global north and west, and by the development of a tertiary sector which services global networks of production and consumption, and which facilitates modes of production that are increasingly digitally mediated.

Duchêne and Heller (2012) have argued that, in these new political and economic conditions, language and communication have taken on a new prominence and that we have seen the creation of new sites of discursive production (outside of, or indirectly related to, state control), where multilingual resources are being drawn upon in new ways. This includes the private sector, supranational bodies (such as the European Union and agencies of the United Nations such as UNESCO), non-governmental organisations (NGOs) and globalising religious organisations. Take, for example, the creation of new sites of discursive production in the private sector where multilingualism is used as a resource. Stroud and Mpendukana (2012) have shown how globalised discourses of consumption and consumer identities are being re-semioticised through the use of multilingual and multimodal resources in billboard advertising in a South African township. In this volume (Chapter 11), Kelly-Holmes and Lenihan provide us with an account of how corporations with a global reach create gateway sites on the web for consumers with different language resources.

Another significant aspect of the role of language in the new globalised economy is the rise of language industries. As da Silva et al. (2007: 187) have noted: "Today, language is still being used in the process of selling products (as a communicational tool) but, more importantly, it has become a product itself (that is, a marketable resource)". Language industries provide a whole range of services, from translation and interpreting to private language teaching, bilingual call centres, outsourced work for publishers, bilingual website design or research and development work by NGOs focusing on language policy and planning. Such industries are becoming more prominent in today's globalised multilingual world with its premium on the rapid circulation of information.

New technoscapes, new communicative practices

Arjun Appadurai (1996) characterised different facets of globalisation in terms of different and rapidly changing 'scapes'. Here, we focus on his changing "technoscapes". With the advent of new digital technologies, with the globalised spread of new technoscapes, there have been major changes in the global communicative order. The pace of communication has quickened and the time–space compression of contemporary social life has made it possible to build and sustain translocal relationships over distance (e.g. within diasporic spaces) through the use of mobile technology, new social media and the internet. In the new communicative landscape of the twenty-first century, we read and write, and we create and use texts in ways that are substantially different from those of only a few decades ago. There is constant diversification of communication media, digital artefacts (e.g. new software) and textual resources (e.g. new genres, such as blogs and tweets). There are also new ways of combining multiple modes of semiosis (e.g. colour, image or sound) with text on screen, so that meaning-making practices are now more multimodal in nature (Kress, 2003; Kress & Van Leeuwen, 2006).

Transnational population flows and new diversities

The intensification of transnational population flows in the last two or three decades has brought about far-reaching changes of a social, cultural, linguistic and demographic nature across the globe. These flows have included increased transnational labour migration and the movement of refugees fleeing war zones and oppressive governments. They have also included the movement of students in the context of 'internationalisation programmes' and expansion in competition between universities with regard to student recruitment. There are also other groups 'on the move': these include the white-collar workers and the elite employees in globalised companies, the increased number of tourists due to the expansion of the tourist industry, journalists working in international media, and staff working with international NGOs, charities and UN agencies.

We focus here on recent research related to transnational labour migration and to the movement of refugees, because it provides the wider context for

8   M. Martin-Jones and D. Martin

several chapters in this volume. New, diverging patterns of migration have given rise to much greater linguistic and cultural diversity in countries that have become key migration destinations. This social and demographic phenomenon is now referred to, across the social sciences, as "superdiversity" (Vertovec, 2007a). Over a decade ago, in his research on the changing patterns of migration to the United Kingdom (UK), Vertovec (2007a: 1024) pointed out that these patterns are characterised by a "dynamic interplay of variables among an increased number of new, small and scattered, multiple origin, transnationally connected, socio-economically differentiated and legally stratified immigrants who have arrived over the last decade". He was drawing attention to the increasingly differentiated composition, social positioning, legal status and precarity of different groups of migrant origin in the twenty-first century. In a separate article, Vertovec (2007b) also pointed out that the concept of superdiversity also takes account of the ways in which different social 'variables', such as country of origin, class, gender, sexuality, disability or generation intersect and are giving rise to greater diversification of diversity.

In recent years, sociolinguists have been turning their attention to the implications of these new patterns of transnational migration and new diversities for the study of multilingualism (e.g. Blommaert, 2010; Blommaert & Rampton, 2011; De Fina et al., 2017). Some have focused on the issues related to intersectionality, with specific reference to gender (e.g. Menard-Warwick, 2009), or with reference to disability (Martin, 2012). Others have observed that urban neighbourhoods, in particular, have become increasingly diverse and, within these spaces, there has been a "meshing and interweaving of diversities" (Martin-Jones et al., 2012: 7), in which new communicative repertoires are developing. These repertoires include local vernacular forms of English, lingua franca and the language resources of different groups of migrants or refugee origin. In addition, as Blommaert (2010) has pointed out, the social networks of migrant groups in contemporary urban neighbourhoods are both local and translocal, both real and virtual. New diasporic lines of connectedness are shaping the development of communicative repertoires and language and literacy practices.

Investigating contemporary diversities: new conceptual compasses

As a number of sociolinguists have observed, the range and complexity of the social and linguistic changes that have been taking place in the wake of globalisation pose a major challenge for those of us who are concerned with the study of multilingualism. In 2010, Blommaert indicated that investigation of changes of the kind listed above "stretches the limits of existing frameworks for analysing and understanding multilingualism and the dynamics of language change" (2010: 8). He also indicated that we need to "rethink our conceptual and analytic apparatuses" (2010: 1). This process of rethinking approaches to knowledge building has now been set in train. As in

Introduction 9

the past, new conceptual compasses and new ethnographic approaches have emerged from interdisciplinary conversations. These new ways of researching multilingualism have been married with poststructuralist perspectives and are well represented in this volume.

One recurring theme in recent research has been that of 'mobility'. Heller (2011: 56) has argued that we need to turn our gaze "from stability to mobility". She has also made the case for the adoption of a new conceptual compass – that of "trajectory" – as a means of foregrounding the flows of people, resources (material and symbolic), texts and discourses that traverse today's world. She and her colleagues in French Canada have employed this concept in their research into social change, focusing in particular on the new labour migrations that have considerable consequences for French speakers (Heller, 2011; Heller et al., 2015). However, Heller notes that trajectories are not necessarily linear pathways, or equivalent in nature. They are historically and socially situated. Moreover, as Duchêne and Heller (2012: 15/16) put it: "The landscape is uneven, unbounded and fluid, and ... social actors occupy different and differently advantageous positions with respect to access to the resources that circulate across it". Other scholars have also called for a shift of focus to mobility, while focusing in particular on the situated ways in which the communicative repertoires of different social actors are shaped through the experience of migration and the ways in which these resources circulate within transnationally connected networks. Blommaert (2010: 41) has, for example, called for the development of "a sociolinguistics of mobile resources".

Along with this conceptual shift to mobilities, mobile resources and trajectories has come a new interest in taking account of time, as well as space, in the study of language practices. For example, in research that focuses on narratives in the context of transnational migration, Baynham (2009: 131) has called for: "more complex and nuanced accounts of the ways in which orientations in space and time contribute to the construction of oral narratives". While social events, such as the telling of a story related to the experience of migration, occur in particular spaces, at particular times, speakers/storytellers also make indexical references[1] to other spaces and other times. Other worlds and other time periods are thus brought into their utterances. Moreover, as Blommaert (2010: 34) has put it, in indexing other worlds and time periods, speakers are evoking different "images of society" which are, in turn, associated with different "sociolinguistic scales" within a broader social order. For Blommaert, "scales need to be understood as 'levels' or 'dimensions' ... at which particular forms of normativity, patterns of language use and expectations thereof are organised" (Blommaert, 2010: 36). There are higher-scale levels (e.g. where institutional norms prevail) and lower-scale levels (e.g. associated with individual lives and /or local life worlds). Blommaert (2010) argues that we need to develop an approach to sociolinguistic analysis that represents linguistic and semiotic phenomena as being located and distributed across scales, from global to local and, specifically, an approach that interrogates the links between scales.[2]

10   *M. Martin-Jones and D. Martin*

With the adoption of new conceptual compasses such as mobility, mobile resources and time/space scales, the scope of contemporary ethnographic research on multilingualism looks rather different from earlier work in the ethnography of communication (e.g. Gumperz & Hymes, 1972). In that work, the focus was primarily on local social groups and on speech events that were situated at one moment in time. As Rampton et al. (2015) have remarked: "expansion of the spatio-temporal horizon of theory and analysis has been one of the most important developments since Gumperz and Hymes (1972)".

The horizons of research on multilingualism have also been significantly expanded through a broad turn to the visual dimensions of communication. Two fields of transdisciplinary research have developed quite rapidly and are represented in this volume: they include the study of linguistic landscapes in the material world and research into the multimodal and multisemiotic practices involved in the construction of virtual worlds online. In both these fields, the concern has been with the situated ways in which multilingual resources are imbricated with other semiotic resources.

Researchers concerned with linguistic landscapes in the material world have, for the most part, concentrated on detailed description and analysis of urban landscapes in particular streets and neighbourhoods (e.g. Gorter, 2006; Shohamy & Gorter, 2009; Blommaert, 2013). They have shown that critical, ethnographic research conducted in this vein serves as a valuable means of revealing the complex dimensions of diversity in such urban settings. Some of these researchers have focused on particular institutions, such as schools, employing a linguistic landscape approach, along with ethnography, to chart processes of political, social and ideological changes over time (e.g. Laihonen & Tódor, 2015; see also Laihonen & Szabó, Chapter 8, this volume).

Research concerned with the interplay between multimodal and multilingual resources in the online construction of virtual worlds has taken diverse forms, as the digital landscapes of the internet, of mobile technology and social media have changed and diversified (see Androutsopoulos, 2007; Barton & Lee, 2013 for overviews written at different points in time). As this research has shown us, digital communication is becoming increasingly multilingual although, inevitably, access to the new digital technologies is also unevenly distributed. A range of research avenues is now being opened up with regard to multilingual literacy and the use of diverse semiotic resources online. These include the investigation of the creative and nuanced ways in which young people draw on the linguistic resources and semiotic modes available to them as they negotiate virtual identities and relationships, both locally and globally, across diasporic spaces (e.g. McGinnis et al., 2007; Lam & Rosario-Ramos, 2009). It also includes studies of multiple language use in specific online communities of practice, such as those vividly portrayed in Chapters 9 and 10 of this volume, by Barton and Lee and by Leppänen and Kytölä. In addition, it includes research into the use of different scripts in

Introduction   11

online communication (e.g. Warschauer et al., 2002; Lee, 2007 and Chapter 9, by Barton and Lee, this volume).

Methodological innovation and diversification of ethnographic approaches

The interrogation of the different dimensions of globalisation and the adoption of new conceptual compasses such as those that we have just mentioned have given rise to considerable methodological innovation in critical and ethnographic research on multilingualism. The chapters in this volume illustrate key directions in which this methodological innovation is moving. As before, ethnographic approaches are favoured, but they are now being conceptualised in differing ways. Most of the research presented here could be described as "topic-oriented", in Hymes' (1996: 5) original sense: instead of aiming to provide a "comprehensive" picture of the entire way of life of a particular social group, they aim to provide focused insights into the communicative practices of particular social actors in particular institutional or life-world contexts. In these and other studies of the multilingual realities of our times, the design of research projects takes account of the particular way in which the researchers' gaze is oriented and of the particular set of conceptual compasses guiding their research, be it mobility, the shaping and use of mobile resources over time, the connections between different sociolinguistic scales or the interplay between multilingual and multimodal resources in communication online or offline.

Some ethnographic approaches are particularly well adapted to research on language and contemporary mobilities. One of these is multi-sited ethnography. It is represented in two chapters in the volume (Chapter 5, by Zimmermann; Chapter 13, by Creese et al.). Other approaches are well suited to research that takes account of sociolinguistic scales and investigates the links between scales. In Chapter 6 of this volume, Hult shows us how nexus analysis enables researchers to investigate discursive flows across different scales, through what he calls "scalar ethnography".

As researchers address the particular challenges of investigating multilingual and multisemiotic practices online, there is ongoing methodological innovation and diversification of approaches. For example, in Chapters 9 to 11 of this volume, we see resonances with wider methodological debates taking place in the study of language online. We see different vocabularies being used to describe ethnographic work. Barton and Lee (Chapter 9) refer to "ethnographically-informed approaches"; Leppänen and Kytölä (Chapter 10) write about "online ethnography", and Kelly-Holmes and Lenihan (Chapter 11) use the term "virtual ethnography". And, in both Chapters 9 and 10, we see reference to "discourse-centred online ethnography", a term first coined by Androutsopoulos (2007) to designate research that combines discourse analysis of online texts with ethnography.

There has been a process of differentiation in other areas of ethnographic research on multilingualism. This is not only reflected in the use of different

12   M. Martin-Jones and D. Martin

terms, but also in extended metacommentary about different approaches. The current range of terms includes: linguistic anthropology, linguistic ethnography,[3] ethnography of language policy,[4] sociolinguistic ethnography, ethnographic sociolinguistics and critical ethnography. These terminological differences are also evident in this volume, though the boundaries between the different 'strands' of work remain relatively porous.

A further dimension of differentiation lies in the ways in which interpretive research approaches based on different research traditions are combined with ethnography. Take, for example, the linking of narrative analysis (and, in particular, the study of story-telling practices) with ethnography, as in Chapter 2 (Baynham and De Fina); or the matching of ethnography with a case-study design, as in Chapter 4 (Khan); or the emphasis on the need to link discourse analysis of online texts with ethnography – a theme that cuts across Chapters 9–11.

The chapters in this volume also provide a window on the broadening of the range of research methods now employed in ethnographic and interpretive work related to multilingualism. Along with the long-established methods of participant observation, audio- and video-recording of interviews and analysis of moments of interaction and the production of traditional fieldwork texts, such as field notes, transcripts and descriptions of events, we read (in Chapters 12–15, in particular) about the production of a wider range of fieldwork texts, e.g. vignettes, researcher narratives, participant diaries, transcripts of diary-based interviews and different versions of transcripts. This expansion of the scope of ethnographic work has come with greater researcher reflexivity and with greater commitment to bringing the voices of research participants into developing research narratives. In this volume, we also learn of significant moves towards the use of visual and multimodal research methods. This includes the innovative use of drawings by Brigitta Busch in Vienna and her research team to elicit language biographies (Chapter 3); the audio-recording of talk about schoolscape texts by Laihonen and Szabó (Chapter 8) and the audio-recording of children's talk about faith-inspired text-making by Lytra et al. (Chapter 14).

All the chapters in the volume reveal a distinct shift towards researcher reflexivity, with different chapters foregrounding different stages of the research process – from initial fieldwork, to the gathering of data, to transcription, to data analysis and writing up. In Chapters 12–15, there is also evidence of a multilingual turn in research practice, with individual researchers drawing attention to the role of language and semiosis in knowledge building by foregrounding their use of multilingual resources and "the multilingual dynamics of the research process" (Vakser, Chapter 15). There is also evidence of methodological innovation emerging from research in multilingual research teams, especially in Chapter 13 (Creese et al.).

Ethnography oriented to social change

For decades, researchers engaged in social and ethnographic research on multilingualism have expressed concern about the role that they might play

Introduction   13

in relation to social change, especially when, as a result of engagement over time with research participants, they become aware of the ways in which particular language practices and ideologies are contributing to the construction of social inequalities. This concern about the role of the researcher was already a recurring theme in the work of Dell Hymes. In the late 1970s/early 1980s, he put forward the idea of "ethnographic monitoring" (Hymes, 1979, 1980). He did this in the context of wider interdisciplinary discussions relating to research on bilingual education in the USA. This was a time when the educational entitlements of children from linguistic minority groups were being acknowledged and when broader processes of change were taking place through the introduction of bilingual education programmes within the public education system. However, it was also a time when the evaluation of educational programmes was dominated by positivist models of social science and where programme outcomes were defined in primarily quantitative terms. Within this broader institutional and epistemological context, Hymes' proposal for ethnographic monitoring was a radical departure from the dominant tradition in educational research. Hymes argued that an ethnographic approach was "essential" (1979: 73) to the investigation of a far-reaching process of change such as the introduction of bilingual education programmes. He pointed out that the participants in such new educational programmes were not mere "bystanders" but had "the finest possible grasp of the workings of the programs" (1979: 85). For these reasons, he made the case for engaging in "cooperative ethnographic monitoring" with participants, and for undertaking joint knowledge building.

This concern about the role of the researcher with regard to social change surfaced again, in the 1990s, in different strands of sociolinguistic research, as critical approaches and poststructuralist perspectives were being adopted. For example, in critical discourse analysis (CDA) (e.g. Fairclough, 1989), in critical studies of language and gender (Talbot, 1998) and in critical approaches to language policy (Tollefson, 1991, 2002; McCarty, 2011), research was seen as having two broad aims: first that of shedding light on the ways in which language practices, discourses and ideologies contribute to the construction of social inequalities; and, second, that of challenging such discourses and ideologies by raising awareness about them.

These earlier reflections on the role of research in contributing to social change are echoed in three of the chapters in this volume: in Chapter 16, by Haley De Korne and Nancy Hornberger, and in Chapter 17, by Jef Van der Aa and Jan Blommaert, we see an assertion of the contemporary relevance of Hymes' notion of ethnographic monitoring. In Chapter 7, by David Cassels Johnson, we are reminded of the debates that took place in the 1990s about what it means to do critical research related to language policy and planning processes and we learn of specific new proposals by Johnson as to how research projects might be co-designed with educational practitioners so as to enable them to act as "language policy arbiters". In all three chapters, the

14   M. Martin-Jones and D. Martin

emphasis is on the ways in which "collaborative critical analysis" (Murchison, 2010)[5] between researchers and research participants can open up space for dialogue and reflection and can lead to the joint identification of directions for change.

Contributions to the volume

The contributions to the volume have been grouped around the five following themes:

- researching trajectories, multilingual repertoires and identities
- researching discourses, policies and practices on different scales
- researching multilingual communication and multisemioticity online
- multilingualism in research practice: voices, identities and researcher reflexivity
- ethnographic monitoring and critical collaborative analysis for social change.

A theme-based organisation of the volume has been adopted to foreground: the dimensions of globalisation that are particularly pertinent to research on multilingualism and diversities; innovation in research methodology in studies conducted in particular social spaces; and the increasingly multilingual nature of research practice across the social sciences and the opportunities this opens up for researcher reflexivity.

Researching trajectories, multilingual repertoires and identities

The chapter on "Narrative analysis in transnational contexts", by Mike Baynham and Anna De Fina, shows us, in illuminating detail, how narrative analysis can serve as a methodological resource for researching multilingualism in the context of contemporary mobilities and transnational population flows. In the first part of their chapter, Baynham and De Fina survey the theoretical and methodological ground on which the recent research on narratives of mobility and displacement has been developed. They also point out that in sociolinguistic studies of narrative there has been a shift in research focus from stories to story-telling, and to a more practice-oriented approach. In effect, what this means is that there has been a move away from early work on narratives as texts, from the study of their structure and their linguistic features, to more recent work on story-telling practices. In this recent strand of work, the focus is on the ways in which story-telling practices are bound up with the construction of identities, social spaces and social boundaries. In addition, Baynham and De Fina indicate that, in some contemporary research on narrative in migration contexts, there has been a move towards combining narrative analysis with ethnography, so as to build a fuller understanding of the specific values of local research participants and the categories of

Introduction 15

belonging that they see as being significant. In the remainder of the chapter, Baynham and De Fina then trace the development of two different kinds of research on narrative in multilingual migratory contexts and they specify the kinds of insights that are gleaned from each kind: first, research on narrative as embedded within institutional and everyday practices; and, second, research on narratives that occur in interactions between researcher and research participants, e.g. in interviews or in focus-group sessions. This part of the chapter is illustrated with reference to a rich body of research, including some of the ground-breaking research carried out by Baynham and De Fina themselves.

In her chapter on "Biographical approaches to research in multilingual settings: exploring linguistic repertoires", Brigitta Busch outlines some of the advantages that accrue from adopting biographical approaches and she considers the specific nature of this methodological option. She does this in a number of ways. First, she provides a useful genealogy of the language biographical research that has been developed in different areas of social science. She gives examples of the ways in which diaries and other kinds of biographical texts and images have been incorporated into research on child bilingualism, on multilingual literacy practices and on language learning. Second, she shows in considerable detail how biographical approaches are embedded within the broad tradition of qualitative and interpretive research in the social sciences. At the heart of her argument here is the premise that, while all interpretivists agree that there can be no 'objective' account of (social) reality and that all accounts are mediated by the researcher's subjective perceptions, there are differences in the ways in which interpretive work in different strands of social science characterises the biographical subject, and in the ways in which the notions of experience, memory and narration are construed. To substantiate this point, Busch compares three strands of interpretive research: interactionist, phenomenological and poststructuralist approaches.

Busch suggests (in the final section of her chapter) that it would be profitable to combine insights from all three approaches, and she indicates that this is what she is endeavouring to do in her innovative biographical research in different multilingual settings – research that involves the use of multimodal methods in combination with life-history work. Two central concepts in this research are: "linguistic repertoires" and "lived experience of language".

In his chapter on "The risks and gains of a single case study", Kamran Khan demonstrates the affordances of case-study research with just one individual. He does this with considerable nuance and insight. He also shows how the risks involved in opting for a single case study can be anticipated and how alternative strategies can be built into the initial research design. He draws on his own research into the language and literacy practices involved in obtaining British citizenship. The main unit of analysis for this research was the journey to citizenship taken by one individual. Since the early twenty-first century, in the UK, this journey has involved not only paperwork but also

16   *M. Martin-Jones and D. Martin*

assessment of 'skills' in English and assessment of knowledge of life in the UK, through the 'Life in the UK test'. Khan indicates that he first met W – the main participant in his study – when W was enrolled in an ESOL class (English for Speakers of Other Languages). Khan's original research strategy was to investigate the collective citizenship journey of those enrolled in the class, but early on, the focus shifted to just one participant. The research design and the unit of analysis remained the same (i.e. the journey to citizenship) but, as Khan points out, a case study of just one individual enabled him to take account of the wider context of the journey to citizenship. The design of the study was also informed by key principles of ethnography, such as the investment of time by the researcher into 'being there' as a participant observer, and the posing of broader questions such as: "What is happening here?" to open up lines of interpretation and analysis.

In her chapter on "Researching student mobility in multilingual Switzerland: reflections on multi-sited ethnography", Martina Zimmermann makes a strong case for adopting a multi-sited approach to research with people who are 'on the move' across linguistic, institutional and political borders. She does this by presenting a reflexive account of ethnographic research that she has been conducting in Switzerland, with students from the southern region, where Italian is most widely spoken (the Ticino region). A significant number of students from the region opt to do university degrees in the central and north-eastern region of the country, where German is most widely spoken. Zimmermann shows how her research began with a significant period of participant observation in a single research site: a student association in Berne organised by and for Italian-speaking students from the Ticino region. She then shows how this initial research design was extended to include multi-sited ethnography. She began conducting interviews with a wider range of students, in other cities in the German-speaking region of Switzerland (e.g. in Lucerne and in Zurich) and included students who were not members of a student association such as the one in Berne. She also built a picture of special provision for academic support for Italian-speaking students in the universities using German as a medium of instruction. She then travelled to the Ticino region to conduct observations and carry out interviews during an "information day" organised at the local university for students who were potential applicants for higher education degree programmes in Swiss universities outside the region. This is an annual event where universities from across the country market their courses and compete to recruit students. Zimmermann argues that a multi-sited approach has enabled her to identify connections between institutional practices that she has documented in different sites and to grasp the significance of the differences between Italian-speaking students' own accounts of their motivations in opting for mobility and crossing this linguistic border. Some align themselves with a discourse about the value of investing in German-medium higher education, echoing the shifts currently taking place within the linguistic market in Switzerland, and others take a more critical stance (e.g. those involved in the student association in Berne).

Introduction 17

Researching discourses, policies and practices on different scales

In the chapter by Francis M. Hult, on "Nexus analysis as scalar ethnography for educational linguistics", the starting point is with the broad shift towards multi-scalar analysis among scholars engaged in educational linguistic research in multilingual contexts. Hult argues that nexus analysis – as originally conceptualised by Scollon and Scollon (2004) – is particularly well suited to ethnographic research that aims to trace discursive and/or semiotic links across different scales of social and institutional life. This chapter gives us a clear and well-illustrated overview of the core elements of nexus analysis, highlighting the ways in which this approach facilitates multi-scalar research. Hult reminds us of the central principles of nexus analysis: that "the analytic focus is not solely on language but on the social significance of the language-mediated act"; that individual actions constitute "part of specific social systems – sets of practices or a nexus of practice"; and that "the social context of a specific action, meaning how it is situated in a specific nexus of practice, can be mapped discursively". He then goes on to describe and illustrate, with reference to educational settings, the three types of discourse that mediate social actions: the historical body, the interaction order and discourses in place. In the concluding section of his chapter, Hult then demonstrates the value of nexus analysis in research design, especially in research incorporating multiple methods.

In his chapter, "Critical ethnography of language policy: a semi-confessional tale", David Cassells Johnson addresses the question of what it actually means to do critical, ethnographic research on language policy. To do this, he provides a useful genealogy of critical approaches in two fields: research in language planning and policy (LPP) and ethnographic research. He shows how the critical turn in both these fields was part of the broader epistemological shift within the social sciences towards poststructuralism and postmodernism. He also notes that there has been a much longer concern with researcher positionality and subjectivity in ethnographic research and that there has also been a long-standing debate about the writing of ethnographic narratives and about whose storylines are actually developed. In addition, there has also been a shift towards making the history, stance and values of the ethnographer more visible, through what Van Maanen (2011) has called "confessional tales". Johnson welcomes the move towards more acknowledgement of the role of researcher subjectivity in knowledge building and towards greater reflexivity in current "researching-texting practices", but he expresses concern about the "over-focus on the researcher" in some postmodernist accounts. To support these lines of argument, he provides examples from his own research and draws on projects carried out in two different school districts in the United States. He describes this part of his chapter "a semi-confessional tale".

The chapter on "Investigating visual practices in educational settings: schoolscapes, linguistic ideologies and organizational cultures", by

18   *M. Martin-Jones and D. Martin*

Petteri Laihonen and Tamás Szabó, opens up for us a developing area of research into schoolscapes and different aspects of visual communication in educational settings. In the first part of their chapter, they show how guiding concepts in the field have emerged from different research traditions, notably the work of Scollon and Scollon (2003, 2004) on language and meaning-making in the material world, and Kress and Van Leeuwen's (2006) characterisation of discourse as including visual and multimodal elements. They also trace the influences on the development of different strands of empirical work in school settings, focusing in particular on influences from early work in anthropology and education and from more recent, interdisciplinary work on linguistic landscapes. In the second part of their chapter, they go on to consider different research approaches, including quantitative, qualitative and ethnographic research. They weigh up the potential and the limits of different approaches and they illustrate their account with reference to particular studies. In the third part of the chapter, they draw attention to the visual turn in research practice and show how and why some researchers have employed visual resources in gathering data. In the remainder of the chapter, Laihonen and Szabó provide detailed and illuminating examples from their own research on schoolscapes in different school settings in Eastern Europe.

Researching multilingual communication and multisemioticity online

In their chapter on "Methodologies for researching multilingual online texts and practices", David Barton and Carmen Lee show us, in illuminating detail, how researchers investigating multilingualism online have had to develop new research lenses and new ways of working on and offline. Two main arguments underpin their chapter: first, multilinguals do not necessarily engage in the same kinds of communicative practices when interacting with others via the internet as they do in offline contexts. So, for example, methodologies associated with research into face-to-face interaction may not serve as adequate means of providing description and analysis of multilingual communication in online environments. Online communication takes place in a different mode and it involves writing, so some account needs to be taken of this. And, second, in the study of multilingualism online, considerable benefits accrue from *combining* text-based approaches (such as discourse analysis) with more practice-based, ethnographically informed approaches. In this way, researchers can build a fuller account of how web users draw on the multilingual resources in their repertoires and why they do so in the way that they do. By working in ethnographically informed ways, they can also glean insights into the meanings and values associated with different multilingual practices online by users in different contexts. Barton and Lee draw on past and present research into different types of multilingual communication online to support these arguments, including their own innovative research into multilingual practices on Flikr and on multilingual writing, in Chinese and English, on Web 2.0 in Hong Kong.

Introduction 19

In their chapter on "Investigating multilingualism and multisemioticity as communicative resources in social media", Sirpa Leppänen and Samu Kytölä foreground the range of resources that are drawn upon in communication online, including language(s), varieties, styles and genres, along with other semiotic resources such as textual forms and patterns, visuality, still and moving images, sounds and music. They also show how such resources are intertwined and mobilised in processes such as entextualisation (Bauman & Briggs, 1990) and resemiotisation (Iedema, 2003). They do this with reference to examples from their own highly innovative research into new social media. The examples include the use of Twitter by football celebrities, the evaluation of the form and content of tweets in a football discussion forum and the online fan activity of 'shredding' on YouTube. In addition, Leppänen and Kytölä provide a brief genealogy of approaches to the study of social media and point to the increasing convergence in their field with research on the sociolinguistics of globalisation and with changing conceptualisations of linguistic and cultural diversity. Their account highlights two broad shifts in research practice: first, the increasing focus on the participatory nature of digital discourse following the development of Web 2.0 and social media, along with different affordances for digital interaction and production; and, second, the turn towards ethnography and the use of multiple methods. Given that new social media have become complex and dynamic social niches for interaction, for cultural production and for the creation of groups and communities, the turn to ethnography is particularly appropriate.

The chapter by Helen Kelly-Holmes and Aoife Lenihan on "Virtual ethnographic approaches to researching multilingualism online" provides us with detailed insights into the ways in which ethnography has been adapted and developed to study multilingualism online. They start out with an account of the changing landscape of multilingualism on the internet. They then draw attention to some of the issues that arise in virtual ethnographic work. These issues relate to research ethics, to defining the scope of the 'field' and to the sheer quantity of data to archive. They stress, in particular, the challenges posed by the constant changes taking place on the web. In the fourth and fifth sections of their chapter, they give examples of two studies of online multilingualism. The first illustrates the way in which a linguistic landscape approach might be employed in the investigation of commodified uses of multilingualism on corporate websites. The website chosen is that of the multinational fast-food company, MacDonald's. Kelly-Holmes and Lenihan also give examples of the kinds of questions that are addressed in this kind of online research. The second example shows how virtual ethnography can be employed in a study of social networking sites. Here, we read about a detailed study of the use of Irish on Facebook and, in particular, the use of an Irish translation app which was introduced shortly before an ethnographic project conducted by Lenihan. In the final section, Kelly-Holmes and Lenihan conclude the chapter with some valuable pointers for further virtual ethnographic research into multilingualism online.

20   M. Martin-Jones and D. Martin

*Multilingualism in research practice: voices, identities
and researcher reflexivity*

The chapter on "Reflexive ethnographic research practice in multilingual contexts" by Marilyn Martin-Jones, Jane Andrews and Deirdre Martin traces the diverse ways in which reflexive ethnographic approaches to research on multilingualism have been developed over the last two decades and takes stock of what we have learned from these developments. Their account is illustrated with reference to research carried out by individual researchers or by multilingual research teams in different multilingual contexts. It includes references to research on multilingualism in interaction, on multilingual literacy practices and on multimodal practices. The authors show how recent innovation in the production and use of different kinds of fieldwork texts – participant diaries, interview transcripts, field notes, vignettes and field narratives – has opened up new ways of achieving reflexivity and new means of constructing polyphonic research narratives.

In their chapter, "Reflexivity in team ethnography: using researcher vignettes", Angela Creese, Jaspreet Kaur Takhi and Adrian Blackledge draw on over twelve years' experience of ethnographic research on multilingualism in multilingual teams. The particular focus of their chapter is on one of the methodological strategies that they have adopted in team research, namely the use of researcher vignettes. They argue that the autobiographical nature of this particular research genre lends itself well to the development of strategic reflexivity. By means of illustration, they refer to two researcher vignettes written by Jaspreet Kaur Takhi and by Angela Creese while carrying out ethnographic research in a Panjabi complementary school. They show how narrative vignettes such as these provide the reader with insights into the "lived stuff of the research process". They also point to some of the reasons why researcher vignettes are of particular value, methodologically and analytically, in multilingual team ethnography.

The topic of the chapter by Vally Lytra, Eve Gregory and Arani Ilankuberan is "Researching children's literacy practices and identities in faith settings: multimodal text-making and talk about text as resources for knowledge-building". Their chapter focuses on research with children and on ways of designing research practice so that the voice, perspectives and understandings of children can be incorporated into the development of research narratives. They write about one particular aspect of an ethnographic research project carried out in London, which took a multi-method approach to the study of literacy learning and literacy practices in different faith settings. In order to encourage the children involved in the project to represent their experiences of extending their multiscriptal literacy repertoires in a faith setting, they provided them with the materials needed to make multimodal texts 'on paper'. The children engaged in text-making, drawing on a range of resources, including images, text and colour. Once completed, the children's texts provided the focus for a conversation between the children and one

Introduction 21

of the project researchers. The chapter presents a detailed reflection on the nature and significance of the dialogues that took place between researchers and the children around these multimodal texts. At the heart of the chapter, we read about the conversation that took place between Arani Ilankuberan and two children. The children had grown up in London, with Tamil as a heritage language, and their parents were affiliated with the Tamil Hindu/Saiva faith community in the city.

The chapter on "Multilingual dynamics in the research process: transcribing and interpreting interactional data" by Sabina Vakser presents compelling critical reflections on the interpretive and representational processes involved in the production of transcripts of multilingual interaction. As Vakser points out, the interpretive processes involved in the transcription of multilingual data bears the imprint of "the sociolinguistic profile of the interpreter(s), their familiarity with the relevant social contexts and the reasons motivating their transcription choices". In this chapter, she calls for greater transparency and reflexivity at each stage of the transcription process. Her own, detailed reflections are based on research that she carried out with three families in Melbourne, Australia. The adult members of those families all had Russian as a heritage language, but they originated from different regions where Russian is spoken and they had different migration trajectories. As the complexity of communication in the contact zones of the twenty-first century increases, be it in local families, neighbourhoods, classes, workplaces or service encounters, reflexivity of the kind demonstrated in this chapter by Vakser will definitely be needed. There needs to be a clear shift from viewing multilingual transcription as a relatively straightforward step in the research process and much more attention is needed to the specific, situated ways in which data is constructed by individual researchers, or co-constructed in multilingual research teams.

Ethnographic monitoring and critical collaborative analysis for social change

The chapter by Haley De Korne and Nancy Hornberger, "Countering unequal multilingualism through ethnographic monitoring", presents a thought-provoking dialogue with the principles underpinning Hymes' (1979, 1980) notion of ethnographic monitoring. The authors build, in particular, on Hymes' premise that ethnographers can contribute to change as well as describing and interpreting events and practices that are unfolding in particular social contexts. The central focus of the chapter is on the ways in which ethnographic monitoring can contribute to efforts to bring about change in language-in-education policies and programmes, in different sectors of education from primary to higher education, where social inequalities are being created through institutional processes. The chapter is organised around three core aspects of ethnographic monitoring practice: observation and description, analysis and interpretation, and evaluation oriented towards change. The discussion of each of these aspects of ethnographic monitoring is illustrated with reference to five vignettes from the lived experiences of the authors as ethnographers working

22　M. Martin-Jones and D. Martin

in support of educational initiatives designed to counter language inequalities. The examples are drawn from a multilingual education programme in the southern Philippines, from initiatives in two South African universities aiming at the development of bilingual provision involving African languages, from an Indigenous language course at university level in Mexico and from a Sámi language teacher education programme in northern Scandinavia.

In the chapter entitled, "Ethnographic monitoring and the study of complexity", Jef Van der Aa and Jan Blommaert also engage with Hymes' (1979, 1980) concept of ethnographic monitoring, bringing his voice into their text in a similar way. In particular, they consider the implications of ethnographic monitoring for research practice and for the way we conceptualise theory-building. Like De Korne and Hornberger, they stress the value of a long-term commitment to working with the social actors in the field and they argue that the goal of ethnographic monitoring should be that of achieving "epistemic solidarity" with these social actors. They then turn to an account of ways in which they have organised their own research in Belgium, in line with these principles. This research is focusing on the provision of social services in two urban settings: a family care centre in a neighbourhood of Antwerp that is characterised by considerable linguistic and cultural diversity and an asylum centre for refugees in West Flanders. In both settings, there is a researcher in residence who acts as a "long-term academic consultant", enabling staff to reflect on and adapt to the constantly changing conditions of their work. Echoing one of the central themes of the volume, they demonstrate the particular relevance of ethnographic monitoring for the ever-shifting conditions of complexity in contemporary social life.

Notes

1　For detailed discussion of the notion of indexicality, see Silverstein (2003).
2　For further discussion of the notion of scales, see Collins et al. (2009) and Blommaert (2010).
3　For the genealogy of this particular research tradition, see Rampton et al. (2004); Creese (2010); Copland & Creese (2015); Rampton (2007); Shaw et al. (2015); Tusting & Maybin (2007).
4　For the genealogy of this research tradition, see Hornberger & Johnson (2007); Johnson (2009, 2013); McCarty (2011).
5　We first encountered this concept in Chapter 4 by Kamran Khan. It is such an apt term for the final section of this volume that it has been incorporated in the sub-heading for that section.

References

Androutsopoulos, J. (2007) 'Bilingualism in the mass media and on the internet', in M. Heller (ed.), 207–230.

Appadurai, A. (1996) *Modernity at Large: Cultural Dimensions of Globalization.* Minneapolis, MN: University of Minnesota Press.

Barton, D. & Lee, C. (2013) *Language Online: Investigating Digital Texts and Practices.* London: Routledge.

Introduction 23

Bauman, R. & Briggs, C. (1990) 'Poetics and performance as critical perspectives on language and social life'. *Annual Review of Anthropology* 19, 59–88.

Bauman, R. & Sherzer, J. (eds) (1974) *The Ethnography of Speaking*. New York: Cambridge University Press.

Baynham, M. (2009) '"Just one day like today": scale and analysis of space/time orientation in narratives of displacement', in J. Collins, S. Slembrouck & M. Baynham (eds) *Globalization and Language in Contact*. London: Continuum, 130–142.

Blackledge, A. & Creese, A. (2010) *Multilingualism: A Critical Perspective*. London: Continuum.

Blommaert, J. (ed.) (1999) *Language Ideological Debates*. Berlin: Mouton de Gruyter.

Blommaert, J. (2007) On scope and depth in linguistic ethnography. *Journal of Sociolinguistics* 11(5), 682–688.

Blommaert, J. (2010) *The Sociolinguistics of Globalization*. Cambridge: Cambridge University Press.

Blommaert, J. (2013) *Ethnography, Superdiversity and Linguistic Landscapes: Chronicles of Complexity*. Bristol: Multilingual Matters.

Blommaert, J. & Rampton, B. (2011) 'Language and superdiversity'. *Diversities* 13(2), 1–22.

Bourdieu, P. (1977) *Outline of a Theory of Practice*. Cambridge: Cambridge University Press.

Bourdieu, P. (1991) *Language and Symbolic Power*. Cambridge, MA: Harvard University Press.

Bucholtz, M. & Hall, K. (2008) 'All of the above: new coalitions in sociocultural linguistics'. *Journal of Sociolinguistics* 12(4), 401–431.

Castells, M. (2000) *The Information Age: Economy, Society and Culture*. Oxford: Blackwell.

Clifford, M. & Marcus, G.E. (1986) *Writing Culture: The Poetics and Politics of Ethnography*. Berkeley, CA: University of California Press.

Collins, J., Slembrouck, S. & Baynham, M. (eds) (2009) *Globalization and Language in Contact*. London: Continuum.

Copland, F. & Creese, A. (with F. Rock & S. Shaw) (2015) *Linguistic Ethnography*. London: Sage.

Creese, A. (2010) 'Linguistic ethnography', in L. Litosseliti (ed.) *Research Methods in Linguistics*. London: Continuum, 138–154.

Da Silva, E., McLaughlin, M. & Richards, M. (2007) 'Bilingualism and the globalized new economy: the commodification of language and identity', in M. Heller (ed.), 183–206.

De Fina, A., Ikizoglu, D. & Wegner, J. (eds) (2017) *Diversity and Super-Diversity: Sociocultural Linguistic Perspectives*. Washington, DC: Georgetown University Press.

Duchêne, A. & Heller, M. (eds) (2012) *Language in Late Capitalism: Pride and Profit*. New York: Routledge.

Errington, J.J. (2008) *Linguistics in a Colonial World: A Story of Language, Meaning and Power*. Oxford: Blackwell.

Fairclough, N. (ed.) (1989) *Language and Power*. London: Longman.

Foucault, M. (1971) 'Orders of discourse'. *Social Science Information* 10(2), 7–30.

Foucault, M. (1972) *The Archaeology of Knowledge*. London: Tavistock Publications.

Gal, S. (1989) 'Language and political economy'. *Annual Review of Anthropology* 18, 345–367.

Gal, S. & Irvine, J. (1995) 'The boundaries of languages and disciplines: how ideologies construct difference'. *Social Research* 62(4), 967–1001.

24 M. Martin-Jones and D. Martin

Gal, S. & Woolard, K.A. (1995) 'Constructing languages and publics: authority and representation'. *Pragmatics* 5, 155–166.

Gardner, S. & Martin-Jones, M. (eds) (2012) *Multilingualism, Discourse and Ethnography*. Abingdon, Oxon: Routledge.

Giddens, A. (1990) *The Consequences of Modernity*. Cambridge: Polity Press.

Gorter, D. (ed.) (2006) *Linguistic Landscapes: A New Approach to Multilingualism*. Clevedon, UK: Multilingual Matters.

Grillo, R. (1989) *Dominant Languages: Language and Hierarchy in Britain and France*. Cambridge: Cambridge University Press.

Gumperz, J.J. (1972) 'Introduction', in J.J. Gumperz & D. Hymes (eds) *Directions in Sociolinguistics: The Ethnography of Communication*. New York: Holt, Rinehart & Winston, 1–25.

Gumperz, J.J. (1982) *Discourse Strategies*. Cambridge: Cambridge University Press.

Gumperz, J.J. (1996) 'The linguistic and cultural relativity of inferences', in J.J. Gumperz & S.C. Levinson (eds) *Rethinking Linguistic Relativity*. Cambridge: Cambridge University Press, 374–406.

Gumperz, J.J. (1999) 'On interactional sociolinguistic method', in C. Roberts & S. Sarangi (eds) *Talk, Work and Institutional Order*. Berlin: Mouton de Gruyter, 453–471.

Gumperz, J.J. & Hymes, D. (eds) (1964) 'The ethnography of communication', [Special issue]. *American Anthropologist* 60(6), part 2.

Gumperz, J.J. & Hymes, D. (eds) (1972) *Directions in Sociolinguistics: The Ethnography of Communication*. New York: Holt, Rinehart & Winston.

Harvey, D. (1989) *The Condition of Postmodernity*. Oxford: Blackwell.

Heller, M. (1995) 'Language choice, social institutions and symbolic domination', *Language in Society* 24(3), 373–405.

Heller, M. (1999) *Linguistic Minorities and Modernity*. London: Longman.

Heller, M. (ed.) (2007) *Bilingualism: A Social Approach*. Basingstoke, Hampshire: Palgrave Macmillan.

Heller, M. (2011) *Paths to Post-Nationalism: A Critical Ethnography of Language and Identity*. Oxford: Oxford University Press.

Heller, M. & Martin-Jones, M. (eds) (2001) *Voices of Authority: Education and Linguistic Difference*. Westport, CT: Ablex.

Heller, M., Bell, L.A., Daveluy, M., McLaughlin, M. & Noël, H. (2015) *Sustaining the Nation: The Making and Moving of Language and Nation*. Oxford: Oxford University Press.

Hornberger, N.H. & Johnson, D.C. (2007) 'Slicing the onion ethnographically: layers and spaces in multilingual language education'. *TESOL Quarterly* 41(3), 509–532.

Hymes, D. (1969) 'The use of anthropology: critical, political, personal', in D. Hymes (ed.) *Reinventing Anthropology*. Ann Arbor, MI: University of Michigan Press, 3–82.

Hymes, D. (1972) 'Models of the interaction of language and social life', in J.J. Gumperz & D. Hymes (eds) *Directions in Sociolinguistics: The Ethnography of Communication*. New York: Holt, Rinehart & Winston, 35–71.

Hymes, D. (1974) *Foundations of Sociolinguistics: An Ethnographic Approach*. Philadelphia, PA: University of Pennsylvania Press.

Hymes, D. (1979) 'Ethnographic monitoring', in E. Brière (ed.) *Language Development in a Bilingual Setting*. Pomona, California: National Multilingual, Multicultural Materials Center, for the National Dissemination and Assessment Center, Los Angeles, 73–88. (Reprinted in Hymes, 1980).

Hymes, D. (1980) *Language in Education: Ethnolinguistic Essays*. Washington, DC: Centre for Applied Linguistics.

Hymes, D. (1983) *Essays in the History of Linguistic Anthropology*. Amsterdam: John Benjamins.

Hymes, D. (1996) *Ethnography, Linguistics, Narrative Inequality: Towards an Understanding of Voice*. London: Taylor & Francis.

Iedema, R. (2003) 'Multimodality, resemiotization: extending the analysis of discourse as multi-semiotic practice'. *Visual Communication* 2(1), 29–57.

Jaffe, A. (1999) *Ideologies in Action: Language Politics on Corsica*. Berlin: Mouton de Gruyter.

Johnson, D.C. (2009) 'Ethnography of language policy'. *Language Policy* 8, 139–159.

Johnson, D.C. (2013) *Language Policy*. Basingstoke, Hampshire: Palgrave Macmillan.

Kress, G. (2003) *Literacy in the New Media Age*. London and New York: Routledge.

Kress, G. & Van Leeuwen, T. (2006) *Reading Images: The Grammar of Visual Design*. London: Routledge, 2nd edn.

Laihonen, P. & Tódor, E.-M. (2015) 'The changing schoolscape in a Szekler village in Romania: signs of diversity in "rehungarization"'. *International Journal of Bilingual Education and Bilingualism*. (Online) http://dx.doi.org/10.1080/13670050.2015.1051943.

Lam, E. & Rosario-Ramos, E. (2009) 'Multilingual literacies in transnational digital mediated contexts: an exploratory study of immigrant teens in the United States'. *Language and Education* 23(2), 171–190.

Lee, C.K.-M. (2007) 'Affordances and text-making practices in online instant messaging'. *Written Communication* 24(3), 223–249.

Lin, A.M.Y. (1999) 'Doing-English-lessons in the reproduction or transformation of social worlds'. *TESOL Quarterly* 33, 393–412.

Lytra, V., Volk, D. & Gregory, E. (eds) (2016) *Languages, Literacies and Identities: Religion in Young Lives*. New York: Routledge.

McCarty, T.L. (ed.) (2011) *Ethnography of Language Policy*. London and New York: Routledge.

McGinnis, T., Goodstein-Stolzenberg, A. & Saliani, E.C. (2007) '"indnpride": online spaces of transnational youth as sites of creativity and sophisticated literacy and identity work'. *Linguistics and Education* 18(3&4), 305–324.

Makoni, S. & Pennycook, A. (eds) (2007) *Disinventing and Reconstituting Languages*. Clevedon, UK: Multilingual Matters.

Marcus, G.E. & Fischer, M.J. (1986) *Anthropology as Cultural Critique*. Chicago, IL: Chicago University Press.

Martin, D. (2012) 'A critical linguistic ethnographic approach to language disabilities in multilingual families', in S. Gardner & M. Martin-Jones (eds), 305–318.

Martin-Jones, M. & Jones, K. (eds) (2000) *Multilingual Literacies: Reading and Writing Different Worlds*. Amsterdam: John Benjamins.

Martin-Jones, M., Blackledge, A. & Creese, A. (2012) 'Introduction: a sociolinguistics of multilingualism for our times', in M. Martin-Jones, A. Blackledge & A. Creese (eds) *Handbook of Multilingualism*. Abingdon, Oxon: Routledge, 1–29.

Menard-Warwick, J. (2009) *Gendered Identities and Immigrant Language Learning*. Bristol: Multilingual Matters.

Murchison, J.M. (2010) *Ethnography Essentials: Conducting and Presenting Your Research*. San Francisco, CA: Jossey-Bass.

Pavlenko, A. & Blackledge, A. (2004) 'Introduction: new theoretical approaches to the study of negotiation of identities in multilingual contexts', in A. Pavlenko &

A. Blackledge (eds) *Negotiation of Identities in Multilingual Contexts*, Clevedon, UK: Multilingual Matters, 1–33.

Pennycook, A. (2001) *Critical Applied Linguistics*. Mahwah, NJ: Lawrence Erlbaum.

Pietikäinen, S. (2012) 'Experiences and expressions of multilingualism: visual ethnography and discourse analysis in research with Sámi children', in S. Gardner & M. Martin-Jones (eds), 163–178.

Pujolar, J. (2007) 'Bilingualism and the nation-state in the post-national era', in M. Heller (ed.), 71–95.

Ramanathan, V. (2005) *The English-Vernacular Divide: Postcolonial Language Policies and Practice*. Clevedon, UK: Multilingual Matters.

Rampton, B. (2007) 'Neo-Hymesian linguistic ethnography in the United Kingdom'. *Journal of Sociolinguistics* 11(5), 584–607.

Rampton, B., Maybin, J. & Roberts. C. (2015) 'Theory and method in linguistic ethnography', in J. Snell, S. Shaw & F. Copland (eds) *Linguistic Ethnography: Interdisciplinary Explorations*. Basingstoke, Hampshire: Palgrave Macmillan, 14–50.

Rampton, B., Tusting, K., Maybin, J., Barwell, R., Creese, A. & Lytra, V. (2004) 'UK linguistic ethnography: a discussion paper'. Online www.ling-ethnog.org.uk.

Rampton, B. (2007) 'Neo-Hymesian linguistic ethnography in the United Kingdom'. *Journal of Sociolinguistics* 11(5), 584–607.

Rampton, B., Maybin, J. and Roberts. C. (2015) Theory and method in linguistic ethnography. In J. Snell, S. Shaw & F. Copland (eds) *Linguistic Ethnography: Interdisciplinary Explorations*. Basingstoke, Hampshire: Palgrave Macmillan, 14–50.

Rindler Schjerve, R. (ed.) (2003) *Diglossia and Power: Language Policies and Practice in the 19th Century Habsburg Empire*. Berlin: Mouton de Gruyter.

Schieffelin, B.B., Woolard, K.A. & Kroskrity, P.V. (eds) (1998) *Language Ideologies: Practice and Theory*. Oxford: Oxford University Press.

Scollon, R. & Scollon, S. (2004) *Nexus Analysis*. New York: Routledge.

Scollon, R. & Wong Scollon, S. (2003) *Discourses in Place: Language in the Material World*. London: Routledge.

Shaw, S., Copland, F. & Snell, J. (2015) 'An introduction to linguistic ethnography: interdisciplinary explorations', in J. Snell, S. Shaw & F. Copland (eds) *Linguistic Ethnography: Interdisciplinary Explorations*. Basingstoke, Hampshire: Palgrave Macmillan, 1–15.

Shohamy, E. & Gorter, D. (eds) (2009) *Linguistic Landscapes: Expanding the Scenery*. London: Routledge.

Silverstein, M. (2003) 'Indexical order and the dialectics of sociolinguistic life'. *Language and Communication* 23, 193–229.

Stroud, C. (2007) 'Bilingualism: colonialism and postcolonialism,' in M. Heller (ed.), 25–49.

Stroud, D. & Mpendukana, S. (2012) 'Material ethnographies of multilingualism: linguistic landscapes in the township of Khayelitsha', in S. Gardner & M. Martin-Jones (eds), 149–162.

Talbot, M. (1998) *Language and Gender*. Cambridge: Polity Press.

Tollefson, J.W. (1991) *Planning Language, Planning Inequality*. London: Longman.

Tollefson, J.W. (ed.) (2002) *Language Policies in Education: Critical Issues*. Mahwah, NJ: Lawrence Erlbaum.

Tusting, K. & Maybin, J. (2007) 'Linguistic ethnography and interdisciplinarity: opening up the discussion'. *Journal of Sociolinguistics* 11(5), 575–583.

Urla, J. (1993) 'Cultural politics in an age of statistics: numbers, nations, and the making of a Basque identity'. *American Ethnologist* 20(1), 818–843.

Vertovec, S. (2007a) 'Super-diversity and its implications'. *Ethnic and Racial Studies* 30(6), 1024–1054.

Vertovec, S. (2007b) 'Introduction: new directions in the anthropology of migration and multiculturalism'. *Ethnic and Racial Studies* 30(6), 961–978.

Van Maanen, J. (2011) *Tales of the Field: On Ethnographic Writing*. Chicago, IL: Chicago University Press, 2nd edn.

Warriner, D. (2007) 'Introduction. Transnational literacies: immigration, language learning and identities'. *Linguistics and Education* 18(3&4), 201–214.

Warschauer, M., El Said, G.R. & Zohry, A. (2002) 'Language choice on-line: globalization and identity in Egypt'. *Journal of Computer-Mediated Communication* 7(4).

Woolard, K.A. (1985) 'Language variation and cultural hegemony: towards an integration of sociolinguistics and social theory'. *American Ethnologist*, 12, 38–48.

Woolard, K.A. (1989) *Double Talk: Bilingualism and the Politics of Ethnicity in Catalonia*. Stanford, CA: Stanford University Press.

Part 1

Researching trajectories, multilingual repertoires and identities

2 Narrative analysis in migrant and transnational contexts

Mike Baynham and Anna De Fina

Narrative analysis has become one of the most important methodological tools for the study of processes of uprooting, relocation, adaptation to new surroundings and linguistic realities, and the consequent identity struggles of migrants and transnational individuals. It is widely accepted that narratives are a fundamental means through which people make sense of and share their take on experiences, no matter how big or small, how life-changing or insignificant. Narratives are a ubiquitous discourse genre given the many functions that they fulfil in social life. Stories are told to create common ground and to share experiences, to amuse and to instruct, but they can also be used to differentiate, to feed disputes and arguments. They are tools for both sociability and conflict in everyday life; however, they are also often imbricated in institutional practices and public communication and underlie many linguistic struggles. It comes as no surprise then that the study of narrative has attracted the attention of sociolinguists and other scholars interested in the interactions of language and social life and that it has experienced such a surge in popularity in the last decades.

Nonetheless, the use of narrative analysis in the investigation of individuals and communities in transnational and migratory contexts and of their language practices is relatively recent. Early studies of migrants focused on narrative as a text-type. Researchers looked for signs of L2 proficiency in the narrative production of immigrant adults or children, who were evaluated as more or less proficient "bilinguals" (see, e.g. Berman, 1998; Berman & Slobin, 1994). Narratives were dissected in terms of linguistic devices, strategies and topics in order to assess bilinguals' development in the target language. Studies invariably focused on immigrants. Cognitive research also used narrative-eliciting techniques to study cognitive development and/or loss in bilinguals (see Schrauf & Rubin 1998). Thus stories as texts, not storytelling, was the focus of analysis in these early studies, and immigrants were seen as bi- or multilinguals who were always in a state of 'disadvantage' with respect to native speakers.

In this chapter we focus on a very different approach to narrative analysis: one that has been developing throughout the last two decades and that can be characterized as practice-oriented and ethnographic in nature. Within

32   M. Baynham and A. De Fina

this approach, the focus is on storytelling as a meaning-making practice that can throw light on the way immigrants, transnational communities and individuals act within and experience processes of relocation and uprooting, on their identity constructions and negotiations and on the power relations in which they are involved. Below, we provide some background on the main theoretical influences that have contributed to shaping this approach and we highlight the role of narrative analysis in the study of migration, transnationalism and multilingual spaces. We focus on two main areas: studies that have analyzed narrative as embedded within institutional and everyday practices, and research on a variety of topics related to identities, language and the representation of experiences of migration or uprooting through narratives produced in interviews and other research-generated contexts.

Background

It is thanks to the 'narrative turn' in the social sciences (Bruner, 1991; Riessman, 1993) that researchers have started shifting their attention from stories towards storytelling. Indeed, narrative-turn analysts promoted an anti-positivist, poststructuralist stance on research that put the stress on qualitative methods and a re-evaluation of narratives as an essential site for the articulation of subordinate subjects' own voices. As a result, narrative analysis has become a primary method for the elicitation of migrants' and diasporic individuals' talk about their own experiences and stances.

Besides being influenced by general trends towards qualitative instruments and the re-evaluation of subjectivities in the research process, narrative investigation has also responded to a more general shift in sociolinguistics towards flexible, practice-oriented understandings of the connections between discourse phenomena, identities and social processes that have developed in response to the new social relations and forms of communication that characterize globalized, mobile and highly complex late modern societies (Blommaert, 2010). Traditional variationist sociolinguistic frameworks that conceived of stories in structural terms as texts defined by specific discourse and linguistic characteristics reflected the focus of earlier research paradigms on the stability of cultural norms, identities and ways of speaking within well-established communities delimited in terms of class, ethnicity and other fixed variables (see, e.g. Labov, 1972). But such a paradigm can hardly provide a frame for the analysis of discourse in globalized societies that are characterized by a high degree of mobility and by a breaking up of notions of identity as homogeneous and grounded in well-defined territorial spaces. Theoretical developments in identity and postcolonial studies (see Giddens, 1991; Bhabha, 1994) have established a view of late modern identities as essentially fragmented and polyphonic. Polymorphism, mobility and hybridity are even more central concepts to the understanding of processes of identity formation among immigrants and transnational subjects. Indeed, global flows push/pull more and more people to seek new destinations, either to better their

Narrative analysis 33

life perspectives or to flee violence and instability. At the same time, mobility defines the experience of being "in between" that is so prevalent in their lives. Thus, one important strand of narrative analysis has focused on new understandings of the ways people index and negotiate relations between space, discourses and identities (see Baynham & De Fina, 2005).

Another influence on recent developments in narrative analysis has come from sociolinguistic approaches that emphasize the need for the close study of discourse phenomena through ethnographic lenses and with particular attention to the contextualization of meanings in local interactions (Rampton, 2006; Pennycook, 2010). From this perspective, the semiotic processes through which mobile, transient and uprooted individuals and groups represent and negotiate their own experiences need to be investigated, not presupposed. For this reason, narrative studies are increasingly becoming aligned with a view of narratives as social practices (De Fina & Georgakopoulou 2008, 2012), that is, as emergent and embedded within specific contexts of interaction and communication, be they interviews (see also De Fina & Perrino, 2011), or non-research-generated everyday contexts. Within this framework, storytelling needs to be investigated as a process that always involves presuppositions, co-construction and negotiations by participants. Thus, recent research on storytelling has paved the way for the study of how different kinds of narratives, not only canonical ones, are used in a variety of contexts to varied purposes and with different effects.

In the area that we are examining here of narratives in transnational and migratory contexts, for example, even if most work has focused on autobiographical and biographical narratives, there has also been a keen interest in other kinds of narratives. The latter have been studied and defined based on the close analysis of discourse in context and not on the basis of a single model or schema. For example, Baynham (2003) showed how generic narratives were used by Moroccan immigrants to the UK to construct a gendered representation of the process of migration. Carranza (1998) demonstrated the significance of habitual narratives in the discourse of Salvadorans in the USA to explain and motivate their need to leave their country of origins. De Fina (2009) provided an analysis of how accounts given by Mexicans in interviews were designed to answer interviewers' questions and justify personal choices. Relaño Pastor (2010) focused on the role of small stories co-constructed in focus-group interviews with migrant youngsters in Madrid schools in representing processes of "fitting in." Recent work has started to look at the way online narratives are used in identity claims by immigrants and as sites for the negotiation of transnational identities. For example, Kresova (2011) investigated blogs by Russian migrants, while Galasinska and Horolets (2012) analyzed how forum discussions by Polish individuals in the UK contribute to the construction of a grand narrative about migration. In brief, researchers in this tradition underlie the need for ethnographic approaches to data in order not only to understand the value systems, categories of belonging and social representations underlying narratives, but also to describe the kinds of

34 *M. Baynham and A. De Fina*

storytelling practices that are enacted by migrants and translocal individuals and groups.

Research on narrative as embedded within institutional and everyday practices

As mentioned above, a great deal of work on narrative has taken as a starting point data generated in research-related contexts such as interviews and focus groups, particularly in the area of identity and language experiences and ideologies. However, scholars have also investigated contexts in which stories are not elicited but are naturally occurring in order to understand processes connected to migration, settlement, transnationalism and their relationship with linguistic issues. This type of work takes an ethnographic approach in order to study the processes that surround and underlie storytelling. Participant observation is generally adopted as a research strategy and this is often complemented by interviews. Below we discuss examples of this kind of research. For example, research on storytelling in institutions focuses on the rules that regulate the production, entextualization (Bauman & Briggs, 1990) and delivery of different kinds of narratives and on relationships of power that affect story ownership, performance and negotiation. In many cases, such studies are not devoted exclusively to narratives but consider their role within wider social processes. An illustrative example is that of Katrjin Maryns' (2006) ethnographic study of the asylum seeker's process in Belgium, which involves crucially the use of stories. Through careful observation and analysis of transcripts of asylum seekers' interviews Maryns demonstrates how lack of proficiency in the language of the official interviewer and the filtering processes through which stories are entextualized to become acceptable within the institutional process deprives asylum seekers of the real possibility of telling their versions of what happened. Maryns also illustrates the fundamental role that interviewers have in the co-construction of those stories, both through direct intervention and through presuppositions about what a good account needs to look like (see also Jacquemet, 2005 for similar research and Berg & Millbank, 2009 on the narratives of asylum claimants based on sexual orientation).

Roberts and Campbell (2005) have investigated the role of narratives as a form of self-presentation in job interviews and the ways that expectations concerning how a story should be told systematically penalize black and ethnic minority applicants. Roberts (2013: 84) writes about a successful applicant "responding to the question with a vivid personal narrative"; however, the research identifies a preference for a normative Anglo narrative, with non-Anglo applicants being penalized if they are not seen to follow it.

Ethnographies of immigrant or immigrant-origin communities provide accounts of the role of stories in various processes related to identities and intergroup relations. An example of this type of research can be found in De Fina's (2008) study of an all-men card-playing group in which participants were both recent immigrants from Italy and second- or third-generation Italian Americans. De Fina observed the club's meetings for around a year, conducted interviews and tape- and audio-recorded sessions. She found that among the most common stories that the Italian American men told each other in conversation were narratives of trips to Italy, migration stories related to family history and anecdotes about family life. She argued that, at the micro level, individual stories fundamentally contributed to legitimizing members of the club as real "Italians," but that, at the same time, because of their common glorification of Italian traditions, these narratives had an important role in shaping the club as an ethnic organization by building a collective narrative of immigrant success which in turn reflected more general processes of accumulation of cultural capital by Italian Americans in the country.

In another long-term ethnographic study of a new Latino neighborhood in the US, Wortham et al. (2011) investigated a particular kind of story, the "payday mugging narrative," and discuss how it reflects and shapes relations between Mexicans and African Americans residing in the area. Payday mugging narratives revolve around assaults by African Americans against Mexican residents who have just received a paycheck. Wortham et al. trace the trajectories of these types of narratives through ethnographic notes and interviews and describe how such narratives follow paths that go from newspaper reports to talk among residents to interviews about life in the neighborhood, thus shaping and contributing to ideologies of personhood.

These studies are all examples of ways in which the analysis of narratives in naturally occurring contexts can throw light on institutional and even local neighborhood practices of exclusion, and on linguistic ideologies and representations about self and others and the construction of identities.

Narratives in research contexts

Much narrative analysis has relied on data drawn from interviews, specifically the open-ended sociolinguistic or ethnographic interview, and we will begin this section by reviewing studies in which the interview was used as a frame for eliciting narratives and will then go on to research that does not focus specifically on narrative, but uses narrative analysis in interview-based studies.

Researchers representing the first trend, such as De Fina (2003), Relaño Pastor and De Fina (2005), Baynham (2005, 2006), Liebscher and Dailey-O'Cain (2005), Farrell (2008) and (Miller 2012), have made narrative the central focus of their research, using it in open-ended sociolinguistic or ethnographic interviews for the purpose of generating rich and involved talk about fundamental experiences with work, language and personal relations lived by migrants and/or translocal individuals. In this sense, they can be regarded as belonging to a tradition initiated by Labov (1972) which exploits the potential of narrative as a high-involvement genre. This research focuses on issues of identity construction (for example on dimensions such

36   *M. Baynham and A. De Fina*

as agency), and on the representation of self and others (for example on categories used to describe self and others) in the telling of significant experiences. Among such experiences, linguistic and intercultural encounters have had a central role. Indeed, narrative is seen by researchers in this tradition as a central locus for identity work, though this is often assumed rather than openly argued.

In an effort to address this lacuna, Baynham (2015) argues that the affordances of narrative as a genre make it a privileged site for identity work, through narrative characteristics such as *repeatability*, *involvement*, *distribution of evidential responsibility*, and *pragmatic and metapragmatic explicitness*. For example, the repeatability of narrative lends itself to the sedimentation of identity positions in habitus. In his words:

> The characteristic of involvement binds the interlocutor into the identity positions being constructed, hailing them as it were. To use Althusser's other formulation, interlocutors are quite literally interpellated into the narrative through the pragmatic work required of them to make sense of features like shifts in pronoun anaphora, deixis and reference.
>
> (Baynham, 2015: 75)

We will illustrate the first approach (interviews designed to elicit narratives) through the research of Relaño Pastor (2014) and Relaño Pastor and De Fina (2005) on the narratives of first-generation Mexican women in the area of San Diego, California, and through work by Murphy (2010) on the narratives of *sans papiers* (undocumented migrants) in Paris, France. In Relaño Pastor's study, the research questions focus on how Latinas use narrative to talk about language difficulties and issues of access to language resources. A previous investigation (Relaño Pastor & De Fina, 2005) concentrated on the kind of agency these speakers project in their narratives, the kinds of acts of resistance they talk about and on whether there is a gendered dimension to their narrative re-tellings. Agency was defined as "the degree of activity and initiative that narrators attribute to themselves as characters in particular story worlds" (p. 41). According to the authors, agentive reactions to troubles and difficulties can be placed on a continuum from low to high and can be analyzed based on complicating action clauses and evaluations. Complication clauses are divided into: (1) complicating events (CE); (2) reactions (RE); and (3) resolutions (RES). Evaluation is particularly associated with reported speech and emotional language (ibid.: 42–43). Using this framework, Relaño Pastor and De Fina (2005) analyze data on language conflicts. For example, an interviewee recounts how she went to hospital, nobody spoke Spanish there (CE), she felt horrible but filled out the paperwork as best as she could (RE), had an encounter with a doctor who spoke a bit of Spanish and, in the end, could communicate with her (RES). Evaluation of this episode of language difficulty was expressed through the language of emotion *me sentí horrible* (I felt horrible). The analysis demonstrated both how language encounters

Narrative analysis 37

represented highly charged moments in the life of Mexican immigrant women and how these women, contrary to stereotypical visions, presented themselves as strongly agentive characters in story worlds.

Besides investigating substantive issues such as identity and agency via narrative analysis, such research can also contribute to extending the scope of narrative theory. Further contributions in this direction come from recent work on spatial orientations and practices in narrative. Post-Labovian work on narrative (Baynham, 2003) has made a distinction between the spatial/ temporal orientation of narrative as a backdrop against which the story line is played out, and a constitutive, performative understanding of space/time relations in narrative. From this perspective, mobility in space/time *is* the story. This perception is well captured by Giddens:

> We can only grasp time and space in terms of the relations of things and events: they *are* the modes in which relations between objects and events are expressed.
>
> (Giddens, 1991: 31)

An example of work on narrative which problematizes and develops our understanding of the spatiality of narrative is Murphy's (2010) investigation of narratives told by *sans papiers* in France. Murphy's analysis of spatial practices draws on the philosophy of Merleau-Ponty (1992) and Heidegger (1962), on Bachelard's (1994) psychoanalytic work on the poetics of space, on Bakhtin's (1981) chronotope, and on the work on spatial cognition of linguistic anthropologists such as Haviland (2005) and others. It involves eight dimensions:

i embodied space
ii static or dynamic space: shelter and displacement
iii lived space understood as an interactional event
iv spatial identity as discursive activity
v physical space structured by social space
vi cognitive representations of space and spatial terminology
vii fictionalized movement in the discursive expression of space
viii spatial reference in the narrative.

Take, for example, spatial identity as discursively constructed. Murphy starts with a quote from Dixon and Durrheim (2000: 27): "Questions of 'who we are' are often intimately related to questions of 'where we are'". He illustrates this with the example of the *sans papiers* being conceived of as *hors la loi* (outside the law). This echoes Bourdieu's remark that:

> Like Socrates, the immigrant is *atopos*, without place, displaced, unclassifiable … Neither citizen nor foreigner, neither truly on the side of the Same, nor totally on the side of the Other, the "Immigrant" is located

in this "bastard" place of which Plato also speaks, the frontier between social being and non-being.

(Bourdieu, 1991: 9)

Static or dynamic space is illustrated by the dialectics of "at-homeness" and "displacement," drawing on the work of Bachelard (1994).

With regard to the social structuring of physical space, one example Murphy analyzes is the role in the narratives of the *sans papiers* of the major Paris railway station – the Gare du Nord – which is transformed into a place to be feared even though it is a necessary route, because it could betray their illegal status. Indeed, as a transport hub, it presents a high risk of random paper checks by the *Police aux Frontières* (PAF) [Frontier Police], which would expose the immigrants' illegal status.

A great deal of work on narrative, particularly in the context of second language or intercultural studies, has focused and still focuses on life stories. Researchers use these types of elicited narratives particularly to study identity construction and adaptation processes by migrants. Life-story research, partly like research on narratives of personal experience, mostly looks at agency.

Recent developments have started to put greater emphasis on the role of the interviewer and on the interactive, co-constructed characteristics of the research interview (cf. De Fina & Perrino, 2011). Current understandings of this communicative event have been informed by the insights generated by the study of narrative in everyday conversational contexts, and therefore researchers pay closer attention than in the past to the processes through which interviewer and interviewee interactionally achieve and jointly construct meanings. For example, researchers have shown how interview participants build on unspoken presuppositions and ideologies in order to co-construct and interpret narrative accounts dealing with conflictual events in the life of narrators (see Cavallaro Johnson, 2008; Van de Mieerop & Clifton, 2012; De Fina & King, 2011; Miller, 2012).

In addition to research where the study of narrative is the central focus, as is the case in the work of Relaño Pastor and Murphy above, it has become clear in other kinds of investigations that any social science interview of an open-ended ethnographic sort is likely to be rich in narrative features, whether fully performed narratives or momentary shifts into narrative performance. Such momentary shifts have been characterized by Georgakopoulou (2007) and Bamberg and Georgakopoulou (2008) as "small stories," stories told as an example of an argumentative point, generic narratives, hypothetical narratives, and so forth. Along with other kinds of expository, evaluative or argumentative talk, and interacting with them, narrative is thus an intrinsic constituent of the talk generated in the course of such events. We will illustrate this point with examples of studies where narrative is not the primary focus yet which prove to be rich in narrative talk and, indeed, where the functions of narrative prove to be crucial in making sense of the data. We will argue that it is always profitable for the researcher working with interview data to be aware of the way narratives of different sorts are contributing to the meaning-making. We will also argue that it is necessary to move beyond the dichotomy between 'real' or 'authentic' data which is collected in everyday contexts via methods such as participant observation and artificially elicited – hence 'inauthentic' – data gathered, for example, in interviews. As discussed above, current developments in sociolinguistics are problematizing the notion of the 'authentic' in everyday interactional contexts and here we seek to also problematize the notion of the interview as 'inauthentic.'

An interesting case is that of the emergence of unbidden narratives in contexts where researchers were not anticipating their possible significance for data interpretation. For example, Tullio Maranhão recounts how in a study undertaken in north-east Brazil, with no initial orientation towards narrative, designed to elicit local men's classifications of fish and their cognitive planning in sailing and fishing, the fishermen responded to detailed questioning with long, intricate and unexpected narratives of fishing prowess. He eventually discovered that the fishermen were interpreting his detailed learned questioning as an implicit criticism of their fishing and sailing prowess and were telling the narratives to demonstrate their skill and bravery (Maranhão, 1993).

A second category refers to interview-based research which, while not setting out to investigate narrative, nevertheless generates data with a rich variety of text types, including various kinds of narratives. This case is represented by Liebscher and Dailey-O'Cain's (2013) study examining bilingual language use in the German urban immigrant community in Canada. The focus of the research is on immigrant identity and the construction of space, and the role of positioning and membership categorization in identity work. Although the investigation is not specifically on narrative, the researchers are clearly aware of the potential role of narrative in their data, when they describe instructions to fieldworkers "to improvise on follow-ups in order to elicit more information and longer narratives from informants ..." (Liebscher & Dailey-O'Cain, 2013: 9). The interview data they use to exemplify their discussion is indeed full of narratives, for example this illustrative small story (translations are in italics):

```
01 Nanda:   my son used to like the Fischer choir
02 IntW:    ah ja aha.
03 Berta:   ja.und die herz[buben
              yes. and the Herzbuben (name of a band)
04 Nanda:   and when we had German visitors coming, they said oh how can
              you listen to this
05 Suse:    mhm
06 Nanda:   and he was so eh you know eh (...) eingeschnappt (upset) because
              they told him
07          how can you listen to some music like this? (.) but he likes to
              listen to
08 Berta:                                                              [ja
```

40   M. Baynham and A. De Fina

09 Nanda: the German music still [(.) because I brought him up from small on
10 IntW: [ja
11 Nanda: listen to German programs.
12 IntW: ahja.

This small story indexes both a southern German space and Nanda's son's enjoyment of and alignment with it, exemplified by a choice of particular German music, an enjoyment and alignment which is upset when the German visitors position him by challenging his choice. This extract illustrates the pervasiveness of narrative in such ethnographic interview data (which Liebscher and Dailey-O'Cain call "conversational").

In another recent interview-based study, Piller and Takahashi (2013) investigated language work in English and Japanese in a low-cost airline. Again the interview data seems to be rich in narrative as interviewees recount problematic or challenging interactions with customers and others:

> Ryoko: He went like "You are not Japanese! I run a business, but you all are blah, blah, blah. Aren't you ashamed of yourself? Aren't you ashamed to call yourself Japanese?" I was like, "I don't represent Japan." aaa. I don't represent my company either aaa. He made me a representative just because I'm Japanese.

Here Ryoko tells a small story about an encounter with a Japanese customer who is dissatisfied with the service. The customer attempts to position her as an inauthentic Japanese but she resists that positioning argumentatively by insisting that "I don't represent Japan" (Piller & Takahashi, 2013: 109).

These examples give some sense of why narrative is such a rich source of data on identity work, precisely because narrative as a genre both performs and condenses actions and assessments, evaluations and arguments about actions, giving a kind of intensifying affective focus to the recounting of the everyday. In each of these extracts there is a challenge by one actor to some assumptions deeply held by another. Nanda's son's taste in music is put on the line by the German visitors. In Ryoko's case, the offended businessman's negation of her authenticity as a representative of her national culture could potentially be very destabilizing for her sense of identity. Ryoko, however, sees through the gambit and rebuffs it robustly.

It is perhaps obvious from the discussion so far that a vague and generic notion of 'identity' does not quite suffice to account for the interpersonal struggles that are involved in identity work. Notions of positioning, stance and alignment are useful here (cf. Baynham, 2011) as well as membership category analysis. Speakers position themselves in relation to what is being talked about. As such, they take up a stance, aligning with or distancing themselves from particular topics under discussion or other speakers. Du Bois (2007) synthesizes these interrelated concepts in a useful definition:

Narrative analysis 41

Stance is a public act by a social actor, achieved through overt means, of evaluating an object, positioning the self, and aligning with other subjects in respect of any salient dimension of the stance field.

(2007: 163)

Moving on now to membership category analysis, membership was identified as significant in interactional work by Sacks (1992 [1966]). Membership categorization, which can be defined as the analysis of "situated and reflexive use of categories in everyday and institutional interaction" (Benwell & Stokoe, 2006: 38), is often used as a tool to investigate work on identity boundaries. Membership is at stake in both the data examples above: Nanda's son's taste in German music is categorized and othered by the German visitors. The businessman's attempt to offend Ryoko turns on her membership in the category "Japanese," which the businessman attempts to put at stake. Linked to this is the notion of positioning, a typical process in conversation in which interlocutors constantly put themselves and others in specific positions, sometimes aligning with each other, sometimes disassociating from the other, even in such extreme forms that they could be described as "othering." Indeed, both Ryoko and Nanda's son are othered by their interlocutors. All of these interactional devices serve to emphasize the dynamic and performative aspect of identity work, the fact that identity is not something we have as an unchanging attribute but it is rather something we do. As shown in these examples, narrative as a genre is a privileged site for these dynamic and performative characteristics of identity work to emerge, hence its importance in the study of migrants, translocal and transnational communities.

Conclusion

In this chapter, we have reviewed key developments in narrative theory, both in everyday interactional contexts and in research contexts, most notably the open-ended ethnographic interview, glossed as conversational by Liebscher and Dailey-O'Cain (2013) and others, even though we have pointed out the importance of bearing in mind the generic constraints of the research interview. We have shown how ways of conceiving the research interview have been influenced by interactional approaches. Rather than regarding the research interview as a convenient format for grabbing data, we now tend to see it as dynamically co-constructed by participants. Throughout, we have illustrated the discussion with research and data examples taken from work on multilingual and/or diasporic individuals and communities. We have shown how narrative is a privileged site for identity work. This can be explained partly in terms of the constraints and affordances of the genre and partly in terms of the interactional work to which it is put in conversation.

We have seen how identity as a generic construct is not enough to capture the dynamic emergent quality of identity work, which is particularly in

42   M. Baynham and A. De Fina

evidence in narrative. We need more specific notions such as stance, positioning and alignment to engage with the ways that people do identity rather than have identities. This again has been illustrated above.

What narrative can tell us about the social world can perhaps be explained with reference to the notion of tellability (Labov's "so what" factor) and to the immediacy that the creation of story worlds brings about. If Ryoko's Japanese businessman had complimented her on the service and she had thanked him, the actions would have constituted a pleasant conclusion to a service encounter but would not have merited a story. It is because of Ryoko's presentation of her opponent's utterance as so challenging and provocative, so charged with discordant values, in itself creating a divergence, attempting to other Ryoko in a particularly profound way that her response becomes interesting. It is in the challenge and counter-challenge, the attempt at positioning which is resisted and countered by a divergent positioning that the story's tellability lies. Furthermore, narratives are performances that mimic real time and hence audiences become involved in a sequence of events and its consequences and in the evaluative judgments which constitute the disputed social meanings interactively at stake. As such, narrative proves an invaluable resource for researchers interested in how people make sense of their social worlds and work with and against others to construct them.

References

Bachelard, G. (1994) *The Poetics of Space*. Boston, MA: Beacon Press.

Bakhtin, M. (1981) *The Dialogic Imagination*. Austin, TX: University of Texas Press.

Bamberg, M. & Georgakopoulou, A. (2008) 'Small stories as a new perspective in narrative and identity analysis'. *Text and Talk* 28(3), 337–396.

Bauman, R. & Briggs, C. (1990) 'Poetics and performance as critical perspectives on language and social life'. *Annual Review of Anthropology* 19, 59–88.

Baynham, M. (2003) 'Narratives in space and time: beyond "backdrop" accounts of narrative orientation'. *Narrative Inquiry* 13(2), 347–366.

Baynham, M. (2005) 'Network and agency in the migration stories of Moroccan women', in M. Baynham & A. De Fina (eds) *Dislocation/Relocations: Narratives of Displacement*. Manchester: St. Jerome, 11–35.

Baynham, M. (2006) 'Performing self, family and community in Moroccan narratives of migration and settlement', in A. De Fina, D. Schiffrin & M. Bamberg (eds) *Discourse and Identity*. Cambridge: Cambridge University Press, 376–397.

Baynham, M. (2011) 'Stance, positioning and alignment in narratives of professional experience'. *Language in Society* 40, 63–74.

Baynham, M. (2015) 'Identity: brought about or brought along? Narrative as a privileged site for researching intercultural identities', in F. Dervin & K. Risager (eds) *Researching Identity and Interculturality*. London: Routledge, 67–88.

Baynham, M. & De Fina, A. (2005) (eds) *Dislocation/Relocations: Narratives of Displacement*. Manchester: St. Jerome.

Benwell, B. & Stokoe, E. (2006) *Discourse and Identity*. Edinburgh: Edinburgh University Press.

Berg, L. & Millbank, J. (2009) 'Constructing the personal narratives of lesbian, gay and bisexual asylum claimants'. *Journal of Refugee Studies* 22(2), 195–223.

Berman, R.A. (1998) 'Bilingual proficiency/proficient bilingualism: insights from narrative texts', in G. Extra & L. Verhoeven (eds) *Bilingualism and Migration*. Berlin: Mouton de Gruyter, 187–210.

Berman, R.A. & Slobin, D. (1994) *Relating Events in Narrative: A Cross-Linguistic Developmental Study*. Hillsdale, NJ: Lawrence Erlbaum.

Bhabha, H. (1994) *The Location of Culture*. London: Routledge.

Blommaert, J. (2010) *The Sociolinguistics of Globalization*. Cambridge: Cambridge University Press.

Bourdieu, P. (1991) 'Preface' to Abdelmalek Sayad. *L'immigration ou les paradoxes de l'alterité* [Immigration or the paradoxes of the other]. Brussels: De Boeck University.

Bruner, J. (1991) 'The narrative construction of reality'. *Critical Inquiry* 18, 1–21.

Carranza, I. (1998) 'Low narrativity narratives and argumentation'. *Narrative Inquiry* 8(2), 287–317.

Cavallaro Johnson, G. (2008) 'Making visible an ideological dilemma in an interview narrative about social trauma'. *Narrative Inquiry* 18(2), 187–205.

De Fina, A. (2003) *Identity in Narrative: A Study of Immigrant Discourse*. Amsterdam: John Benjamins.

De Fina, A. (2008) 'Who tells the story and why? Micro and macro contexts in narrative'. *Text and Talk* 28(3), 421–442. [Special Issue on "Narrative analysis in the shift from text to practices", edited by A. De Fina & A. Georgakopoulou].

De Fina, A. (2009) 'Narratives in interview – the case of accounts: for an interactional approach to narrative genres'. *Narrative Inquiry* 19(2), 233–258.

De Fina, A. & Georgakopoulou, A. (2008) 'Analysing narratives as practices'. *Qualitative Research* 8(3), 379–387.

De Fina, A. & Georgakopoulou, A. (2012) *Analyzing Narrative*. Cambridge: Cambridge University Press.

De Fina, A. & King, K. (2011) 'Language problem or language conflict? Narratives of immigrant women's experiences in the US'. *Discourse Studies* 13(2), 163–188.

De Fina, A. & Perrino, S. (2011) 'Narratives in interviews, interviews in narrative studies'. *Language in Society*, 40, 1–11. [Introduction to a Special Issue on "Interviews vs. 'natural' contexts: a false dilemma", edited by A. De Fina & S. Perrino].

Dixon, J. & Durrheim, K. (2000) 'Displacing place-identity: a discursive approach to locating self and other'. *British Journal of Social Psychology* 39, 27–44.

Du Bois, J. (2007) 'The stance triangle', in Robert Englebretson (ed.) *Stancetaking in Discourse: Subjectivity, Evaluation, Interaction*. Amsterdam: John Benjamins, 139–182.

Farrell, E. (2008) *Negotiating Identity: Discourses of Migration and Belonging*. Unpublished PhD dissertation, Department of Linguistics, Macquarie University, Australia.

Galasinska, A. & Horolets, A. (2012) 'The (pro)long(ed) life of a "grand narrative": the case of internet forum discussions on post-2004 Polish migration to the UK'. *Text and Talk* 32(2), 125–143.

Georgakopoulou, A. (2007) *Small Stories, Interaction and Identities*. Amsterdam: John Benjamins.

Giddens, A. (1991) *Modernity and Self-Identity: Self and Society in the Late Modern Age*. Stanford, CA: Stanford University Press.

Haviland, J.B. (2005) 'Dreams of blood: Zinacantecs in Oregon', in M. Baynham & A. De Fina (eds) *Dislocation/Relocations: Narratives of Displacement*, Manchester: St. Jerome, 87–127.

44   M. Baynham and A. De Fina

Heidegger, M. (1962) *Being and Time*. New York: Harper & Row.

Jacquemet, M. (2005) 'Transidiomatic practices: language and power in the age of globalization'. *Language & Communication* 25, 257–277

Kresova, N. (2011) 'Storytelling on Web 2.0: the case of migrants' personal blogs.' Paper presented at *Narrative Matters 2012*, UAP, Paris, France, May 31. Available from www.vitartis.com/analysis.php, retrieved 7 July 2014.

Labov, W. (1972) 'The transformation of experience in narrative syntax', in W. Labov (ed.) *Language in the Inner City: Studies in the Black English Vernacular*. Philadelphia, PA: University of Pennsylvania Press, 354–396.

Liebscher, G. & Dailey-O'Cain, J. (2005) 'West Germans moving east: place, political space, and positioning in conversational narratives', in M. Baynham & A. de Fina (eds) *Dislocation/Relocations: Narratives of Displacement*. Manchester: St. Jerome, 61–85.

Liebscher, G. & Dailey-O'Cain, J. (2013) *Language, Identity, and Space in Migration*. Basingstoke, Hampshire: Palgrave Macmillan.

Maranhão, T. (1993) 'Recollections of fieldwork conversations, or authorial difficulties in anthropological writing', in J. Hill & J. Irvine (eds) *Responsibility and Evidence in Oral Discourse*. Cambridge: Cambridge University Press, 260–288.

Maryns, K. (2006) *The Asylum Speaker: Language in the Belgian Asylum Procedure*. Manchester: St. Jerome.

Merleau-Ponty, M. (1992) *The Phenomenology of Perception*. New York: Humanities Press.

Miller, E.R. (2012) 'Agency, language learning and multilingual spaces'. *Multilingua* 31(4), 441–468.

Murphy, M. (2010) *La Mise en Récit des Espaces et des Relation Identitaires de Trois Femmes "Sans Papiers" en France*. [The Narration of Space and Identity by Three Undocumented Women Migrants in France]. Unpublished PhD thesis, Université Paris Descartes.

Pennycook, A. (2010) *Language as a Local Practice*. London: Routledge.

Piller, I. & Takahashi, K. (2013) 'Language work aboard the low-cost airline', in A. Duchêne, M. Moyer & C. Roberts (eds) *Language, Migration and Social Inequalities: A Critical Sociolinguistic Perspective on Institutions and Work*. Bristol: Multilingual Matters, 95–117.

Rampton, B. (2006) *Language in Late Modernity: Interaction in an Urban School*. Cambridge: Cambridge University Press.

Relaño Pastor, A.M. (2010) 'Ethnic categorization and moral agency in 'fitting in' narratives among Madrid immigrant students'. *Narrative Inquiry* 20(1), 82–105.

Relaño Pastor, A.M. (2014) *Shame and Pride in Narrative: Mexican Women's Language Experiences at the U.S.–Mexico Border*. New York: Palgrave Macmillan.

Relaño Pastor, A.M. & De Fina, A. (2005) 'Contesting social place: narratives of language conflict', in M. Baynham and A. De Fina (eds) *Dislocation/Relocations: Narratives of Displacement*. Manchester: St Jerome, 36–60.

Riessman, C.K. (1993) *Narrative Analysis*. Thousand Oaks/London: Sage.

Roberts, C. (2013) 'The gatekeeping of Babel: job interviews and the linguistic penalty', in A. Duchêne, M. Moyer & C. Roberts (eds) *Language, Migration and Social Inequalities: A Critical Sociolinguistic Perspective on Institutions and Work*. Bristol: Multilingual Matters, 81–94.

Roberts, C. & Campbell, S. (2005) 'Fitting stories into boxes: textual and rhetorical constraints on candidates' performance in British job interviews'. *Journal of Applied Linguistics* 2(1), 45–73.

Sacks, H. (1992 [1966]) '"We"; Category-bound activities', in G. Jefferson (ed.) *Harold Sacks: Lectures on Conversation*, Vol. 1. Oxford: Blackwell, 333–340.

Schrauf, R. & Rubin, D.C. (1998) 'Bilingual autobiographical memory in older adult immigrants: a test of cognitive explanations of the reminiscence bump and the linguistic encoding of memories'. *Journal of Pragmatics* 39(3), 437–457.

Van De Mieerop, D. & Clifton, J. (2012) 'The interactional negotiation of group membership and ethnicity: the case of an interview with a former slave'. *Discourse & Society* 23(2), 163–183.

Wortham, S., Allard, E., Lee, K. & Mortimer, K. (2011) 'Racialization in payday mugging narratives'. *Journal of Linguistic Anthropology* 21, 56–75.

3 Biographical approaches to research in multilingual settings

Exploring linguistic repertoires

Brigitta Busch

Introduction

Linguistic diversity has become a central feature in daily lives. It has also become a central feature of societies whose self-understandings were or still are deeply rooted in a monolingual paradigm. In sociolinguistics, traditional approaches which assumed a stable link between language and national, ethnic or social belonging and were based on the idea of languages conceived as pre-established, clear-cut, bounded entities are increasingly being abandoned in favour of approaches that foreground speakers' heteroglossic language practices and repertoires. Whereas Gumperz' (1964) original notion of linguistic repertoire takes the outside perspective of the observer, biographical approaches emphasise the perspective of the experiencing and speaking subject. They contribute to an understanding of the linguistic repertoire as reflecting individual life trajectories, heterogeneous life worlds and discourses about language and linguistic practices referring to specific time-spaces (Blommaert, 2009; Busch, 2012). Biographical research has proven to be particularly productive in addressing topics such as subject positions or identity constructions, language and emotion, fears and desires associated with ways of speaking or language attitudes linked to language ideologies or discourses on language (Kramsch, 2009; Busch, 2015a).

The interest in language biographies is related to developments, sometimes referred to as the 'biographical turn', that have been taking place in other disciplines such as ethnography, sociology or history since the 1980s. A particular stimulus has come from feminist and post-colonial studies in which stories related to biographical experiences have been valued as an important source (e.g. Chilisa, 2012), especially among researchers who are particularly interested in the 'hidden' symbolic power relations of everyday practices. One of the aims of biographical research is to give voice to positions excluded from the dominant discourse, and – in light of the collapse of the Grand Narratives postulated by Jean François Lyotard (1979) – to give recognition to the heterogeneity and singularity expressed in individual stories. However, it is worth noting that, in sociology, first works drawing on biographical data go back to the 1920s, when Thomas and Znaniecki (1996) published their

Biographical approaches 47

ground-breaking migration study *The Polish Peasant in Europe and America.* A further incentive for biographically oriented research and oral history narratives stemmed from the interest in collecting and understanding first-hand experiences of Nazism, exile and the Holocaust. Over the last decades, biographical methods have been developed particularly in the German-speaking scientific space, which has benefited from a strong tradition in phenomenological thought. As Fischer-Rosenthal, one of the promotors of biographical research in sociology, states: "Biographical research moved from being a mere tool for empirical social research (like the interview, questionnaire, participant observation) into a full-fledged sociological sub-discipline, aimed at developing empirically grounded theories on contemporary society" (1995: 259). Fischer-Rosenthal understands biographical work as dialogical and interactive and as offering an alternative to the concept of stable identities: in contrast to the concept of identity that assumes belonging in a once-and-for-all sense, "[b]iography refers to an interpretatively open process of 'becoming'." (ibid.: 258). In his view, the notion of biography does not reproduce the split between individual and society but rather structures both spheres (ibid.: 259).

The following section will give a brief overview of studies in multilingualism employing a biographical approach. I will then situate biographical research within the interpretative paradigm in social and cultural studies, and I will discuss data collection and interpretation as well as ethical implications. In the last section, drawing on my own research, I will show how (multimodal) biographical approaches can contribute to a better understanding of heteroglossic life worlds and multi-layered linguistic repertoires.

An overview of language biographical research

Biographically oriented research in Applied Linguistics first established itself in the fields of second language acquisition and foreign language learning, where it continues to be prolific. It is also important to note that some early work on child bilingualism followed a biographical approach and yielded results that diverged from the monolingual paradigm prevalent at the time. Ronjat's (1913) and Leopold's (1939–1949) famous diary studies, considered to be milestones in psycholinguistic research, document not only the language development of their respective children but, to some extent, also the diarists' own reactions, sorrows and joys. Both works highlight the fact that the children whose trajectories were documented in the diaries oriented to different languages in different phases of their lives, sometimes more towards one language, sometimes to the other. This suggested that their languages could not simply be considered as clearly separated. Other diary-based studies, observing children's bi- or multilingual language development, have emerged since these early contributions.

There has also been keen interest in language-learning diaries and the use of biographical texts in the field of Applied Linguistics (for an overview, see Pavlenko, 2007). In a poststructuralist and feminist approach, Norton

48   *B. Busch*

(2000), working with migrants in Canada, used language-learning diaries to initiate a process in which the participants reflected collectively on their individual experiences and explored their suppressed potential. In a similar line of thought, Kramsch (2009) has been working for many years with learners' autobiographical texts which demonstrate "heightened perceptions and emotions, imagined identities, projected selves, idealizations or stereotypes of the other, awareness of one's body, feelings of loss or enhanced power" (Kramsch, 2006: 99).

Diaries and other biographical texts and images continue to provide important data for other kinds of research in multilingual settings. In ethnographic studies of multilingual literacy practices, diary-based research has been developed in different ways. For example, Jones et al. (2000) reviewed the ways in which they carried out diary-based interviews in different research projects, working from literacy diaries which were compiled in note form by participants. They found that this approach enabled them to capture the situated ways in which different literacies traversed the daily routines of participants. They also noted that working in this way also contributed to the shifting of researcher–researched positionings, enabling the emic perspectives of participants to be voiced and making the research process more dialogic in nature.

An early, unjustly neglected, publication appeared in French in 1985 under the title *Du bilinguisme* (Collectif, 1985). This contrasted with the then dominant paradigm in bilingualism studies. This publication followed a colloquium in Rabat, Morocco, which brought together writers, linguists and psychotherapists, many of them with a North African background. Most of the authors reflected their own experience of lived bilingualism under the conditions of (post-)colonialism and migration, thereby addressing the interrelations of language, subjectivity and power. Derrida's essay "Monolingualism of the other or the prosthesis of origin" (Derrida, 1998) can be read as an echo of the Rabat colloquium. He draws on his own experience as a French-speaking Algerian Jew to discuss the colonial mechanisms of traumatically lived exclusions from language. In recent research on multilingualism, literary texts and language memoirs have also become an important resource for the exploration of how linguistic diversity is experienced and lived (Pavlenko, 2007; Busch & Busch, 2008; Kramsch, 2009).

Since the 1990s, we have witnessed an increasing interest in establishing research based on qualitative narrative interviews as a biographical method in Applied Linguistics. This method is indebted to the above-mentioned German sociological tradition in biography studies. Studies within this strand revolve around questions of language learning, language practices and identity construction in multilingual environments in the context of migration and minority situations (e.g. Nekvapil, 2001; Franceschini, 2003; Treichel, 2004). Some studies focus more on the social dimensions of language change linked to political disruptions and reconfigurations (e.g. Fix & Barth, 2000), others more on individual language maintenance, transmission and loss (e.g.

Betten, 2010). In addition, there is growing interest in multimodal approaches in applied linguistics, and in biographically oriented research. Visual and creative methods and, in particular, the so-called language portraits, are increasingly employed to explore speakers' heteroglossic repertoires (e.g. Krumm & Jenkins, 2001; Busch, 2006, 2012; Farmer, 2012). I will come back to this approach later in this chapter.

Epistemological and methodological considerations

Biographical research is located within the broader framework of qualitative and interpretative approaches.[1] Basically, what this means is that they do not aim at detecting laws that allow for prognostics but, instead, they aim at building an understanding of social phenomena through reconstruction. Though interpretative approaches agree on the assumption that (social) reality cannot be observed objectively but only mediated by perception, they differ considerably in how they conceive the biographical subject, and how they understand the notions of experience, memory and narration. Which basic perspective to adopt, which stance to take will depend on the phenomena researchers are interested in, on the specific research questions and on their preferred theoretical orientations. When combining elements and methods which have their origins in different approaches, one must obviously be aware of such distinguishable perspectives and reflect on how they can be integrated with regard to the underlying theoretical assumptions. Schematically, I shall contrast three theoretical positions within the interpretative paradigm: approaches based on interactionist, on phenomenological and on poststructuralist thinking.

I will first turn to studies that rely on **interactional approaches**. These approaches are inspired by symbolic interactionism (e.g. Goffman, 1959), ethnomethodology (Garfinkel, 1967) and dialogism (Bakhtin, 1981), among others. They focus on phenomena of social interaction situated in a here and now. Interaction is conceived as a dialogical process in which the interlocutors, explicitly or implicitly, constantly refer by means of indexicality (Silverstein, 2006) to other persons, things, times and spaces. In this view, the subject is not a stable category but is seen as continuously (co-)constructed in interaction with and in relation to others. Experience is seen as having an explicitly social dimension, because experience itself already implies an interpretation (of the sign) according to an already acquired referential, socio-ideological framework (Vološinov, 1973: 36). Memory is accessible only by the detour of looking at (biographical) accounts as situated re-enactments of the past. Borrowing Jakobson's (1960) terminology regarding functions of communication, interactional approaches can be described as being primarily interested in the phatic function of language, i.e. the means by which social contact is established and constantly renegotiated between the inter-actors. The researcher takes the stance of an outside observer – a third-person perspective, as it were. Biographical interviews are considered more as providing

50   *B. Busch*

additional data about how speakers interpret their own linguistic behaviour (Hymes, 1977: 31) than as a reliable source on how they act. Biographically oriented research on multilingualism rooted in Conversation Analysis or Linguistic Anthropology is still fairly scarce (e.g. Koven, 2001; De Fina, 2003; Baynham & De Fina, 2005; Blommaert, 2009). However, these approaches offer a rich set of analytical tools for the micro-analysis of narrative features – such as framing, indexicality, sequencing, turn taking or (double-) voicing – that is frequently borrowed from for biographical research following other epistemological approaches.

Most biographical studies in the social sciences, mainly in the German-speaking area, are located within the **phenomenological tradition** that draws on Husserl's (1982) idea of the intersubjective nature of perception. They take the bodily constituted, perceiving, feeling, speaking and meaning-making subject as their point of departure and thereby open the path to a first-person perspective, allowing for the exploration of lived experiences, feelings, emotions and reflections. While bodily lived experience is conceived as a central category, memory is understood as an effort to re-open the past starting from the implications of the present. In a phenomenological view, time is centred in the present and embodies recollections of the past and anticipations of the future. The biographical account is thus seen as a process that results in the retrospective reconstruction of a coherent, meaning-making life trajectory. Referring again to Jakobson's (1960) terminology, the main interest in this case is on the expressive function of language, the addresser's representation of self. Language is, before anything else, seen as the bodily gestural capacity to relate oneself to the world and to the other (Merleau-Ponty, 2002). Research in sociology within this paradigm has developed a rigorous methodology for conducting, processing and analysing biographical interviews (e.g. Rosenthal, 1995, 2006). However, Rosenthal's (1995) assumption that the coherence of biographical accounts is a (normative) goal that has to be achieved[2] is problematic, as is the assumption that case reconstructions can establish a sort of truth 'outside' of the account. Phenomenological approaches have been applied successfully in studies of multilingualism (e.g. Treichel, 2004). The strength of this approach is that it can contribute substantially to the understanding of how living in multilingual life worlds is experienced.

The phenomenological assumption of a pre-existing, coherent subject is contested by **poststructuralist approaches**, which in turn draw on post-Marxist and post-Freudian thinking. In a poststructuralist view, subjectivity can only be considered in terms of subjectification, i.e. how, in a specific historical-political context, the subject is constituted in being addressed by ideological interpellation (Althusser, 1971) and the performative power (Butler, 1997) of already uttered discourses, norms and categorisations. One could say that poststructuralist approaches focus on what Jakobson (1960) termed the conative function of language, i.e. the way in which the addressee is constructed through language. They address the biographic

Biographical approaches 51

subject from a second-person perspective, submitting it to a deconstructive reading and rewriting of the biography as "a product of the historical processes to date which has deposited in you an infinity of traces without leaving an inventory" (Gramsci, 1971: 324). In working with biographical accounts, importance is attached to the ways in which the narrator's and the researcher's perceptions, experiences, memories, thoughts and narratives are shaped by historically determined power relations and subject practices. Poststructuralist approaches attach less importance to the construction of biographical continuity and coherence but focus rather on disruptions and on what is excluded or made invisible by dominant discourses and "techniques of the self" (Foucault, 1982). Due to the profound scepticism of poststructuralism vis-à-vis any kind of consolidated methodology, research in this field does not draw on a pre-established toolset. In sociology (Schäfer & Völter, 2005; Tuider, 2007), as well as in multilingualism research (McNamara, 2010; Busch, 2012), possibilities of how theoretically to integrate biographical research and poststructuralist understandings of discourse are on the agenda. In his above-mentioned essay, Derrida (1998) exemplifies practices of deconstruction, submitting his own language biography to a critical reading.

Although most current biographical studies on multilingualism are based on extensive biographical interviews, I will not discuss in any detail how such interviews are conducted and analysed, as biographical interviews can be considered as a specific form of the qualitative interview which is amply discussed in different manuals. Of course, audio or video recordings of the interviews, the choice of an appropriate transcription system and careful transcriptions corresponding to linguistic criteria are indispensable. It is not a coincidence that the question of language choice is debated, as the language in which biographical interviews are conducted influences the ways in which a life story is told or in which subjectivity is constructed (Koven, 2001; Pavlenko, 2007). I would insist that opening a space for code switching or language crossing (Rampton, 1995) will not only ease the interaction but can also be highly significant for its analysis (Tylim, 2002).

Inspiring recommendations on how to conduct biographical interviews can also be found in Bourdieu's (1999) methodological contribution to the collection of interviews published under the title *The Weight of the World*, in which he argues that the interviewer should take the role of an empathic, active and methodical listener who, during the interview, adopts the subject perspective of the interviewee. Working with others' biographies requires particular attention and awareness about the power asymmetry in the relationship between researcher and interviewees (Bourdieu, 1999). The loss of ownership of one's life story can be experienced as extremely harmful and disempowering (Cuellar, 2005). Particularly in feminist (e.g. Haug, 1990) and post-colonial (e.g. Tuhiwai Smith, 2012; Chilisa, 2012) studies, participatory forms of research are developed that are highly relevant when working with others' biographies.

52 B. Busch

Language ideologies, language experience and the linguistic repertoire

As shown above, biographical approaches are applied in a range of fields in multilingualism research and differ considerably in their theoretical and methodological foundations. In the following part I will discuss an approach developed in the framework of my research based on the concepts of the lived experience of language and the linguistic repertoire and briefly illustrate how it is applied in practice.

Recent research on multilingualism frequently refers to the notion of repertoire and conceives it – as Gumperz has already done – as multi-layered. In Gumperz' (1964: 140) view, languages and dialects "form a behavioural whole, regardless of grammatical distinctness, and must be considered constituent varieties of the same verbal repertoire". He linked the notion of the linguistic repertoire to particular speech communities: "[the verbal repertoire] contains all the accepted ways of formulating messages. It provides the weapons of everyday communication. Speakers choose among this arsenal in accordance with the meanings they wish to convey." (ibid.: 138) Later, Gumperz (2001: 37) conceded that in his earlier work he had underestimated the influence of "ideology in relation to subconsciously internalized background knowledge" in order to be able to account for the basic issues of hegemony or symbolic domination.

Whereas Gumperz' original concept is rooted in an interactional paradigm, I recommend elaborating on it, drawing on thinking inspired by poststructuralism and phenomenology. I make this recommendation because it provides us with a means to seek an understanding of how ideology – or discourse – when translated into bodily and emotionally lived experience of language, impacts on the linguistic repertoire. Discourses that tell us who we are exert power in a twofold way (Foucault, 1982): by coercion or interdiction and through the process of subjectification, i.e. the ways in which we appropriate identifications as (mis-)recognitions by discourse. Language ideologies or discourses on language and language use, on linguistic normativity, appropriateness, hierarchies, taboos, etc., translate into attitudes, into the ways in which we perceive ourselves and others as speakers, and into the ways in which these perceptions are enacted in language practices that confirm, subvert or transform categorisations, norms and rules (Busch, 2012). This translation into embodied attitudes and practices presupposes, following Merleau-Ponty (2002), that language is not mainly seen as a conventionalised, sedimented system of signifiers but primarily as an intersubjective bodily emotional gesture which relates the experiencing/speaking subject to the other and to the world. Whereas lived experience of language can hardly be observed from an outside perspective, it can be approached through first-person accounts. To give an example, language biographical accounts frequently mention feelings of shame that arise in situations when one becomes aware of speaking with a 'wrong' accent or making a 'mistake'. From a phenomenological point of view, shame is a bodily feeling that is experienced as a move of withdrawal from the world, which sometimes results in momentary lapses into silence. From a discourse perspective, the 'mistake' is not a personal shortcoming but an infringement against a discursively set norm that can become internalised precisely through such experiences. Lived experience of language (*Spracherleben*) thus plays a pivotal role in mediating between discourses about language and the linguistic repertoire (Busch, 2015b).

From this perspective, the linguistic repertoire cannot simply be considered as a toolbox or a reservoir of competences but should be conceived as a space of potentialities linked to life trajectories. Although it responds immediately to the needs of the present, it also points towards the past and the future. Discontinuities in personal biographies (e.g. a change of location) inscribe their traces in the same way as societal discontinuities (e.g. regime change). Drawing on a broad range of earlier voices, discourses, and codes, the linguistic repertoire forms a contingent space both of restrictions and of potentialities, which includes anticipations, imaginations, fears and desires. With every situated linguistic interaction we position ourselves not only in relation to what is directly present – i.e. the respective interaction partners and interaction contexts – but also implicitly in relation to what is absent. This absence runs or resonates in the background and is therefore, whether welcome or not, also present: there are relevant others, other spaces and times by which we orientate ourselves or which demand our loyalty.

Biographical approaches based on the notions of lived experience of language and the linguistic repertoire seem particularly productive for multilingualism research as they allow us to consider languages not as bounded and separated entities but rather to embrace a concept which is best captured referring to Bakhtin's notion of heteroglossia (Todorov, 1984: 56): linguistic diversity is understood as a multiplicity of discourses in relation to which we position ourselves, voices which we appropriate as styles, and language varieties which reflect the socio-cultural spaces in which we move. The concept of the heteroglossic repertoire allows us to address from a speaker-oriented perspective phenomena such as language acquisition, language shift or linguistic creativity. The starting point is not a single language but a "dialog of languages" (Bakhtin, 1981: 294), a "highly specific unity of several 'languages' that have established contact and mutual recognition with each other" (ibid.: 295).

A multimodal, creative method to explore heteroglossic repertoires

The Spracherleben [Lived Experience of Language] Research Group at the Institute of Linguistics at the University of Vienna began ten years ago to use a multimodal biographic method in research on linguistic diversity (Busch, 2006, 2012) and has since collected and evaluated several hundred language portraits in the context of various projects.

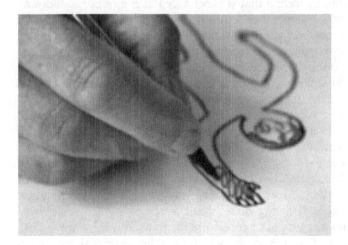

Figure 3.1 Participants are asked to map their 'languages' and 'ways of speaking' with regard to a body silhouette. The silhouette can be downloaded at www.heteroglossia.net.

Participants are asked to either use the body silhouette supplied (see Figure 3.1) or to draw one themselves, to choose different colours for their different languages and ways of speaking and to place them with regard to the body silhouette.

They are invited to think about ways of speaking that are relevant for them in their daily life but also about languages that were important in the past or might become important in the future, as well as about languages which they relate to particular persons, places or situations. The prompt leaves it to the participants to determine what they consider to be a language or way of speaking. Not only are conventional languages and dialects represented in portraits and attached explanatory legends but, frequently, other ways of categorising speech and communication are also portrayed. These include categories such as 'sister language', 'secret language', 'language of anger', 'musical language'. Through the body silhouette on the white paper, a framing is laid down for the language portrait, one that is taken up, exhausted or supplemented. The picture repeatedly serves as a point of reference in the account elicited by the drawing, and these references to the picture – such as body or colour metaphors – structure the interpretation and reconstruction of the narrative in a way that differs from responses to interview questions organised around a participant's language biography. As a multimodal method, the language portrait provides two sets of data that permit inferences to be drawn concerning how speakers interpret their linguistic repertoire: a visual one and a narrative one. Meaning is created through both modes; one is neither the translation nor simply the illustration of the other. Whereas narrations are structured in a rather linear and sequential way, the visual mode

Biographical approaches 55

steers one's vision toward the whole and toward the connections between the parts. Whereas the verbal mode favours diachronic continuity and synchronic coherence, the visual mode allows contradictions, fractures, overlappings and ambiguities to remain unresolved more easily. As with any kind of biographical representation, the language portrait cannot be considered as a depiction of the repertoire 'as it is' but as a production corresponding to a specific interactional situation. Selection, interpretation and evaluation take place in the visual mode as much as in the verbal mode, and representation and reconstruction do not occur independently of social discourses.

Today, language portraits are widely applied in language awareness and in teacher training and function as an empirical method in a range of research projects relating to multilingualism. In her arts-informed work on migration and schooling in Canada, Farmer (2012) has developed a modified form of the language portrait using a body silhouette derived from photographs taken by the students. Using language portraits, Singer and Harris (forthcoming), in their sociolinguistic study on language survival among speakers in a highly multilingual Australian Indigenous community, identify features of small-scale multilingualism which do not correspond to expectations derived from established knowledge about societal multilingualism in this context. In Cape Town and Vienna, we have developed a modular approach, the so-called school language profiles, which use language portraits – created in workshops with learners – in combination with other ethnographic methods, to explore the current local language regime and to negotiate a tailor-made school language policy (Busch, 2010). The research project *Multilingualism and Resilience* – an interdisciplinary project involving psychiatrists, trauma therapists and linguists – aims at identifying linguistic resources that can be mobilised to strengthen resilience through conversations with patients following the drawing of language portraits. We hope that this project will bring new impetus to diagnostic and therapeutic practice in the context of posttraumatic stress disorder, and also deepen the understanding of the connection between emotion and language (Busch, 2015b).

Even a brief discussion of language biographical approaches as presented in this contribution can give an idea about what interesting outlooks open up when the perspective of observing language in interaction is brought into dialogue with a perspective that foregrounds the speaking subject. Although biographic approaches rely on individual accounts, they are not primarily interested in the uniqueness of the particular life story as such but in what its apparent singularity can reveal about specific dimensions of language practices and ideologies that are neglected when taking an assumed 'average' speaker as representative of a certain group. Exploring situations that have so far rarely been in focus because they were considered exceptional or marginal can lead to a deeper understanding of language in linguistically diverse contexts, as in such situations the liminality of speech is lived and it becomes vital to develop strategies of translingual understanding. It is particularly in accounts of experiences of social exclusion and precarity that participants

56   B. Busch

bring forward unexpected language practices, resources, fears and desires. Especially when framed as action research, biographical research can contribute to the raising of an awareness of power relations and language ideologies that label certain linguistic practices as deficient. It can also reveal the potentially transformative power of the linguistic resources and strategies speakers can rely on. Taking the speakers' perspective and the linguistic repertoire as point of departure helps to avoid overly rapid 'objectivisations' into pre-established categories such as first, second or foreign languages. It can also enable us to develop an understanding of linguistic diversity in the Bakhtinian sense, as heteroglossia, as entanglement of multiple discourses, voices and languages.

Notes

1 A few studies in research on multilingualism employ biographical data in combination with quantitative methods, e.g. Schmid (2004) or Stevenson (2013).
2 For a critical discussion of narrative coherence, see Adamzik and Roos (2002).

References

Adamzik, K. & Roos, E. (eds) (2002) 'Biografie linguistiche – Biographies langagières- Biografias linguistica- Sprachbiografien' [Language biographies]. *Bulletin Vals-Alsa* no. 76, Neuchâtel.

Althusser, L. (1971) 'Ideology and ideological state apparatuses (Notes towards an investigation)', in Louis Althusser, *Lenin and Philosophy, and Other Essays*. London: New Left Books, 127–188.

Bakhtin, M. (1981) 'Discourse in the novel', in Mikhail Bakhtin, *The Dialogic Imagination* (ed. by M. Holquist). Austin, TX: University of Texas Press, 259–422.

Baynham, M. and De Fina, A. (2005) *Dislocations/Relocations: Narratives of Displacement*. Manchester: St. Jerome.

Betten, A. (2010) 'Sprachbiographien der 2. Generation deutschsprachiger Emigranten in Israel: zur Auswirkung individueller Erfahrungen und Emotionen auf die Sprachkompetenz'. [Language biographies of 2nd generation German-speaking emigrants in Israel: on the impact of individual experiences and emotions on linguistic competence] *Zeitschrift für Literatur und Linguistik* 40, 29–57.

Blommaert, J. (2009) 'Language, asylum, and the national order'. *Working Papers in Urban Language & Literacies*, Paper 50, 2–21. Online. Available from the Centre for Language, Discourse and Communication, Kings College, London: www.kcl.ac.uk/sspp/departments/education/research/ldc/publications/workingpapers/search.aspx.

Bourdieu, P. (1999) 'Understanding', in P. Bourdieu et al. *The Weight of the World: Social Suffering in Contemporary Society*, trans. Priscilla Parkhurst Ferguson. Stanford, CA: Stanford University Press, 607–626.

Busch, B. (2006) 'Language biographies for multilingual learning: linguistic and educational considerations,' in B. Busch, A. Jardine & A. Tjoutuku (eds) *Language Biographies for Multilingual Learning*. Cape Town: PRAESA Occasional Papers No. 24, 5–17.

Busch, B. (2010) 'School language profiles: valorizing linguistic resources in heteroglossic situations in South Africa'. *Language and Education* 24, 283–294.

Biographical approaches 57

Busch, B. (2012) 'The linguistic repertoire revisited'. *Applied Linguistics* 33, 503–523.

Busch, B. (2015a) '"Without language, everything is chaos and confusion": bodily and emotional language experience and the linguistic repertoire', in U. Lüdtke (ed.) *Emotion in Language: Theory – Research – Application*. Amsterdam: John Benjamins, 273–288.

Busch, B. (2015b) 'Expanding the notion of the linguistic repertoire: on the concept of Spracherleben – the lived experience of language'. *Applied Linguistics*. doi:10.1093/applin/amv030.

Busch, B. & Busch, T. (eds) (2008) *Mitten durch meine Zunge. Erfahrungen mit Sprache von Augustinus bis Zaimoğlu. [Right through my Tongue: Experiences with Language from Augustine to Zaimoğlu]*. Klagenfurt/Celovec: Drava.

Butler, J. (1997) *Excitable Speech: A Politics of the Performative*. New York: Routledge.

Chilisa, B. (2012) *Indigenous Research Methodologies*. Los Angeles, CA: Sage.

Collectif (ed.) (1985) *Du Bilinguisme: Actes du Colloque*. [On Bilingualism: Proceedings of the Colloquium] Paris: Denoël.

Cuellar, A.C. (2005) 'Unraveling silence: violence, memory and the limits of anthropology's craft'. *Dialectical Anthropology* 29, 159–180.

De Fina, A. (2003) *Identity in Narrative: A Study of Immigrant Discourse*. Amsterdam: John Benjamins.

Derrida, J. (1998) *Monolingualism of the Other or the Prosthesis of Origin*. Stanford, CA: Stanford University Press.

Farmer, D. (2012) 'Portraits de jeunes migrants dans une école internationale au Canada'. ['Portaits of young migrants in an international school in Canada']. *La Revue Internationale de l'Education Familiale* 31, 73–94.

Fischer-Rosenthal, W. (1995) 'The problem with identity: biography as solution to some (post)-modernist dilemmas'. *Comenius* 15, 250–265.

Fix, U. & Barth, D. (2000) *Sprachbiographien. Sprache und Sprachgebrauch vor und nach der Wende von 1989 im Erinnern und Erleben von Zeitzeugen aus der DDR [Language Biographies. Language and Language Use before and after the Fall of the Iron Curtain 1989, through the Recollections and Experiences of Contemporaries of the German Democratic Republic]*. Frankfurt am Main: Peter Lang.

Foucault, M. (1982) 'The subject and power', in M. Foucault (ed.) *Beyond Structuralism and Hermeneutics* (ed. by H. Dreyfus & P. Rainbow). Chicago, IL: The University of Chicago Press, 208–226.

Franceschini, R. (2003) 'Unfocussed language acquisition? The presentation of linguistic situations in biographical narration'. *Forum Qualitative Sozialforschung / Qualitative Social Research*. Online journal. Available www.qualitative-research.net.

Garfinkel, H. (1967) *Studies in Ethnomethodology*. Englewood Cliffs, NJ: Prentice Hall.

Goffman, E. (1959) *The Presentation of Self in Everyday Life*. Garden City, NY: Doubleday Anchor Books.

Gramsci, A. (1971) *Selections from the Prison Notebooks*. London: Lawrence & Wishart.

Gumperz, J.J. (1964) 'Linguistic and social interaction in two communities'. *American Anthropologist* 66, 137–153.

Gumperz, J.J. (2001) 'Contextualization and ideology in intercultural communication', in A. Di Luzio, S. Günthner & F. Orletti (eds) *Culture in Communication: Analyses of Intercultural Situations*. Amsterdam: Benjamins, 35–53.

Haug, F. (1990) *Erinnerungsarbeit [Reminiscence]*. Hamburg: Argument.

Husserl, E. (1982) *Ideas Pertaining to a Pure Phenomenology and to a Phenomenological Philosophy – First Book: General Introduction to a Pure Phenomenology*. The Hague: Nijhoff.

58   B. Busch

Hymes, D. (1977) *Foundations in Sociolinguistics: An Ethnographic Approach.* London: Tavistock.

Jakobson, R. (1960) 'Linguistics and poetics', in T.A. Sebeok (ed.) *Style in Language.* New York: Wiley, 350–377.

Jones, K., Martin-Jones, M. & Bhatt, A. (2000) 'Constructing a critical, dialogic approach to research on multilingual literacy: participant diaries and diary interviews', in M. Martin-Jones & K. Jones (eds) *Multilingual Literacies: Reading and Writing Different Worlds.* Amsterdam: John Benjamins, 319–351.

Koven, M. (2001) 'Comparing bilinguals' quoted performances of self and others in tellings of the same experience in two languages'. *Language in Society* 30, 513–558.

Kramsch, C. (2006) 'The multilingual subject'. *International Journal of Applied Linguistics* 16, 98–110.

Kramsch, C. (2009) *The Multilingual Subject.* Oxford: Oxford University Press.

Krumm, H.-J. & Jenkins, E.-M. (2001) *Kinder und ihre Sprachen – lebendige Mehrsprachigkeit: Sprachenportraits gesammelt und kommentiert von Hans-Jürgen Krumm* [*Children and Languages – Living Multilingualism: Language Portraits, Collated and Annotated by Hans-Jürgen Krumm*]. Vienna: Eviva.

Leopold, W.F. (1939–1949) *Speech Development of a Bilingual Child: A Linguist's Record* (four volumes). Evanston, IL: Northwestern University Press.

Lyotard, J.-F. (1979) *La Condition Postmoderne: Rapport sur le Savoir.* [*The Postmodern Condition: A Report on Knowledge*]. Paris: Minuit.

McNamara, T. (2010) 'Reading Derrida: language, identity and violence'. *Applied Linguistics Review* 1, 23–44.

Merleau-Ponty, M. (2002) *Phenomenology of Perception.* London: Routledge & Kegan Paul.

Nekvapil, J. (2001) 'From the biographical narratives of Czech Germans: language biographies in the family of Mr. and Mrs. S'. *Journal of Asian Pacific Communication* 11, 77–79.

Norton, B. (2000) *Identity and Language Learning: Gender, Ethnicity and Educational Change.* Harlow: Longman.

Pavlenko, A. (2007) 'Autobiographic narratives as data in applied linguistics'. *Applied Linguistics* 28, 163–188.

Rampton, B. (1995) 'Language crossing and the problematisation of ethnicity and socialisation'. *Pragmatics* 5, 485–513.

Ronjat, J. (1913) *Le Développement du Langage Observé chez un Enfant Bilingue.* [*The Development of Language Observed in a Bilingual Child*]. Paris: Champion.

Rosenthal, G. (1995) *Erlebte und erzählte Lebensgeschichte: Gestalt und Struktur biografischer Selbstbeschreibungen* [*Life Stories in Experience and Narrative: Format and Structure of Biographical Self-Representations*]. Frankfurt am Main: Campus Verlag.

Rosenthal, G. (2006) 'The narrated life story: on the interrelation between experience, memory and narration', in K. Milnes et al. (eds) *Narrative, Memory & Knowledge: Representations, Aesthetics, Contexts.* Huddersfield: University of Huddersfield Press.

Schäfer, T. & Völter, B. (2005) 'Subjekt-Positionen. Michel Foucault und die Biographieforschung' ['Subject positions. Michel Foucault and Biographical Research], in B. Völter, B. Dausien, H. Lutz & G. Rosenthal (eds) *Biographiefroschung im Diskurs* [*Biographical Research in Discourse*]. Wiesbaden, Verlag für Sozialwissenschaften, 161–189.

Biographical approaches   59

Schmid, M. (2004) 'Identity and first language attrition: a historical approach'. *Estudios de Sociolingüística* 5, 41–58.

Silverstein, M. (2006) 'Pragmatic indexing', in K. Brown (ed.) *Encyclopaedia of Language and Linguistics*, Vol. 6, 2nd edn. Amsterdam: Elsevier, 14–17.

Singer, R. & Harris, S. (forthcoming) 'What practices and ideologies support small-scale multilingualism? A case study of unexpected language survival in an Australian Indigenous community'. *International Journal for the Sociology of Language*.

Stevenson, P. (2013) 'SprachGeschichten mit Migrationshintergrund: demografische und biografische Perspektiven auf Sprachkenntnisse und Spracherleben' ['Migrants' language histories: demographical and biographical perspectives on language skills and language experiences'], in *Das Deutsch der Migranten* [*Migrants' German*]. Berlin: Walter de Gruyter, 193–221.

Thomas, W.I. & Znaniecki, F. (1996) *The Polish Peasant in Europe and America: A Classic Work in Immigration History*. Edited by Eli Zaretsky. Urbana, IL: University of Illinois Press.

Todorov, T. (1984) *Mikhail Bakhtin: The Dialogical Principle*. Manchester: Manchester University Press.

Treichel, B. (2004) 'Suffering from one's own multilingualism: biographical processes of suffering and their linguistic expression in narrative interviews with Welsh speakers of Welsh and English', in R. Franceschini & J. Miecznikowski (eds) *Leben mit mehreren Sprachen / Vivre avec plusieurs langues. Sprachbiographien / Biographies langagières*. [Living with several languages – language biographies]. *Transversales* 9. Frankfurt am Main: Peter Lang, 47–74.

Tuhiwai Smith, L. (2012) *Decolonizing Methodologies*. London: Zed Books.

Tuider, E. (2007) 'Diskursanalyse und Biographieforschung: zum wie und Warum von Subjektpositionierung' ['Discourse analysis and biographical research: on the how and why of self-positioning']. *Forum Qualitative Sozialforschung/ Qualitative Social Research* 8, Art. 6. Online journal. Available www.qualitative-research.net.

Tylim, I. (2002) 'Symbolization, multilingualism, and countertransference', in R. Lasky (ed.) *Symbolization and desymbolization: Essays in Honor of Norbert Freedman*. New York: Other Press, 164–181.

Vološinov, V.N. (1973) *Marxism and the Philosophy of Language*. New York: Seminar Press.

4 The risks and gains of a single case study

Kamran Khan

Introduction

This chapter examines the question of how to work with a sole, main participant for a study. The study I am drawing on (Khan, 2013) involved W, a Yemeni migrant. It focused on the period when he was becoming a UK citizen. W's participation was one component in an overall research design and data-collection process. The chapter discusses the research design (and associated practicalities) with reference to an underlying philosophical foundation based on Foucault's "polyhedron of intelligibility" (Foucault, 1991). I show how it was necessary to manage each aspect of the research process separately while also aiming to achieve overall coherence.

Since 2001, there has been a focus on the language requirements to becoming a British citizen. Following the 2001 social disturbances in the north of England involving British Asian youths, far-right extremists and the police, there was a drive for a 'common identity' through citizenship. A language requirement was introduced through ESOL (English for Speakers of Other Languages) with citizenship classes or the Life in the UK (LUK) test. As a consequence, there has been considerable research interest in the last few years in citizenship, immigration and language (e.g. Blackledge, 2005; Shohamy, 2006).

The individual in this research is W. He is a male in his mid twenties and he came to the UK from Yemen in 2006. He works in a factory during the day and attends ESOL classes in the evenings. When I first met him, he had aspirations to attend a British university. W had not been able to go to university in Yemen for financial reasons and this is something that he has tried to address in the UK. I met him through the ESOL classes and this is where data collection started. Both W and I have similarities which enriched our relationship: we are both males, we are both Muslim and we live in the same part of the city. The importance of shared religion was crucial in developing the informant–researcher relationship. These shared characteristics allowed me to gain a thorough insight into how W experienced the process of applying for and gaining citizenship.

The data-collection period lasted eleven months. As will be demonstrated later, the study was defined as an ethnographically informed case study. My

The risks and gains of a single case study   61

initial interest went from following W's participation in an ESOL class on a journey to citizenship to his wider experience. This meant that the research themes moved from classroom practices to issues such as language testing, community and integration as well as the citizenship process itself. By focusing on just one participant, it was possible to capture a greater variety of sociopolitical themes.

Baseline and evolving practicalities

At the very beginning of the study, I was interested in building an understanding of the lived experience and linguistic practices involved in becoming a British citizen. There were two issues to address at the point of departure: first, it was necessary to define the baseline and the main focus of the study. The baseline was that of investigating the language and linguistic practices involved in becoming a British citizen. In order to become a British citizen there are now criteria regarding residence in the UK and language proficiency requirements to be fulfilled. According to Joppke (2007: 44), "what ordinary people associate with citizenship is one of the biggest lacunae in the literature". Blackledge (2005) has also called for research into the journey to citizenship which places the citizen at the centre of the study. Thus, the baseline was partly informed by existing gaps in the literature.

The second important issue was that of defining the unit of analysis which, in this case, was the process of becoming a citizen. This was important as, at times, the unit of analysis could be easily blurred in ways which deviated from the main aim. For example, at times, the study could have become a biographical account of W. However, the aim was not to tell W's life story but to articulate W's journey towards citizenship.

Originally, I had intended to follow sessions of an approved ESOL with citizenship class. My initial interest was in observing the class. However, having met W, I was convinced that understanding his life outside of the class would add extra texture to the study. The focus was no longer solely on the class but on the wider context of W's life. In this respect, W led some of the research and it appeared to be a much richer line of enquiry. The study was now no longer centred on the classroom as part of the citizenship journey but on the citizenship journey itself. I had a back-up plan as an insurance policy as I realized the risks of relying only on W. The college was happy to permit me to use a plan B and this was negotiated with the ESOL tutors. Thus, I took on the role of a special needs assistant in another ESOL class at the college. The college used my experience to assist a teacher and I was able to spend more time at the college.

W and I had originally met in an ESOL class when I was helping him with his English. We then began meeting outside of the college. We arranged to meet on a Saturday night and W chose where we should meet and where we could go. I was impressed by his willingness and enthusiasm to show me his community. This was not a problem for me as we always remained in the

62   *K. Khan*

neighbourhood where we both live. It was *his* journey which provided the basis for the study reported here. His guidance required me to make decisions on which avenues to pursue for my work.

The scope of my research project changed from focusing on a class to focusing on a person, from a collective citizenship journey to an individual one. W became the focus of the study as the main participant. Hammersley and Atkinson (2007) describe this process of cumulative focus as a "funnel structure" which moves from a general interest to a specific interest, and which must be "transformed and its scope must be clarified and delimited, and its internal structure explored" (Hammersley & Atkinson, 2007: 160). It is usual for a study to gain in focus as a clarity of aims emerges (Seliger & Shohamy, 1989; Blommaert & Dong Jie, 2010).

From the first idea to the final idea, I had maintained a commitment to the original orientation of the study: to investigate the language and linguistic practices involved in becoming a British citizen. The unit of analysis was also the same; that is to say, the process of becoming a citizen. The study evolved through the actual practicalities of dealing with the research, some of which were quite constraining, and through my developing understanding of how the study could be enhanced through advice from W. This flexibility was only possible within the structure of an existing research design (RD).

Initial interest and research design

In order to manage the data-collection period, there was an initial process of discerning the most appropriate RD to operationalize and orient the overall study. An RD governs how a research interest is translated into research practice. It is through an analysis of RDs and appropriate selection that the research can move forward smoothly from mere interest or idea to operationalized research. Here, I focus only on RD and not on research methods. Methods depend on the type of RD selected.

RD is reflected in an array of metaphors in the research literature: the navigation of a ship to its destination (Maxwell, 1996), architectural plans (Hakim, 2000), choreography (Janesick, 2000), a construction plan (De Vaus, 2001) and journey planning (LeCompte & Schensul, 2010). Despite such metaphoric diversity, the commonality shared by the above examples is located in how they move from research question to research conducted through a particular form of planning and orientation, from idea to argument (Cresswell, 2009; Hancké, 2009).

RD does not only ensure that a research question/problem is appropriately answered but also determines *how* it is researched. Cresswell (2009) views RD as a point of convergence between philosophy, strategies and specific methods. The nature of a research problem and question demands a research design that is "governed by the notion of 'fitness for purpose'" (Cohen et al., 2007: 75); in other words, the most appropriate selection of a RD in relation to the problem to be solved or research interest to be pursued. RD connects

The nature of the research question to the manner of research undertaken and data collected (De Vaus, 2001).

As indicated above, the RD selected for my study was an ethnographically informed case study. Although ethnography and case-study research may appear interchangeable, not all case studies are ethnographic. The ethnographic principles of 'being there' and investment of time in an area were adhered to (Erickson, 1990). The 'unit of analysis' was W's journey. I must emphasize that the subject of this study was not W, nor was it a biographical account. It was necessary to understand the context of W's life in order to understand the citizenship process. The study was an account of his journey, including details of everyday life on the road to becoming a member of British society in the context of the legal requirements for acquiring citizenship.

The ethnographic dimension

The study involved the legal aspects of applying for citizenship as well as more quotidian and affective features of this *process* of becoming British. Heller argues that "ethnography is about processes ... not objects" and "occurs in natural settings ... undertaken to record processes of change" (2008: 252). Ethnography became a logical choice in tracking the process of becoming British.

The value of ethnography is in uncovering areas that we do not know enough about (Hymes, 1996). This is especially the case in building a better understanding of the role of languages in social life. Some of the most pertinent questions in relation to this study regard how language is used in becoming a citizen. Heller (2008: 250) explains as follows:

> Ethnographies allow us to get at things we would otherwise never be able to discover. They allow us to see how language practices are connected to the very real conditions of people's lives, to discover how and why language matters to people in their own terms, and to watch processes unfold over time. They allow us to see complexity and connections, to understand the history and geography of language. They allow us to tell a story; not someone else's story exactly but our own story of some slice of experience, a story which illuminates social processes and generates explanations for why people do and think the things they do.

Heller (2008) highlights two notable points here. First, an ethnographic approach can act as a searchlight within the darker recesses of the unknown. Initially, the overarching research question was to examine the process (or journey) of citizenship as well as investigating the linguistic practices involved. This represents a "what is happening here?" question (Erickson, 1990: 83).

My study deliberately struck a balance between broad initial research questions which allowed for an emergent and flexible RD to investigate the unknown and providing sufficient direction and guidance. The RD required "a constant interplay between the topical and the generic, or the substantive and the formal" (Hammersley & Atkinson, 2007: 25) in which the research questions were chiselled and refined as they calibrated to the direction and sharpness of focus involved in the evolution of this study (Blommaert & Dong Jie, 2010). To portray my study as being centred on clearly defined research questions at the outset would betray the requisite process of development.

Second, the unknown for the ethnographer is the reality for those researched. Hymes (1996: 13) states that ethnography is "continuous with real life. Much of what we seek to find out in ethnography is knowledge that others already have". Ethnography deliberately seeks real-life, naturalistic settings which are placed in the luminescence of analytic rigour (Richards, 2003; Hammersley & Atkinson, 2007). This permits the researched to be placed at the centre of a study but, far from marginalizing the researcher to the role of front-stage presenter, it entrusts the researcher with the task of explaining *why* and *how* processes may occur. The quality of analysis here is what separates an ethnography which is sharp in analysis and thorough in rigour from story-telling (Aunger, 1995).

Case study

A case study is "an in-depth description and analysis of a bounded system" (Merriam, 2009: 40). Yin (2009: 18) states that through a case study it is possible "to understand a real-life phenomenon in depth". The focus of a case study is the particular unit or a set of units (Richards, 2003). Hakim (2000) posits that the individual is the simplest form of unit choice. In the research project considered here, it was the journey to citizenship of an individual. This resulted in a clearly defined, bounded project.

Case study offers "detailed insights into mechanisms, motives of actors, and constraints they face at particular moments" (Hancké, 2009: 62). It is particularistic in examining a case in detail, descriptive in providing "thick description" and heuristic in illuminating an under-known phenomenon (Merriam, 2009). Given that the project sought to investigate the process of becoming a citizen, the case study would facilitate a detailed account of this.

Thomas (2011a) offers a nuanced overview of case-study design types. I will now outline the specific nature of the case study in the RD for my study. The subject was a "local knowledge case" (Thomas, 2011a: 93). My local knowledge of the community and the neighbourhood aided the research. The purpose of the case study was explanatory in that it sought to explain how the process of citizenship is experienced. The approach was interpretative. As Thomas (2011a: 124) observes, interpretative research "assumes an in-depth understanding and deep immersion in the environment of the subject". This is where the overlap between ethnography and case study occurs. For this reason, both ethnography and case-study research had an important role to play in the development of this study.

A case study RD is extremely useful in presenting a holistic account of researching the ESOL classroom and beyond. For the purposes of this study, "the proximity to reality which the case study entails and the learning process that it generates for the researcher will often constitute a prerequisite for advanced understanding" (Flyvbjerg, 2006: 235). The bounded nature of case studies neatly offers the context of a journey to citizenship that can be followed to the end of the citizenship process.

Ethnography provides a RD that affords entry into the world of the participant(s) and allows the researcher the advantage of 'being there'. It takes into consideration the natural setting of the participant(s) and provides insights into how they make sense of their world by placing them at the centre of the research. Case studies offer a rich insight into a unit of analysis as well as being conveniently bounded research which can facilitate in-depth study. Both designs in conjunction are ideal for examining a process of becoming.

The choice of one

The choice to base the study principally around one informant was not premeditated. Instead, it was the result of evolving research interests and an emergent research design which was guided as much by W as it was by me, the researcher. My choice was also informed by my reading of other studies and the relevant research literature, especially that relating to the "choice of one case" and to the handling of single units of analysis (Yin, 2009).

In Kinginger's (2004) study, Alice was the sole subject of a four-year study. Kinginger charted Alice, an American student of French, throughout her time before, during and after her time as a study-abroad student in France. Much like English for W, learning French for Alice came with a 'promise'. That is to say, acquiring French was tied to personal aspiration, social mobility and professional development. This difference between what was promised and what occurred in reality resulted in a sense of disappointment for Alice. Furthermore, Kinginger notes how learning French related to access to social networks as well as constructing and negotiating a sense of identity.

Like Kinginger (2004), Teutsch-Dwyer (2001) also followed a language learner in non-native settings. Karol, a Polish migrant, was the subject of Teutsch-Dwyer's study in San Francisco. With a particular emphasis on masculinity and identity in relation to language learning, Teutsch-Dwyer tracked Karol's experience of learning English over a period of fourteen months. Teutsch-Dwyer concludes that much of Karol's sense of social acceptance was rooted in being accepted by those in his female social circles.

Kinginger and Teutsch-Dwyer were able to focus on a number of factors while using a single participant as an object of enquiry. Kinginger was able to draw in references to wider sociopolitical ideologies around her central research narrative, which involved a personal journey involving a particular history and experience and a sense of imagination and desire about the future. As Kinginger suggests, this involved placing an emphasis on an experience

66   *K. Khan*

which was at once "dramatic and mundane" (Kinginger, 2004: 219). It was dramatic in that a 'mundane' journey was personalized and explored before being presented within an academic context. Thus, what may appear banal in one context may have been of great interest beyond that context. Likewise, Teutsch-Dwyer provided a representation of Karol's trajectory (both real and imagined). There was a distinct emphasis on very real relationships but also language practices and what they meant in broader personal trajectories and journeys.

Both studies demonstrate a commitment to a personal trajectory and processes of identification through learning a language. In the case of W, I invested eleven months of data collection and many more in analysis and writing, in understanding and conveying the bureaucratic and personal journey to becoming a British citizen. While W's journey was the unit of analysis, there was a sense of "multivocality" as a social process which "includes multiple and varied voices" (Tracy, 2010: 844). Others beyond W contributed accounts which aided my developing understanding of his journey. Some of those interviewed did not know W, but they were able to contribute to the analysis through specific knowledge and/or professional expertise and experience about becoming a citizen.

I also chose to interview people at different levels of status from the policy level down to the personal. I interviewed (1) a UK Border Agency (UKBA) policy maker, who gave insight into the wider context around W's linguistic practices; (2) the assistant principal at W's college, who was able comment on his journey as an ESOL student and the pressures that the institution was under; (3) W's ESOL teacher, who was able to talk more specifically about classroom practices; (4) an ESOL teacher who taught the LUK test and validated the type of preparatory skills that W employed for the test; and (5) another ESOL teacher, who could comment on my own position as a special educational needs assistant in the college. Each person brought an extra layer of insight and contributed towards a multidimensional understanding of W's journey. For example, in one case, an ESOL tutor drew parallels between W's preparation methods for the LUK citizenship test and the strategies that she employed:

> TUK: It's a little bit harder. Basically, like what you mentioned about the Arabic speaker ... right translate everything ... I actually have it in here. I basically did English, Chinese ... there's two parts. There's English on this side and the Chinese on this side and then found the key words. Firstly, for these people they haven't been to ... university or whatever.

Transferability

Kinginger (2004) and Teutsch-Dwyer (2001) highlight a way of refracting a multitude of issues through a case study with one person. In their work there is a sense of "transferability" (Tracy, 2010) in applying the points of interest from these studies to other studies and situations. Tracy (2010: 845) refers to transferability which "is achieved when readers feel as though the story of the research overlaps with their own situation and they intuitively transfer the research to their own action". This can be viewed as adding external validity to the analysis of the study. In the literature on research methodology, external validity refers to how generalizable the results may be beyond the studies. External validity has been defined as "the degree to which results have relevance beyond the study itself" (Angrosino, 2007: 60). It can be argued that "even the most exact replication of research methods may fail to produce identical results" (LeCompte & Goetz, 1982: 35). Of course, the strength of ethnography is not in generalizability but in "the depth of understanding and insight" (Pole & Morrison, 2000: 111) and in unraveling "different layers of universality and particularity" (Erickson, 1990: 108). This impacts on external validity by moving from erroneous aspirations to generalizability towards more apt terms for the research world such as "transferability".

It is not possible to generalize from one case study directly, as a case is a case (De Vaus, 2001) due to its "critical uniqueness" (Stake, 1995). This uniqueness is lent to "transferability" by "thick description" (Onwuegbuzie & Leech, 2006) and "focuses on explicating the unique, idiosyncratic meanings and perspectives constructed by individuals, groups or both who live/act in a particular context" (Cho & Trent, 2006: 328). As with ethnography, it is not the goal of a case study to aim for generalizability. Therefore, it would be unfair to judge a case study on a standard to which it does not aspire (Yin, 2009; Thomas, 2009, 2011a, 2011b). Instead, case studies offer theoretical or analytic statements rather than statistical generalizations (Flick, 2009; Yin, 2009). This kind of research constructs what Thomas (2011b: 32) calls hermeneutically inspired "exemplary knowledge". A case study provides "understanding presented from another's 'horizon of meaning', but understood from one's own" (ibid.).

With regard to this multi-dimensionality of case studies, I refer to Foucault's term "the polyhedron of intelligibility" (Foucault, 1991: 77). This term is used by Thomas (2011a) in describing the need to examine the subject of enquiry in a multi-directional manner rather than solely from "one direction". It must also be added that although I have mentioned five interviews above, there were actually seven participants in my study. W was the main participant. I also become a participant who was (re)presenting his journey in my study. While Thomas makes brief reference to "the polyhedron of intelligibility", I would like to engage with Foucault's idea in greater detail and consider its implications for my study.

The polyhedron of intelligibility

The "polyhedron of intelligibility" emerged from Foucault's idea of "eventalization" (Foucault, 1991). Eventalization means "rediscovering the connections, encounters, supports, blockages, plays of forces, strategies

68   *K. Khan*

and so on which at a given moment establish what subsequently counts as being self-evident, universal and necessary" (Foucault, 1991: 76). This means understanding and taking into account the wider influences which contribute to what may appear at first glance to be 'normal'.

Eventalization is useful as it constructs an analysis around a single event (Foucault, 1991) yet seeks a multifaceted analysis and engagement. Foucault (1991: 77) specifically describes the polyhedron of intelligibility when stating that it is "the number of whose faces is not given in advance and can never properly be taken as finite". Thus, there is an emergent nature to adopting such an orientation of analysis. Foucault (1991) refers to a sense of "polymorphism" as analysis develops. For Foucault, the deeper one engages with the processes of analysis, "the more one is enabled and indeed obliged to construct their external relations of intelligibility" (Foucault, 1991: 77). Foucault uses the example of analysing the process of "incarceration", which later informed his work on discipline in schools, hospitals and prisons (see Foucault, 1977).

There are two paradoxes which Foucault captures through the polyhedron of intelligibility. The first is that although there is a single event, or unit of analysis, there is a multiplicity of processes to be grasped. It is this convergence between the unity of event and the multiplicity of processes which my study sought to capture. The processes at work included political, linguistic, socio-historic ones, along with personal subjectivity, within a single journey to citizenship. The second paradox is between the details of the internal aspects of the study in evidencing the everyday aspects, on the one hand, and understanding and relating this to external relations. Foucault is at pains to suggest that the internal details do not come at the expense of relating them to wider contexts; instead, a deeper analysis of the internal must include an exhaustive analysis of the external.

The journey of citizenship as a polyhedron of intelligibility

In the case of the case of W's journey to citizenship (Yin, 2009), the analysis of the details of this process, taking account of W's own narrative, and the multiple voices involved, led to the identification of four different themes. The four themes were (1) language testing, (2) integration, (3) adult ESOL education policy and (4) the acquisition of citizenship. Through the single event of becoming a citizen, a range of issues emerged which heightened the relevance to the study of the various people interviewed. The points of divergence and convergence added to the richness and complexity of the study, and my analysis was rooted in the everyday life and language practices of W yet resonated with policy and broader sociopolitical issues. For example, the issue of integration was examined by analysing who W spent time with and why. The ESOL teachers, who were familiar with the lives of the students, also confirmed the account of W's experiences. These experiences were then viewed against the discursive backdrop of policy and politics. Through W's

The risks and gains of a single case study   69

journey, there was sufficient latitude to examine key sociopolitical issues while remaining rooted in the data and everyday practices. Thus, the detail in the data analysis had theoretical and political resonance in a wider context.

Finally, I would like to make a distinction between "giving the participant a voice" and "collaborative critical analysis" (Murchison, 2010). I feel that giving the participant a voice pre-imposes certain frames of power in which the researcher is positioned at a higher level by virtue of being able to tell others about these settings. In this research, it would mean that I assume that my research was as important to W as it was to me. Instead, I prefer to describe the nature of this study as a form of collaborative critical analysis in which the collaboration was guided by W, and I made decisions on the direction of the study. For example, on one occasion, W suggested where we should meet and what we should see. On another occasion, I had considered asking W to do a literacy diary showing what languages he used during a whole day. W felt this was not useful and instead he told me the same information. In this way, W was able to guide me in establishing what method to use.

There are always risks with single case studies. Focusing on W meant there was always a possibility that the central pillar of the study might fall if he was unable to continue. As a safeguard, I was also a special educational needs classroom assistant. I am a former ESOL teacher and so I offered my services to the college on a voluntary basis. The college staff knew that adopting this role in an ESOL class was a plan B for data collection. There was thus a useful interaction between my professional experience and the needs of the college. The arrangement was beneficial to both parties. In this way, a potential problem was foreshadowed at the outset with the support and collaboration of the college.

Another risk is that a single case study may appear to lack direction and orientation. Dealing with a plan A and a plan B may seem to be a vague way of conducting research, giving the impression of a lack of focus. This may be true to some extent, but instead, I gained in terms of fluidity and flexibility. It was possible to adjust to the settings and the data emerging. This was far easier to do in dealing with one person than with an institution or a class.

Conclusions

The study I have referred to throughout this chapter matched methodological elements of ethnography and case study with the ontological dimensions of the polyhedron of intelligibility. Ethnography permits an examination of processes and everyday practices (Heller, 2008; Blommaert & Dong Jie, 2010) with a focused emphasis on capturing the continuity of everyday life (Hymes, 1996). The case study element allows for the adoption of a finite and manageable object of enquiry (Thomas, 2011b). In this study, the object of enquiry was the journey to citizenship that ends at the citizenship ceremony. The polyhedron of intelligibility calls for a form of analysis, involving a polymorphic orientation, which demands multi-dimensionality and a level

70 K. Khan

of reflexivity from the researcher in adjusting to the emergent nature of the data collection. Furthermore, using Foucault's approach, there is an interplay between the details of everyday life and wider contexts, beyond the immediacy of quotidian practices.

This ensures a sense of transferability (Tracy, 2010) and an approach which can be applied to other studies, much in the same way that I was able to draw upon Kinginger (2004) and Teutsch-Dwyer (2001) to inform this study. I hope that this chapter will, in some way, be beneficial to other studies which centre around a sole, main participant. Far from being restrictive, a singular focus can be flexible and fluid in creating, rather than limiting, avenues of research.

As I have already indicated, there are inherent benefits and risks. The benefits lie in focusing on details which can be taken into account with regard to a number of diverse (and significant) issues. In investigating W's journey, it was possible to examine citizenship testing, integration, ESOL education and the process of citizenship itself. Furthermore, it was still possible to include other voices to add greater texture to the study. Thus, a number of issues and dimensions could be added to the central participant's experiences and account.

The risks lie in the possibility of a study lacking direction or a back-up plan. Both possibilities can be anticipated. For me, the key to maintaining direction lay in grounding the study on a clear baseline and unit of analysis. This meant that no matter how the study was progressing, it was always oriented in a particular way. The clarity of the unit of analysis meant that, whenever there was a danger that the study might veer, no matter how subtly, into irrelevant areas, it was possible to maintain focus. Through collaboration with the college, it was possible to foreshadow the potential problem of participant attrition with the assurance of a back-up plan.

References

Angrosino, M. (2007) *Doing Ethnographic Observational Research*. London: Sage.
Aunger, R. (1995) 'Storytelling or science?' *Current Anthropology* 36(1), 97–130.
Blackledge, A. (2005) *Discourse and Power in a Multilingual World*. Amsterdam: John Benjamins.
Blommaert, J. & Dong Jie (2010) *Ethnographic Fieldwork*. Bristol: Multilingual Matters.
Cho, J. & Trent, A. (2006) 'Validity in qualitative research revisited'. *Qualitative Research* 6, 319–340.
Cohen, L., Manion, L. & Morrison, K. (2007) *Research Methods in Education*, 6th edn. London: Routledge.
Cresswell, J.W. (2009) *Research Design*, 3rd edn. London: Sage.
De Vaus, D.A. (2001) *Research Design in Social Research*. London: Sage.
Erickson, F. (1990) 'Qualitative methods', in R. Linn & F. Erickson (eds) *Research in Teaching and Learning, Vol. 2*. New York: Macmillan, 71–194.
Flick, U. (2009) *An Introduction to Qualitative Research*, 4th edn. London: Sage.
Flyvbjerg, B. (2006) 'Five misunderstandings about case study research'. *Qualitative Inquiry* 2(2), 219–245.

The risks and gains of a single case study   71

Foucault, M. (1977) *Discipline and Punish*, trans. Alan Sheridan. Harmondsworth: Penguin Books.

Foucault, M. (1991) 'Questions of method', in G. Burchell, C. Gordon & P. Miller (eds) *The Foucault Effect*. Chicago, IL: University of Chicago Press, 73–86.

Hakim, C. (2000) *Research Design*, 2nd edn. London: Routledge.

Hammersley, M. & Atkinson, P. (2007) *Ethnography: Principles and Practice*, 3rd edn. London: Routledge.

Hancké, B. (2009) *Intelligent Research Design*. Oxford: Oxford University Press.

Heller, M. (2008) 'Doing ethnography', in L. Wei & M.G. Moyer (eds) *The Blackwell Guide to Research Methods in Bilingualism and Multilingualism*. Malden, MA: Blackwell, 249–262.

Hymes, D. (1996) *Ethnography, Linguistics, Narrative Inequalities*. London: Taylor & Francis.

Janesick, V.J. (2000) 'The choreography of qualitative research design', in N.K. Denzin & Y.S. Lincoln (eds) *Handbook of Qualitative Research*, 2nd edn. London: Sage, 379–399.

Joppke, C. (2007) 'Transformation of citizenship: status, rights and identity'. *Citizenship Studies* 11(1), 37–48.

Khan, K. (2013) *Becoming British: A Migrant's Journey*. Unpublished PhD thesis, University of Birmingham and University of Melbourne.

Kinginger, C. (2004) 'Alice doesn't live here anymore', in A. Pavlenko & A. Blackledge (eds) *Negotiation of Identities in Multilingual Contexts*. Clevedon, UK: Multilingual Matters, 219–242.

LeCompte, M.D. & Goetz, J.P. (1982) 'Problems of reliability and validity in ethnographic research'. *Review of Educational Research* 52(1), 31–60.

LeCompte, M.D. and Schensul, J.J. (2010) *Designing and Conducting Ethnographic Research*, 2nd edn. Plymouth, MD: Altamira Press.

Maxwell, J.A. (1996) *Qualitative Research Design: An Interactive Approach*. London: Sage.

Merriam, S.B. (2009) *Qualitative Research*. San Francisco, CA: John Wiley & Sons.

Murchison, J.M. (2010) *Ethnography Essentials: Designing, Conducting and Presenting Your Research*. San Francisco, CA: Jossey-Bass.

Onwuegbuzie, A.J. and Leech, N.L. (2006) 'Validity and qualitative research: an oxymoron?' *Quality & Quantity* 41, 233–249.

Pole, C.J. & Morrison, M. (2000) *Ethnography for Education*. Maidenhead: Open University Press.

Richards, K. (2003) *Qualitative Inquiry in TESOL*. Basingstoke: Palgrave Macmillan.

Seliger, H.W. & Shohamy, E.G. (1989) *Second Language Research Methods*. Oxford: Oxford University Press.

Shohamy, E. (2006) *Language Policy: Hidden Agendas and New Approaches*. London: Routledge.

Stake, R.E. (1995) *The Art of Case Study Research*. London: Sage.

Teutsch-Dwyer, M. (2001) '"How am I to become a woman in an American vein?" Transformations of gender performance in second language learning', in A. Pavlenko, A. Blackledge, I. Piller & M. Teutsch-Dwyer (eds) *Multilingualism, Second Language Learning, and Gender*. The Hague: Mouton De Gruyter, 175–198.

Thomas, G. (2009) *How To Do Your Research Project*. London: Sage.

Thomas, G. (2011a) *A Guide to Doing Your Case Study*. London: Sage.

Thomas, G. (2011b) 'The case: generalisation, theory and phronesis in case study'. *Oxford Review of Education* 37(1), 21–35.

Tracy, S.J. (2010) 'Qualitative quality: eight "big tent" criteria for excellent qualitative research'. *Qualitative Inquiry* 16(10), 837–851.

Yin, R. (2009) *Case Study Research: Design and Methods*, 4th edn. London: Sage.

5 Researching student mobility in multilingual Switzerland

Reflections on multi-sited ethnography

Martina Zimmermann

Introduction

Even though multi-site studies were already being conducted in the mid twentieth century (see, for instance, Redfield's 1941 study on the folk culture of Yucatan), classic ethnography – the practice of long-term stays in a chosen field – dominated social research for a long time (Amit, 2000). Marcus's (1995) article "Ethnography in/of the world system: The emergence of multi-sited ethnography", reflecting on the need for multi-sited ethnography, initiated a debate on the design and practice of fieldwork and on the need for methodological changes. The debate continues today. Marcus argued that not all social phenomena can be studied by concentrating on a single site and that 'multi-sited ethnography' was particularly well suited to research in late modern times. He encouraged thinking about how we might track social phenomena across space and about how we might map the trajectories of people, things, associations and relationships.

For a while, there was profound scepticism towards this new methodology (Hage, 2005; Candea, 2007). However, there is now growing recognition among social researchers of the need for a refocusing of the 'object' and 'site' of study in social research, due to the significant epistemological shifts that have taken place in the social sciences and the unpacking of notions of place, culture, community and nation in recent social theory (e.g. Anderson, 1991; Appadurai, 1996). There has been a significant reconceptualisation of the nature of the field (Appadurai, 1990; Hendry, 2003) and a turn towards multi-sited research (cf. Falzon, 2009; Gallo, 2009). Numerous researchers have now provided their own accounts of what multi-sitedness implies and have demonstrated how this approach proved to be of value in their work (cf. Hannerz, 2003; Falzon, 2009; Coleman & von Hellermann, 2011; Marcus, 2011). For instance, Hannerz (2003) highlights the opportunity it affords to examine movements or processes that traverse localities.

A multi-sited approach is also increasingly being leveraged in sociolinguistic research due to the shift to a focus on linguistic and social processes associated with contemporary mobilities and social change (cf. Heller, 2008a; Blackledge & Creese, 2010; Moyer, 2012; Takahashi,

74   *M. Zimmermann*

2013; Pietikäinen & Pitkänen-Huhta, 2014). This shift has led to a concern with the investigation of the circulation of communicative, symbolic and material resources, as well as the tracking of the trajectories of social actors across different discursive spaces. In particular, research in critical sociolinguistic ethnography has been concerned with capturing not only the "sites of the production and distribution of these resources, but also the circulation of resources and actors through those sites" (Heller, 2008a: 517).

In the first part of this chapter, I discuss the role of multi-sited ethnography in studies focusing on mobility. Since this is the social phenomenon that first led to the development of a multi-sited approach, I sketch out some of the benefits that accrue from the decision to go beyond a single site and I point to some of the issues that arise. In the second part, I demonstrate how and why this approach turned out to be helpful in my own research and in enhancing my understanding of student mobility across language regions in Switzerland. Finally, I offer some concluding remarks.

Multi-sited ethnography and mobility

If we agree that ethnographic data serve as a "contingent window into complexity", as Candea puts it (2007: 179), we are better prepared, as ethnographers, for the complex settings in which the particular individuals or communities we are interested in act and circulate. We are also likely to anticipate that the local realities of these individuals and communities are shaped by social processes at work elsewhere (Marcus, 2011: 20). If the subjects of our research are mobile and/or spatially dispersed, then the practice of participant observation has to reflect this (Clifford, 1992). In Falzon's (2009: 9) terms, this is "fieldwork as travel practice".

In the nineteenth and early twentieth centuries, anthropologists moved about 'in the field' like the people they were working with: they went about on foot. Moreover, because they undertook fieldwork in just one location over an extended period of time, the main travel involved was that of going to and from the field. However, in multi-site research focusing on mobilities, the ethnographer is often 'on the move'. Take, for example, Hannerz's (2003) research with journalists working internationally, or Heller's (2011) multi-site research in different geographical and social spaces in French Canada, as she tracked – over several decades – changes in the discursive construction of *la francophonie* in these spaces. Heller's research involved extensive travel by road and by air, at different points in time, and numerous field trips. Other researchers have focused on the movement of research participants within one particular urban environment. For example, Lamarre and Lamarre (2009) carried out a research project with multilingual urban youth in the city of Montreal which involved accompanying the research participants as they traversed different social spaces and networks within the city and documenting their language practices across different spaces and networks.

As Fitzgerald (2006: 3) has observed, a multi-sited approach enables us to "take seriously" the movement that contributes to the processes related to mobility. However, the meaning of movement for the research participants involved might sometimes be overestimated (cf. Gallo, 2009) or, as Hage (2005: 470) has argued, it may be "unpredictable". In his study on the Lebanese diaspora, Hage (2005) shows that for one of his participants the move from a village in the Lebanon to Boston was less vital than moving in, together with his wife, to the house of his uncle. He argues that the meaning attributed to mobility should not be taken for granted but rather investigated. Similarly, Xiang (2013) has noted that we should critically reflect on the relevance of different kinds of movement (and the sites involved) for those participating in our research.

When working with mobile subjects, research conversations about prior places of residence, 'homes' or regions of origin are frequent. Reference is made to other spaces but also other times. If researchers have the opportunity to visit the points of departure for their research participants, then it might be possible to overcome the dichotomy between a 'closed past' and an 'open present' (Waldinger & Fitzgerald, 2003: 24) and it might make it possible to re-historicise present forms of mobility (cf. Gallo, 2009). Reflection on future destinations or potential homes might also be helpful. This would involve taking research conversations beyond the 'here and now'.

It is rather common for ethnographic work to be adapted to particular conditions; a multi-sited approach is sometimes adopted because researchers realise that the conventional single-site fieldwork originally planned is not appropriate. However, we should be cautious about thinking that multi-sitedness is an assured means of producing a 'complete' picture. Our research object will always be characterised by some fluidity and complexity and, as Falzon (2009: 13) has observed, "it is best studied by focussing on a limited slice of action".

In the following, I explain how I focused on a limited slice of action in my study of student mobility in Switzerland. I show how the research evolved due to my experiences in the field and I offer my reflections on my own experience of doing multi-sited ethnography. I start with my initial research objectives and my selection of a research site. I then explain how, in the process of doing the ethnographic work, questions arose that led me beyond this single site and pointed to the inclusion of other sites. Finally, I offer some thoughts on the advantages that accrued from adopting a multi-sited approach.

Research with students crossing linguistic borders to enter university

Mobility across language regions in order to study has a long tradition in Switzerland. There have been universities in the French region (in the west), and in the German region (in the centre and the north-east) since the sixteenth century. In the Ticino, the Italian-speaking region (in the south),

76   *M. Zimmermann*

the local economy was not strong enough to support the establishment of a university. Only in 1995 did we see the founding of a university in this southern region. However, the university has just four faculties and does not meet the needs of all prospective students. So, students from the Ticino have three options with regard to higher education: they can remain in their region and choose a subject offered by the local university, they can move to another language region in Switzerland or they can leave the country. In 2011, when I started being interested in student mobility, about 80 per cent of the students moved out of the region, with about half of them opting for a university in the German-speaking part of Switzerland.[1]

The focus of my ethnographic research has been on young people in Switzerland ending their schooling in the Italian-speaking region and moving on to higher education in the German-speaking region. I was interested in their linguistic and social practices in their new place of residence and study. When I was seeking ways of gaining access to the field, my attention was drawn to a student association established in Berne. The members of this association speak Ticino-dialect and/or Italian and they all come from the Ticino. I contacted the association and obtained access after having explained the aims of my project during an association event when newly arrived students from the Ticino were being welcomed, and I gradually built relationships with some of the people in the association. There were approximately 150 members altogether and I built a relationship with people who were regularly present at association gatherings. My aim was to understand how their day-to-day language practices were connected to the very real conditions of their lives and to gauge how language mattered to them. I undertook ethnographic research at this site, bearing in mind the account of ethnography presented in Mason (2007) and Heller (2008b). During the 2011/2012 academic year, I participated in a range of activities organised by members of this association, including welcoming events, movie nights, weekly meetings, parties and barbecues. The data I collected consisted of audio-recordings of interactions between students (e.g. meetings of the committee), ethnographic interviews (with members of the association), photographs (taken by members of the association and published on their website), field notes and institutional documents (e.g. the statute of the association, minutes of meetings, flyers for association events). As I began to collate and take stock of this preliminary data, new insights emerged which eventually guided me to other sites in other places: first of all to Lucerne and Zurich, two cities in the German-speaking region and, second, to the Ticino, the region of origin for most of the students.

Apart from organising many events, the members of this student association in Berne met informally every Monday evening in a bar near the University of Berne. On one of these evenings in the autumn of 2011, Mauro,[2] a member of the student association, started talking about his experience with Swiss German dialect when arriving in Berne. Other members sitting around the

Reflections on multi-sited ethnography 77

table joined in. The following is an extract from the field notes I wrote after the conversation:

> Mauro told us that his start in Berne was horrible. In the Ticino, he had learned German at school. Before starting at the university he had gone to Heidelberg for three months where he had taken intensive German classes. In Heidelberg he had not had any problems. Then he had come to Berne. That was very difficult. Some of the people he met were not able to speak standard German and many misunderstandings arose. Ennio said he had done his Bachelor's degree in Zurich and added that he had had a traumatising start there because of the omnipresent Swiss German dialect.
>
> (Field notes 14.11.2011)

Speaking to each other in Italian,[3] these students were highlighting the linguistic difficulties they had faced in the German-speaking part of the country, partly due to the local diglossic situation in which the local Swiss German dialect and the German standard coexist, and where the Swiss German dialect serves as a key marker of regional identity. Conversations among these Ticinese students often turned to their linguistic difficulties. Of course, I need to take account of the fact that, as a first language speaker of Swiss German, my presence may well have had an influence on the topics that surfaced. The students may also have been expressing pride in their abilities to overcome these difficulties and/or pride in a shared identity and regional origin – pride of the sort described by Duchêne and Heller (2011). I had also become aware that, within the networks around the student association in Berne, the discourses which had greatest legitimacy were those in which reference was made to the experience of being from the Italian-speaking minority in Switzerland and in which the expression of negative attitudes to Swiss German was commonplace.

As I listened to these conversations, I found myself asking questions such as the following: If studying in the German-speaking region is a "traumatising experience" – as Ennio put it – how come so many Italian-speaking students still choose a university in the German-speaking region rather than studying in their home region (or abroad, e.g. in Italy)? How do students make the decision to invest in study in a German-speaking region? What interests are driving their decisions? How do languages become part of the argument legitimising their choice of university? Moreover, how do students cope with the challenges when they are not part of an association providing support?

On Thursday or Friday nights, the members of the association travelled back to the Ticino, transiting either in Lucerne or Zurich (both are about an hour by train from Berne). There, other Ticinese students boarded the train to spend the weekend back home. During these joint trips, possibilities and conditions for Italian-speaking students at different universities in the German-speaking part of Switzerland were discussed and compared. When

78   *M. Zimmermann*

this came to my attention, I realised that I needed to go beyond the sample of students from the association in Berne and contact newcomers enrolled at universities in Lucerne and in Zurich in order to tackle some of the questions listed above.

Via the university's admission offices, I therefore got in touch with students from Lucerne and Zurich, with whom I conducted several interviews. I decided not to limit the interviews to the inter-urban social network of the members based in Berne, not wanting to reduce my focus to those who are generally favourable to the Ticinese student associations that can also be found in Lucerne and Zurich. One of these new interviews took place in a cafe near the university's main building in Lucerne. This interview was with Ilona, a Ticinese student who had recently arrived in Lucerne and who was studying law. We talked about her decision to move to this German-speaking region.[4]

MZ: How come you have chosen to study law in Lucerne/. you could have gone to other pla:ces/
IL: mhm. I said to myself … law can be studied in different places. also in the French-speaking part of Switzerland. for instance in Lausanne and Fribourg if I am not wrong/
MZ: yes
IL: ehm. well. from the very beginning I excluded the French speaking part because I said to myself … my French is more or less ok/
MZ: yes
IL: it is similar to Italian and therefore let's say I can learn it in little time/ German however is much more important … and spoken by three quarters of Switzerland\. and I am still struggling with German. thus I prefer studying in German … like that my German gets better and I'll have advantages for the. for the future\

At this point in her university career, Ilona was clearly investing in German-medium higher education because she saw it as a means of securing better prospects for herself in the future. So, in addition to other discourses underpinning student mobility, such as the limited number of subjects offered in the university in the Ticino, the higher reputation of universities in other regions of Switzerland, and the difficulties involved in learning German, here we see a discourse about the value of the German language within the wider linguistic market in Switzerland. We see it being valued as a form of linguistic and symbolic capital with regard to future employment prospects.

Several scholars have drawn attention to the ways in which symbolic resources such as language have become more prominent within the new, globalised, economic order of late capitalism (Urciuoli, 2008; Duchêne & Heller, 2011). Here, we get a brief glimpse of this phenomenon. Ilona's thinking also reflects the shifts taking place with regard to language ideologies

Reflections on multi-sited ethnography 79

in Switzerland, with German, and now English, gaining ground within the national linguistic market at the expense of French and Italian.

This extract from my interview with Ilona shows how she rationalised and legitimated her decision to leave the Ticino and come to the German-speaking part of the country. Since her discourse about the German language was different from that of the students in the association in Berne, I needed to include in my sample other students like her who had a similar background, that is, students from the Ticino at a different university in a different city, who were not yet part of a specific network with its own dominant discourse. Rather than focusing on the difficulties involved in learning German, Ilona stressed the value of German as a resource in the job market and showed a commitment to investing in the learning of the language.

During my interview with her, Ilona also referred on several occasions to the time before her migration from the Ticino as she explained her decision in favour of the University of Lucerne. She pointed out to me that a delegation from Lucerne had taken part in an information day for prospective students in the Ticino where all the universities in Switzerland were represented. This drew my attention to the fact that not only students but also universities crossed the linguistic border. Teams of university representatives travelled south to this event each year. This led me to questions about the universities' role in marketing courses, in recruiting students, thereby promoting mobility (or, in the case of the university based in the Ticino, promoting immobility). I added two further research questions to my study: How is the choice of university made *before* leaving the Ticino and coming to the German-speaking region? And under what conditions does language play a role in this process?

With these questions in mind, I thus travelled to a third site – the Ticino. This trip turned out to be helpful for two reasons. First, undertaking the same journeys that my research subjects based in Berne made, almost every weekend, to their homes in their region of origin, enabled me to have lived experience of these journeys – journeys which were an omnipresent topic of conversation amongst the students. The four hours or so spent travelling back to the region of origin were described by the students as 'lost', and there was also much comment on the sickness induced by the tilting motion of the train. I could only comprehend these discussions once I had done this trip too (including feeling sick!). Second, travelling to the Ticino and doing participant observation at one of these information days enabled me to follow the decision-making of a small group of prospective students. It also gave me the chance to track the movement of university staff across linguistic borders and to observe their on-site practices. Situated on the campus of the university in the Ticino, delegations from all Swiss universities took part and presented their courses of study. I was able to participate, observe and talk to prospective students. I also met students who were already enrolled in courses in universities outside the Ticino region who were representing these universities. I collected flyers, leaflets and other documents produced by different institutions.

80   *M. Zimmermann*

The following extracts, taken from the official programme created, in Italian, for the information day, illustrate how the different universities presented themselves to potential 'clients'. For example, the University of Zurich entitled one of its presentations: "30 institutes, 1000 opportunities: combine a lot at the Faculty of Literature and Philosophy".[5] A presentation by the Economics Faculty at the University of the Italian-speaking part of Switzerland was billed as: "How to win black jack and other mathemagic games". A third presentation bore the simple title "The pleasure of studying at the University of Lausanne". Only one university offered degrees in Italian, while the whole programme for the day was written in Italian and nearly all the presentations were done by Italian-speaking professors and/or students who had travelled to the Ticino in order to present their institution, to answer questions and to convince future students of the excellence of their department or of their subject of study.

A key point to note here is that there is keen competition between Swiss universities to recruit students. The universities are public institutions and receive subsidies from the government on the basis of student numbers. They therefore have to try to recruit students from all language regions. Thanks to the inclusion of this third research site involving a form of spatial decentredness (that is geographical in nature), I became aware of the importance of this event for the different actors involved. In particular, it enabled me to understand the student perspective and the issues that concerned them. I realised why they engaged in repeated comparison of different institutions. I also came to see why the students took up elements of the discourses manifested in universities' advertisements (e.g. in their peer interactions or in their interviews with me). For instance, the students in my study often talked about the linguistic accommodation practices of university authorities in the German-speaking region, such as offering introductory language courses, special examination rules (e.g. the option of using Italian). Forms of support such as these were promised (in Italian) by some university representatives at the information day in the Ticino. My study is still underway; however, it is already clear that language is a key resource for gaining access to prestigious higher education pathways and it is a central marker of distinction for universities and students alike. Moreover, within the higher education system in Switzerland, language is increasingly bound up with the ideology of competitiveness and with neo-liberal management practices (Kauppi & Erkkilä, 2011; Block et al., 2012).

Reflections on multi-sitedness: benefits and limits

My ethnographic work in the student association in Berne brought up questions that led me to Lucerne and Zurich, where further interviews were conducted. In these interviews, the period before the migration became a subject of discussion, guiding me, in turn, to the Ticino – the region of origin for the students. So to conclude this chapter, I present the benefits associated

Reflections on multi-sited ethnography 81

with a multi-sited ethnographic approach in projects of this kind and I offer my reflections. I also touch on the challenges and the limits of multi-sited research, focusing in particular on the constraints on extended engagement with research participants in all sites.

As I have endeavoured to show, several benefits accrued from adopting a multi-sited approach in this study: first, my research questions were taken to a new level during the research process. I was able to identify sites, relationships and contours that were not initially evident. Marcus (1995) made a similar point. The study developed from being one focusing on the linguistic and social practices of Italian-speaking students in just one setting in Berne to one designed to build an understanding of the processes involved in gaining access to linguistic and cultural capital (Bourdieu, 1983) through mobility, from one language region to another, and from one sector of the Swiss higher education system to another. Second, the multi-site research enabled me to develop an in-depth understanding of the linkages between practices in different sites, e.g. the marketing of courses by Swiss universities in the Ticino region; the significance of the linguistic accommodation policies and practices of universities in the German-speaking region; or the role of the student association in Berne as a space for providing support to newcomers from the Ticino and for (re-)constructing a Swiss Italian identity as distinct from a Swiss German one. In describing some of my research journey here, one of my aims has been to illustrate the fact that ethnography (and maybe multi-sited ethnography in particular) is not about "holding knowledge" but about "making knowledge" (Marcus, 2011: 17). As ethnographers, we are in constant reflection about our research questions and in regular dialogue with the actors in the field. In my case, this involved crossing linguistic, spatial and institutional borders, tracing the trajectories of different actors and building an account of their practices and their discourses about language.

Traditional ethnography has always stressed the importance of a prolonged stay in a chosen field. However, the classical model presents an idealised version of research practice. There are, of course, constraints on time and funding in contemporary research. But, also, as I found in doing multi-site research, in some sites, it is not possible to achieve the same depth of focus or to engage with participants over an extended period due to constraints on access, or due to the nature of the field itself. For example, while I conducted a classical form of participant observation, for about a year, in the student association in Berne, participating in various events, informal conversations and leisure activities, I faced quite different conditions at the information day at the university in the Ticino. There I participated in the programme for only a day and, like all the other participants, the future students, students already enrolled and the academic staff from other universities, I had to rely on the gathering of textual data such as institutional documents and leaflets, along with attendance at specific presentations and conducting short informal interviews with the people present. These conditions merely reflected the terms on which the prospective students circulated and interacted with the representatives of various Swiss universities.

The same information day event takes place every year in the Ticino, with broadly the same format, albeit with a different set of actors. According to Muir (2004: 210), multi-sited research should be conceived of as being about "scenes and spaces" rather than "sites or places". He also highlights the "spatial and temporal ephemerality" characterising multi-sites studies. I certainly concur with Muir's (2004) representation of the 'sites' of multi-sited research as being "scenes or spaces", given the complex ways in which different social actors can construct these spaces over time. However, I take issue with the argument that multi-sited research is always characterised by "spatial and temporal ephemerality". As I have shown in this account of my own multi-sited ethnographic work in Switzerland, extended participant observation in one site, achieving depth of focus, can be combined with fieldwork in other social spaces where new insights can be gleaned, albeit through research with less depth of focus, because the activities being observed have a shorter duration. The limited period of observation at the information day in Ticino did give me valuable insights into the situated, institutional use of Italian in the marketing of university courses. This is a practice that I could not have anticipated had I located my study only in the German-speaking region. Furthermore, discussing with prospective students before their 'departure' not only helped me to understand the relevance of the recurring topics in the conversations of Italian-speaking students already enrolled with regard to the present phase of their lives in the German-speaking part of Switzerland, it also helped me to comprehend their past as an element in their present. In addition, I learned more about the local education system, about their lives before going to university and about their worries related to the move away. This shed new light on the students' justifications for their choice of a university in the German-speaking region rather than in the French-speaking region.

As Sheller and Urry (2006) have pointed out, research 'on the move' has proved to be beneficial when it comes to tracking, in various ways, the intermittent movement of people, images, information and objects. Such research has also included travelling in person with research subjects. This is relevant in my study since the students I was working with went back and forth across linguistic and cultural borders in Switzerland, to/from the Ticino. Following the students as they crossed these borders presented a challenge, putting me out of my "comfort zone", as Haraway (1991) put it, but through this kind of ethnography 'on the move', I was able to glean greater insight into the emic understandings and perceptions of the students regarding the higher educational pathways they had chosen.

Multi-sited ethnography certainly makes it possible to build an account of complex connections across sites of investigation. It often involves the use of different languages by ethnographers as they move across different spaces. Moreover, it is often transdisciplinary in nature, being applied across

Reflections on multi-sited ethnography 83

the social sciences, in disciplines such as linguistic anthropology, social geography, sociology and sociolinguistics. The ongoing transdisciplinary conversations about multi-sited research have enriched our understanding of its characteristics and its potential. In the new times in which we live, traditional ethnographic methods of inquiry and units of analysis need to be challenged and we need to unpack research methodologies that focus on just one group in one particular setting (Gille & Ó Riain, 2002). We need to develop new conceptual frameworks and research methodologies so as to be able to grasp the variable roles and values that are attributed to languages by different actors. The questions that we are addressing in the new sociolinguistics cut across the boundary of a single field (Kurotani, 2004).

By adopting a multi-sited approach, one is nevertheless faced with multiple challenges, including the difficulty of anticipating the next location for investigation and the difficulty of making sense of unanticipated contradictions and relationships (Grätz, 2003; Werthmann, 2003). Despite these challenges, the particular advantage of multi-site fieldwork lies in its potential for moving beyond the traditional 'single tribe, single scribe' way of doing ethnographic research. It enables us to identify the connections between social and linguistic practices occurring in different sites and to take account of social and institutional processes at work beyond local social groups.

In the case of my research on the mobility of students across linguistic regions in Switzerland, multi-sited ethnographic research enabled me to build an understanding of the contrasts in the language practices and ideologies of different students and to make links with more general institutional processes (e.g. the marketing of university courses in the German-speaking region) and with more general discourses (e.g. about the value of German as a form of linguistic capital) produced by institutional and individual actors within the higher education system. The extended period of ethnographic fieldwork and participant observation with members of the student association in Berne and the ethnographic interviews in Lucerne and Zurich also enabled me to gain insights into the discursive stances that students assumed vis-à-vis the discourses about German, with some taking on elements of the dominant discourse and others adopting a more critical stance.

Notes

1 Bundesamt für Statistik: STAT-TAB, Übersicht, Bildungswesen. Studierende der universitären Hochschulen bei Jahr, Wohnkanton vor Studienbeginn und Hochschule (2011). www.pxweb.bfs.admin.ch/ [cited, 13.09.2014].
2 This and all other names in this chapter are fictitious. They have been used, for ethical reasons, to preserve confidentiality.
3 All the conversations between the members of the association took place in Italian. The Italian transcriptions and my German field notes have been translated into English for the purposes of this chapter.
4 The conventions used in transcribing extracts such as this one were as follows:

. short pause
... long pause

84 *M. Zimmermann*

:   stretching preceding sound or letter
/   rising intonation
\   falling intonation

5 All these presentations and texts were in Italian. They have been translated into English for this chapter.

References

Amit, V. (2000) 'Introduction: constructing the field', in V. Amit (ed.) *Constructing the Field: Ethnographic Feldwork in the Contemporary World.* New York: Routledge, 1–18.

Anderson, B. (1991) *Imagined Communities: Reflections on the Origin and Spread of Nationalism.* New York: Verso.

Appadurai, A. (1990) 'Disjuncture and difference in the global cultural economy'. *Theory, Culture, and Society* 7, 295–310.

Appadurai, A. (1996) *Modernity at Large: Cultural Dimensions of Globalization.* Minneapolis, MN: University of Minnesota Press.

Blackledge, A. & Creese, A. (2010) *Multilingualism: A Critical Perspective.* New York: Continuum.

Block, D., Gray, J. & Holborow, M. (2012) *Neoliberalism and Applied Linguistics.* London: Routledge.

Bourdieu, P. (1983) 'Ökonomisches Kapital, kulturelles Kapital, soziales Kapital' [Economic capital, cultural capital, social capital], in R. Kreckel (ed.) *Soziale Ungleichheiten* [Social Inequalities]. Göttingen: Schwartz, 83–198.

Candea, M. (2007) 'Arbitrary locations: in defence of the bounded field-site'. *Journal of the Royal Anthropological Institute* 13(1), 167–184.

Clifford, J. (1992) 'Traveling cultures', in L. Grossberg et al. (eds) *Cultural Studies.* New York: Routledge, 96–116.

Coleman, S. & von Hellermann, P. (eds) (2011) *Multi-Sited Ethnography: Problems and Possibilities in the Translocation of Research Methods.* New York: Routledge.

Duchêne, A. & Heller, M. (eds) (2011) *Language in Late Capitalism: Pride and Profit.* New York: Routledge.

Falzon, M.-A. (ed.) (2009) *Multi-Sited Ethnography: Theory, Praxis and Locality in Contemporary Research.* Farnham: Ashgate.

Fitzgerald, D. (2006) 'Towards a theoretical ethnography of migration'. *Qualitative Sociology* 29(1), 1–24.

Gallo, E. (2009) 'In the right place at the right time? Reflections on multi-sited ethnography in the age of migration', in M.-A. Falzon (ed.) *Multi-Sited Ethnography: Theory, Praxis and Locality in Contemporary Research.* Farnham: Ashgate, 87–102.

Gille, Z. & Ó Riain, S. (2002) 'Global ethnography'. *Annual Review of Sociology* 28, 271–295.

Grätz, T. (2003) 'Les chercheurs d'or et la construction d'identités de migrants en Afrique de l'Ouest' [The gold seekers and the construction of migrant identities in West Africa]. *Politique Africaine* 91, 155–169.

Hage, G. (2005) 'A not so multi-sited ethnography of a not-so imagined community'. *Anthropological Theory* 5(4), 463–475.

Hannerz, U. (2003) 'Being there … and there … and there! Reflections on multi-site ethnography'. *Ethnography* 4(2), 201–216.

Reflections on multi-sited ethnography 85

Haraway, D. (1991) *Simians, Cyborgs, and Women: The Reinvention of Nature.* New York: Routledge.

Heller, M. (2008a) 'Doing ethnography', in L. Wei & M. Moyer (eds) *The Blackwell Guide to Research Methods in Bilingualism and Multilingualism.* Oxford: Blackwell, 249–262.

Heller, M. (2008b) 'Language and the nation-state: challenges to sociolinguistic theory and practice'. *Journal of Sociolinguistics* 12(4), 504–524.

Heller, M. (2010) 'The commodification of language'. *Annual Review of Anthropology* 39, 101–114.

Heller, M. (2011) *Paths to Post-Nationalism: A Critical Ethnography of Language and Identity.* Oxford: Oxford University Press.

Hendry, J. (2003) 'An ethnographer in the global arena: globography perhaps?' *Global Networks* 3, 497–512.

Kauppi, N. & Erkkilä, T. (2011) 'The struggle over global higher education: actors, institutions, and practices'. *International Political Sociology* 5, 314–326.

Kurotani, S. (2004) 'Multi-sited transnational ethnography and the shifting construction of fieldwork', in L. Hume & J. Mulcock (eds) *Anthropologists in the Field: Cases in Participant Observation.* New York: Columbia University Press, 201–215.

Lamarre, P. & Lamarre, S. (2009) 'Montreal "on the move": pour une approche ethnographique non-statique de pratiques langagières des jeunes multilingues' [Towards a non-static ethnographic approach to the language practices of young multilinguals], in T. Bulot (ed.) *Segregations et discriminations urbaines (formes et norms sociolinguistiques)* [Urban segregations and discriminations (sociolinguistic forms and norms)]. Paris: L'Harmattan (Collection Espaces Discursifs), 105–134.

Marcus, G.A. (1995) 'Ethnography in/of the world system: the emergence of multi-sited ethnography'. *Annual Review of Anthropology* 24, 95–117.

Marcus, G.A. (2011) 'Multi-sited ethnography: five or six things I know about it now', in S. Coleman & P. von Hellermann (eds) *Multi-Sited Ethnography: Problems and Possibilities in the Translocation of Research Methods.* New York: Routledge, 16–34.

Mason, J. (2007) *Qualitative Researching.* London: Sage.

Moyer, M. (2012) 'Sociolinguistic perspectives on language and multilingualism in institutions', in S. Gardner & M. Martin-Jones (eds) *Multilingualism, Discourse and Ethnography.* London: Routledge, 34–47.

Muir, S. (2004) 'Not quite at home: field envy and new age ethnographic dis-ease', in L. Hume & J. Mulcock (eds) *Anthropologists in the Field: Cases in Participant Observation.* New York: Columbia University Press, 185–200.

Pietikäinen, S. & Pitkänen-Huhta, A. (2014) 'Dynamic multimodal language practices in multilingual Indigenous Sámi classrooms in Finland', in D. Gorter, V. Zenotz & J. Cenoz (eds) *Minority Languages and Multilingual Education: Bridging the Local and the Global.* Dordrecht: Springer, 137–157.

Redfield, R. (1941) *The Folk Culture of Yucatan.* Chicago, IL: University of Chicago Press.

Sheller, M. & Urry, J. (2006) 'The new mobilities paradigm'. *Environment and Planning* 38(2), 207–226.

Takahashi, K. (2013) *Language Learning, Gender and Desire: Japanese Women on the Move.* Clevedon, UK: Multilingual Matters.

Urciuoli, B. (2008) 'Skills and selves in the new workplace'. *American Ethnologist* 35(2), 211–228.

86 M. Zimmermann

Waldinger, R.D. & Fitzgerald, D. (2003) 'Immigrant "transnationalism" reconsidered'. Department of Sociology, UCLA. Online: http://escholarship.org/uc/item/067683p8 (accessed 19 August 2014).

Werthmann, K. (2003) *Bitteres Gold. Historische, Soziale und Kulturelle Aspekte des Nicht-industriellen Goldbergbaus in Westafrika* [Bitter Gold: Social and Cultural Aspects of Non-Industrial Gold Mining in West Africa]. Unpublished habilitation thesis, Johannes Gutenberg-Universität Mainz.

Xiang, B. (2013) 'Multi-scalar ethnography: an approach for critical engagement with migration and social change'. *Ethnography* 14(3), 282–299.

Part 2

Researching discourses, policies and practices on different scales

6 Nexus analysis as scalar ethnography for educational linguistics

Francis M. Hult

Introduction

As experiences with globalization and mobility have increasingly become a focus of research, attention to the nature of the connections humans forge across time and space and their significance for meaning-making have intensified in educational linguistics. How do educators, students, and community members make use of historically and geographically situated semiotic resources to locate themselves and each other in moments of space and time? How do semiotic resources that circulate across time and space intersect to mediate experiences in particular moments of interaction? How do circulating ideas from policy, (new) media, and popular culture, among other areas, become part of classroom experiences? As questions like these suggest, what seems to interest many contemporary educational linguists is the nature of flows and connections (e.g. Bigelow & Ennser-Kananen, 2015). Along with this interest comes a growing desire to reconcile methodologically how such flows across continua of scale should be systematically investigated (Blommaert, 2005, 2010; Hornberger, 2003; Hult, 2010a).

In this chapter, I take up nexus analysis (Scollon & Scollon, 2004), an ethnographic sociolinguistic[1] approach to the study of discursive flows across scales, and I consider its applicability to educational linguistic research. I begin with a brief discussion that situates multidimensional inquiry in educational linguistics, highlighting the conceptual relevance of scales. Then, turning to nexus analysis, I provide an exposition of some of its fundamental principles and how they facilitate scalar research. Next, I discuss how these principles allow nexus analysis to be used as a meta-methodology to guide the selection and integration of multiple methods for data collection and analysis, since multi-method research is often called for in educational linguistics. Finally, I reflect on how the principled yet flexible nature of nexus analysis makes it useful as a guide to research design in educational linguistics.

Educational linguistics and social scales

Educational linguistics, as a field, is transdisciplinary (Hornberger & Hult, 2008; Hult, 2010a), meaning that investigating the full range of issues related

90   *F. M. Hult*

to language (in) education requires multiple vantage points, ranging from the psycholinguistic to the sociolinguistic. The kinds of issues educational linguists take up with respect to multilingualism and education are necessarily multidimensional because they involve the interplay of actions taken by individuals (e.g. students, teachers, and parents) and the nested social contexts (e.g. classrooms, schools, communities, countries) in which those actions are situated (Larsen-Freeman & Cameron, 2008; Martin-Jones, 2015).

In an earlier discussion about theme-based research and transdisciplinarity in educational linguistics (Hult, 2010a: 23–24), I drew upon key summary works (Hornberger, 2008; Spolsky & Hult, 2008) to highlight some of the major areas of inquiry in the field:

language ecology and education
language education policy and management
linguistically and culturally responsive education
literacy development
second and foreign language learning
language testing and assessment.

At first glance, the multidimensional nature of educational linguistics becomes readily apparent as one can easily imagine how these major areas relate to each other. For instance, investigating how learning does or does not take place in linguistically and culturally responsive ways in a particular school or classroom will likely also involve taking into account the relationships among languages and speakers in the language ecology of the school and surrounding community (e.g. Creese & Martin, 2003; Hornberger, 2003). Language policy and management is, of course, related to all of the other areas as educators must interpret policy in their daily educational practices (e.g. Johnson, 2013; McCarty, 2011; Menken & García, 2010). No single focus of research is ever truly isolated.

In their work drawing on complex systems theory, Larsen-Freeman and Cameron (2008: 200–203) remind us that investigating any single moment, like a group of students completing a language-learning task, calls on educational linguists to consider what other dimensions are (potentially) related to that moment: from smaller dimensions like the individual students and their minds to larger dimensions such as the lesson, the school, the regional or national curriculum, and the wider sociopolitical context. Fundamentally, this means that as educational linguists we must pay attention to scales, or the idea that human experiences are socially constructed and made meaningful on varying interconnected dimensions of space and time (Blommaert, 2007; Blommaert et al., 2014).

Different ways of conceptualizing scales have come into applied/educational linguistics from complexity theory (Larsen-Freeman & Cameron, 2008; Lemke, 2000) and social geography (Blommaert, 2007). In a basic sense, the concept of scales draws attention to different dimensions of social

Nexus analysis as scalar ethnography 91

organization and how connections across them can be theorized. As Lemke (2000: 276) puts it: "there is always a higher level process already in place, already running on its own longer timescale, and this sets the context that constrains what is likely and what is socially appropriate at the next scale below". At the same time, larger scales are also constructed by actions on smaller scales (Lemke, 2000: 276). In educational research, for instance, a scalar perspective facilitates a view of schools and classrooms as points of intersection for discursive flows, where every moment can be seen as an instance of 'layered simultaneity' in that "it occurs in a real-time, synchronic event, but it is simultaneously encapsulated in several layers of historicity, some of which are within the grasp of the participants while others remain invisible but are nevertheless present" (Blommaert, 2005: 130). Analytically, thinking in terms of scales calls on us, as educational linguists, to consider what discourses from different dimensions of time and space are relevant to understanding any particular instance and to map the layers that are simultaneously co-present.

Scales are discursive constructions; they are the ways in which aspects of time and space are conceptualized, labeled, and therefore made meaningful and socially significant (Blommaert et al., 2014: 3). Lemke (2000: 277) notes that the semiotization of phenomena ranging from chemical to cosmological processes facilitates making sense of the very nature of life and the universe itself. Within the parameters of human existence, Scollon and Scollon (2004: 168) show us how phenomena ranging from breaths and heartbeats, to speech events and work days, to individual lifespans and multiple generations are made meaningful and become discursively interconnected. Like pebbles or stones dropped in a pond, smaller (marginal) discourses ripple for a short period over a small space while larger (dominant) ones may ripple longer over a greater space (Hult, 2010b: 19). One ripple may affect others. Scales become meaningful *emically* for understanding how research participants organize their experiential reality and *etically* as lenses (i.e. powers of analytical magnification) that researchers can use to situate and interpret data within social systems (Hult, 2010b: 14; Blommaert et al., 2014: 4–6; Creswell, 1998: 60).

Nexus analysis and the ethnographic sociolinguistics of scales

At its core, nexus analysis is an approach to investigating social phenomena as multidimensional, meaning how single moments of social action are nexus points for discourses across various scales (Scollon & Scollon, 2004: 8). With this multidimensional aim in mind, Scollon and Scollon developed nexus analysis by integrating principles from three different research traditions that respectively facilitate analytical foci on complementary scales: interactional sociolinguistics, linguistic anthropology, and critical discourse analysis. Interactional sociolinguistics emphasizes interpersonal scales, linguistic anthropology emphasizes community scales, and critical discourse analysis emphasizes societal scales. Of course, each of these traditions also attends in varying degrees to relations among different scales, which allows them to be combined fruitfully. Indeed, they have been woven together in various configurations by researchers over the past several decades (Bucholtz & Hall, 2008). The practice of using these and other orientations together in ethnographic sociolinguistic research often becomes eclectic due to the need to match theories and methods to social phenomena as they arise, yet this eclecticism must also be done in a principled manner (Blommaert, 2005: 16). With nexus analysis, Scollon and Scollon offer a framework to guide such principled eclecticism.

On the one hand, then, nexus analysis is not a radical departure from the methodological traditions of discourse analysis or ethnographic sociolinguistics (Scollon, 2005: 485). On the other hand, nexus analysis provides a distinct analytical mechanism that represents the ongoing evolution of contemporary ethnographic sociolinguistics. In short, it provides a kind of protocol, much like Hymes' (e.g. 1974) earlier SPEAKING mnemonic for capturing the dynamic nature of sociolinguistic scales and discursive flows. Specifically, nexus analysis makes social action, rather than language or discourse, the central focus (Scollon, 2005: 485; Scollon & Scollon, 2004: 11–12). It then directs the researcher to the task of mapping the discourses that emerge on different scales, along with the ways in which they intersect in a moment of action in order to mediate it (see Figure 6.1).

Social action

Nearly all human actions are *social* actions, as Scollon and Scollon (2004: 11) suggest, because human behavior is deeply situated in social context and processes of meaning-making. Even private actions that we take in isolation, like picking one's nose, are imbued with socially situated values that we carry with us. Actions may be physical, like walking in one direction instead of another, or semiotic, like writing graffiti on a sign or making a statement in conversation. Semiotic actions, much like speech acts, are actions, meaning that the analytical focus is not solely on language but on the social significance of the language-mediated act. Some actions, such as those taken by teachers and students during a lesson, may be observed in real time. Others, such as signs in the print environment of a school (e.g. Dressler, 2012) or specific lines in an educational policy text (e.g. Hult, 2012), can be seen as 'frozen actions', that is to say, traces of previously taken social actions (Pietikäinen et al., 2011).

Actions in nexus analysis are social in another sense. They are part of specific social systems – sets of practices or a nexus of practice (Scollon & Scollon, 2004: 12). When a teacher utters a statement to begin a task in an ESL classroom, for example, that utterance can be seen as part of different nexuses of practice. For example, one might wish to understand the utterance in relation to educating English language learners, including how training in TESOL relates to classroom practices. Alternatively, one might wish to

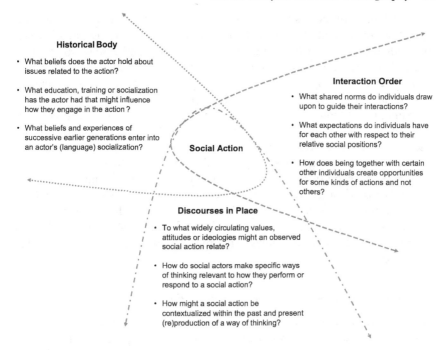

Figure 6.1 Intersecting discourses in nexus analysis.

understand the utterance in relation to policy interpretation/implementation, including how classroom practices are shaped by an ESL curriculum crafted in relation to a national educational language policy. Other nexuses of practice are also possible. Which nexus one follows will depend on one's focus and research questions.

In the relationship between a social action and a nexus of practice, we see the dialectic of scale as Lemke (2000) explains it. It is through the iteration of actions that a larger scale or nexus of practice is socially (re)produced. At the same time, the existence of the larger scale, for example the education of English language learners, as previously (re)produced, provides a discursive context for a specific social action (Scollon & Scollon, 2004: 168–169). As such, any single social action must be seen in relation to other related social actions as well as to the nexus of practice as a whole. By conducting a study in this way, a researcher can "[make] sure that the study does not become obsessively narrowed to single moments, speech acts or events, or participants without seeing how these connect to other moments, acts, events, and participants which make up the full nexus" (Scollon & Scollon, 2004: 9).

The social context of a specific action, meaning how it is situated in a specific nexus of practice, can be mapped discursively. As shown in Figure 6.1, the framework of nexus analysis provides a guide for how to trace specific

94   *F. M. Hult*

relationships between a social action and other scales. Scollon and Scollon posit that social actions are mediated by three types of discourse[2] which they call the *historical body*, the *interaction order*, and *discourses in place* (2004: 20). Each type is dynamic in its own right, flowing, as Scollon and Scollon (2004: 27) suggest, like the water cycle. Water rains down, picks up new elements from the air and ground, evaporates, rains down again, and so on. Similarly, discourses are expressed, changed in sociohistorical context, and expressed again in potentially altered ways. Each of the three types of discourse, then, is usefully considered as a cycle. These cycles may manifest themselves on differing scales of space and time. One aspect of nexus analysis is to trace the evolution of the respective cycles that are germane to a particular nexus of practice. Another aspect of nexus analysis, as highlighted in Figure 6.1, is to examine how relevant elements of the respective cycles intersect in a moment of social action thereby mediating it. Concretely, it is these two aspects of nexus analysis that make it useful as a methodology for scalar inquiry.

Three types of discourse that mediate social action

The *historical body* discourse cycle draws attention to life histories and the experiences of the social actors involved in the action being analyzed (Scollon & Scollon, 2004: 160–161). Spatially, it is about an individual or personal scale. Thus, the kinds of questions we might want to ask include: What beliefs does the actor hold about issues related to the action? What education, training or socialization has the actor had that might influence how they engage in the action? Temporally, the historical body is mainly about the lifespan of an individual; however, depending on the nature of one's research focus, it could be broader or narrower (Bhalla, 2012), including questions such as: What beliefs and experiences of successive earlier generations enter into an actor's (language) socialization? What experiences during a specific period of life, such as teacher education or professional apprenticeship, is particularly relevant to an action being studied?

Scollon and Scollon borrow the term 'historical body' from the Japanese philosopher Nishida, who explains that the concept is not just about the individual but about the dialectic between individual and society:

> Something created is both an expression of the artist's subjective idea and, at the same time, it is an objective thing as well ... Then, too, an art work is made by oneself but it does not remain one's own – it becomes a public thing. For example, when the carpenter builds the house, the house does not remain his alone, but becomes a public thing.
>
> (Nishida, 1937/1998: 40)

In this way, the historical body invokes the role of agency and the potential for individual influence on society. An action is mediated by the life experiences

Nexus analysis as scalar ethnography 95

of the individual, and once committed, the action has the potential to influence the life experiences of others (Blommaert & Huang, 2009). To extend Nishida's analogy, the way a house is built by one actor will affect how another lives in it. A prolific architectural or construction firm may have a wide influence on how an entire society lives. Lane's (2010) work on language shift in a Norwegian Kven community illustrates the point further. She traces the ideological trajectories underlying her participants' experiences, mapping how current values and language-use practices can be connected diachronically to language ideologies about Kven and Norwegian language use. Using nexus analysis in a more synchronic perspective, Compton (2010) investigates the implementation of language policy for Deaf education in Texas, showing how the individually held beliefs about deafness and language development by key actors mediate very different interpretations of policy texts and concomitant consequences for students' learning. Thus, mapping the historical body cycle is one useful perspective for understanding how a certain action (or set of actions) takes shape the way it does.

Actions also take place in the context of relationships among social actors. Accordingly, drawing on the work of Erving Goffman, Scollon and Scollon (2004: 13) suggest that mapping the *interaction order* is another useful perspective for understanding how an action takes shape. Spatially, the interaction order is mainly about the immediate interpersonal scale or interactional context co-constructed by actors. As Goffman explains,

> Once individuals ... come into one another's immediate presence, a fundamental condition of social life becomes enormously pronounced, namely, its promissory, evidential character. It is not only that our appearance and manner provide evidence of our statuses and relationships. It is also that the line of our visual regard, the intensity of our involvement, and the shape of our initial actions, allow others to glean our immediate intent and purpose, and all this whether or not we are engaged in talk with them at the time.
>
> (1983: 3)

Thus, we can ask questions such as the following (cf. Scollon & Scollon, 2004: 157): What shared norms do individuals draw upon to guide their interactions? What expectations do individuals have for each other with respect to their relative social positions? How does being together with certain other individuals create opportunities for some kinds of actions and not others? Temporally, the immediate scope of the interaction order is the duration of the encounter itself, which may vary: classroom lessons, policy negotiation meetings, parent–teacher conferences, among other possibilities. Norms and expectations may be (re)negotiated during encounters. At the same time, it must be recognized that norms and expectations often also emerge and change sociohistorically in communities over multiple generations even if they are instantiated in the moment of action. As with the historical body cycle,

96   *F. M. Hult*

depending on one's research focus, it may be useful to map the evolution of the interaction order to gain a broader perspective on why it functions as it does. Alternatively, it might be sufficient to consider the interaction order in its immediate synchronic function in mediating a specific action.

In our study of the making of a language policy at a Swedish university (Källkvist & Hult, 2016), we attended to the immediate nature of the interaction order while also placing it in sociocultural context. In analyzing the interaction among policy committee members, we observed the special function of the chair in managing the contributions of members. The shared norms about committee deliberation and expectations about the role that a chair plays facilitated the chair's ability to introduce ideas into policy deliberation as well as to guide how other members' ideas were made relevant. We noted, in particular, how with respect to certain issues, the chair created substantial interactional space for individuals with unique expert knowledge about those issues. The chair's ability to create such space was certainly legitimized by his immediate discourse role as committee chair. We also determined ethnographically that his behavior in these instances reflected a culturally situated consultative approach to leadership in which listening is valued and specialized expertise is heavily weighted. This approach has developed historically in the Scandinavian context and has come to be (re)produced broadly across institutions over time (e.g. Jönsson, 2010) and, in the immediate context of our study, over the year-long sequence of committee meetings. Thus, the historical body allows the researcher to focus deeply on elements of subjectivity while the interaction order aids the contextualization of an action in the context of intersubjectivity.

The third type of discourse cycle that Scollon and Scollon proffer is *discourse in place*. Actions are mediated not only by the values and experiences of actors (historical body), and intersubjectivity (interaction order), but also by wider circulating discourses that are already present (i.e. in place) when the action occurs:

> All places in the world are complex aggregates (or nexus) of many discourses which circulate through them. Some of these circulate on slow time cycles like the aging of the built or architectural environment of a shopping mall ... Some of these discourses circulate more rapidly like the conversational topics among three friends walking through the same shopping mall.
>
> (Scollon & Scollon, 2004: 14)

Gee's (1999: 13) conceptualization of discourse includes 'ways of thinking' as well as ways of 'using tools and objects.' The physical layout of a classroom, for example, is based on ways of thinking about teaching and learning which are manifested in how objects like desks, boards, and books are positioned. The configuration of desks will serve as an affordance for actions during student–student and teacher–student interactions. In a similar way, beliefs

Nexus analysis as scalar ethnography 97

about language (i.e. language attitudes and ideologies) circulate in society and may be in place locally where they mediate a particular action.

While discourses in place become relevant, for both participants and researchers, at the moment of action, they emerge and circulate on wider scales of space and time. Temporally, ways of thinking (e.g. values, attitudes, ideologies) may be (re)produced over years and decades, if not hundreds of years. Spatially, they may span communities, regions, countries, or even the world (e.g. through global professional networks or religious movements). Discourses become concrete in moments of social action because they are made relevant and observable in a tangible way which also highlights the role of human agency in (re)producing ways of thinking (Scollon, 2008: 34–35). As Blommaert remarks with respect to investigating language ideological debates, "the story of language must not be an abstract *histoire d'idées* ... Rather, it should be a story of different conflicting, disharmonious practices performed by identifiable actors, in very specific ways, and by means of very specific instruments" (1999: 426). Tracing how discourses in place mediate a particular social action suggests questions such as: To what widely circulating values, attitudes or ideologies might an observed social action relate? How do social actors make specific ways of thinking relevant to how they perform or respond to a social action? How might a social action be contextualized within the past and present (re)production of a way of thinking?

Mapping discourses in place allows the researcher to see connections, including those participants themselves might not see, between actions that occur locally and ideas circulating in society on wider scales. In her study of a German bilingual school in Canada, Dressler (2012) demonstrates how discourses in place about the social value of German dialects and the psycho-social benefits of bilingualism mediate how teachers and parents experience the school's curriculum and its implementation. Similarly, in my own work on language education policy in Sweden, I have mapped how discourses entextualized in national policy documents are taken up by educators as they formulate understandings of classroom practice (Hult, 2012). Identifying relevant discourses in place and determining how they come to be related to social actions makes values, attitudes, and ideologies tangible and traceable across scales, allowing the researcher to document discursive flows.

As with the other two types of discourse (historical body and interaction order), it may also be useful to map the evolution of the discourse in place cycle itself. How has the discourse evolved and through what pathways did it flow from other scales to be put 'in place'? Doing so sheds light on how different ideas become intertwined in framing a certain way of thinking. In our study (Hult & Pietikäinen, 2014) of a language ideological debate about the position of Swedish in Finnish educational policy, Pietikäinen and I examine how ideas about the legitimacy of Finland as a bilingual nation were braided together with the framing of questions about how Swedish as a subject should be organized. We bring to light how historically situated values about bilingualism in Finland were carried into the present debate but also how new

98   *F. M. Hult*

values entered into the cycle thereby slightly shifting the framing of bilingualism. In this way, we provide insight into what the discourse of Finland as a bilingual nation can mean in contemporary social context and, in turn, offer ways to interpret it 'in place' as it is drawn upon by politicians and educators in understanding classroom practice (e.g. Boyd & Palviainen, 2015).

Nexus analysis as a meta-methodology

Hornberger (2006) explains that when conducting problem-centered inquiry, educational linguists must attend to what she calls "methodological rich points." Extending Agar's ethnographic concept of rich points, Hornberger (2006: 222) writes that methodological rich points are "points of research experience that make salient the differences between the researcher's perspective and mode of research and the world the researcher sets out to describe." In other words, when conducting problem-based research, how do researchers know what to focus on and, once they decide on a focus, do they have the right methodological tools for the job? In designing and implementing a study in educational linguistics, making such determinations is not easy. Since problems are often complex, it can be a challenge to determine the most fruitful path of inquiry. Methodologically, educational linguistics is a transdisciplinary field in which a broad spectrum of theories and methods may be used. Selecting among them can be a process that is less than transparent (Hult, 2010a). With its grounding in the traditions of linguistic anthropology, interactional sociolinguistics, and critical discourse analysis and its analytical focus on how social actions are mediated by three types of discourse, nexus analysis can serve as a meta-methodology that can guide the selection of paths to follow in scalar inquiry and the combination of methods for data collection and analysis (Hult, 2010b: 10).

Research in educational linguistics begins with identifying an issue or problem which, rather than a theory or method, becomes the starting point for inquiry (Hornberger, 2001; Hult, 2010a). Using nexus analysis, a problem can be defined in relation to social actions (Scollon & Scollon, 2004: 152). How and why are certain (sets of) actions taken in particular ways? In order to make sense of these actions what needs to be understood about the types of discourses that mediate them? How might changing the cycle of one or more of the three types of discourse also change how actions unfold?[3] By further drawing attention to the three types of discourse and how they potentially intersect in social actions, nexus analysis facilitates inquiry that brings to light the multiple scales, or 'layered simultaneity,' relevant for the problem being investigated. Following discursive flows related to each type of discourse suggests possibilities for data collection and analysis.

Mapping the historical body cycles of actors involved in an issue means engaging with individuals and collecting data that will yield information about their beliefs, memories, routines, habits, professional training, and previous experiences, *inter alia* (Scollon & Scollon, 2004: 160–161). Obtaining such

Nexus analysis as scalar ethnography 99

information calls for the use of methods that focus on introspective data. The most obvious of these might be ethnographic interviewing, but it could also include focus groups, narrative elicitation, and surveys, among others (Bhalla, 2012; Compton, 2010; Dressler, 2012; Scollon & Scollon, 2004: 157–158).

Gaining insight into the interaction order in which actions are situated calls for the observation of how actors behave in relation to one another. In scalar inquiry, a primary consideration in this regard is selecting sites. When conducting a study focused on discursive flows across scales, research is often multi-sited (Falzon, 2009; Marcus, 1998) because different scales may suggest different sites (e.g. schools, district offices, and legislative chambers). Since it is impossible to observe every site potentially relevant to a nexus of practice, choices must be made about where the most useful data can be obtained and the set of sites most likely to yield meaningful information about discursive flows (Hult, 2010b).

Once sites are selected, moments of interaction when actions occur can be determined and observed, gaining information about the norms and expectations for language use, how expectations might change based on the social positions of the actors, and how interaction among actors constitutes a context for an action (Scollon & Scollon, 2004: 157). Drawing upon anthropological approaches such as the ethnography of communication, data may usefully be collected through field notes about observations of speech situations, events, and acts (Hult, 2014a; Hymes, 1974; Saville-Troike, 2003). Interactional sociolinguistic analysis of audio-/video-recorded data may also be beneficial for providing close insight into how specific linguistic and paralinguistic features contribute to the positioning of actors in relation to each other and the action as well as for identifying specific instances where discursive connections are made by actors to other scales (Källkvist & Hult, 2016; Scollon & Scollon, 2004: 136).

Finally, considering discourses in place guides attention to the wider discursive context in which actions are situated. The analyst's task is to figure out what possible discourses might enter into the place where an action occurs and determine which ones are most relevant in mediating it. As Scollon and Scollon clarify:

> Some of these discourses are very distant and of little direct relevance to particular social actions occurring in that place such as the design specifications of the table at which two friends are having coffee. Some of these discourses are directly relevant such as the menu from which the snack selection is made.
>
> (Scollon & Scollon, 2004: 14)

Ascertaining which discourses could possibly be relevant involves investigating what discourses are circulating more widely in relation to the issue or problem being studied (Scollon, 2008: 34–35). Discourses related to physical space (e.g. architecture, design, or signage) are potentially germane

100 F. M. Hult

and so, too, are discourses of ideological space. The tools of critical discourse analysis are useful in this regard, and in the case of visual data, so are the tools of linguistic landscape analysis (Hult, 2014b; Pietikäinen, 2010). The analysis of policy documents, media texts, public signage, or advertising, for instance, brings to light specific ways of thinking about an issue (Hult & Pietikäinen, 2014; Johnson, 2011; Scollon & Scollon, 2004: 156–157). Other methodological tools can also be useful for identifying circulating discourses, including ethnographic observations and language attitude surveys. With an understanding of the available discourses, the researcher can then search for evidence of intertextuality and interdiscursivity as concrete examples of specific discourses being taken across one scale such as policy to another scale such as the moment of action (Blommaert, 2005: 29; Hult, 2015; Johnson, 2015; Scollon, 2008: 22).

Principled yet flexible research design for scalar inquiry

In arguing for the relevance of complexity theory in applied linguistics, Larsen-Freeman and Cameron call for:

> An increased awareness of the *interconnectedness* of the components of a system in producing the whole, and of the system and its context. We cannot properly understand a system and how it behaves without understanding how the different parts of the system interact with each other; it is not enough to understand the parts just in themselves.
>
> (2008: 38–39, emphasis in original)

Nexus analysis facilitates research design for scalar inquiry by providing terms and concepts to identify 'the parts' and a mechanism for understanding how they 'interact with each other' to form a system. The visualization of nexus analysis in Figure 6.1, with social action in the center and three types of discourses flowing through it, is not a prescriptive heuristic for categorizing data. Rather, it is a way to theorize how discourses flow across scales through the social actions that construct a system, and it is a set of conceptual instruments for mapping those flows. As such, nexus analysis is a principled yet flexible approach to the kind of theoretical and methodological eclecticism that Blommaert (2005: 16) describes as necessary for the investigation of the complex issues of mobility, globalization, and the creative use of semiotic resources.

It is principled in providing clear and specific analytical foci: social action and the cycles of the historical body, interaction order, and discourses in place. Each of these foci suggest certain kinds of data to collect and, concomitantly, the kinds of tools that may be useful in gathering and analyzing those data, thereby helping educational linguists navigate methodological rich points (Hornberger, 2006). They also indicate the kinds of pathways to follow in tracing discourses across scales. While every nexus of practice will manifest itself in unique ways, the three foci indicate the types of discourses

Nexus analysis as scalar ethnography 101

to be mindful of and point the researcher in the direction of the sorts of cycles or flows of discourse that are useful to document.

It is flexible in offering a dynamic way to conceptualize discourses in time and space. While the three types of discourse point to scales with different scopes, they should not be misunderstood as identical to the tripartite micro–meso–macro distinction (Hult, 2010b; Blommaert et al., 2014: 3). Rather, they allow for more detailed accounts of how discourses can be both synchronic and diachronic, how they operate across a continuum of broad and narrow social spaces, and how the semiotic construction of time and space relates to human agency and experience. Moreover, they are not singular categories. In the investigation of any particular nexus of practice, there may be, for instance, multiple discourses in place that are relevant and take shape over different scales of space or time. In any particular study, it may also be the case that not all three types of discourse emerge as equally relevant analytically.

In sum, nexus analysis offers one approach to ethnographic sociolinguistic research design for the kinds of complex and multifaceted issues that are of interest to contemporary educational linguists. It is a way to conceptualize scales and discourses as they relate to human agency, and it is a meta-methodology to guide the integration of theories and methods that are needed to map discursive flows within and across social actions.

Notes

1 The disciplinary lines across linguistic ethnography, sociolinguistics, and discourse studies are fuzzy as theories and methods from various traditions have been integrated and refined over the past several decades (Tusting & Maybin, 2007). Bucholtz and Hall (2008) suggest 'sociocultural linguistics' as a cover term while Blommaert (2005: 16) offers 'ethnographic-sociolinguistic analysis of discourse'. An historical trace of terms and disciplines is beyond the scope of this chapter. I refer to the contemporary enterprise of the broad analysis of language in sociocultural context as 'ethnographic sociolinguistics' (Bucholtz & Hall, 2008).
2 Following Scollon and Scollon (2004), I use discourse here in Gee's (1999) sense to mean the relationship between language and "ways of thinking, acting, interacting, valuing, feeling, believing, and using symbols, tools, and objects ... [in order to] give the material world certain meanings, distribute social goods in a certain way, make certain sorts of meaningful connections in our experience, and privilege certain symbol systems and ways of knowing over others" (as cited in Scollon & Scollon, 2004: 4).
3 The three phases of a nexus analysis that Scollon and Scollon (2004) identify are engaging, navigating, and changing a nexus or practice. These resonate with (critical) ethnography in that the researcher enters a community, gradually becomes more acquainted and involved with its members, and identifies opportunities for social change.

References

Bhalla, S. (2012) *Experiencing Globalization as South Asian Teaching Assistants: Navigating Tensions in Professional and Social Identities.* Unpublished PhD dissertation, University of Texas at San Antonio.

102   F. M. Hult

Bigelow, M. & Ennser-Kananen, J. (eds) (2015) *The Routledge Handbook of Educational Linguistics*. London: Routledge.

Blommaert, J. (ed.) (1999) *Language Ideological Debates*. The Hague: Mouton de Gruyter.

Blommaert, J. (2005) *Discourse: A Critical Introduction*. New York: Cambridge University Press.

Blommaert, J. (2007) 'Sociolinguistic scales'. *Intercultural Pragmatics* 4(1), 1–19.

Blommaert, J. (2010) *The Sociolinguistics of Globalization*. New York: Cambridge University Press.

Blommaert, J. & Huang, A. (2009) 'Historical bodies and historical space'. *Journal of Applied Linguistics* 6(3), 267–282.

Blommaert, J., Westinen, E. & Leppänen, S. (2014) 'Further notes on sociolinguistic scales'. *Tilburg Papers in Cultural Studies*, 89, 1–11. Available from www.tilburguniversity.edu/research/institutes-and-research-groups/babylon/tpcs/item-paper-89-further-notes-on-sociolinguistic-scales.htm.

Boyd, S. & Palviainen, Å. (2015) 'Building walls or bridges? A language ideological debate about bilingual schools in Finland', in M. Halonen, P. Ihalainen & T. Saarinen (eds) *Language Policies in Finland and Sweden: Interdisciplinary and Multi-Sited Comparisons*. Bristol: Multilingual Matters, 57–89.

Bucholtz, M. & Hall, K. (2008) 'All of the above: new coalitions in sociocultural linguistics'. *Journal of Sociolinguistics* 12(4), 401–431.

Compton, S. (2010) *Implementing Language Policy for Deaf students from Spanish-speaking Homes: The Case of Agents in a Texas School District*. Unpublished Master's thesis, University of Texas at San Antonio. Available from: http://gradworks.umi.com/14/75/1475894.html.

Creese, A. & Martin, P. (eds) (2003) *Multilingual Classroom Ecologies: Inter-relationships, Interactions and Ideologies*. Clevedon, UK: Multilingual Matters.

Creswell, J.W. (1998) *Qualitative Inquiry and Research Design: Choosing Among Five Traditions*. Thousand Oaks, CA: Sage.

Dressler, R.A.H. (2012) *Simultaneous and Sequential Bilinguals in a German Bilingual Program*. Unpublished PhD thesis, University of Calgary, Canada.

Falzon, M. (ed.) (2009) *Multi-Sited Ethnography: Theory, Practice and Locality in Contemporary Research*. Burlington, VT: Ashgate.

Gee, J.P. (1999) *An Introduction to Discourse Analysis: Theory and Method*. London: Routledge.

Goffman, E. (1983) 'The interaction order'. *American Sociological Review* 48, 1–17.

Hornberger, N.H. (2001) 'Educational linguistics as a field: a view from Penn's program on the occasion of its 25th anniversary'. *Working Papers in Educational Linguistics* 17(1–2), 1–26. Available from www.gse.upenn.edu/wpel/archive/f2001.

Hornberger, N.H. (ed.) (2003) *Continua of Biliteracy: An Ecological Framework for Educational Policy, Research, and Practice in Multilingual Settings*. Clevedon, UK: Multilingual Matters.

Hornberger, N.H. (2006) 'Negotiating methodological rich points in applied linguistics', in M. Chalhoub-Deville, C.A. Chapelle & P. Duff (eds) *Inference and Generalizability in Applied Linguistics: Multiple Perspectives*. Philadelphia, PA: John Benjamins, 221–240.

Hornberger, N.H. (ed.) (2008) *Encyclopedia of Language and Education*, 2nd edn. New York: Springer.

Nexus analysis as scalar ethnography   103

Hornberger, N.H. & Hult, F.M. (2008) 'Ecological language education policy', in B. Spolsky & F.M. Hult (eds) *Handbook of Educational Linguistics*. Malden, MA: Blackwell, 280–296.

Hult, F.M. (2010a) 'Theme-based research in the transdisciplinary field of educational linguistics', in F.M. Hult (ed.) *Directions and Prospects for Educational Linguistics*. New York: Springer, 19–32.

Hult, F.M. (2010b) 'Analysis of language policy discourses across the scales of space and time'. *International Journal of the Sociology of Language* 202, 7–24.

Hult, F.M. (2012) 'English as a transcultural language in Swedish policy and practice'. *TESOL Quarterly* 46, 230–257.

Hult, F.M. (2014a) 'Covert bilingualism and symbolic competence: analytical reflections on negotiating insider/outsider positionality in Swedish speech situations'. *Applied Linguistics* 35(1), 63–81.

Hult, F.M. (2014b) 'Drive-thru linguistic landscaping: constructing a linguistically dominant place in a bilingual space'. *International Journal of Bilingualism* 18, 507–523.

Hult, F.M. (2015) 'Making policy connections across scales using nexus analysis', in F.M. Hult & D.C. Johnson (eds) *Research Methods in Language Policy and Planning: A Practical Guide*. Malden, MA: Wiley, 217–231.

Hult, F.M. & Pietikäinen, S. (2014) 'Shaping discourses of multilingualism through a language ideological debate: the case of Swedish in Finland'. *Journal of Language and Politics* 13, 1–20.

Hymes, D. (1974) *Foundations in Sociolinguistics: An Ethnographic Approach*. Philadelphia, PA: University of Pennsylvania Press.

Johnson, D.C. (2011) 'Critical discourse analysis and the ethnography of language policy'. *Critical Discourse Studies* 8(4), 267–279.

Johnson, D.C. (2013) *Language Policy*. New York: Palgrave Macmillan.

Johnson, D.C. (2015) 'Intertextuality and language policy', in F.M. Hult & D.C. Johnson (eds) *Research Methods in Language Policy and Planning: A Practical Guide*. Malden, MA: Wiley, 166–180.

Jönsson, S. (2010) 'Ledarskap som recept: "mycket av vad jag lärde mig på Sandvik körde vi sedan in på ASEA"' [Leadership as a panacea: "a lot of what we did at Sandvik we later implemented at ASEA"], in S. Jönsson & L. Strannegård (eds) *Ledarskapsboken* [The Leadership Book]. Malmö: Liber, 332–350.

Källkvist, M. & Hult, F.M. (2016) 'Discursive mechanisms and human agency in language policy formation: negotiating bilingualism and parallel language use at a Swedish university'. *International Journal of Bilingual Education and Bilingualism* 19(1), 1–17.

Lane, P. (2010) '"We did what we thought was best for our children": a nexus analysis of language shift in a Kven community'. *International Journal of the Sociology of Language* 202, 63–78.

Larsen-Freeman, D. & Cameron, L. (2008) *Complex Systems and Applied Linguistics*. New York: Oxford University Press.

Lemke, J.L. (2000) Across the scales of time: artifacts, activities, and meanings in eco-social systems. *Mind, Culture, Activity* 7(4), 273–290.

McCarty, T.L. (ed.) (2011) *Ethnography and Language Policy*. London: Routledge.

Marcus, G.A. (1998) *Ethnography Through Thick and Thin*. Princeton, NJ: Princeton University Press.

Martin-Jones, M. (2015) 'Classroom discourse analysis as a lens on language-in-education policy processes', in F.M. Hult & D.C. Johnson (eds) *Research Methods in Language Policy and Planning: A Practical Guide*. Malden, MA: Wiley, 94–106.

Menken, K. and García, O. (eds) (2010) *Negotiating Language Policies in Schools: Educators as Policymakers*. London: Routledge.

Nishida, K. (1937/1998) 'The historical body', in D.A. Dilworth, V.H. Vigliemo & A.J. Zavala (eds) *Sourcebook for Modern Japanese Philosophy*. Westport, CT: Greenwood Press, 37–53.

Pietikäinen, S. (2010) 'Sámi language mobility: scales and discourses of multilingualism in a polycentric environment'. *International Journal of the Sociology of Language* 202, 79–101.

Pietikäinen, S., Lane, P., Salo, H. & Laihiala-Kankainen, S. (2011) 'Frozen actions in the Arctic linguistic landscape: a nexus analysis of language processes in visual space'. *International Journal of Multilingualism* 8(4), 277–298.

Saville-Troike, M. (2003) *The Ethnography of Communication: An Introduction*. Malden, MA: Blackwell.

Scollon, R. (2005) 'The discourses of food in the world system'. *Journal of Language and Politics* 4(3), 465–488.

Scollon, R. (2008) *Analyzing Public Discourse: Discourse Analysis in the Making of Public Policy*. London: Routledge.

Scollon, R. & Scollon, S.W. (2004) *Nexus Analysis*. London: Routledge.

Spolsky, B. & Hult, F.M. (eds) (2008) *Handbook of Educational Linguistics*. Malden, MA: Wiley-Blackwell.

Tusting, K. & Maybin, J. (2007) 'Linguistic ethnography and interdisciplinarity: opening the discussion'. *Journal of Sociolinguistics* 11(5), 575–583.

7 Critical ethnography of language policy

A semi-confessional tale

David Cassels Johnson

The confessional tale (Van Maanen, 2011) – in which researchers reflect on fieldwork and their research findings in ways that illuminate researcher subjectivity – is a popular genre in ethnographic writing. They are "confessional" because the authors open up about lingering concerns relating to analytical decisions, relationships in the field, or the portrayal of participants. They are almost always written in the first person, directing the attention away from the participants and towards the researcher. Confessional tales are important contributions in the pantheon of ethnographic writings because they reveal precisely what more objectivist accounts obfuscate – how frustrating, difficult, and confusing the research process can be, especially when given the benefit of time and reflection. I do not want this chapter to be a confessional tale but I agree with Ramanathan (2011) that it is increasingly crucial for language planning and policy (LPP) scholars to openly question the ethics that motivate our decisions, rendering transparent the typically gauzy façade that shrouds our researching-texting practices. That goal motivates this chapter.

This chapter is also inspired by the 2013 conference on *Researching Multilingualism*, organized by the MOSAIC Centre for Research on Multilingualism, and held at the University of Birmingham. A topic of discussion and debate concerned the term "critical": What does it mean to conduct "critical" research and how is it different from research that is *not* critical? If most researchers of multilingualism and language policy lay claim to the term, does it really have meaning any longer? Indeed, some will argue that its overly liberal usage has made it vacuous – an extraneous term tagged onto an ever-increasing variety of disciplines – but I am going to argue in this chapter that it is still meaningful, especially with regard to ethnographic research on language policy. I will begin by reviewing the evolution of the term and how it is applied in language policy and ethnographic research. I will then introduce some of my own ethnographic data as illustration, and end with a proposal for how and why critical ethnographies of language policy are as vital as ever.

The critical in critical language policy

The evolution toward critical language policy research (see Ricento, 2000) reflected a similar trend in the language sciences more generally, which

106   *D.C. Johnson*

featured critiques of earlier approaches that attempted to divorce linguistic data from sociocultural context. Chomsky's (1965: 3) famous line about how linguistic theory should focus on an "ideal listener-speaker, in a completely homogeneous speech community" became a sort of rallying cry as researchers (e.g. Hymes, 1972) sought distance from generative linguistics and structuralist approaches. Instead, the social context in which language is used became the focus and, in particular, how relationships between language and power are engendered by sociocultural and sociolinguistic discourses (Fowler et al., 1979; Fairclough, 1989). Thus, the criticism of early language planning research – that it ignored the ideological and political nature of language planning; that it focused on individual decisions instead of social, political, and economic forces; that it was overtly and overly positivist or technocratic – reflected a more general intellectual movement towards approaches influenced by post-modernism, post-structuralism, and critical social theory.

The critical turn in language policy research goes back, at least, to Richard Ruiz' very influential (1984: 2) article, "Orientations in Language Planning," in which he argues:

> Orientations are basic to language planning in that they delimit the ways we talk about language and language issues ... they help to delimit the range of acceptable attitudes toward language, and to make certain attitudes legitimate. In short, orientations determine what is thinkable about language in society.

While he does not cite him, this Foucaultian (1978) perspective on language and power reverberates in much of the language policy research being conducted and written about today. Still, Tollefson's (1991) seminal monograph *Planning Language, Planning Inequality* offered the earliest fully formed conceptualization of what the "critical" in critical language policy research might look like. Tollefson's withering critique of earlier language planning research (which he referred to as "neo-classical") accompanied a new proposal – the historical-structural approach – which put the focus squarely on the "economic, social, and political factors which constrain or impel changes in language structure and use" (Tollefson, 1991: 3). Tollefson leveraged social theoretical tools from Habermas (1973), Giddens (1971), and Foucault (1970) to conceptualize language policy as integral to a social structure that privileges particular languages and their speakers, while marginalizing others. While this was a watershed moment in the LPP field, it was also reflective of discursive changes across different disciplines, as neo-Marxist theories gained a foothold within the minds and hearts of a new generation of researchers.

Later, Tollefson (2002) outlined the interplay between critical linguistics (Fowler et al., 1979; Hodge & Kress, 1996), critical discourse analysis (Fairclough, 1989), and critical language policy and helpfully clarified the "critical" in language policy research, which: (1) is critical of traditional, neo-classical language planning research; (2) is influenced by critical theory;

Critical ethnography of language policy 107

(3) emphasizes the relationships among language, power, and inequality, which are held to be central concepts for understanding language and society; and in particular, it "aggressively investigates how language policies affect the lives of individuals and groups who often have little influence over the policy-making process" (p. 4); and (4) entails social activism. About (4), Tollefson argues that language policy researchers are

> responsible not only for understanding how dominant social groups use language for establishing and maintaining social hierarchies, but also for investigating ways to alter those hierarchies ... thus, research and practices are inextricably linked through this important social and political role of linguists and their work.
>
> (2002: 4)

In a later publication, Tollefson (2006) positions this commitment to social justice as concomitant to, and reliant upon, a critical examination of interactions with participants: "[Critical language policy] researchers seek to develop a 'critical method' that includes a self-reflective examination of their relationship with the 'Others' who are the focus of research."

It is this last characteristic of the "critical" in critical language policy that I want to tease out and further elaborate because, while the field is filled with studies that exemplify the first three characteristics in Tollefson's framework, it has been less common to openly examine researcher positionality and epistemology in LPP studies. There are undoubtedly social activists among us and much of the research focuses on social justice; still, the "activism" and the "research" are often separated, thus perpetuating divisions between participants and observers in ways that reify objectivist epistemologies.

Perhaps it has become accepted as a given that most language policy scholars are "critical" since so much of the research is focused on power and/or committed to social justice; however, the interrogation of researcher positionality in LPP studies has only recently begun to gain traction. For example, De Costa (2014) argues that a consideration of ethical decisions in critical ethnographic research requires that we not only describe, critique, and transform discriminatory practices and social inequality but also maintain critical reflexivity regarding the position of the researcher. Similarly, in Angel Lin's (2015) interrogation of researcher epistemology in LPP studies, she argues that a critical or emancipatory perspective includes self-reflection on one's position in institutional hierarchies and an interrogation of how such institutional hierarchies produce and reproduce domination and subordination. Instead, the goal of the researcher should be knowledge co-construction: "In the critical research paradigm, both the researcher and the researched are subjects of knowing and enter into a dialogue on equal footings" (p. 26).

Another compelling example is the work of Ramanathan (2006, 2011), who openly grapples with her own ideological conflict in researching texting practices. She criticizes a body of LPP scholarship that tends to present its

108   D.C. Johnson

textual products in hermetically sealed ways – "a modus operandi that often leaves little room for addressing uncertainties and tensions in the researching-texting process" (Ramanathan, 2011: 256) – and emphasizes that the meanings we make in our texts should instead be rendered "porous, unstable, and changeable" (p. 247). She argues that, within LPP research, it is crucial that we interrogate the ideological aspects of ethnography as, itself, a social practice, while also permitting a way to "complexify the researcher's voice" (p. 268). Similarly, Canagarajah and Stanley argue that the genre of academic writing makes it challenging to give voice and agency to minority communities, yet it is essential that LPP scholars push back against positivistic writing genres that attempt to synthesize research findings into generalizable and monolithic "truths":

> Since the subjects exist in the report only through the voice of the researcher, there is a tendency for their complexity to be suppressed and their identity to be generalized (or essentialized) to fit the dominant assumptions and theoretical constructs of the researcher and the disciplinary community.
>
> (Canagarajah & Stanley, 2015: 41;
> cf. also Lather, 1993)

Ricento (2000) divides the LPP field into three distinct phases: (1) classic language planning research (1960s–1970s); (2) an intermediary phase where earlier frameworks were questioned and alternatives offered (1970s–1980s); and (3) critical approaches focusing on power, ideology, and discourse (1990s–2000s). At the time of this writing, my sense is that a new phase is underway that is probably not so easily encapsulated because the field has grown so diverse. However, perhaps one hallmark is that more and more researchers are *publicly* questioning what it means to be a language policy scholar and asking questions like: What is our responsibility to the speech communities in which we work? How can we be effective advocates in debates about multilingual education? How do we generate our own dominant discourses that reject monolingual and deficit orientations? How do we reconcile our social justice aims with objectivist epistemologies and discourses that influence the production of our research? And, what does it mean to be an ethical language policy researcher? In the words of Michael Agar (1980/1996): Who are we to do this?

The critical in critical ethnography

Agar's question has permeated discussion and debate about ethnography since he first published *The Professional Stranger* in 1980. The question, in and of itself, critiqued more traditional naturalistic ethnographic studies, which were inspired by naturalism, with researchers attempting to blend in with some foreign culture in order to observe "natural" human behavior

Critical ethnography of language policy 109

without influencing it. As Hammersley and Atkinson (2007) note, it was often considered a rite of passage for a new anthropologist to set out to some foreign society to pay their dues in the field. Borrowing from research traditions in biology, ethnographers attempted to discover observable truths, accessed through empirical observation, a cornerstone of what is often referred to as positivism. Discussions aside about what truly constitutes positivism or post-positivism – and whether or not it is primarily used as a term of abuse by anti-positivists, as Hammersley (2007: 691) claims (a claim with which I agree) – there is no doubt that naturalistic ethnographic studies adopted and adapted methods from the natural sciences as models for how best to gather and analyze data.

The perception of what counted as true science influenced earlier work, which has been characterized by a "fly on the wall" perspective because the researcher attempts to be as unobtrusive as possible, an objective observer of (hopefully) natural behavior. The other option is to "go native" by blending in as much as possible with the new culture by adopting similar modes of dress, language use, and other norms. Roman (1993) argues that being a fly on the wall can lead to "intellectual tourism" and an uncritical acceptance of unequal power relationships among research participants, while going native lends itself to voyeurism and uncritical valorization of the research subjects' experiences. She recounts struggles with her own positionality in her ethnography of a punk rock subculture in the USA when, confronted with misogyny and domestic abuse, she could not (and did not want to) either objectively observe or completely blend in. Neither approach, Roman (1993: 282) argues, adequately analyzes power relations that mediate fieldwork.

Most contemporary ethnographers would orient themselves somewhere between (or above) these two ends of the flies–natives continuum of positionality. Agar (1980) uses the term "detached involvement" to describe researchers who are both part of, and distant from, the community in which they are studying. Geertz (1973: 13) envisions the researcher's position as that of a conversationalist, attempting to engage the participants on their own turf: "We are not ... seeking either to become natives or to mimic them. Only romantics or spies would seem to find point in that. We are seeking ... to converse with them, a matter a great deal more difficult ... than is commonly recognized." Both Agar and Geertz argue against the notion that ethnography is ever orderly, complete, objective, or without researcher biases. As Geertz puts it, "Cultural analysis is (or should be) guessing at meanings, assessing the guesses, and drawing explanatory conclusions from the better guesses ... [It] is intrinsically incomplete. And, worse than that, the more deeply it goes the less complete it is" (pp. 20, 29). Or, perhaps in a more succinct depiction of the chaos ethnographers find themselves in during fieldwork, Agar (1980: 44) argues that: "An ethnographer is like a drunk pretending to walk a straight line in a dark room with a gale-force wind blowing through it." Eventually, the ethnographer must emerge from the metaphorical storm, ready to analyze data and write the text, only to find new challenges in attempting to depict what has been seen with fidelity, coherence, and "validity". As in the beginning of our research, when we may have the disorientation associated with culture shock, a new sort of disorientation is possible when faced with the arduous task of writing something that represents what we saw and heard. Geertz reminds us that our data are constructions of participant perceptions, which are, themselves, constructions – constructions of constructions, so to speak: "[Our] writings are themselves interpretations, and second and third order ones to boot. (By definition only a 'native' makes first order ones: it's [their] culture.) They are thus fictions; fictions in the sense that they are 'something made', 'something fashioned'" (Geertz, 1973: 15).

Debates and interrogations about the subjectivity of the ethnographer have been around for decades without being called "critical"; however, the distinction seems to arise when the primary focus of the research project is to reveal systemic injustice on behalf of those who are marginalized. As Thomas (1993) argues, the notion that ethnography should be emancipatory is an explicitly value-laden position: "Critical ethnography begins from the premise that the structure and content of culture make life unnecessarily more nasty, brutish, and short for some people" (Thomas, 1993: 33). If earlier theorists like Geertz and Agar set aside the shackles of 'objectivity,' Thomas focused ethnographer subjectivity towards explicit social justice aims, arguing that ethnographic tools are effective for illuminating relations of power and thus disrupting the taken for granted and the status quo. "Conventional ethnography describes what is; critical ethnography asks what could be" (Thomas, 1993: 4). However, while critical ethnography is directed at social ills, Thomas still stresses that researchers should never impose their own beliefs onto the data, and the "scientist" must never gather data to prove a point or be ruled by passion. He repeatedly defends ethnography as a science and ethnographers as scientists who "objectively report on the subjectivity of subjects" (Thomas, 1993: 17).

It is perhaps Thomas's commitment to, or depiction of, facts and science that inspired later critical and post-critical ethnography (Noblit et al., 2004). Like Thomas, Madison (2012) argues that critical ethnography begins with an ethically minded focus on social injustice and the goal of disrupting the status quo by illuminating obscure operations of power. However, she expands upon Thomas's conceptualization, implicitly critiquing Thomas's notions of objectivity along the way by, instead, focusing on and contextualizing researcher positionality, "thereby making it accessible, transparent, and vulnerable to judgment and evaluation" (p. 9). In this way, she argues for a dissolution of the barriers between researcher and subject and, with echoes of Geertz, suggests that we are all subjects in dialogue: "[C]ritical ethnography is always a meeting of multiple sides in an encounter with and among others, one in which there is negotiation and dialogue toward substantial and viable meanings that make a difference in others' worlds" (p. 10). Thus, both the researcher and the participants are responsible for knowledge production. Still, Madison stops short of celebrating what she

Critical ethnography of language policy 111

characterizes as an *over*-focus on the researcher and raises questions about auto-ethnography and post-modernist accounts that focus exclusively on the researcher, since the goal of ethnography is always to understand the "empirical world of others."

Critiques of critical

Post-structuralism and post-modernism have permeated a wide variety of disciplines as new scholars adopt an overtly political position in their research; yet, criticisms of this "critical" turn in education and language studies are worth considering. A major criticism of Foucault's theories is that they are overly deterministic and conceptualize a set of intractable discourses that operate outside of the control of discoursers, thus leaving little room for improvisation, subversion, and human creativity – to wit, agency – even if, in later writings, Foucault does leave room for "counter-discourses" (e.g. Foucault, 1982). For Foucault (1978: 49), discourses are "practices that systematically form the object of which they speak." For example, the history and proliferation of discourses on human sexuality constituted a "whole restrictive economy," which managed, systematized, analyzed, and policed sexual experience and identity. In other words, the power to control human sexuality – and to pathologize homosexuality – relied upon the language to describe it ("an entire medico-sexual regime", 1978: 42). "We must not forget that the psychological, psychiatric, medical category of homosexuality was constituted from the moment it was characterized" (1978: 43). Thus, discourse is both an effect and an instrument of power, which has the ability to constitute and thus control entire categories of being.

Foucault's theories are integral to post-modernism, yet while Benjamin Whorf (Carroll, 1956) and Edward Sapir (1921) are rarely (if ever?) cited by educational post-modernists, language scholars will recognize connections to linguistic determinism, the so-called strong version of the Sapir-Whorf hypothesis, which proposes that our thoughts are controlled by our language. Influenced much more by French philosophers than US linguistic anthropologists, critical educational scholarship in the US has often assumed this power of language without question (see discussion in Livia & Hall, 1997). Especially among post-modernists, Foucault's theories are applied in a deterministic way, foregrounding how discourse "worlds the world" (Lather, 1993: 675). And, because academic writing is a product of epistemological hegemony, changing the status quo requires a disruption of academic discourses (Britzman, 1995), often through intentionally obscure or otherwise transgressive prose (Lather, 1993; Richardson, 1993). As Lather (1993: 676–677) argues, "to not revert to the dominant foundational, formulaic and readily available codes of validity requires the invention of counter discourse/practices of legitimation." Because academic research in general, and academic writing in particular, are a product of the "legitimation of knowledge in contemporary postpostivism" and the

112   *D.C. Johnson*

challenges of representing social practices (with another social practice, aka writing), counter-strategies are proposed:

> Contrary to dominant validity practices where the rhetorical nature of scientific claims is masked with methodological assurances, a strategy of ironic validity proliferates forms, recognizing that they are rhetorical and without foundation, post-epistemic, lacking in epistemological support. The text is resituated as a representation of its failure.
>
> (Lather, 1993: 677)

If linguistic determinism is rejected, many of the essential tenets of post-modernism lose their appeal. Furthermore, as it has been applied in US educational research especially, post-modernism has been criticized as nihilistic armchair radicalism, with scholars safely writing arcane theoretical squibs from their office, while social problems continue outside. While they focus on changing the way we think through disrupting our ideological domestication and the taken-for-granted status quo, the critic immediately wonders how and why post-modernists are uniquely positioned to transcend dominant discourses and ideological domestication. Such a patronizing position perhaps compromises the purported commitment to an interrogation of researcher subjectivity. Resisting dominant discourses in academic writing becomes the "protest," a type of ivory tower elitism (as critics would argue) that has no impact on real social problems. For example, in a strong critique of post-modern feminism, Nussbaum (2000) argues that this type of metaphysical abstraction is a form of moral passivity and sharply criticizes "feminist thinkers ... [who] appear to believe that the way to do feminist politics is to use words in a subversive way, in academic publications of lofty obscurity and disdainful abstractness" (2000: 2). Nussbaum argues that while obfuscatory prose creates an aura of importance, the ideas are actually quite thin and, more importantly, the notion that "hip quietism is a comprehensible response to the difficulty of realizing justice in America ... collaborates with evil" (2000: 6). Very similarly, in an interview with Atherton, Noam Chomsky argues that:

> Postmodernism is a very useful invention to keep intellectuals in their preferred status of conformist subservients to those in power ... [I]t turns out to be a way for intellectuals to be more radical than thou, but do nothing except talk to each other in academic seminars and not get involved with the general public in real activism.
>
> (Atherton, 2009: 96)

A similar criticism is that critical research is blinded by the exclusive and *a priori* focus on unequal power relations. For example, Blommaert (2005: 32) argues that in critical discourse analysis (CDA), "Texts are found to have a certain ideological meaning that is forced upon the reader" and "Power relations are often predefined and then confirmed by features of

Critical ethnography of language policy   113

discourse ... politicians *always* and *intentionally* manipulate their constituencies, doctors are *by definition* and always the powerful party in doctor–patient relationships, etc." Similarly, while there is a recognition that discourse operates across many levels and analysts should consider local and societal discourses, and the connections between the two, a multi-layered conceptualization of context is less developed in CDA. What operates as a "dominant" discourse in one layer may not be the case for another, and what may be viewed as "subversive" (by analysts) in, say, micro-level texts and discourses may be considered quite common, mainstream, or even dominant by the humans responsible for creating and interpreting those texts and discourses, at least in the context they were created. As Blommaert and other linguistic anthropologists would argue, what is lacking in these critical approaches is a full analysis of how the context shapes discourse. On the other hand, it is not as if CDA practitioners are not cognizant of these limitations, and important contributions that combine CDA with ethnography are abundant (e.g. Kryżanowski, 2011).

Interrogating my own researching-texting practices

The data in this section are drawn from two ethnographies of language policy, the first of which engendered my doctoral thesis, *Language Policy Within and Without the School District of Philadelphia* (Johnson, 2007), with the second (and ongoing) being conducted in Washington State, USA. A series of events led to a re-evaluation of my researching-texting practices. First, some readers were offended by my depiction of Lucía Sanchez in my doctoral study. Sanchez was the director of ESOL/bilingual programs in the School District of Philadelphia (SDP) during the second half of my fieldwork. Previous to Sanchez taking over, under the guidance of the ESOL/bilingual programs office, bilingual education programs were developed and expanded, thus providing access to bilingual instruction for a growing number of students. Groups of administrators and teachers organized to develop a dual language initiative and an official SDP language policy which promoted bilingual education. In my participant observation with these groups, bilingual education was promoted as an effective means for incorporating the multilingual and multicultural resources of students in classrooms. Halfway through my fieldwork, however, there was an upheaval in administration, with many personnel changes, and Sanchez took over as head of the ESOL/bilingual programs. My arguments about how Sanchez changed the SDP policy were supported by three types of data collection: (1) field notes and recordings in language policy meetings with teachers; (2) two recorded interviews with Sanchez; and (3) a document she created to help guide language policy decisions (a language education "handbook"). Guided by deficit-oriented beliefs, Sanchez attempted to shift the additive bilingual programs to transitional and English-focused programs and she did so without any input from teachers.

114   *D.C. Johnson*

In fact, she seemed to silence teacher input at language policy meetings, which were largely a venue for Sanchez to lecture on the new direction of language policy. For example, in one meeting ...

Teacher: Who or where did the decision make ... come from to [transition students]?
Sanchez: Because, because, number 1, we looked at all the programs that are effective based on Krashen's research ... and the beginning of Title III of the No Child Left Behind Act, which is long, and there's nothing we can do to change that.

And, later in the same meeting, while defending her decisions:

Sanchez: Everyone knows about Stephen Krashen – he's a linguist that has devoted most of his research to education, but he's a *linguist*. He's a scientist that studies different linguistic patterns but he really – we heard about the silent period through Krashen, we heard about comprehensible input, that's Krashen. We heard about the lowering the affective filter, that's Krashen, error correction, that's Krashen, so all of that is good research that we all as language teachers need to know. And he said, *he* is the expert, and he said that, yes, you can introduce English right away – Yes it is important that we know what the research says.

(12.1.05)

I have written at length about this excerpt because it was a stark moment of silencing teachers. A seemingly simple and predictable question "Where did this decision come from?" (especially given the abrupt shift in SDP language policy) was met with a list of reasons – Krashen's research (or some would argue a misapplication of it), other effective programs (which were not explained), and Title III of No Child Left Behind (which was emphasized as impossibly long and intractable) – which excluded Sanchez as the actual decision-maker. In other words, even though these decisions are coming from Sanchez, in an attempt to legitimate the decisions, Sanchez appeals to an abstract rationale that is elevated to something out of the teacher's control. Blommaert (2007) would describe this discursive move as "scale-jumping." Then the diatribe about Stephen Krashen further serves to silence the teachers. One might argue that Sanchez is mis-appropriating the research for tactical reasons, but that is almost beside the point. By her positioning of Krashen (1985) – or Sanchez' depiction of him – as a *linguist*, a *scientist*, and *expert*, the teachers are simultaneously positioned as none of these and therefore rendered unqualified to provide input in language policy decisions. It is through these discursive moves that Sanchez strips them of their agency.

In order to more fully understand Sanchez' rationale for these changes, and her educational philosophy in general, I conducted two interviews with her. I found the following excerpt particularly enlightening:

Critical ethnography of language policy 115

Sanchez: When you talk about bilingual education, in many research based models, it is uh – considered a way to help children, or assist students who are second language learners, to acquire English – The problem we have seen historically with bilingual education is that – somehow even students who are born ... in the United States have been placed in bilingual education programs just ... because, even though they're native speakers of English, they come in with some gaps with their linguistic development due to maybe speaking another language at home or even *hearing* another language at home.

(Tape-recorded interview, 6.13.05)

While the administrators who preceded Sanchez viewed bilingual education as an educational model that drew on linguistic resources to help students become bilingual and biliterate, Sanchez sees bilingual education as a program for *acquiring English*. Furthermore, she emphasizes who is not a good candidate for bilingual education, which may include: (1) students born in the US, (2) native speakers of English, or (3) students with gaps in their linguistic development, perhaps because they come from multilingual households. As a result of this interview, Sanchez' beliefs about language and language education were clarified, and I argued that she was drawing on deficit and monolingual discourses and language ideologies about 'semilingualism'[1] when making her language policy decisions. I stand by these assertions.

In a more recent research project, which focused on bilingual education and language policy in a Central Washington (USA) school district, we interviewed Scott Finder, a superintendent in a district that had an active bilingual education program. Research participants had informed us that Finder was skeptical about the value of bilingual education and was actively seeking to transition to English-focused programs. So, we interviewed him to try to understand his educational vision. When asked about whether research is utilized when making language policy decisions, he replied:

Finder: That's a good question – I just make stuff up (laughter) ... I just don't see a ... most of the studies I read, and I'm not going to tell you I read them all, but the ones that I've looked at, they always end with *more research is needed* in this area (laughter).

And, later, when reflecting on who bilingual education programs are for, he said:

Finder: So, if a kid comes to us and they're just a low language kid, low level of Spanish vocabulary, low level of English vocabulary, they're going into all English instruction. Because there's no point in, they don't have a Spanish, a strong Spanish language to take advantage of.

We argued that Finder, like Sanchez, was drawing on deficit and monolingual discourses – and a language ideology of 'semilingualism' – along with a skeptical

116   D.C. Johnson

relationship with academic research, to inform his language policy decision-making. I stand by this analysis as well. However, when presented at an academic conference, these interview excerpts elicited laughs from the audience, and while I was pleased by the reception at the time, I felt increasingly uneasy about my selection of interview excerpts and the public portrayal of research participants.

Both events made me reflect at length on Madison's (2012: 153) entreaty that when participants are placed in a questionable or negative light, "[Y]ou must consider the context of their lives in relation to structures of power that consti-tute their actions." For example, one might consider the position of Sanchez as a Latina female in a position of authority, in a school district where most of the administrators have historically been white men. I might have considered her life history, or how her rise to a fairly powerful position within a large school district was shaped by dominant and historical racist and sexist discourses, and how she responded. I did none of these things, which raises questions about how "critical" I was. Furthermore, there is no doubt that the ubiquitous and ceaseless obsession with test scores in the US is a result of educational policies that punish school districts for low scores, and the actions of educators must be interpreted in this light. While Finder's beliefs about language educational research conflict with the consensus within the field, his doubts about the research and the conse-quences of low test scores reveal the rationality of his actions.

The structure of US educational language policy perhaps encourages deficit discourses and certainly helps promote English-focused approaches (Menken & Shohamy, 2008). While we attempt to illuminate agency in educa-tional language policy processes, the power of policy as discourse (Ball, 1993, 2006) is formidable and should not be underestimated. Furthermore, we need to take stock of how researchers have not necessarily reached the people they need to reach, nor impacted educational processes in ways that ensure equal educational opportunities for everyone (Johnson & Johnson, 2015).

Language policy engagement and action research

It is difficult to escape our own influences, to transcend the dominant discourses that have shaped our personal and professional lives. And although critical scholars suggest that illuminating these discourses reduces their power, I tend to agree with Agar (1980: 48) that: "Professional training further widens the blinders of bias." Even if part of that training is to identify dominant and marginalizing discourses in Others' education, it does not necessarily turn the spotlight on dominant discourses that guide our *own* training. The emphasis on researcher subjectivity can be taken too far, especially in post-modernist research on education in which researchers are so debilitated by the dangers of participant depiction that they are reduced to focusing almost exclusively on themselves. However, the part of post-modernism that encourages healthy speculation of researcher subjectivity would be a valuable addition to LPP writings.

This discussion leads us into a logical quandary. If we agree that part of being critical means focusing on power imbalances, and if we further agree

Critical ethnography of language policy 117

that an ethnographic perspective emphasizes human agency, then there must be human agents who are responsible for imbalances, who will inevitably be placed in a questionable light. One solution is to revert to a critical focus on structural inequality and blame the system as opposed to individuals. If you believe in the power of policy as discourse (which I do), this makes sense. However, if you believe in the power of humans as creative agents (which I also do), one must further the investigation to determine how participants appropriate policy discourses. Inevitably, many educators will reify them, implement them, institutionalize them, and champion them. It is at such moments that interrogations of our subjectivity as critical ethnographers of language policy are the most important. How do we balance the need to accurately depict the "empirical world of others" – which has resulted in important findings in our field about how deficit discourses interact with language policy – with the need to empower educators who can champion cultural and linguistic diversity? How can we be critical and yet develop epistemic solidarity (Van der Aa & Blommaert, this volume) with participants *at the same time*?

I have elsewhere (Johnson, 2013) proposed Educational Language Policy Engagement and Action Research (ELPEAR), which includes collaboration between language policy agents from multiple levels of institutional authority to engage in LPP processes and do research on educational language policies and programs, together with outside researchers. Language policy action research is conducted throughout the language policy cycle – creation, interpretation, appropriation, and instantiation – and is used to inform and improve these processes. The focus is:

(1) how macro-level language policies are interpreted and put into practice;
(2) how micro-level language policies are created, interpreted, and put into practice;
(3) multilingual education and the educational opportunities of minority language users.

It involves teachers and administrators from multiple levels of institutional authority and ideally includes input from students and parents, as well as university scholars. Language policy action research provides the research team with an opportunity to interrogate how they are creating, interpreting, and appropriating language policy and educating students from diverse linguistic and cultural backgrounds, and changing if needed. It also provides the opportunity for the research team to challenge inequalities in schools which emerge from the subordination of minority languages, and thus there is an inherent agenda of social justice. Finally, it provides the research team with the opportunity to critically examine institutional discourses and challenge those aspects that marginalize teachers as mere implementers of language policy and to reposition them as policy decision-makers, i.e. *language policy arbiters* (Johnson & Johnson, 2015).

118   *D.C. Johnson*

In order to challenge marginalizing discourses, the participation frameworks and participation statuses of the participants within meetings often need to be critically examined, challenged, and changed. Goffman (1979) proposes the concept of 'footing,' which refers to the participants' alignment or positions in an interaction. The relative footing of participants in an interaction characterizes what Goffman refers to as the *participation framework*, which is engendered by the *participation status* of each of the participants. I argue that non-traditional participation frameworks – in which teachers and administrators engage in egalitarian decision-making and language policy action-research projects – can alter traditional hierarchical power structures and lead to the positioning of teachers as language policy arbiters, not just in policy implementation and classroom teaching, but in bottom-up policy *creation* and *interpretation* and *appropriation* of top-down policy. On the other hand, when school district administrators, who are typically invested with more language policy power, rely on hierarchical participation frameworks that position teachers as lacking the expertise to make language policy decisions, teacher agency is stripped.

Note

1   For a critique of this notion, see Martin-Jones and Romaine (1986).

References

Agar, M. (1980/1996) *The Professional Stranger: An Informal Introduction to Ethnography*. New York: Academic Press.
Atherton, C. (2009) '"Who drank the hemlock?": an interview with Noam Chomsky'. *Writing on the Edge: A Journal about Writing and Teaching Writing* 19(2), 91–99.
Ball, S.J. (1993) 'What is policy? Texts, trajectories and toolboxes'. *Discourse* 13(2), 10–17.
Ball, S.J. (2006) *Education Policy and Social Class: The Selected Works of Stephen J. Ball*. London: Routledge.
Blommaert, J. (2005) *Discourse: Key Topics in Sociolinguistics*. Cambridge: Cambridge University Press.
Blommaert, J. (2007) 'Sociolinguistic scales'. *Intercultural Pragmatics* 4(1), 1–19.
Britzman, D. (1995) '"The question of belief": writing poststructural ethnography'. *International Journal of Qualitative Studies in Education* 8(3), 229–238.
Canagarajah, S. & Stanley, P. (2015) 'Ethical considerations in language policy research', in F.M. Hult & D.C. Johnson (eds) *Research Methods in Language Policy and Planning: A Practical Guide*. Malden, MA: Wiley-Blackwell, 33–44.
Carroll, J.B. (1956) *Language, Thought, and Reality: Selected Writings of Benjamin Lee Whorf*. Cambridge, MA: MIT Press.
Chomsky, N. (1965) *Aspects of the Theory of Syntax*. Cambridge, MA: MIT Press.
De Costa, P.I. (2014) 'Making ethical decisions in an ethnographic study'. *TESOL Quarterly* 48(2), 413–422.
Fairclough, N. (1989) *Language and Power*. London: Longman.

Critical ethnography of language policy 119

Foucault, M. (1970) *The Order of Things: An Archeology of the Human Sciences.* New York: Vintage Books.

Foucault, M. (1978) *The History of Sexuality.* New York: Random House.

Foucault, M. (1982) 'The subject and power'. *Critical Inquiry* 8 (Summer), 777–795.

Fowler, R., Hodge, B., Kress, G. & Trew, T. (1979) *Language and Control.* London: Routledge & Kegan Paul.

Freeman, R. (2004) *Building on Community Bilingualism.* Philadelphia, PA: Caslon.

Geertz, C. (1973) *The Interpretation of Cultures: Selected Essays.* New York: Basic Books.

Giddens, A. (1971) *Capitalism and Modern Social Theory: An Analysis of the Writings of Marx, Durkheim, and Max Weber.* Cambridge: Cambridge University Press.

Goffman, E. (1979) 'Footing'. *Semiotica* 25(1–2).

Habermas, J. (1973) *Theory and Practice.* Boston, MA: Beacon Press.

Hammersley, M. (2007) 'Reflections on linguistic ethnography'. *Journal of Sociolinguistics* 11(5), 689–695.

Hammersley, M. & Atkinson, P. (2007) *Ethnography: Principles and Practice*, 3rd edn. London: Routledge.

Hodge, B. and Kress, G. (1996) *Language and Ideology.* London: Routledge.

Hymes, D. (1972) 'On communicative competence', in J.B. Pride & J. Holmes (eds) *Sociolinguistics: Selected Readings*, Harmondsworth: Penguin Books, 269–293.

Johnson, D.C. (2007) *Language Policy Within and Without the School District of Philadelphia.* Unpublished PhD thesis, Philadelphia: University of Pennsylvania.

Johnson, D.C. (2013) *Language Policy.* Basingstoke, UK: Palgrave Macmillan.

Johnson, D.C. & Johnson, E.J. (2015) 'Power and agency in language policy appropriation'. *Language Policy* 14(3), 221–243.

Krashen, S. (1985) *The Input Hypothesis: Issues and Implications.* New York: Longman.

Kryżanowski, M. (2011) 'Ethnography and critical discourse analysis.' *Critical Discourse Studies* 8(4). (Thematic issue edited by M. Kryżanowski).

Lather, P. (1993) 'Fertile obsession: validity after poststructuralism'. *The Sociological Quarterly* 34(4), 673–693.

Lin, A.M.Y. (2015) 'Researcher positionality', in F.M. Hult & D.C. Johnson (eds) *Research Methods in Language Policy and Planning: A Practical Guide.* Malden, MA: Wiley-Blackwell, 21–32.

Livia, A. and Hall, K. (1997) '"It's a girl!" Bringing performativity back to linguistics', in A. Livia & K. Hall (eds) *Queerly Phrased: Language, Gender, and Sexuality.* New York: Oxford University Press, 3–18.

Madison, D.S. (2012) *Critical Ethnography: Method, Ethics, and Performance*, 2nd edn. Los Angeles: Sage.

Martin-Jones, M. & Romaine, S. (1986) 'Semilingualism: a half-baked theory of communicative competence'. *Applied Linguistics* 7(1), 26–38.

Menken, K. & Shohamy, E. (2008) 'No child left behind and US language education policy'. *Language Policy* 7(3) (special issue).

Noblit, G.W., Flores, S.Y., Murillo Jr., E.G. (eds) (2004) *Postcritical Ethnography: Reinscribing Critique.* New York: Hampton Press.

Nussbaum, M.(2000) *Sex and Social Justice.* Oxford: Oxford University Press.

Ramanathan, V. (2006) 'Of texts AND translations AND rhizomes: postcolonial anxieties AND deracinations AND knowledge constructions'. *Critical Inquiry in Language Studies* 3(4), 223–244.

120 D.C. Johnson

Ramanathan, V. (2011) 'Researching-texting tensions in qualitative research: ethics in and around textual fidelity, selectivity, and translations', in T. McCarty (ed.) *Ethnography and Language Policy*. New York: Routledge, 255–270.

Ricento, T. (2000) 'Historical and theoretical perspectives in language policy and planning'. *Journal of Sociolinguistics* 4(2), 196–213.

Richardson, L. (1993) 'Poetics, dramatics, and transgressive validity: the case of the skipped line'. *The Sociological Quarterly* 34(4), 695–710.

Roman, L.G. (1993) 'Double exposure: the politics of feminist materialist ethnography'. *Educational Theory* 43(3), 279–308.

Ruiz, R. (1984) 'Orientations in language planning'. *NABE Journal* 8(2), 15–34.

Sapir, E. (1921) *Language: An Introduction to the Study of Speech*. New York: Harcourt, Brace & Co.

Thomas, J. (1993) *Doing Critical Ethnography*. London: Sage.

Tollefson, J.W. (1991) *Planning Language, Planning Inequality*. London: Longman.

Tollefson, J.W. (2002) 'Introduction: critical issues in educational language policy', in J.W. Tollefson (ed.) *Language Policies in Education: Critical Issues*. Mahwah, NJ: Lawrence Erlbaum Associates, 3–15.

Tollefson, J.W. (2006) 'Critical theory in language policy', in T. Ricento (ed.) *An Introduction to Language Policy: Theory and Method*. Malden, MA: Blackwell, 42–59.

Van Maanen, J. (2011) *Tales of the Field: On Ethnographic Writing*, 2nd edn. Chicago, IL: The University of Chicago Press.

8 Investigating visual practices in educational settings

Schoolscapes, language ideologies and organizational cultures

Petteri Laihonen and Tamás Péter Szabó

Introduction

In our chapter, we provide an overview of approaches to the study of linguistic landscapes (e.g. Shohamy & Gorter, 2009; Shohamy, 2012; Blommaert, 2013) and semiotic practices in educational settings, taking account of both theory and method. We also illustrate this area of research with reference to schoolscapes in Eastern Europe. The field of linguistic landscape studies has various roots and methodological traditions (see Shohamy, 2012 for a recent summary). In this account we mainly deal with *schoolscapes* (Brown, 2012), and we discuss research that focuses on schools, their classrooms and their foyers and on activities taking place within school walls.

We consider the investigation of schoolscapes to be relevant to research into the visual socialization of children, into the ways in which they are oriented to visual literacy and into the visual literacy practices of both children and adults. That is, we view visual literacy not only as the ability to interpret visual signs but also as a social practice – one in which teachers and students exercise agency in engaging in visual communication in educational settings. We also focus on language ideologies reflected in schoolscapes. We argue that, like classroom interaction and other educational practices, schoolscapes can also be analyzed as displays or materialization of the 'hidden curriculum' regarding language values (cf. Johnson, 1980; Brown, 2012).[1]

The development of different terms and concepts across research traditions

Cohen (1971: 19) captured an early semiotic perspective on education as follows:

> [M]any anthropologists are agreed that in their daily lives people in all societies respond to cultural symbols rather than to objective reality [...] the symbolizations of cultural life [...] are learned as the result of systematic and consistent experiences to which the individual is exposed in the course of growing up.

122 *P. Laihonen and T.P. Szabó*

Building on Cohen's work, Johnson (1980) took further the idea that children are socialized through regular exposure to cultural visualizations and looked into the ways in which children produce such symbolizations and artifacts themselves. He also drew attention to the ideological component of signs and artifacts in schools. Aronin and Ó Laiore (2012) have recently reviewed similar research in multilingual educational settings.

Working in the realm of educational anthropology, Brown was the first to propose the term *schoolscape* to cover school-based material environments where text, sound, images and artifacts "constitute, reproduce, and transform language ideologies" (Brown, 2012: 282).

The notion of *visual literacy* grew out of the New Literacy Studies tradition with its commitment to the ethnography of literacy and the uses of texts. This tradition was extended by Kress and Van Leeuwen when they introduced the notions of multimodality and multimodal discourse. As the title of their seminal book, *Reading Images* (2006), indicates, pictures, artifacts, figures and the like can be interpreted and understood in the same way that texts are "read." Meanings and values are also produced and reproduced through visual communication practices

In two volumes, *Discourses in Place* (2003) and *Nexus Analysis* (2004), Scollon and Wong Scollon employed two terms – *visual semiotics* and *geo-semiotics* – to capture the increasing shift toward visual communication in contemporary social life. Their work built on and extended the tradition of critical discourse analysis. They argued that the study of *visual semiotics* represents a turn "from spoken, face-to-face discourses to the representations of that interaction order in images and signs" (2003: 82). They define *geosemiotics* as "the study of the meaning systems by which language is located in the material world. This includes not just the location of the words on the page you are reading now but also the location of the book in your hand and your location as you stand or sit reading this" (Scollon & Wong Scollon, 2003: x).

Finally, work on the linguistic landscapes of schools fits well with the recent critical and ethnographic strand of research on multilingualism and heteroglossia (Martin-Jones et al., 2012), extending it by taking in a broader range of resources for meaning-making.

Researching schoolscapes: differing research lenses and methodologies

Research into schoolscapes has been characterized by the same diversity as the broader field of linguistic landscape research and has generated similar methodological debates. Here, we will take a look at different approaches and weigh up their strengths and limitations. Our account will be illustrated with reference to studies in different types of multilingual school settings.

In a recent study of the schoolscapes of seven schools in the Basque country, Gorter and Cenoz (2014) adopted a quantitative approach, building on the methods associated with the quantitative strand of linguistic landscape

Investigating visual practices in education   123

research. They focused on schools where teaching took place in Basque and Spanish and, in some cases, in English, too. Their main finding was that the use of Basque predominated in the signage in the schools, while Spanish predominated in wider public spaces beyond the school. Quantitative methods such as those adopted in this study allow researchers to capture broad patterns of language use across schoolscapes. In this specific context, we see that the minority language schools succeeded in creating a distinct visual environment within a wider national setting where Spanish – the dominant language – held sway.

However, in order to gain deeper insights into the local meanings associated with particular kinds of signs and into the concerns of particular sign producers, we need to narrow our research lenses. Gorter and Cenoz (2014) sought to do this by assigning all the signs within the schoolscapes of the seven schools into one of nine categories, e.g. the category "decoration." The categories were devised by the researchers themselves rather than on the basis of interviews with teachers and students, that is, with the producers and readers of the signs. Despite the systematic and insightful nature of this study, the researchers missed an opportunity to gain insights into the meaning and significance of different kinds of signs for those participating in their study. As Pennycook (2009: 304) has noted, in research of this kind, "analysis remains predominantly between the text and the analyst." The use of quantitative methodology has also been questioned (e.g. Blommaert, 2013) since it reinforces popular thinking about languages being separate, countable entities with neat borders. In many linguistic landscapes (especially those online), languages are often intertwined or juxtaposed in meaningful ways.

Some researchers have combined quantitative and qualitative approaches to the linguistic landscape (e.g. Hult, 2009). Other researchers have chosen to prioritize qualitative work. As we indicated earlier, there is now a well-established tradition of ethnographic research on the organization of visual and material culture in local schoolscapes. This research involves extended observation in particular school settings and work with different data sources. It also involves the identification of patterns of signing across different school spaces (e.g. school foyers, classrooms, staff rooms, school canteens). Thus, for example, Johnson (1980) was able to show the role of nation-state discourses in the organization of material culture in public-school classrooms in the United States. He kept a detailed record of the material items in classrooms, their placement, their material qualities and the techniques employed in producing them, as well as the "aesthetics and style" of the items (1980: 178). He also identified particular themes that resonated across schools. Thus, for example, he encountered frequent displays of images relating to Thanksgiving. His interpretation of his findings was that: "material culture is an index of the relative degree of symbolic integration between local school communities and national society and culture" (1980: 173). In fact, in all the schools he visited, there was a high degree of symbolic integration and there were few signs relating to local social or cultural traditions.

124   *P. Laihonen and T. P. Szabó*

More recent schoolscape research involves dialogue with research participants (teachers, students, school administrators, parents and so on) about the meanings associated with different signs. Ethnographic research of this kind seeks to build an understanding of the emic perspectives of research participants and to uncover the language ideologies and discourses underpinning sign use and production. Since ethnographic research involves extended observation over time, sometimes involving several return visits to the field, this enables the researcher to capture changes taking place over time, too. Consider, for example, changes triggered by the introduction of a new national or regional language policy, by new patterns of transnational migration or by a major change in the wider social or political context. Take, for example, the research carried out by Brown (2012) into a schoolscape in Estonia. This study was designed as an "intensive school-based ethnography." It included interviews with teachers and extended observation of school life, as well as still photography. Brown took account of the range of signs and artifacts in different spaces in the school, including the school foyer, the classrooms and the school museum. Her study was carried out in a region of Estonia where a local language – Võro – was widely spoken. The wider social and political context for the study was that of the revitalization of Estonian as a national language in a context where Russian had long been dominant. Working across different spaces in the school, Brown noted that the school foyer was dedicated to the use of Estonian and prestigious European languages. Since the foyer was the public face of the school, Brown concluded that the choice of languages for this space served "to elevate the ideological importance of Europe and the Estonian nation-state" (Brown, 2012: 287–288). The school museum gave particular prominence to the Estonian language and, according to Brown (2012: 293), this functioned as a "school-based linguistic chronicle." There was no reference to the Võro language variety in either of these spaces. However, in the classrooms, Võro occasionally "came out of hiding" in fleeting ways. Classroom practice sometimes involved use of Võro texts, but these texts were mostly provisional in nature. For example, they were handwritten on a blackboard and then erased after class. Mass-produced printed texts of a more enduring nature were only in Estonian or in English. Brown (2012: 296) emphasized the role of teachers as key social actors in making occasional use of Võro in these classroom contexts and in transforming "the physical environment into one more connected with the immediate community."

Multi-sited ethnography, involving comparison of schoolscapes across different schools, has also proved to be a fruitful approach, albeit more demanding in terms of time. Khan (2012) carried out a study of schoolscapes in different kinds of schools in different regions of Pakistan. The schoolscapes of two private schools offering some instruction through the medium of English were, for example, compared and contrasted with that in a public-school offering instruction through the medium of Urdu (the national language). Khan found that, in the private schools where English was one of the

Investigating visual practices in education 125

languages of instruction, the use of English-only noticeboards was commonplace in public spaces such as school foyers. Since English is a highly prized commodity on the private educational market in urban Pakistan, Khan concluded that this was a marketing strategy that was aimed at the parents of prospective students. The predominance of English in the visual landscape of the schools contrasted with the multilingual practice in some of the classrooms. Khan also noted that the students he worked with in this study had little understanding of the content of the notices pinned up on the noticeboards in English.

Visual practices in research in multilingual settings

As the scope of research in multilingual schools and classrooms has been broadened to incorporate schoolscapes and different visual and semiotic practice, researchers have also begun to build a visual dimension into their own research practice. Visual methods such as photography or the use of drawings have been employed in research in multilingual settings, at the stage of data gathering and also at the stages of data interpretation and analysis. In this section of our chapter, we illustrate the visual turn in research on multilingualism with reference to four studies: two that focused on out-of-school contexts and two that were linked to language teaching and learning in school and to the raising of language awareness among students. The first study in an out-of-school context was that conducted by Pietikäinen (2012). In a study carried out with Sámi children from Northern Finland, Pietikäinen focused on the ways in which the children represented their Sámi language experiences by means of photography and drawings. She argued that, by drawing on multimodal and visual resources in research in revitalization contexts, we can minimize the impact that researchers have in shaping the data. Moreover, participants' voices and agency are foregrounded in the final research narrative.

The second study is described by Martin-Jones (2011) in a volume on the *Ethnography of Language Policy*. This was an ethnographic project that was conducted in Wales with young bilinguals aged 16–19. The focus of the research was on the bilingual literacy practices, in Welsh and in English, of the young people during the time they spent at college and during out-of-college hours. The young people in the study were asked to keep diary notes about their out-of-college literacy practices over two days. They were also asked to take photographs of particular literacy events in their out-of-college lives. Martin-Jones and her colleagues then conducted diary-based interviews and photo-based interviews with the young people, in the language of their choice. Each of the interviews was audio-recorded. The data gathering was organized in this way so as to facilitate dialogue between the researchers and the young people participating in the study, and to gain insights into the young people's emic perspectives and understandings of their own practices. As in the study by Pietikäinen (2012), the voices of the participants were

126   *P. Laihonen and T.P. Szabó*

incorporated into the research narrative about bilingual literacy practices in this context.

In addition to ethnographic projects such as those discussed above, there have been a number of practically oriented research projects that have been linked to language teaching and learning or to the raising of critical language awareness. They have provided revealing insights into students' perceptions of linguistic and cultural diversity. We give two examples here: the first is a study by Dagenais et al. (2009) which was carried out in Vancouver and Montreal. Dagenais and her colleagues designed their research so as to capture the ways in which children in a local school perceived the linguistic landscape of their neighborhood. The research was part of a wider pedagogic initiative that aimed at fostering critical language awareness. The second study was conducted by Nikula and Pitkänen-Huhta (2008). This study focused on Finnish adolescents learning English. The adolescents were asked to take photographs of themselves in situations where they were learning or using English. The researchers found that the students linked the notion of 'learning' to formal situations (e.g. classes at school). They did not take account of their informal learning activities (e.g. skate-boarding with friends or using English terminology when speaking Finnish in local life worlds of this kind).

Researching schoolscapes: case studies in Hungary and in Hungarian minority settings

In this part of our chapter we present and discuss the methodology and some selected findings from our own work in two contrasting research sites: (1) state and private schools in Budapest, Hungary (Szabó, 2015); and (2) a school in a region of Romania where there is a large Hungarian-speaking population (Laihonen & Tódor, 2015). We will also demonstrate how we developed our approach to interviewing so as to build an account of research participants' own *emic* understandings of their local schoolscapes.

State and private schools in Hungary

Szabó (2015) investigated differences between two types of organizational culture in a comparative study of schoolscapes in two state schools and two private schools in Budapest. His study was carried out in 2013. The research corpus includes five extended interviews and almost 900 photographs. With a view to incorporating the emic perspectives of those participating in the research, Szabó adapted the *walking tour* methodology (Garvin, 2010: 255–256) to fit the specific characteristics of educational institutions, calling this the *tourist guide technique*. As he was photographing signs in the school building, he interviewed the person who was guiding him through the corridors, classrooms and other spaces in each particular school. This was generally a person with some authority, such as a teacher. First, Szabó asked this person to make comments on the choice of language, texts and

Investigating visual practices in education 127

other symbols on display. The conversation proceeded as if the teacher was a tourist guide and Szabó was a tourist. Then, responding to the utterances of the 'institutional guide,' Szabó occasionally asked for further details. These conversations were audio-recorded as they occurred. In effect, Szabó and each 'guide' co-constructed a narrative (cf. Laihonen, 2008) as they surveyed the material environment together. This was a kind of joint exploration, in which Szabó was able to gain new insights by incorporating an insider angle into his schoolscape study.

As mentioned above, Johnson (1980) highlighted the impact of nation-state discourses on schoolscapes in an early study in the United States. In the two state schools in this study in Budapest, nation-state discourses were also clearly manifested in the general schoolscapes and were quite similar to those identified by Johnson. To begin with, the two state schools were named after national figures, such as the composer of the Hungarian national anthem. In some classrooms, portraits of eighteenth- to twentieth-century artists and statesmen hung on the walls. Furthermore, when the schools were commemorating the 1848 revolution, portraits of the protagonists who figure in the national narrative about this historical event were thumbtacked or taped on the walls, along with student artwork relating to some aspect of the revolution. Nineteenth-century Hungary was a multiethnic and multilingual state and many of the revolutionaries had an ethnic background other than the dominant Hungarian one. In spite of this, the history of 1848 was visually retold, in the Hungarian language, as a story about Hungarians. For example, only copies of the Hungarian version of the multilingual revolutionary leaflets were on display. Szabó interpreted this as a practice of *erasure* (Irvine & Gal, 2000) within state school practices (for details, see Szabó, 2015).

Top-down homogenization in the schoolscape was also stronger in the case of the state schools, while the educational practitioners in the private schools engaged in some negotiation with students over visual communication practices. One of the most salient differences related to the classrooms – the space designated for teacher–student interaction. In the state schools, the arrangement of the classroom furniture anticipated a mode of classroom interaction that was predominantly teacher-centered. This is the type of classroom described by Scollon and Wong Scollon (2004: 39) as the "panopticon classroom." According to Scollon and Wong Scollon (2004: 39), this arrangement is typical for "lectures, musical and dramatic performances, political speeches, and so forth," where the attention is focused on one person who dominates and regulates communication. Figure 8.1 shows an example of a classroom layout of this kind. In contrast, in the private schools in this study, desks were usually arranged in (semi)circles, anticipating small group discussions or individual work. Teacher-fronted arrangements of the classroom furniture were rare. As Scollon and Wong Scollon (2004: 39) put it, this significant difference can be interpreted as a manifestation of another culture of communication in which "a group of people conduct a line of discussion with relatively

Figure 8.1 Panopticon classroom (designed for teaching music).

equal status in their rights to take the floor and speak". Figure 8.2 provides an example of this kind of arrangement.[2]

There were also differences between state and private schools in the policy on counter-culture and the use of graffiti. In one state and one private school, the discussion during the interview with the school 'guide' turned to graffiti on the wall and on the desks. While transgressive signs such as graffiti were prohibited by the principal in the state school, in the private school, a decision was taken, during the school assembly, to assign the wall of a side corridor for the purpose of graffiti. The involvement of students in the decision-making process and in the implementation of school policies of this kind indexed a different organizational culture and different ideologies about transgressive signs.

Languages were also represented in different ways in the state and private schools. Szabó's analysis focused on both the representation of the forms of the languages and on the ways in which they were linked to nation-states. We focus here on the latter form of representation.

Foreign languages were taught in the state schools in classrooms designed for the specific purpose of foreign language teaching, and reference to languages other than Hungarian was very rare outside those rooms. In the private schools, English appeared more often and in a wider range of spaces, e.g. as inscriptions on the students' artwork.

Investigating visual practices in education 129

Figure 8.2 Classroom for group and individual work (designed for teaching arts).

Languages were clearly portrayed as being tied to nation-states and a standard variety was promoted. For instance, in one of the state schools, English was explicitly linked to the United Kingdom. National symbols such as the Union Jack flag were used, along with other stereotypical visualizations of the country (e.g. London scenes). Figure 8.3 depicts the door at the entrance to the English classroom.

The visual impression of the dominance of 'British English' in foreign language education in this school was reinforced in the account of the teacher who guided Szabó round the school. Relevant aspects of the school policy were explained in the following terms[3,4]:

(1)

Tamás: [...] and as I see, British English is preferred
Éva: Definitely, yes. [...] well, obviously for us it's the basis, so [the students] should learn British English first and after that, maybe, American English.

In the other state school, Szabó came across visual references to other English-speaking countries. In this secondary school, the classroom designed for teaching English had maps of the United Kingdom and the USA on the wall. These were accompanied by various information boards about Canada, New Zealand, Australia and Ireland. Figure 8.4 shows one of these boards. During Szabó's 'tour' of this school, the guide was a teacher of English. Szabó initiated discussion with her on policy regarding the teaching of varieties of

Figure 8.3 The dominance of 'British English'.

English. As a prompt, he made brief reference to the standardist ideology that there should be a central, prioritized variety in language teaching:

(2)

Tamás: What is the central variety? So is it BBC English or rather something else?
Zsuzsa: You mean in the school?
Tamás: Yes.
Zsuzsa: Well, yes, we teach British English because you see Oxford University Press gained ground maximally, I think, in the majority of schools, and, well, it is what they distribute.

This English teacher positioned herself as a representative of the whole school community ("We teach"), and then she legitimized the current practice with reference to the consequences of marketing by a British publisher. Later on, Szabó mentioned that students might encounter other varieties such as American English in their spare time, and indicated that these varieties might appear in their actual usage as well:

Investigating visual practices in education 131

Figure 8.4 Beyond 'British English'.

(3)

Tamás:	And if somebody writes such a form in a test, then
Zsuzsa:	In principle, if I follow how matriculation examinations should be marked, I shouldn't accept that.
Tamás:	Uh huh, I see.
Zsuzsa:	I underline [the word] in the test, I accept that and I make a note [such as] 'but you know that in an exam situation it wouldn't carry any marks, don't you?'

The teacher then turned to her own practice. She described a typical situation where she would have to make a pragmatic decision. She alluded to the expectations of the school authorities and the regulation of matriculation examinations, while legitimizing her own more liberal practices.

Hungarian-medium minority schools

A detailed study in one Hungarian minority school in Romania

From 2012 to 2013, Laihonen and Tódor (2015) carried out a detailed study of changes in the schoolscape in a Hungarian minority school in Szeklerland,

132 P. Laihonen and T.P. Szabó

Romania. Their research involved the gathering of photographic data, ethnographic observation, the taking of field notes and interviews with school staff and current and former students. The history of the village was evident in the different kinds of signs that made up the schoolscape. Laihonen and Tódor focused on the changes that had been generated by the far-reaching political change ushered in by the fall of the Ceauşescu regime in 1989, by the transformation of Romania from a centralized dictatorship to a liberal economy and democratic culture where local initiatives could gain more space, and by the 'rehungarization' process in the region. They also investigated the problems related to the learning and use of the Romanian language. In particular, they were interested in identifying the ways in which the political transition and the processes involved in the reassertion of a Hungarian identity and the revival of public displays of religiosity had changed the ways in which languages were conceptualized and actually employed in this local schoolscape.

Their approach was ethnographic and multi-method in nature. They designed the research so as to take account of the emic interpretations of the schoolscape by local villagers, parents, and current and previous students, as well as their own etic interpretations. They carried out fieldwork in the village and its school over the course of a year. In July 2012, Laihonen conducted 20 interviews in Hungarian, with people such as the present and former school director, parents, and local villagers. He also took 61 photographs inside and outside the school (in addition to approximately 300 photographs in the village itself). Tódor lives near the village and she speaks both Hungarian and Romanian. She visited the school three times in the autumn of 2012 and in the spring of 2013, interviewing staff (13 interviews in all). She also observed Romanian classes, along with history and geography classes. The history and geography classes were chosen because the language of instruction had officially changed from Romanian to Hungarian in 2012. During the same fieldwork visit, Tódor took 205 photographs in different spaces within the school.

In addition, Tódor undertook a small-scale survey of students. She had prepared a questionnaire that was filled in by 66 pupils (girls and boys between the ages of 11 and 15). The focus was on language use and language learning. The survey was undertaken for three reasons: first, to widen the picture being built up through the ethnographic work, the classroom observations, the photography and the interviews; second, to include the perspectives, preferences and experiences of a range of young people regarding the Hungarian and Romanian language, and third, to prepare the ground for an audio-recorded discussion with a sub-sample of students, based on the themes emerging from the survey. The discussion took place during a class organized by Tódor.

At the interpretation and analysis stage of this study, Laihonen and Tódor began with the photographic data. Their analysis focused on the differentiation of signs along functional and symbolic lines. They found that Romanian was being used for official state administrative purposes and that Hungarian indexed local heritage, along with local cultural and religious practices and

Investigating visual practices in education 133

everyday life at school. They also found that most texts were produced monolingually. For example, basic texts on the homepages of the school were only in Hungarian, but certain administrative materials such as the subject curricula were only in Romanian. Materials that were judged to be of interest to students and parents (e.g. notices about special events) were all in Hungarian but, on occasion, the title of the text (but not its content) appeared in Romanian as well. Due to the salience of the differentiation between state and minority language, other symbols, languages and language varieties occupied less space.

From their interviews, Laihonen and Tódor learned that there had been a distinct trend towards greater use of Hungarian in the schoolscape, along with a conscious replacement of Romanian and bilingual signs from the dictatorship period (i.e. before 1990). Hungarian-only signs predominated during the period when the study was carried out (for details, see Laihonen & Tódor, 2015). The students attending the school regularly encountered cultural symbols and visual texts depicting Hungarian-ness. The signs depicting images of modernization and citizenship of the Romanian nation-state had been changed into signs indexing local identity and a broader transnational sense of Hungarian-ness. From the perspective of language education, few displays of bilingual signage and specially tailored Romanian signs had been developed by the local teachers, which indicated that Romanian was taught so that the pupils' language background (Hungarian first language and a beginner-level Romanian) was taken into account.

Comparative research in different emerging nation-states in Eastern Europe

Schools with Hungarian as the (dominant) language of instruction can be found in other countries around Hungary, especially in areas where Hungarians form the regional majority. In addition to Szeklerland in Romania, these include areas in Subcarpathia in Ukraine and rural areas of Southern Slovakia. Laihonen did multi-sited fieldwork in all three regions from 2011 to 2013. These regions form linguistic and cultural peripheries and are rarely given a mention in the national narratives of these young states. Attempts at integration of these Hungarian-speaking regions into the nation-states in which they are located through public education have given rise to various tensions. The choice, display and placement of national symbols in Hungarian-medium minority schools has been a topic of constant debate since the end of the Cold War in 1990.

During his fieldwork, Laihonen compared the ways in which local tensions were played out in different national settings and the ways in which the imposition of national symbols was negotiated, and occasionally subverted. Local practices ranged from the parallel display of nation-state symbols and Hungarian symbols to the predominant use of local Hungarian symbols or a complete ban on the use of certain Hungarian symbols in the public spaces of a school. In all three national contexts, nation-state symbols had

Figure 8.5 Hidden Slovak national symbols in a Hungarian minority school.

to be displayed in certain spaces. For instance, in Slovakia, all schools were required to display the coat of arms, the first passages of the Constitution and the national anthem of Slovakia (in Slovak). In one Hungarian minority school that Laihonen visited in Slovakia, he found that these symbols were barely visible in one classroom. Figure 8.5 shows a corner of the classroom where the national symbols were almost hidden behind large artifacts used for teaching and learning.

In schools where the display of Hungarian national symbols was restricted, new ways to display them had been invented. For example, in another Hungarian-medium school in Slovakia that was visited by Laihonen, the students were learning the Hungarian alphabet with the help of illustrated alphabet cards, as shown in Figure 8.6. Z stood for *Zászló* ('flag') and the visual image associated with this letter was the Hungarian flag with the Hungarian coat of arms.

Concluding comments

Our aims in this chapter were as follows: (1) to draw attention to the growing body of research on the visual dimension of meaning-making in multilingual educational settings; (2) to provide glimpses into the range of research that

Figure 8.6 Hungarian national symbols displayed through alphabet cards in Slovakia.

has been undertaken in different cultural and historical contexts, along with examples of the kinds of research questions that have been posed; and (3) to give some insights into the ways in which research projects have been designed and the range of research approaches and research methods that have been employed.

The growing research interest in this field of multilingualism and education is partly due to the changes ushered in by globalization: by political changes taking place on a global scale which are having an impact on schools, by the advent of the internet and mobile technology and by the rapidity of the shift towards the use of visual and semiotic resources in communication in contemporary social life. The theoretical ground for this new strand of empirical work was first laid over a decade ago by a number of scholars. Those who broke particularly important new ground were Scollon and Wong Scollon (2003, 2004), who focused our attention on language in the material world and on the internet, and Kress and Van Leeuwen (2006), who first characterized discourse as including a visual and increasingly multimodal nature. And, as we have shown, empirical work on the characteristics of contemporary schoolscapes has its roots in the wider field of linguistic landscapes (e.g. Gorter, 2006; Shohamy & Gorter, 2009). It also has roots in the long tradition of research in anthropology and education (e.g. Cohen, 1971; Johnson, 1980; Brown, 2012).

Earlier in this chapter, we mentioned that there has been a strand of work that is largely applied in nature. This has been linked to pedagogical initiatives with different aims, such as raising students' critical awareness of the social significance of different forms of communication, verbal and visual, on page and on screen (e.g. Clemente et al., 2012; Lotherington & Ronda, 2014), or generating discussion about ways of engaging with the linguistic and cultural diversity of contemporary social life (e.g. Dagenais, 2009; Hancock, 2012)

136   *P. Laihonen and T.P. Szabó*

or enabling a wider range of voices to be heard in classrooms (Pietikäinen & Pitkänen-Huhta, 2013).

However, despite the current lively research interest in schoolscapes and in wider visual practices in local linguistic landscapes, it would be premature to say that there has been a parallel visual turn in education – in schools or in higher education. There clearly needs to be more dialogue between researchers and educators, and there needs to be movement towards the fostering of critical awareness of visual literacy and the development of students' capacity to engage in multimodal ways of reading the material world (Clemente et al., 2012). Of all the research approaches we have discussed here, ethnography is best suited to the creation of opportunities for dialogue between researchers and practitioners, because of its commitment to extended engagement with research participants.

Notes

1   We are grateful to Marilyn Martin-Jones for encouraging us to submit a chapter and for her insightful mentoring of earlier drafts.

Research for this article by Laihonen was financed by the Academy of Finland Grant 137718.

Research by Szabó was funded by the European Union's Research Executive Agency under a Marie Curie Intra-European Fellowship for Career Development within the EU's Seventh Framework Programme for Research (ref. 626376) and the Kone Foundation in Finland (ref. 44–9730).

2   All the photographs in this chapter were taken by the authors. Figures 8.1–8.4 are © Szabó, and Figures 8.5 and 8.6 are © Laihonen.

3   The names of the teachers represented in the extracts from the interviews presented here are fictitious. They have been adopted to preserve confidentiality and to avoid revealing the identities of the research participants.

4   The original tour-guide conversations took place in Hungarian. This extract and those that follow have been translated into English by Szabó.

References

Aronin, L. & Ó Laoire, M. (2012) 'The material culture of multilingualism', in H.F. Marten, D. Gorter & L. van Mensel (eds) *Minority Languages in the Linguistic Landscape*. Basingstoke, Hampshire: Palgrave Macmillan, 299–318.

Blommaert, J. (2013) *Ethnography, Superdiversity and Linguistic Landscapes: Chronicles of Complexity*. Bristol: Multilingual Matters.

Brown, K.D. (2012) 'The linguistic landscape of educational spaces: language revitalization and schools in southeastern Estonia', in H.F. Marten, D. Gorter & L. van Mensel (eds) *Minority Languages in the Linguistic Landscape*. Basingstoke, Hampshire: Palgrave Macmillan, 281–298.

Clemente, M., Andrade, A.I. & Martins, F. (2012) 'Learning to read the world, learning to look at the linguistic landscape: a study in the first years of formal education', in C. Hélot, M. Barni, R. Janssen & C. Bagna (eds) *Linguistic Landscape, Multilingualism and Social Change*. Frankfurt: Peter Lang, 267–285.

Cohen, Y.A. (1971) 'The shaping of men's minds: adaptations to imperatives of culture', in M.L. Wax et al. (eds) *Anthropological Perspectives on Education*. New York: Basic Books, 19–50.

Investigating visual practices in education 137

Dagenais, D., Moore, D., Sabatier, C., Lamarre, P. & Armand, F. (2009) 'Linguistic landscape and language awareness', in E. Shohamy & D. Gorter (eds) *Linguistic Landscape: Expanding the Scenery*. London: Routledge, 253–269.

Garvin, R. (2010) 'Responses to the linguistic landscape in Memphis, Tennessee: an urban space in transition', in E. Shohamy, E. Ben-Rafael & M. Barni (eds) *Linguistic Landscape in the City*. Bristol: Multilingual Matters, 252–271.

Gorter, D. (ed.) (2006) *Linguistic Landscape: A New Approach to Multilingualism*. Clevedon, UK: Multilingual Matters.

Gorter, D. & Cenoz, J. (2014) 'Linguistic landscapes inside multilingual schools', in B. Spolsky, M. Tannenbaum & O. Inbar (eds) *Challenges for Language Education and Policy: Making Space for People*. New York: Routledge, 151–169.

Hancock, A. (2012) 'Capturing the linguistic landscape of Edinburgh: a pedagogical tool to investigate student teachers' understandings of cultural and linguistic diversity', in C. Hélot, M. Barni, R. Janssen & C. Bagna (eds) *Linguistic Landscape, Multilingualism and Social Change*. Frankfurt: Peter Lang, 249–266.

Hult, F.M. (2009) 'Language ecology and linguistic landscape analysis', in E. Shohamy & D. Gorter (eds) *Linguistic Landscape: Expanding the Scenery*. London: Routledge, 88–103.

Irvine, J.T. & Gal, S. (2000) 'Language ideology and linguistic differentiation', in P. Kroskrity (ed.) *Regimes of Language: Ideologies, Polities and Identities*. Santa Fe, NM: School of American Research, 35–84.

Johnson, N.B. (1980) 'The material culture of public school classrooms: the symbolic integration of local schools and national culture'. *Anthropology & Education Quarterly* 11(3), 173–190.

Khan, M.A. (2012) *Social Meanings of Language Policy and Practices: A Critical, Linguistic Ethnographic Study of Four Schools in Pakistan*. Unpublished PhD thesis, Lancaster University, UK.

Kress, G. & Van Leeuwen, T. (2006) *Reading Images: The Grammar of Visual Design*, 2nd edn. London: Routledge.

Laihonen, P. (2008) 'Language ideologies in interviews: a conversation analysis approach'. *Journal of Sociolinguistics* 12, 668–693.

Laihonen, P. & Tódor, E.-M. (2015) 'The changing schoolscape in a Szekler village in Romania: signs of diversity in "rehungarization"'. *International Journal of Bilingual Education and Bilingualism*. Online: http://dx.doi.org/10.1080/13670050.2015.1051943.

Lotherington, H. & Ronda, N. (2014) '2B or Not 2B? From pencil to multimodal programming: new frontiers in communicative competencies', in J.P. Guikema & L. Williams (eds) *Digital Literacies in Foreign and Second Language Education*. San Marcos, TX: CALICO, 9–28.

Martin-Jones, M. (2011) 'Languages, texts, and literacy practices: an ethnographic lens on bilingual vocational education in Wales', in T.L. McCarty (ed.) *Ethnography and Language Policy*. New York: Routledge, 231–254.

Martin-Jones, M., Blackledge, A. & Creese, A. (eds) (2012) *The Routledge Handbook of Multilingualism*. London: Routledge.

Nikula, T. & Pitkänen-Huhta, A. (2008) 'Using photographs to access stories of learning English', in P. Kalaja et al. (eds) *Narratives of Learning and Teaching EFL*. New York: Palgrave Macmillan, 171–185.

Pennycook, A. (2009) 'Linguistic landscapes and the transgressive semiotics of graffiti', in E. Shohamy & D. Gorter (eds) *Linguistic Landscape: Expanding the Scenery*. London: Routledge, 302–312.

Pietikäinen, S. (2012) 'Experiences and expressions of multilingualism: visual ethnography and discourse analysis in research with Sámi children', in S. Gardner & M. Martin-Jones (eds) *Multilingualism, Discourse and Ethnography*. New York: Routledge, 163–178.

Pietikäinen, S. & Pitkänen-Huhta, A. (2013) 'Multimodal literacy practices in the Indigenous Sámi classroom: children navigating in a complex multilingual setting'. *Journal of Language, Identity, and Education* 12, 230–247.

Scollon, R. & Wong Scollon, S. (2003) *Discourses in Place: Language in the Material World*. London: Routledge.

Scollon, R. & Wong Scollon, S. (2004) *Nexus Analysis: Discourse and the Emerging Internet*. London: Routledge.

Shohamy, E. (2012) 'Linguistic landscape and multilingualism', in M. Martin-Jones, A. Blackledge & A. Creese (eds) *The Routledge Handbook of Multilingualism*. London: Routledge, 538–551.

Shohamy, E. & Gorter, D. (eds) (2009) *Linguistic Landscape: Expanding the Scenery*. London: Routledge.

Szabó, T.P. (2015) 'The management of diversity in schoolscapes: an analysis of Hungarian practices'. *Apples: Journal of Applied Language Studies* 9(1), 23–51. Online: http://apples.jyu.fi/article/abstract/353.

Part 3

Researching multilingual communication and multisemioticity online

9 Methodologies for researching multilingual online texts and practices

David Barton and Carmen Lee

There has been a growing body of research in the past few years devoted to multilingualism on the internet. It is clear that as the web becomes more globalized, it is giving rise to more opportunities for multilingual encounters which were not possible in face-to-face contexts (as described in Barton & Lee, 2013). Most of the research so far on multilingualism on the internet has adopted the discourse analytic or interactional linguistic approaches used in existing studies of 'offline' contexts, such as language choice and code-switching patterns in face-to-face conversations. With a few exceptions (e.g. Sebba, 2012), rarely do existing studies look into what people do with their mixed-language texts online. However, in reality, especially with the advent of Web 2.0 social media, our research and the research of others suggest that multilingual web users do not simply carry over their face-to-face offline practices to online web contexts. Data in our studies also reveal that even people who are considered 'monolinguals' in offline contexts are regularly involved in multilingual interactions in their online participation.

Whilst most research has started from examining texts, our research has been more concerned with the practices people are participating in. The overall aim of this chapter is to discuss the importance of paying attention to both texts and practices in researching multilingualism online. To do this we focus on three studies of multilingual writing online that have drawn upon both traditional and newer methods of research, including observations, interviews, auto-ethnography and technobiography. We first discuss the question of alternative methodologies as starting points when researching language online. We also ask what can be gained from discourse-based studies which start out by examining texts versus more ethnographic approaches which focus on people's language practices. Through the three case studies, we introduce the approaches we have taken in our research that combine both texts and people's practices. This chapter argues that while it is important to describe patterns of language choice and mixed-language texts, a situated and contextualized approach that draws upon ethnographic data is useful in revealing the actual social activities and practices surrounding multilingual writing online.

142   *D. Barton and C. Lee*

Approaches to researching multilingualism online

In this chapter, the term 'multilingualism' is used in a broad sense. It refers to the co-existence of two or more languages, or 'codes', in any communicative context. In our research, multilingual practices online may also broadly refer to activities in which two or more languages are central. A 'code' may refer to a variety or form of representation of a language (e.g. Romanized Cantonese and Cantonese represented in characters are treated as two distinct codes as they serve different functions in online writing). The examples used here are taken from our own research and refer primarily to Spanish–English or Chinese–English multilingual encounters.

The emerging research area of 'multilingualism online' or the 'multilingual internet' is a multifaceted one. Existing studies of multilingualism online tend to fall into two major categories – first, quantitative studies of linguistic diversity online and, second, the investigation of patterns of mixed-language texts and practices in a specific form of computer-mediated communication (CMC) or across different forms of CMC. At a macro level, public surveys and other quantitative forms of research have been conducted to measure linguistic diversity on the internet. Statistical findings generated from such studies tend to focus on the distribution between English and other languages by recording the dominant language of individual web pages, or by identifying the native language of web users. Some of the most cited public surveys about the internet population by language include Internet World Stats (www.internetworldstats.com/) and W3Tech (http://w3techs.com/technologies/overview/content_language/all), both of which are hosted by marketing companies. The methodologies adopted in these marketing surveys should always be treated with caution. First, the estimates generated are often based on multiple sources from different countries, which may not share the same set of methods to measure their internet penetration rates. Second, amongst the many sources of these surveys are governments and marketing companies who might have presented their findings to their own interest, thus leading to biased results or over-estimates. As Paolillo (2007) has noted, estimates of internet user populations are far from sufficient in representing multilingualism online, and therefore he has called for more empirical research on actual instances of language use online. Certainly, a more meaningful and comprehensive investigation of multilingualism online involves understanding what web users actually do with their multiple linguistic resources in authentic contexts and why they do so. Combining people's multilingual texts and practices online is what this chapter is interested in.

A recurring issue for researchers of language online more broadly is the overall framing and where to begin. Should the research start out by observing the mixed-language texts on our chosen research site? Or should it begin by gathering details of what people do with their language resources online, i.e. their practices? This is the distinction between discourse-based studies on

Researching online texts and practices   143

the one hand and more ethnographic approaches on the other. The answer to these questions is closely tied to the aims of the research.

It is worth providing a brief overview of recent research in the area. The first key collection of studies on multilingualism online is notably Danet and Herring's (2007) *The Multilingual Internet*. This volume covers a wide range of topics from general discussions of linguistic diversity online to language choice and identities online. To date, however, most of the literature on the multilingual internet focuses on two key issues, documenting either language choice or code-switching practices among multilingual web users. *Language choice* online is concerned with the codes or linguistic resources available to web users and how they negotiate their choice when communicating online with people with or without shared languages. Existing research covers a wide range of platforms and documents users' choices between a number of languages, especially between English and other languages such as Egyptian Arabic (Warschauer et al., 2007), Swahili (Mafu, 2004), Jamaican Creole (Hinrichs, 2006), Cantonese (Lee, 2007), Mandarin Chinese (Su, 2007), and Thai (Tagg & Seargeant, 2012). Lee (2007), for example, documents the various codes available to Cantonese–English bilingual students in Hong Kong when they participate in email and instant messaging. Some of these studies, including Warschauer et al. (2007), have pointed out that people who rarely use English in their everyday speech and writing may decide nevertheless to communicate only in English when online.

The other common direction of research is *code-switching* (CS). CS research in CMC has been interested in whether patterns of CS in online interaction conform to or deviate from conversational CS in face-to-face contexts. Classic theories and frameworks in face-to-face code-switching have been applied in CMC contexts, including Myers-Scotton's (1998) markedness model as well as Auer's (1999) conversational approach. For example, Auer's classification of code-switching patterns (insertional switching, insertional mixing, alternational switching, and alternational mixing) is adopted in Leppänen's (2007) study of the CS practices among Finnish young people, as well as in Siebenhaar's (2006) study of Swiss-German Internet Relay Chat (IRC) chatrooms. Traditional models of CS based on spoken interaction may not fully account for CS in digital communication, which is largely written in mode and may have distinct forms of interaction (Sebba, 2012). It is clear that sometimes code-switching online does not follow the conventions of CS in offline interaction, as exemplified in Excerpt (1) below, which is part of an email written by a Cantonese–English bilingual university student from Hong Kong:

Excerpt (1)

The ocamp is ok *la*, except that the beach programs and nite journey were cancelled because of the bad weather. And ah sun quarreled with "ha jong" *lor*, as u know his character *ga la*. But in our ocamp gp ah sun

144   *D. Barton and C. Lee*

and jessic got along very well with the cores and freshmen *geh*. Ok *la*, keep contact thru email. One yr is not very long.

When Hong Kong Cantonese–English bilinguals code-switch in face-to-face interaction, Cantonese is the matrix code to which lexical items from English are inserted. Excerpt (1), however, shows the opposite – the dominant language is English, while Cantonese discourse particles in romanized form (italicized in the example) are inserted at the end of the English sentences. This practice is found to be extremely common in computer-mediated interaction among Hong Kong people (as discussed in James, 2001; Lee, 2007). This needs to be explained within a framework that moves beyond the conventional conversation analysis model in speech to a model that takes into account situational factors in other modes of communication (see chapters in Sebba et al., 2012 for further discussion). Perhaps what is more important and meaningful is to look at what multilingual resources web users value and to see how these resources are employed strategically to convey social meanings in different instances of online interaction. In addition to text analysis, understanding practices requires more practice-based, ethnographic-style approaches to research.

Ethnographically informed approaches to multilingualism online

Many studies of multilingualism online can be thought of as 'ethnographically informed': they are not full ethnographies with the extent of immersion expected in an anthropological study but their orientation and methodology draw upon ethnography. They locate instances of language use in their broader cultural context. There is a focus on people's perspectives, aiming to understand how they make sense of an activity and what it means to them. To do this, 'practices' become a basic unit of analysis. When carrying out a study, researchers often draw upon a range of methods, with participant observation being particularly fruitful. Finally, the role of the researcher in the research always needs to be identified. (More about ethnographic approaches and how they are developing to take account of online contexts can be found in Page et al., 2014: 104–115.)

Ethnographically informed approaches to studying multilingualism online make it possible to rethink the meanings of texts, and to consider how texts are produced in authentic contexts of use. Most importantly, these approaches provide insights into why people employ different linguistic strategies in different contexts of use. As an example of this, Eva Lam has carried out extensive research on the out-of-school second language literacy practices of young Chinese immigrants to the United States. In her work, Lam adopts a largely ethnographic approach and focuses on participants' insider perspectives. For instance, one study, Lam (2009), draws upon interview data to reveal how Chinese students in the US represent and reconstruct their second language learner identities and build transnational networks in online chat. Elsewhere,

Researching online texts and practices 145

Androutsopoulos (2007) has carried out work on German-based web environments, including a study of sociolinguistic styles and identity constructions on sites devoted to hip-hop culture. Androutsopoulos (2008) calls for further research that adopts what he calls "discourse-centered online ethnography" (DCOE), an approach that combines observation of discourse online and insights from direct contact with web users. In doing DCOE on such sites, Androutsopoulos starts with systematic observation of the discourse of the sites, moving on to interviewing internet actors to elicit insiders' perspectives.

Another study which combines texts and practices is research by Lexander (2012). She proposes a model for understanding multilingual SMS as literacy practices in which she also combines text analysis with ethnographic interviews. An important point about these methodological approaches is that neither texts nor people's practices should be seen as the sole point of departure in research. Rather, researchers often need to go back and forth between textual data and data relating to people's practices in understanding the interplay between what is visible on the screen and what people actually do with languages online. When observing the words on a website, we frequently get to learn something about the life of the text producers, such as where they are from, what they do for a living, their interests and hobbies, their linguistic repertoire in online and offline situations, and so on. With Flickr, for instance, looking at people's profiles and the language used in various writing spaces can provide a great deal of information about the linguistic and cultural identities that the users are presenting.

Combining texts and practices: three case studies of multilingualism online

In this section, we provide detailed descriptions of the methods of data collection adopted in three of the research projects involving different forms of new media online that we have carried out. These use ethnographically informed approaches for understanding multilingualism within a social-practice theory of language and literacy. The three studies in question involve research into multilingual and multiscriptual practices on instant messaging (IM), research on multilingual practices on Flickr, and a study of multilingual writing on Web 2.0 in Hong Kong. All three studies aimed at bringing together multilingual features observed from the texts available online and the practices surrounding the production and use of the words. They are described in more detail in Barton and Lee (2013: ch. 12); here the focus is on the studies as examples of multilingual methodologies.

Connecting traditions of linguistic analysis with practice-based research requires new methodological design and the reshaping of traditional methods in response to the changing affordances of new media. We have utilized a mixed-method approach, as no one single method can be employed to address all the research questions relevant to both the texts and the practices surrounding them. Sometimes we need to combine the advantages of both

146   *D. Barton and C. Lee*

quantitative and qualitative methods; at the same time, we move back and forth between face-to-face methods and online methods. Overall we recognize the importance of being explicit about the research methods and instruments used in online research so as to present and discuss issues and challenges involved in doing online research more generally.

Study 1: Code choice in instant messaging

The IM project was the earliest of the three studies. The data was collected in 2006 and 2007 and the methods adopted drew upon what was available at that point in time. Its overall aim was to understand how young people in Hong Kong deployed their multilingual, multiscriptual, and multimodal resources when participating in IM. Because the overall objective of the study was to understand the situated nature of language deployment on IM, it generally took a qualitative and multiple-case-study approach. Data were collected from a group of nineteen young people in Hong Kong, aged between 20 and 28. Identifying informants who were willing to participate was not an easy task given the amount of personal and private communication involved in IM. New informants emerged at different points in time. Some started participating at a very early stage while some were identified later by way of existing informants, the approach commonly known as 'snowballing'.

It is worth drawing attention to two aspects of the methodology: first, it was a 'responsive' methodology in that not all participants were researched with the same research procedure. Second, individual participants followed different pathways through the data collection. Some participants were studied through the first pathway below, which involved a mixture of traditional ethnography and online methods, with the following stages:

(i)   *Initial observation in the participants' homes or student residences*: The researcher sat behind them taking field notes as they sat at their computer chatting with friends online. This close observation in the participants' private spaces of communication revealed additional online practices, such as multi-tasking, where participants switched between other applications, such as using MS Word for student assignments, with IM in the background at the same time.

(ii) *Collection of chat logs*: The participant printed out the chat history from phase (i). This ensured the authenticity of the textual data.

(iii) *Face-to-face interview*: Based on the researcher's field notes, an immediate face-to-face interview was conducted with the participant.

(iv) *Initial analysis*: Then the researcher went away and analysed all the data collected from (i)–(iii), starting with discourse analysis of the chat texts. Linguistic features identified in texts then became themes for follow-up interviews.

(v)   *Follow-up*: Based on these emerging themes, follow-up interviews were conducted either face-to-face or online, depending on participants' availability. Keeping in touch with the informants revealed changes in their IM usage. For example, towards the end of a semester, some participants moved beyond interpersonal chat and began to use IM for project discussion with classmates.

As the research progressed, the methodology was responsive in that an alternative procedure was developed, taking more account of the participants' everyday digital lives. In this second pathway, the participants were studied primarily through online methods.

(i)   *Electronic logbook*: Each participant was asked to keep a seven-day diary documenting their daily IM and other online activities. They copied and pasted their chat logs onto the diary and emailed it to the researcher.
(ii) *Initial analysis*: The logbooks were analysed and coded for content. Topics were identified for follow-up interviews.
(iii) *Online interview*: Follow-up interviews were mostly done through IM. This method was particularly suitable for students the researcher did not know well, or who were not able to meet with the researcher face-to-face.

Close observation of the IM messages was important in understanding textual features. In addition, insights from qualitative data such as interviews and logbooks allowed the researcher to understand participants' lives and how their IM text-making could be mediated by other online practices. For each participant, a profile was created from field notes and the various sources of data. Across-case analysis was also conducted, aiming to identify emerging themes and patterns.

Study 2: Multilingual writing on Flickr

The original research aim of the Flickr study was to understand how people deployed their linguistic resources when interacting with an international audience. We began the study by eliciting data about the level of linguistic diversity and the overall distribution of languages on Flickr. This was done by conducting an exploratory observation of 100 Flickr sites selected from one of the largest interest groups on Flickr, called *FlickrCentral*. This was also an effective way of identifying active users, which was our main target group. We observed the first 100 users we came across on *FlickrCentral*, considering only those who had actively contributed written content. From these 100 sites, we obtained descriptive statistics about the presence and distribution of English and other languages in major writing spaces, including profiles, titles and descriptions of photos, tags and comments. As much as possible, we also noted languages used by the users and their locations. Despite this being set up as an English-medium site, we noted the presence of many other languages, and half of the sites in the initial analysis included languages other than English, as reported in Barton and Lee (2013). We then collected multilingual

148   D. Barton and C. Lee

texts on the site and contacted the producers of these texts through Flickr's own email. Our starting point, or our primary unit of analysis, was users' individual Flickr sites. We collected mixed-language texts from four distinct writing spaces which contained user-generated writing: profiles, titles and descriptions, tags and comments.

Having obtained a snapshot of the multilingual situation on Flickr, the next step was to take a closer look at individual users' multilingual practices in these different writing spaces on Flickr. Separate from the 100 sites described above, we identified a set of sites where English and other languages co-existed. We were able to select 30 active users, 18 Chinese speakers and 12 Spanish speakers. These 30 focal participants came from various geographical areas where Chinese or Spanish were the main languages, but apart from that criterion, we studied the first active users we came across. They were invited to complete an online survey questionnaire about their linguistic background and their general Flickr practices. The survey covered questions about what they used Flickr for, what languages they would use in different areas on the site and why. There was a 50 per cent response rate to our initial request, which we considered high for an online request to strangers. The reason for this high response rate may well be that all participants were first approached through FlickrMail, which is only available to members; in that initial email, we identified ourselves as fellow Flickr users as well as academic researchers; the survey was posted on a free online survey site which was easily accessible to the respondents.

The survey was then followed up by a series of email interviews so as to identify different ways of participating in Flickr and ways in which these people deployed their linguistic resources on their own sites. As we got to know the participants, we sometimes switched to personal email accounts, according to their preference. All the informants had a large number of photos and one recurrent issue in online research is how to sample from what can potentially be too much data. To narrow down the scope, for each participant in the research, we examined the 100 most recent photos they had uploaded. In the interviews, our questions then focused on specific areas of these Flickr sites as well as the answers to the initial survey questionnaire. For example, we would provide a link to a user's photo page and ask the user to explain why they wrote the caption in two languages. In so doing, we were able to pay close attention to details about actual situations of Flickr use. The interview data were then coded and categorized according to emerging themes from the transcripts. As our research interest here arose from our personal participation in Flickr, we also carried out auto-ethnographies of our own multilingual activities on Flickr. (We pursue this in greater detail below when discussing the researcher's stance.)

Study 3: Techno-linguistic biographies of Hong Kong University students

The third study of multilingualism online was a study of Web 2.0 writing activities among university students in Hong Kong (Lee, 2014). In addition

Researching online texts and practices 149

to identifying major Web 2.0 activities, the research looked into the ways in which a group of bilingual undergraduate students deployed their multiple linguistic resources on Web 2.0 sites, and how that related to their identity performance online. This study was carried out from 2010 to 2011. There were two phases of data collection in this multi-method study. The first phase aimed to elicit demographic information from the students through an online questionnaire-based survey sent to all undergraduates at the Chinese University of Hong Kong. Over 170 students responded. This was followed by 'persistent observation' (a term used in Herring, 2004) of the most frequented Web 2.0 sites of selected participants, as identified in the questionnaire. As with the Flickr research, the survey questionnaire for this study also covered questions about the participants' linguistic practices in different online and offline domains, such as the language(s) they said they would use when writing an email to a professor, or when they looked up information for their assignments on the web. This first phase then served as a basis for designing an interview protocol for the second phase of the study.

The core data came from detailed technobiographic-style interviews with 20 participants. *Technobiographies*, in short, are people's narratives of life stories in relation to technologies. The notion itself is inspired by the traditional narrative approach to interviews, where an interviewee tells a story about certain significant events in life (Linde, 1987). In her major work on women's technology-related lives, Kennedy (2003) defines technobiographies as participants' accounts of everyday relationships with technology. Technobiographies can be viewed as participants' encounters with technology "at various times and in various locations throughout their histories" (Ching & Vigdor, 2005: 4). In a technobiographic interview, questions may range from participants' past experiences with technology, to their current uses and anticipated future uses. More details of this approach can be found in Page et al. (2014: ch. 7). Technobiographic interviews are also highly reflexive in nature. How people feel about what they do with technologies is crucial in understanding possible changes in their practices.

The Hong Kong student participants tended to share a similar set of linguistic resources. That is, they spoke Cantonese as their primary language in everyday life, while having knowledge of standard written Chinese, a standard variety taught in school and used in institutional contexts. Written Cantonese, a non-standard local variety of writing, may also be used for informal purposes. English is one of the official languages in Hong Kong and is taught as a second language in school. Mixing Chinese and English in utterances has become a prevalent linguistic practice among these young people. Each technobiographic interview started with a screen-recording session, where a participant was asked to go online for about 30 minutes with their screen activities recorded using the screen-recording software *Camtasia*. This was followed by a face-to-face interview lasting between 30 and 50 minutes, in which the screen-recording was played back and the participant went through and discussed the recorded online activities with the researcher. The

150   D. Barton and C. Lee

interview questions revolved around their linguistic practices in online and offline contexts in different phases and domains of their lives, as well as new topics that emerged during the conversation. Follow-up interviews were carried out via the private message function on Facebook (as all participants were active Facebook users).

The analysis developed in two ways. First, each participant was treated as an individual case, a vertical slicing of the data, as discussed in Barton and Hamilton (1998/2012: ch. 4). Second, themes across the whole data set were explored, representing a horizontal slicing. For each participant, a profile was first created according to the information obtained from field notes and the various stages of data collection described above. All of the transcripts were coded using the qualitative data analysis software *ATLAS.ti* to examine emerging patterns across participants. What the participants wrote on Facebook, their blogs, and IM was also analysed as data related to technobiographies. These new media provide new affordances and ways for online users to write about themselves, thus allowing them to create and constantly update their own autobiographies in real time. For this particular work, we extended the meaning of technobiography and coined the term 'techno-linguistic biography' as these narratives are primarily concerned with language use in people's technology-related lives.

The researcher's stance and identity

Finally in this discussion of methodology, we highlight our multiple roles as researchers of multilingualism online. Just as good qualitative research makes other aspects of its methodology explicit (Barton, 2012), it is essential for researchers themselves to make their relationship to the research, that is, their stance, explicit in their analyses and writing. As data collection and analysis proceeded, we became aware of the multiple roles we played at different stages of these studies. First of all, our interests in researching new media, be it IM, Flickr, or Facebook, had all grown out of our own personal participation on these sites. As well as studying the sites and users, we constantly reflected upon our own participation and on numerous multilingual encounters online, thus carrying out our own auto-ethnographies, or in Kosinets' terms, our "auto-netnographies … autobiographical personal reflection on online community membership" (Kozinets, 2010: 188). In the IM research, for instance, the researcher's familiarity with IM-specific language features in Hong Kong (such as code-switching and a range of Asian emoticons) allowed her to compare her own experience and knowledge with the informants' practices, thus discovering the diversity in text-making practices surrounding IM. In our Flickr research, both of us have been active users of Flickr for more than eight years. We make contact with Flickr users from all parts of the world and comment on their photos in different languages. We both know an additional language besides English – one of us is a Chinese–English bilingual and the other has knowledge of Spanish, coincidentally the two

Researching online texts and practices 151

most used languages on Flickr after English. Our multilingual experiences on Flickr inform our understanding of the relationship between English and other languages online, adding insider perspectives to our research. To the research participants, we were sometimes their Flickr contacts or friends; at other times, we were their site visitors and researchers. Some of these roles were consciously and immediately reflected upon as we interacted with our informants, while others became apparent as we analysed the data.

Throughout our language online research, we have combined traditional research methods with online methods such as online interviewing. We see virtual ethnography (Hine, 2000) as an additional way of understanding participants' lives rather than something that competes with or challenges traditional methods. It also does not mean that the researcher has to shift their research site entirely to an online context – the online and the offline work closely with each other in our approach. This can also be referred to as connective ethnography (Hine, 2007; Leander, 2008). A language-focused approach to digital literacies research, supported by traditional and online research methods, provides a rich array of data for us to understand the relationship between online and offline lives or, more precisely, how the online is embedded in participants' everyday lives. This is crucial in understanding participants' text-making as situated literacies. When applied to linguistics or discourse-based research, virtual ethnography also proves extremely useful in understanding the social functions of computer-mediated discourse.

Conclusion and directions for future research

We began the chapter by reviewing methods that have been adopted in research on multilingualism online. While previous studies tended to document interactional patterns in relation to models developed in face-to-face conversations, we have highlighted the approaches adopted in our own research projects on multilingualism online. Through the three case studies of IM, Flickr, and Web 2.0 sites, we have demonstrated the importance of investigating both multilingual texts and the practices they are part of.

There is now a body of research on multilingual practices in digital communication, but it is still limited compared to English-based studies. Language choice and multilingual practices, whether online or offline, change over time. Many web users have now had many years of experience of new media use, and longitudinal studies need to be carried out to trace changes in linguistic practices at different stages of people's lives. It is also becoming obvious that existing theories and methods of multilingualism cannot capture the new forms of multilingual encounters taking place on the web as a result of global flows of people, objects and ideas (Barton, 2011; Martin-Jones et al., 2012). Other concepts such as superdiversity (Blommaert & Rampton, 2011), polylingualism (Jørgensen, 2008), translanguaging (Li Wei, 2011) and metrolingualism (Otsuji & Pennycook, 2010) have been taken up by sociolinguists to rethink the notion of 'multilingualism' and to

152 *D. Barton and C. Lee*

move on from more static notions such as 'speech community'. Such developments are essential to account for the fluidity of language practices and the mobility of people online and offline (see Androutsopoulos (2015) for some ways in which these concepts fit in with research on language in social media). In response to these new practices, mixed-methods research that combines text analysis and ethnographic data that pays attention to details of people's actual writing activities can shed more light on the ever-changing nature of digital communication.

References

Androutsopoulos, J. (2007) 'Language choice and code-switching in German-based diasporic Web forums', in B. Danet & S.C. Herring (eds) *The Multilingual Internet: Language, Culture, and Communication Online.* New York: Cambridge University Press, 340–361.

Androutsopoulos, J. (2008) 'Potentials and limitations of discourse-centered online ethnography'. *Language@Internet*, 5, article 8. Online: www.languageatinternet.de/articles/2008.

Androutsopoulos, J. (2015) 'Networked multilingualism: some language practices on Facebook and their implications'. *International Journal of Bilingualism* 19(2), 185–205.

Auer, P. (1999) 'From codeswitching via language mixing to fused lects: towards a dynamic typology of bilingual speech'. *International Journal of Bilingualism* 3(4), 309–332.

Barton, D. (2011) 'People and technologies as resources in times of uncertainty'. *Mobilities* 6(1), 57–65.

Barton, D. (2012) 'Ethnographic approaches to literacy research', in C.A. Chapelle (ed.) *The Encyclopedia of Applied Linguistics.* Oxford: Wiley-Blackwell.

Barton, D. & Hamilton, M. (1998/2012) *Local Literacies: Reading and Writing in One Community.* London: Routledge.

Barton, D. & Lee, C. (2013) *Language Online: Investigating Digital Texts and Practices.* London: Routledge.

Blommaert, J. & Rampton, B. (2011) 'Language and superdiversity: a position paper', *Working Papers in Urban Languages and Literacies*, paper 70.

Ching, C.C. & Vigdor, L. (2005) 'Technobiographies: perspectives from education and the arts', paper presented at the First International Congress of Qualitative Inquiry, Champaign, IL.

Danet, B. & Herring, S.C. (eds) (2007) *The Multilingual Internet: Language, Culture, and Communication Online*, New York: Cambridge University Press.

Herring, S.C. (2004) 'Slouching toward the ordinary: current trends in computer-mediated communication'. *New Media and Society*, 6(1), 26–36.

Hine, C. (2000) *Virtual Ethnography.* London: Sage.

Hine, C. (2007) 'Connective ethnography for the exploration of e-science'. *Journal of Computer-Mediated Communication* 12(2), 618–634.

Hinrichs, L. (2006) *Codeswitching on the Web: English and Jamaican Creole in Email Communication.* Amsterdam: John Benjamins.

James, G. (2001) 'Cantonese particles in Hong Kong students' English emails'. *English Today* 17, 9–16.

Researching online texts and practices 153

Jørgensen, N.J. (2008) 'Polylingual languaging around and among children and adolescents'. *International Journal of Multilingualism* 5(3), 161–176.

Kennedy, H. (2003) 'Technobiography: researching lives, online and off'. *Biography* 26(1), 120–139.

Kozinets, R.V. (2010) *Netnography*. London: Sage.

Lam, W.S.E. (2009) 'Multiliteracies on instant messaging in negotiating local, translocal, and transnational affiliations: a case of an adolescent immigrant', *Reading Research Quarterly* 44(4), 377–397.

Leander, K.M. (2008) 'Toward a connective ethnography of online/offline literacy networks', in J. Coiro, M. Knobel, C. Lankshear & D.J. Leu (eds) *Handbook of Research on New Literacies*. New York: Lawrence Erlbaum, 33–66.

Lee, C. (2007) 'Linguistic features of email and ICQ instant messaging in Hong Kong', in B. Danet & S.C. Herring (eds) *The Multilingual Internet: Language, Culture, and Communication Online*, New York: Cambridge University Press, 184–208.

Lee, C. (2014) 'Language choice and self-presentation in social media: the case of university students in Hong Kong', in P. Seargeant & C. Tagg (eds) *The Language of Social Media: Community and Identity on the Internet*. London: Palgrave Macmillan, 91–111.

Leppänen, S. (2007) 'Youth language in media contexts: insights into the functions of English in Finland'. *World Englishes* 26(2), 149–169.

Lexander, K.V. (2012) 'Analyzing multilingual texting in Senegal: an approach for the study of mixed language SMS', in M. Sebba, S. Mahootian & C. Jonsson (eds) *Language Mixing and Code-Switching in Writing*. New York: Routledge, 146–169.

Li, Wei (2011) 'Moment analysis and translanguaging space: discursive construction of identities by multilingual Chinese youth in Britain'. *Journal of Pragmatics* 43(5), 1222–1235.

Linde, C. (1987) 'Explanatory systems in oral life stories', in D. Holland & N. Quinn (eds) *Cultural Models in Language and Thought*. New York: Cambridge University Press, 343–366.

Mafu, S. (2004) 'From the oral tradition to the information era: the case of Tanzania'. *International Journal of Multicultural Societies* 6(1), 53–78.

Martin-Jones, M., Blackledge, A. & Creese, A. (2012) 'Introduction: a sociolinguistics of multilingualism for our times', in M. Martin-Jones, A. Blackledge & A. Creese (eds) *The Routledge Handbook of Multilingualism*. Abingdon, Oxon: Routledge, 1–29.

Myers-Scotton, C. (1998) 'A theoretical introduction to the markedness model', in C. Myers-Scotton (ed.) *Codes and Consequences: Choosing Linguistic Varieties*. New York: Oxford University Press, 18–38.

Otsuji, E. & Pennycook, A. (2010) 'Metrolingualism: fixity, fluidity and language in flux'. *International Journal of Multilingualism* 7(3), 240–254.

Page, R., Barton, D., Unger, J. & Zappavigna, M. (2014) *Researching Language in Social Media*. London: Routledge.

Paolillo, J.C. (2007) 'How much multilingualism? Language diversity on the Internet', in B. Danet & S.C. Herring (eds) *The Multilingual Internet: Language, Culture, and Communication Online*. New York: Cambridge University Press.

Sebba, M. (2012) 'Researching and theorising multilingual texts', in M. Sebba, S. Mahootian & C. Jonsson (eds) *Language Mixing and Code-Switching in Writing*. New York: Routledge, 1–26.

Sebba, M., Mahootian, S. & Jonsson, C. (eds) (2012) *Language Mixing and Code-Switching in Writing*. New York: Routledge.

154   *D. Barton and C. Lee*

Siebenhaar, B. (2006) 'Code choice and code-switching in Swiss-German internet relay chat rooms'. *Journal of Sociolinguistics* 10 (4),481–509.

Su, H.-Y. (2007) 'The multilingual multiorthographic Taiwan-based internet', in B. Danet and S.C. Herring (eds) *The Multilingual Internet: Language, Culture and Communication Online*. New York: Oxford University Press, 64–86.

Tagg, C. & Seargeant, P. (2012) 'Writing systems at play in Thai–English online interactions'. *Writing Systems Research* 4(2), 195–213.

Warschauer, M., El Said, G.R. & Zohry, A.A. (2007) 'Language choice online: globalization and identity in Egypt', in B. Danet & S.C. Herring (eds) *The Multilingual Internet: Language, Culture, and Communication Online*. New York: Cambridge University Press, 303–318.

10 Investigating multilingualism and multisemioticity as communicative resources in social media

Sirpa Leppänen and Samu Kytölä

Introduction

This chapter discusses the role of multilingualism and multisemioticity as key resources in communication in contemporary interest-driven social media. We approach social media as translocal arenas for social interaction and (trans)cultural activities (Leppänen, 2008, 2012; Kytölä, 2016) which complement and intertwine with participants' offline realities in different ways. In particular, we show how the investigation of such activities can benefit from a multidimensional framework drawing on insights from several fields, including online ethnography, the study of multimodality, and research into computer-mediated discourse (CMD).

In this chapter, we show that communication in contemporary social media involves resources provided by language(s), varieties, styles and genres, alongside other semiotic resources – textual forms and patterns, visuality, still and moving images, sound, music, and cultural discourses – as well as their mobilization in processes of *entextualization* (Bauman & Briggs, 1990; Blommaert, 2005) and *resemiotization* (Iedema, 2003; Leppänen et al., 2014). We thus explore the ways in which the 'language' of social media can be a bricolage of multiple, intertwined semiotic materials (Kress & Van Leeuwen, 2001; Scollon & LeVine, 2004; Leppänen et al., 2014) which are socially significant to the participants, groups, or communities of practice (Wenger, 1998) involved in digitally mediated social actions and engaged in different ways with the (super)diversity (Vertovec, 2007) that they encounter. Finally, we draw attention to the cultural aspects of much of today's social media discourse, and we argue that the deployment of multilingual and multisemiotic communicative means is integral to contemporary forms of collaborative and participatory knowledge construction and cultural production.

Our contributions to the themes of this volume are thus the following: Since the new sociolinguistics of multilingualism should take "account of the new communicative order and the particular cultural conditions of our times" (Martin-Jones & Martin, this volume), we argue that social media are increasingly important and meaningful sociocultural and communicative niches for participatory prosumer cultures (Burgess & Green, 2009; Leppänen

156 S. Leppänen and S. Kytölä

et al., 2014) building around shared activities. Reflecting the mobility patterns in the current phase of globalization and the increased availability of digital communication technologies, social media practices have become translocal and transcultural to an extent hitherto not experienced (Peuronen, 2011; Leppänen, 2012; Jousmäki, 2014; Kytölä, 2016). Moreover, as research on late modern forms of multilingualism ought to retain "a central concern with the processes involved in the construction of social difference and social inequality" (Martin-Jones & Martin, this volume), we want to draw attention to the construction and evaluation of difference in informal interest-driven social media settings.

Methodologically, the study of these resources calls for an ethnographic and multidimensional theoretical and methodological approach (Blommaert & Rampton, 2011; Martin-Jones et al., 2012; Leppänen, 2012). In what follows we argue for the usefulness of combining insights from the study of bi-/multilingualism with online ethnography, (computer-mediated) discourse studies, cultural studies, and the study of multisemioticity (multimodality).

Defining social media

Social media are often seen fairly narrowly (see e.g. boyd & Ellison, 2007) as referring to *social networking sites* within which participants construct a (semi-)public profile, establish connections with friends with whom they share content and interact in various ways, view and traverse their list of connections and those made by others. We wish to broaden this perspective on social media and define them as any digital applications that build on the ideological and technological premises and foundations of Web 2.0 (e.g. Herring, 2013) allowing the creation, exchange, and circulation of user-generated content (Kaplan & Haenlein, 2010) and enabling interaction between users. This broader view of social media encompasses both applications explicitly building on the idea of mutual exchange of content and digital environments in which the main content can consist of single-authored or monophonic discourse (such as blogging or YouTube videos) but that also offer an opportunity to authors and recipients to interact with one another (such as discussion sections of blog sites). In principle, this broader definition could even be extended to include more traditional media, too, as long as they make it possible for participants to interact with each other, i.e. to be 'social'. This multifaceted conceptualization of social media suggests that the scope of social media research can, in fact, be much more wide-ranging than is often the case, involving different types of (social, print-based, audio-visual, and aural) media as well as their interconnections.

Combining insights from several approaches

In what follows, we outline the key research lines for our study of social media, followed by an illustration with two empirical examples. First, we draw on recent

Language and semiosis in social media research   157

developments in the study of multilingualism (see Creese & Blackledge, 2010; Leppänen & Peuronen, 2012), where empirical and theoretical orientations to non-digital (offline) contexts have adapted and responded to the social changes brought about by globalization. This is shown in critical and ethnographic work within the new sociolinguistics (e.g. Heller, 2007, Blommaert, 2010), entailing the inclusion of a more holistic understanding of the diversity of linguistic styles and varieties (Coupland, 2007; Jørgensen et al., 2011), and heteroglossia (Bailey, 2007; Androutsopoulos, 2011; Lähteenmäki et al., 2011), as well as the significance of space and social semiotics in multilingual environments (e.g. Scollon & Scollon, 2003; Blommaert, 2005, 2010, 2013). Many of these studies have highlighted the convergence between linguistic ethnography and discourse studies.

Second, we have the recent advances in research into CMC/CMD (computer-mediated communication, computer-mediated discourse, respectively), where scholars have noted how the latest advances in social media, or Web 2.0 (e.g. Androutsopoulos, 2008; Thurlow & Mroczek, 2011a; Tannen & Trester, 2013), further complicate contemporary digital discourses due to their growing multimodality and interactive participation options. Iconic formats of Web 2.0 currently include Facebook, Twitter, YouTube and Instagram; each application allows different kinds of affordances and constraints for linguistic and other forms of semiotic expression, and, importantly, each one has been adopted and appropriated differently for personal and community-based usages by different groups of people (Thurlow & Mroczek, 2011a; Androutsopoulos, 2011; Peuronen, 2011; Leppänen et al., 2014).

In contrast to the more text-based 'first wave' and the 'second wave' (retrospective labels) of CMC and CMD research, the 'third wave' (Androutsopoulos, 2008; Herring, 2013; Kytölä, 2013) is interested in connections between online and offline social activities, by default defining (and accepting) diversity, heteroglossia, and complexity as research targets. The participatory character of digital discourse (Androutsopoulos, 2013) is rapidly changing, too: Anyone with an internet connection and a device can now be a producer as well, "writing the self" online (Barton & Lee, 2013: 67–85) on their own. Participation and digital production are becoming more accessible and at least potentially democratic. As Kytölä (2013: 190) points out, "this may be reflected in increasing affordances to use more and more languages online compared with the present, and compared to the English-dominated prehistory of the internet."

Just as many researchers on multilingualism have adopted a more ethnographic perspective (e.g. Blommaert, 2010; Creese & Blackledge, 2010; Blommaert & Rampton, 2011), similar lines have been outlined by scholars of CMC (e.g. Hine, 2000). A prime example is Androutsopoulos's discourse-centered online ethnography (DCOE) (Androutsopoulos, 2008; Kytölä & Androutsopoulos, 2012), which entails venturing beyond screen-based, 'log data' observations through long-term observation of and contact with the individuals and communities online. Such a multi-method approach adds

158 S. Leppänen and S. Kytölä

perspectives on interpretations of both online discourse events and offline social activity; methodologically, DCOE is eclectic, versatile, and triangulative, including participant observation, informal interviews, contact by online messaging contact, or participating in moments of digital discourse with the people being researched (Androutsopoulos, 2008; Peuronen, 2011; Kytölä & Androutsopoulos, 2012).

The study of multimodality/multisemioticity (e.g. Kress & Van Leeuwen, 2001; Iedema, 2003; Scollon & Scollon, 2003; Scollon & LeVine, 2004; Thurlow & Mroczek, 2011a) offers key insights into the study of contemporary digital practices, in which meaning-making occurs in increasingly complex multisemiotic ways. A central tenet from this field that enhances our understanding of diversity in digitally mediated practices is the *a priori* equal salience of different modes and modalities of communication: Even language and discourse scholars should not give by default greater preference to verbal language in contemporary digital communication. Instead, the social meanings and communication preferences of different communities and individuals should be investigated carefully, with ethnographic grounding. In addition to the growing role of pictures and videos in the diversity of digital practices, we should pay attention to issues of layout, design and positioning, as well as complex mediation chains and sequences between online (and offline) spaces.

As digital social media are increasingly multisemiotic and interconnected both translocally and 'rhizomatically'[1] across boundaries of nations, ethnicities, languages, genres, and formats, the notions of *resemiotization* and *entextualization* are useful means to conceptualize and model the complex interconnections between the various layers of elements in contemporary digital communication. We define them as follows:

Resemiotization: the unfolding and rearticulation of meaning across modes and modalities, from some groups of people to others; emphasizes the need for socio-historical exploration and understanding of the complex processes which constitute and surround meaning-makings (Iedema, 2003; Leppänen et al., 2014).

Entextualization: earlier socially, culturally, and historically situated, unique pieces of discourse are lifted out of their original context and transmitted, by quoting/echoing them, by inserting them into another discourse (Bauman & Briggs, 1990: 73; Blommaert, 2005: 47; Leppänen et al., 2014; Androutsopoulos, 2014).

Resemiotization and entextualization are crucial in the investigation of social media discourse since, in them, the circulation and appropriation of discourse is multiplied, accelerated, and highlighted. Resemiotization and entextualization are potential but so far under-used models and concepts for the description of the complex interrelations between moments and nexuses of social action between online and offline sites.

Language and semiosis in social media research 159

The investigation of interest-driven social media practices also needs to draw on insights from cultural studies as digital practices are often geared towards the creation, appropriation, sharing, and evaluation of culture, i.e. towards active 'prosumption' (consumption cum production) of cultural products and practices. Social media build on the existence of participatory convergence culture that enables individuals to engage in collective meaning-making practices (Jenkins, 2008; Burgess & Green, 2009: 10). Meaning-making practices are no longer organized primarily along local, ethnic, or national identifications; rather, it is the engagement with transcultural flows and translocal identification lines which both consist of and go beyond the local and the global (Leppänen et al., 2009). Translocality (Kytölä, 2016; Leppänen et al., 2009) can be manifested in various ways, but for our present purposes, its mutually constructive relationship with language and other semiotic practices is particularly significant. It is often a motivated and meaningful option for participants to draw on resources provided by more languages than one (Leppänen, 2012; Leppänen & Peuronen, 2012; Kytölä, 2013) and to deploy them in ways that resonate with or contest the normative expectations of the specific discourse contexts.

Multilingual and multisemiotic social media discourses and practices: two empirical cases

We will now turn to two empirical examples which illustrate recurrent types of multilingual and multisemiotic digital discourses and practices through which the participants make sense of and construct their social and cultural identities and realities online. The first example is that of Finnish footballers' Twitter usages and the uptake and responses they arouse within a football community, while the second example analyzes a particular cultural practice of crafting transgressive music videos, known as *shredding*.

In the analysis of the examples we engage with the interface between epistemology and methodology, interrogating theories of how language, discourse, and meaning-making work in social realities and weighing up methodological choices and ways of approaching and investigating the complexity of discourse. In more concrete terms, this means that, with the help of the two cases, we wish to demonstrate how the analysis crucially draws on (i) our long-term ethnographic study of social media cultures, environments and practices which enables us to gain emic understandings and develop thick descriptions of social media practices, (ii) linguistic, discourse, and multimodal analysis to describe and interpret the forms, discourse functions, and local sociocultural meanings of participants' semiotic choices, (iii) new sociolinguistics to describe resources provided by language/s, registers, and styles, and their meanings and effects, and (iv) cultural studies, new media studies, and fan studies to describe and explain the 'culturality' of the practices.

160 S. Leppänen and S. Kytölä

From professional footballers' jocular online performance to metapragmatic policing: entextualization of multilingual resources

Football (soccer) culture is rich ground for research on multilingual and multisemiotic practices, because football is a highly translocal, transcultural and polycentric sport, which is reflected in texts and talk about football (Kytölä, 2013). Despite the significant role that football and football culture play in the formation of many trans- and multicultural contexts, its study has not been properly incorporated into studies on multilingualism and diversity (Kytölä, 2013). Our first example entails an entextualization and resemiotization chain of online and offline social activities by three Finnish football professionals (Mikael Forssell, b.1981; Mika Väyrynen, b.1981; Tim Sparv, b.1987), who use the extremely popular micro-blog platform Twitter as a means of self-expression, contact with their friends and fans, and socializing with each other. The life and career trajectories of these Finnish footballers are characterized by mobility and transculturality, with contract-based sojourns in Britain, the Netherlands, Germany, Sweden, Denmark, and Finland. Their digital writing, thus, has diverse audiences transnationally, and their Twitter updates (tweets – quick messages limited to 140 characters) show orientation to multiple centers and audiences (Kytölä & Westinen, 2015), with linguistic choices varying between Finnish, Swedish, English, German, and Dutch. Furthermore, they display great 'intra-linguistic' variety of register and styles, with Sparv leaning toward (and being close to) standard varieties, and the other two leaning toward colloquial, non-standard, slang style(s).

English is perceivably the dominant language choice in tweets by each of them, but they frequently use other languages and mix between them. They also post pictures, hyperlinks to websites, indications of the addressee of the tweet (indicated by the '@' sign) and the popular indexing practice called 'hashtagging' (indicated by '#'), which enables Twitter users to quickly index, search for, or follow particular keywords or phrases. Figure 10.1 is a brief sample from Forssell's Twitter (August 2011), involving interaction with Tim Sparv.

This excerpt illustrates how the footballers can direct their tweets to each other yet make them publicly visible for their followers, often as performance aimed at entertainment. They use (features from) English for this recipro-cal communication, although they also share Swedish (home language) and Finnish (the main language in Finland) – languages which they would prob-ably use in face-to-face contact without non-Finnish interlocutors. Forssell's style is much more informal and non-standard than Sparv's; the linguistic/ stylistic diversity of their tweets notwithstanding, this sample seems rather representative in this respect.

Kytölä's long-time observation and online ethnography of Finnish football fandom (Kytölä & Androutsopoulos, 2012; Kytölä, 2013) identified a 'thick momentum' in the Twitter activity of the three players (Forssell, Sparv, and

Language and semiosis in social media research 161

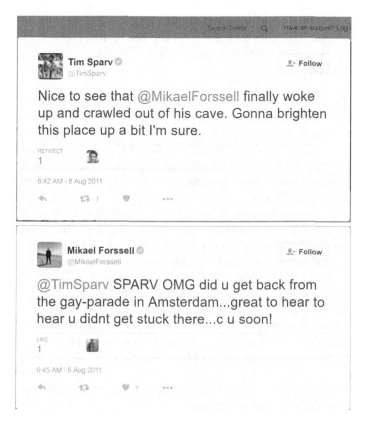

Figure 10.1 Mikael Forssell's Twitter.

Väyrynen), where they deployed several recurring linguistic features that can be associated with African American Vernacular English, or the register of 'gangsta' talk (see also Kytölä & Westinen, 2015). Below are two examples (text only, no screenshot) of tweeting sequences:

Väyrynen: @MikaelForssell wtf bro?harvoin kuullu et jäbä tyytyväinen jos et oo maalannu tai pelannu ... still keep ya head up n c ya next week
Translation from (colloquial) Finnish: wtf bro?<u>rarely heard ya happy when ya ain't scored or played</u> ... still keep ya head up n c ya next week
Forssell: @MikaVayrynen10 no enhän mä ookkaan mut gotta be happy for the lads ... ne ansaitsee ... mun aika tulee kun tulee ... u know bro! C u this week!!
Translation from (colloquial) Finnish: <u>well i'm not but</u> gotta be happy for the lads ... <u>they deserve ... my time comes when it comes</u> ... u know bro! C u this week!!

[...]
Sparv: @MikaelForssell Hey seriously, you got chocolate in your room??
Forssell: @TimSparv of course I do ... &4 a few euros I could offload a few grams to you ... but the price has 2 be right ... u know ... financial-crisis mate

The choice of Twitter, along with varieties and styles of English, for the jocular communication between the players highlights the affordances of Twitter: the discourse is simultaneously private and public, restricted and open, intimate and international, for friends and fans. Moreover, this is only a brief episode in the flow of Twitter updates and rhizomatic connections for Forssell, Sparv, Väyrynen and their colleagues, and for the diverse translocal audiences picking up their tweets.

To illustrate the open-endedness, hyperlinkability, and rhizomaticity of such digital discourses, let us explore the 'next stage' of the digital mediation chain (though this also happens nearly simultaneously). This online communication occurs within a community of Finnish football fans at the bustling online hub Futisforum2.org (Kytölä, 2012, 2013), who initiate and maintain metapragmatic, normatively oriented discussions on the acceptability and authenticity of the language of these tweets, notably non-standard English usages (see also Kytölä & Westinen, 2015). Examples of the community-based evaluations of the Twitter writing by Forssell, Väyrynen, and Sparv are shown below (translations from colloquial Finnish by SK):

> Could someone teach that lad how to write, when the media gets interested too? What do they now think about us etc.

> As if he would need any more space for his brainfarts – he has a hard time forming even 160 characters of text

On Futisforum2, there is entextualization of the tweets by Forssell, Väyrynen, and Sparv into the digital format and space of the web discussion forum. (Their tweets had earlier been representations, and thus entextualizations, of their offline social activity of physical exercise, chocolate eating and so on.) Along with quoting the players' tweets, the forum participants add a layer of metapragmatic evaluation and commentary on them, judging them as "bad English," "ridiculous," "pathetic," or alternatively, "entertaining," "wicked," or "lol stuff." These evaluations are made mostly in the mode of verbal language, emoticons (such as the sad face or the laughing face above), and hyperlinks; and they vary from explicit metapragmatic evaluations (e.g. "this

Language and semiosis in social media research   163

is retarded") to implicit metapragmatics whereby similar, 'mock gangsta' talk is used ("'Da Gangsta'. Str8 from da ghetto").

However, the meta-level evaluation further evolves into the adoption and appropriation of similar linguistic and stylistic features: some participants at Futisforum2 start using features that were mocked earlier and they use them in ways in which the line between mocking and 'second-order entertainment' gets blurred (see Kytölä & Westinen, 2015):

> "i feel rly stoopid right now, mate! gotta get me sum choco! ZÄDÄM!"
> "Yo dawg! Gr8 2 have u bak, 4real, man! Yo!"
> ("ZÄDÄM!" is a written representation of a colloquial, relatively infrequent Finnish exclamation that, to our best knowledge, has no primary meaning. It is likely to express e.g., enthusiasm, coming into sight, conjuring "a magic trick", etc.)

Finnish football enthusiasts' appropriation of these styles is not limited to new expressions and coinages in verbal language. A case in point is the cultural practice of Futisforum2 members (and no doubt many other online communities) to create stylized multisemiotic mockery by means of image manipulations juxtaposed with minimal excerpts of verbal language. For instance, one prolific member, nicknamed "Aarne Ankka," has become appreciated within the community and across various online sites for his minimalistic and obscene comic strips (with four panels), one of which mocked both Forssell's tweeting and his 'gangsta' English. Such creations represent another kind of multimodal resemiotization that has great potential for online circulation via social media. (We refrain from reprinting such examples here, but a Google image search with the search words "Aarne," "Ankka," and "Futisforum" will show a few examples.)

All these phases and discourse events show different attitudes and stances towards cultural diversity and multilingual language use, which remain negotiable and ambivalent; on the one hand, the footballers' tweeting and related social activities are considered entertaining and carefully crafted, on the other, they are portrayed as ridiculous and 'retarded.' The open-endedness and rhizomaticity of such digital practices is further illustrated by tracing the trajectories of Forssell's (and others') Twitter behavior into other online contexts and spaces (e.g. by searching for combinations of keywords with a search engine). The digital styles and practices emerging in the footballers' Twitter accounts spread not only to the hub Futisforum2 but also to blogs, comments sections of institutional online media, institutional media articles and, iteratively, to new social media platforms (Kytölä & Westinen, 2015).

In sum, the constellation of multilingualism (and, to a degree, multimodality) is influenced by and constructed through the transcultural domain of football (where actors are *mobile*), the present participants' life trajectories, and the fluid, transnational communities of practice (of fans, followers, colleagues, and media people). Moreover, they are characterized by the

164   S. Leppänen and S. Kytölä

affordances of digital media (Twitter, web forums, etc.) and the open-ended, rhizomatic connections between online (and offline) sites.

Shredding – multisemioticity as a key resource in cultural production in social media

Our second example illustrates a translocal, informal, and interest-driven cultural practice which crucially draws on and thrives on resemiotization – *shredding*. Shredding is a particular type of online fan activity which involves either "a style of guitar playing characterized by extremely fast flurries of notes and extremely distorted tones" or a parodic representation of such musical performances involving the extraction of "the audio track from a video (usually featuring an overblown, overrated rock guitarist)" and replacing it "with perfectly synchronized, very well played rubbish" (*Urban Dictionary*). The outcomes of shredding, our focus here, are shreds – music videos published on YouTube or the shredders' own websites – and these are the focus of active commentary and discussion by avid fans of shredding.

Shredding is typically conducted by devoted prosumer-fans of popular culture who, as members of a particular participatory culture, engage in activities of crafting, disseminating, and exchanging cultural content with their appreciative audiences. Shredding offers them a means of actively engaging with the objects of their interest and other fans: These include a range of semiotic resources for ridiculing highly revered popular music performances and artists. Shredders and their followers self-identify as members of their fan culture, and, through their own shredding activities and responses to and interactions around shreds by others, establish, negotiate, and maintain forms of appropriate practice and their indexicalities. These forms of practices and their indexicalities constitute a basis for judgments as to who is sufficiently authentic to legitimately pass as a member of shredder culture (see also Leppänen, 2012; Varis & Wang, 2011; Kytölä, 2012).

To illustrate shredding as a fundamentally interventional practice involving complex multisemioticity, we discuss a shred by one of its best known practitioners, StSanders. StSanders (aka Santeri Ojala) is a Finnish professional computer animator and media artist who has extended his expertise to shredding and has produced numerous shreds on well-known rock and pop bands and musicians. Thanks to his professionalism, musicality, versatility, and meticulousness, he has, in fact, become an online micro-celebrity (Senft, 2008). His work is followed, admired, discussed, imitated, and circulated by shredders and audiences both in Finland and around the world. He has become so popular that he has even attracted the attention of mainstream media, again, both in Finland and elsewhere. His shredding has also been acknowledged and admired by some of the musicians whom he has ridiculed. For example, a feature article in the *Wired*

Figure 10.2 The PISS shred (© Santeri Ojala, aka StSanders; reproduced by permission).

magazine in 2007 – itself an instance of resemiotization of StSanders' work – stated that

> [...] after links to the videos were posted [...], even some musicians were caught criticizing the (as one poster put it) "insanely bad" stylings of Clapton and Van Halen – only to later laugh along with everyone else once properly informed of the gag.
>
> (Phan, 2007)

One of the most popular of StSanders' works is a video of the US glam rock band KISS, which has been active since the 1970s. The shred is entitled PISS (see Figure 10.2), and it is a prime example of multimodal interventional resemiotization of content originally produced by someone else, so typical of late modern social media participatory cultures (see e.g. Leppänen et al., 2014).

The resemiotizations conducted by StSanders include the music, which has been recomposed, rearranged, and reperformed by StSanders, producing a piece that is melodically simple and rhythmically abrupt and angular, involving singing with a high-pitched, slightly off-key voice. StSanders also created new lyrics for the song and mediated these not only via the singing but also through subtitles. Further, the lyrics are designed so that they are in perfect lip sync with the original mouthings by the KISS singer on the video. In doing this, StSanders is, in fact, relying on the so-called *mondegreen*, or *soramimi*,

166 S. Leppänen and S. Kytölä

technique which is used in other transgressive social media practices (such as *buffalaxing*, see Leppänen & Häkkinen, 2012). Such practices involve a deliberate mishearing of utterances or lyrics, on the basis of which new lyrics and/or subtitles are created. These new lyrics and subtitles are as closely homophonic as possible with the words said or sung in the original footage. In this shred, because the homophonic lyrics are created on the basis of how they coincide with the original mouthing patterns by the KISS singer, the lyrics of the shred turn out to as an absurd string of one-liners which do not convey any coherent narrative at all. As an illustration, consider the beginning of the shred:

Extract from the PISS lyrics

> Ha ha ho ho Yah
> Ah! Wow, oh Bobby!
> [whistles]
> Kiai!
> I will never go to school
> 'cause it's not so nice
> and it's just so bizarre a place
> I just wanna eat pizza
> Bruce likes a tryphy!
> I feel so bad for you!
> I'm so good for me!
> For me!
> But I was paid to fly with you, Batman!
> Why you're bad, Phil
> And I can't stand the smell
> 'cause you make me...
> Ewww!
> Oh my!

Even though the new lyrics are thus basically nonsensical, in the context of the video, they are not totally senseless. This is because they could be interpreted as incrementally building up an image of the protagonist and/or singer as someone who really doesn't have a message to deliver at all. StSanders also represents this character as a sociolinguistically hybrid creature by assigning him a range of impressionistic accents, which approximate American, Italian, and more generic non-native English pronunciations.

The overall parodic effect of the shred is not only created on the basis of a range of resemiotizing operations, but also by complementing and juxtaposing them with some of the semiotic material of the original video, especially its ways of representing the performance of the band cinematically. The overall effect of all of these semiotic operations is a multidimensional parody of KISS, highlighting the superficiality, absurdity, and even narcissism of the kind of glam rock music genre they represent.

Language and semiosis in social media research   167

StSanders' shreds – as an example of translocal social media practice driven by a shared interest in globally prominent and influential popular cultural products – have themselves become globally viral and celebrated. For our purposes, they are an apt illustration of ways in which multisemioticity is drawn on in social media, and the ways it is taken up, appropriated, and disseminated as resources with which participants can identify. Participants engage with the particular activity culture, express themselves, communicate, interact and build up shared sociocultural worlds. StSanders' work also illustrates another important and recurrent facet of many interest-driven social media cultures: his trend- and norm-setting social media products have become an inspiration for others, and countless versions, adaptations, samplings, and imitations. In this sense, the virality of his products could even be argued to be creating affordances for the development of expertise. They exemplify how viral practices are quickly taken up, rehearsed, and applied by others – more or less successfully. In short, in their own ways, they function as vehicles for learning, as lessons in the multimodal 'language' and resemiotization activities of informal and interest-driven transgressive social media. As is already witnessed by StSanders himself and his micro-celebrity, which has brought him visibility and, no doubt, new work and financial opportunities, in the increasingly media(tion)-saturated world, such expertise can turn valuable and can have applicability in other (educational, professional, institutional) contexts, on- and offline.

Conclusion

In this chapter we have argued that in social media diversity 'happens' in multilingual and multisemiotic and highly mediated ways, necessitating a multidimensional theory-as-method approach. Our multidisciplinary approach and analyses of fluid and open-ended mediated discourse admittedly raise some thorny methodological challenges that need careful consideration and close, long-term contact with and observation of the sites, actors, and discourses one aims at investigating. These include the following:

- ensuring that the investigation of complex social media practices is 'multi-sited enough' so that salient aspects of the discourses and phenomena in focus are convincingly covered;
- identification of meaningful nexuses of practice and sites of engagement (Scollon & Scollon, 2004) in which particular multilingual or multisemiotic practices and styles emerge, thrive, circulate, are transformed, and possibly wither away;
- the delimitation and focusing of investigations to determine where to stop tracing the trajectories in qualitative research with the aim of holistic yet detailed description;
- treating digital practices as grassroots cultural production in which the borderline between producers and consumers of digital discourse is a blurred one, in a world where anyone with an internet connection and a digital device can copy, imitate, edit, and circulate different discourses.

168   *S. Leppänen and S. Kytölä*

In our discussion of two empirical cases, we have highlighted discourses and practices which are typical not only of informal, interest-driven social media but also, increasingly, of late modern, mediated *superdiversity* (Vertovec, 2007; Creese & Blackledge, 2010; Blommaert & Rampton, 2011) in more general terms – its recurrent and symptomatic complexity, mobility, and circulation (Arnaut, 2012; Leppänen & Häkkinen, 2012; Häkkinen & Leppänen, 2014). We have shown how these complex activities and meaning-makings are socially significant and culturally valuable to the participants and groups. Some degree of agency is always involved as participants and groups mobilize these resources as prosumers in sociocultural niches regulated by polycentric, 'post-Panopticon' normativities.

Our analysis also raises some more general points for the study of contemporary forms of cultural and semiotic diversity. Our first example highlighted multilingualism: Certain forms of multilingualism can be enhanced and enabled via certain digital media (affordances and constraints). The Finnish footballers' mutual but public Twitter exchanges and their various 'aftermaths' were shown to be a case in point. The second example showed that the same applies in the case of multisemioticity: In digital media, as with linguistic and discursive resources, it is a crucial means for communication and interaction.

Our examples can also emphasize the 'nothing new' caveat. The multilingual resources, as well as competence in the use of multimodal literacies, have to 'reside' *a priori* in the individuals and communities themselves. Despite the open-ended possibilities to 'copy-and-paste' from various online sources in the process of producing online discourse, there have to be certain prior experiences, 'competences,' and literacies available in order for the complex discourses to make sense, to produce the desired social meanings, or at least 'just enough' unambiguity in the middle of ambivalence for successful (and often entertaining) communication.

Note

1   We adopt this metaphor from Deleuze & Guattari (1987). This metaphorical usage represents an adaptation of a term in biology (the rhizome) and its extension to the social sciences. As opposed to linear, tree-like ("arborescent" in Deleuze & Guattari, 1987) structures, "rhizomatic structures" create connections between individuals, communities, or nodes of social action that are, by default, non-linear, non-chronological, non-hierarchical, and non-binary. The metaphor of the rhizome, therefore, allows for more complex and unpredictable connections, being suitable to the conceptualization of the social life of late modern digital discourses.

References

Androutsopoulos, J. (2008) 'Potentials and limitations of discourse-centered online ethnography', in J. Androutsopoulos & M. Beißwenger (eds) *Data and Methods in Computer-Mediated Discourse Analysis*. Special issue, *Language@Internet* 5. www.languageatinternet.org/articles/2008.

Language and semiosis in social media research 169

Androutsopoulos, J. (2011) 'From variation to heteroglossia in the study of computer-mediated discourse', in Thurlow & Mroczek (eds), 277–298.

Androutsopoulos, J. (2013) 'Participatory culture and metalinguistic discourse: performing and negotiating German dialects on YouTube', in Tannen & Trester (eds), 47–72.

Androutsopoulos, J. (2014) 'Moments of sharing: entextualization and linguistic repertoires in social networking'. *Journal of Pragmatics* 73 (Nov 2014), 4–18.

Arnaut, K. (2012) 'Super-diversity: elements of an emerging perspective'. *Diversities* 14(2), 1–16.

Bailey, B. (2007) 'Heteroglossia and boundaries', in Heller (ed.), 257–274.

Barton, D. & Lee, C. (2013) *Language Online: Investigating Digital Texts and Practices*. Abingdon: Routledge.

Bauman, R. & Briggs, C.L. (1990) 'Poetics and performance as critical perspectives on language and social life'. *Annual Review of Anthropology* 19, 59–88.

Blommaert, J. (2005) *Discourse*. Cambridge: Cambridge University Press.

Blommaert, J. (2010) *The Sociolinguistics of Globalization*. Cambridge: Cambridge University Press.

Blommaert, J. (2013) *Ethnography, Superdiversity and Linguistic Landscapes: Chronicles of Complexity*. Bristol: Multilingual Matters.

Blommaert, J. & Rampton, B. (2011) 'Language and superdiversity'. *Diversities* 13(2), 3–21.

boyd, d.m. & Ellison, N.B. (2007) 'Social network sites: definition, history, and scholarship'. *Journal of Computer-Mediated Communication* 13(1), 210–230.

Burgess, J. & Green, J. (2009) *YouTube: Online Video and Participatory Culture*. Cambridge: Polity Press.

Coupland, N. (2007) *Style: Language Variation and Identity*. Cambridge: Cambridge University Press.

Creese, A. & Blackledge, A. (2010) 'Towards a sociolinguistics of superdiversity'. *Zeitschrift Für Erziehungswissenschaft* 13(4), 549–572.

Deleuze, G. & Guattari, F. (1987) *A Thousand Plateaus: Capitalism and Schizophrenia*, trans. Brian Massumi. Minneapolis, MN: University of Minnesota Press.

Häkkinen, A. & Leppänen, S. (2014) 'YouTube meme warriors: mashup videos as satire and interventional political critique', in *Texts and Discourses of New Media* (Studies in Variation, Contacts and Change in English 15). Helsinki: VARIENG. Available at www.helsinki.fi/varieng/series/volumes/15/.

Heller, M. (ed.) (2007) *Bilingualism: A Social Approach*. Basingstoke: Palgrave Macmillan.

Herring, S.C. (2013) 'Discourse in Web 2.0: familiar, reconfigured, and emergent', in Tannen & Trester (eds), 1–25.

Hine, C. (2000) *Virtual Ethnography*. London: Sage.

Iedema, R. (2003) 'Multimodality, resemiotization: extending the analysis of discourse as multi-semiotic practice'. *Visual Communication* 2(1), 29–57.

Jenkins, H. (2008) *Convergence Culture: Where Old and New Media Collide*. New York: New York University Press

Jørgensen, J.N., Karrebæk, M., Madsen, L. & Møller, J. (2011) 'Polylanguaging in superdiversity'. *Diversities* 13(2), 23–37.

Jousmäki, H. (2014) 'Translocal religious identification in Christian metal music videos and discussion on YouTube', in L. Kaunonen (ed.) *Cosmopolitanism and Transnationalism: Visions, Ethics and Practices*. Helsinki: Helsinki Collegium for Advanced Studies, 138–158.

170 S. Leppänen and S. Kytölä

Kaplan, A.M. & Haenlein, M. (2010) 'Users of the world, unite! The challenges and opportunities of social media'. *Business Horizons* 53(1), 59–68.

Kress, G. & Van Leeuwen, T. (2001) *Multimodal Discourse: The Modes and Media of Contemporary Communication*. London: Oxford University Press.

Kytölä, S. (2012) 'Peer normativity and sanctioning of linguistic resources-in-use: on non-Standard Englishes in Finnish football forums online', in J. Blommaert, S. Leppänen, P. Pahta & T. Räisänen (eds) *Dangerous Multilingualism: Northern Perspectives on Order, Purity and Normality*. Basingstoke: Palgrave Macmillan, 228–260.

Kytölä, S. (2013) *Multilingual Language Use and Metapragmatic Reflexivity in Finnish Internet Football Forums. A Study in the Sociolinguistics of Globalization*. Doctoral thesis, University of Jyväskylä, Finland.

Kytölä, S. (2016) 'Translocality', in A. Georgakopoulou & T. Spilioti (eds) *Handbook of Language and Digital Communication*. London: Routledge, 371–388.

Kytölä, S. & Androutsopoulos, J. (2012) 'Ethnographic perspectives on multilingual computer-mediated discourse: insights from Finnish football forums on the Web', in S. Gardner & M. Martin-Jones (eds) *Multilingualism, Discourse and Ethnography*. New York: Routledge, 179–196.

Kytölä, S. & Westinen, E. (2015) "I be da reel gansta": a Finnish footballer's Twitter writing and metapragmatic evaluations of authenticity. *Discourse, Context & Media* 8, 6–19.

Lähteenmäki, M., Varis, P. & Leppänen, S. (2011) 'The shifting paradigm: towards a re-conceptualisation of multilingualism'. *Apples: Journal of Applied Language Studies* 5(1), 2–11.

Leppänen, S. (2008) 'Cybergirls in trouble? Fan fiction as a discursive space for interrogating gender and sexuality', in C.R. Caldas-Coulthard & R. Iedema (eds) *Identity Trouble: Critical Discourse and Contested Identities*. Basingstoke: Palgrave Macmillan, 156–179.

Leppänen, S. (2012) 'Linguistic and discursive heteroglossia on the translocal internet: the case of web writing', in M. Sebba, S. Mahootian & C. Jonsson (eds) *Language Mixing and Code-Switching in Writing: Approaches to Mixed-Language Written Discourse*. New York: Routledge, 233–254.

Leppänen, S. & Häkkinen, A. (2012) Buffalaxed super-diversity: representing the other on YouTube. *Diversities* 14(2), 17–33.

Leppänen, S. & Peuronen, S. (2012) 'Multilingualism on the Internet', in M. Martin-Jones, A. Blackledge & A. Creese (eds) *The Routledge Handbook of Multilingualism*. Abingdon, Oxon: Routledge, 384–402.

Leppänen, S., Pitkänen-Huhta, A., Piirainen-Marsh, A., Nikula, T. & Peuronen, S. (2009) 'Young people's translocal new media uses: a multiperspective analysis of language choice and heteroglossia'. *Journal of Computer-Mediated Communication* 14(4), 1080–1107.

Leppänen, S., Kytölä, S., Jousmäki, H., Peuronen, S. & Westinen, E. (2014) 'Entextualization and resemiotization as resources for identification in social media', in P. Seargeant & C. Tagg (eds) *The Language of Social Media: Identity and Community on the Internet*. Basingstoke: Palgrave Macmillan, 112–136.

Martin-Jones, M., Blackledge, A. & Creese, A. (2012) 'Introduction: a sociolinguistics of multilingualism for our times', in M. Martin-Jones, A. Blackledge & A. Creese (eds) *The Routledge Handbook of Multilingualism*. Abingdon, Oxon: Routledge, 1–29.

Language and semiosis in social media research 171

Peuronen, S. (2011) '"Ride hard, live forever": translocal identities in an online community of extreme sports Christians', in C. Thurlow & K. Mroczek (eds), 154–176.

Phan, M. (2007) 'Hilarious YouTube parodies "shred" guitar gods'. *Wired 10.17.07.* Available at http://archive.wired.com/entertainment/music/news/2007/10/shredders.

Scollon, R. & LeVine, P. (2004) 'Multimodal discourse analysis as the confluence of discourse and technology', in P. LeVine & R. Scollon (eds) *Discourse & Technology: Multimodal Discourse Analysis.* Washington, DC: Georgetown University Press, 1–6.

Scollon, R. & Scollon, S.W. (2004) *Nexus Analysis: Discourse and the Emerging Internet.* New York: Routledge.

Scollon, R. & Wong Scollon, S. (2003) *Discourses in Place: Language in the Material World.* Abingdon, Oxon: Routledge.

Senft, T. (2008) *Camgirls: Celebrity and Community in the Age of Social Networks.* New York: Peter Lang.

Tannen, D. & Trester, A.M. (eds) (2013) *Discourse 2.0. Language and New Media.* Washington, DC: Georgetown University Press.

Thurlow, C. & Mroczek, K. (2011a) 'Introduction: fresh perspectives on new media sociolinguistics', in Thurlow & Mroczek (eds), xix–xliv.

Thurlow, C. & Mroczek, K. (eds) (2011b) *Digital Discourse: Language in the New Media.* New York: Oxford University Press.

Varis, P. & Wang, X. (2011) 'Superdiversity on the internet: a case from China'. *Diversities* 13(2), 71–83.

Vertovec, S. (2007) 'Super-diversity and its implications'. *Ethnic and Racial Studies* 30(6), 1024–1054.

Wenger, E. (1998) *Communities of Practice: Learning, Meaning, and Identity.* Cambridge: Cambridge University Press.

11 Virtual ethnographic approaches to researching multilingualism online

Aoife Lenihan and Helen Kelly Holmes

In this chapter, we apply virtual ethnographic methods to the study of multilingualism in online contexts. The chapter begins with a brief outline of the evolution and current situation of multilingualism in online contexts. This is followed by an overview of virtual ethnography as a research method, before demonstrating its application to researching multilingualism. We also include a review of ethical issues in researching multilingualism online. Following this, we describe two of our own studies, which illustrate how virtual ethnography can be used to study top-down multilingualism in monologic web spaces, and also bottom-up multilingualisms in dialogic Web 2.0 contexts.

Multilingualism online

While the early development of the internet was dominated by English, leading to a concern that it would prove yet another threat to multilingualism, the evolution of the web, particularly in the last decade, has been largely multilingual. Linguistic diversity on the World Wide Web has grown due a variety of technological, political and economic factors (Internet Corporation for Assigned Names and Numbers, 2011; Unicode Consortium, 2012; Anderson, 2004) from a situation of English plus a limited number of large languages to a situation where the provision of multiple languages and the ability to use one's own language has, more and more, become the norm, albeit with major caveats. Facebook is available in 108 languages, Google in 132 and Wikipedia in 287. The computer no longer just speaks English (Crystal, 2011), rather there is a belief that other languages, such as Chinese, the second most used language online (Internet World Stats, 2016), will challenge the status of English on the web in the not too distant future (Phillipson, 2009; Wilhelm, 2010). In addition, smaller, lesser-used languages and languages not previously used in written form have also found space on the dialogic web, where speakers are jointly codifying their language (see Wright, 2006) and localising global content into their language (see Lenihan, 2013).

However, as it has become more multilingual, in terms of spatial, temporal and linguistic reach, this borderless space has, arguably, become increasingly characterised by a growing number of boundaries and controls. These are

Virtual ethnographic approaches 173

used to categorise and confine individuals to national boundaries and national language groupings (cf. Lenihan, 2011, 2014; Kelly-Holmes, 2006a, 2013). At the same time, these boundaries and controls have enabled the emergence of highly localised spaces of communication and interaction (Androutsopoulos, 2006). There has been, on the one hand, an emergence and growth of top-down multilingualism, as evidenced by the speed with which corporations and organisations seek to provide a greater variety of language options for consumers and users (Kelly-Holmes, 2006a, 2013), and, on the other, bottom-up multilingualism, whereby individuals are using spaces on the web to interact in hybrid multilingual ways, in 'lesser-used' languages (Van Dijk, 2009) and in languages that were previously unwritten (Wagner, 2011), and are creating new, mixed practices (Androutsopoulos, 2009, 2011). There is also a convergence of these two practices online, whereby web users are being looked to by corporations and organisations as a source or resource for multilingualism online, with many major WWW entities outsourcing their localisation efforts to their communities of users (O'Keeffe, 2009). They do so by crowdsourcing (Howe, 2006), whereby a piece of translation work, traditionally given to a professional translator, is now outsourced to a large group of people (hence 'crowdsourcing') who are typically not trained or specialist in that area. For example, Facebook, Mozilla Firefox, and Google have all used crowdsourcing for multilingualising their interface and content, with such groups being facilitated, supported and constrained by the relevant design and technology. The roles of both individual users and communities are thus 're-scaled' (Coupland, 2010), facilitated by technological developments and implemented by corporations and organisations.

Finally, it is important to remember that despite the continually increasing global reach and multilingualism of the web, many languages, speakers and communities continue to be excluded from the developing multilingual internet (Thurlow & Mroczek, 2011; Cunliffe, 2007). Furthermore, and potentially detrimental to future linguistic diversity, languages online are often conceptualised as being in competition with each other (Androutsopoulos, 2010), or dependent on and affecting each other in this cyberecology (Ivkovic & Lotherington, 2009), which often reproduces common-sense hierarchies and inequalities between languages offline.

Virtual ethnography

Virtual ethnography offers a useful means of researching the types of issues outlined above. Researching multilingualism online requires the multi-method, adaptive approach which virtual ethnography offers (cf. Domínguez et al., 2007; Fay, 2007; Greenhow, 2011). Ethnographic studies are very useful for investigating multilingual choices, options and practices on websites, since an ethnographic sensitivity "makes explicit the taken-for-granted and often tacit ways in which people make sense of their lives" (Hine, 2000: 5). Ethnographic approaches to everyday life, institutions and indeed the media are now all

174   *A. Lenihan and H. Kelly Holmes*

well established, and in recent years, the web has also come to be a focus for ethnographic approaches. The concept of travel to a site, which is inherent in traditional ethnography, is particularly useful in web-based ethnography, since the web enables new forms of mobility and 'travel', which result from the compression of time and space enabled by digital technology. Hine (2000) and others (e.g. Cavanagh, 1999) promote an ethnographic approach or the adoption of an ethnographic sensitivity to exploit: "ways in which ethnographic perspectives can be adapted to cast light on the construction of the Internet in use and focus on the locally situated occasional character of Internet use" (Hine, 2000: 5).

Virtual ethnography involves and permits different types of engagement with a range of sites: surfing the web and logging that surfing experience; observing a particular site; and lurking, the term for more systematic and long-term engagement with a site without open participation (Paccagnella, 1997) but involving downloading or archiving of material and the gathering and storing of screen shots, for example. The ethnography may then develop towards active engagement with and participation in the site (Hine, 2008; Markham, 1998). For example, the researcher may wish to reveal their identity and conduct interviews with the owners of the site and the participants in or members of the site (Hine, 2000). Not every ethnographic study will involve or require all these stages of engagement; the level of engagement should be determined by the research questions and purpose of the study. For some purposes, lurking/observing and downloading/archiving may be sufficient in order to document multilingualism on the web, although interviews with site originators and participants can enhance the data gathered.

When researching multilingualism online using a virtual ethnographic approach, the researcher must first suspend what is taken for granted in using the web; for example, the normal language with which they surf or look for a particular website. The process of searching and surfing and the relevant website(s) need to be fully documented in field notes and screenshots. In addition, the researcher should document and follow up on inter-textual and hyper-textual links in order to capture trajectories to and from the site through the web. For example, in some localised country- or region-specific sites, the links from those sites lead to sites/pages in English or another super-central language, or are not available, thus limiting how far one can 'travel' in a particular language. We can only really experience what this is like for the user by emulating the trajectory they would follow. This enables consideration of the gap between multilingual claims (Kelly-Holmes & Milani, 2011) and provision by corporate and new media entities. The researcher needs to be prepared to go where the hyperlinks lead. It is important to be flexible, since virtual ethnography works best as "an adaptive ethnography which sets out to suit itself to the conditions in which it finds itself" (Hine, 2000: 65). For example, when considering Facebook's approach to multilingualism, a link to its patent application for the Translations application was included in a post examined and this application was then accessed and examined as part of

Virtual ethnographic approaches 175

the study (cf. Lenihan, 2013). It is only through ethnographic engagement in sites that many supporting sites and documents can be discovered and investigated. Changes over time should be documented to enable a longitudinal analysis of the site(s). Screenshots are a major methodological tool, as they enable the researcher to document traversals and unique viewing and engagement experiences on the web (Lemke, 2002). Virtual ethnography accepts that every viewing experience is different and that a holistic account of a particular site is not possible. Instead, what can be said holds true for that particular view by that particular individual at that particular point in time and space. It is not stable or static and is constantly changing. So, rather than attempting to freeze the site in time and trying to stop the runaway world (Giddens, 2003) and fight against it, the concept of traversal allows the researcher to embrace it instead.

Ethical concerns

The use of virtual ethnography to examine multilingual interaction and multilingual communities online raises a number of ethical issues, including: how to gain informed consent in this domain, how to successfully render participants anonymous and whether to use direct quotations when reporting, given how easily searchable the web is. One of the primary ethical concerns here is whether communication online is public or private in nature. Both users and researchers are polarised in their views; some feel it is totally public in nature and therefore open to researchers without consent, while others view areas of the internet (such as chat rooms) as private (Flicker et al., 2004). Cavanagh (1999) believes that the public/private definition of interactive contexts is "relative to the definitions of those who occupy it". Recent work by Sveningsson (2005) finds that internet users do not perceive personal information they post online, such as their profile, diary and photo album, as private, leading her to conclude that "not only do users seem to be aware of the risk of having their material observed by others but also the attention from others is often what they seek" (Sveningsson Elm, 2009: 82). Sveningsson Elm (2009) outlines a number of possible questions to ask to gain a deeper understanding of the context of interest when considering whether an online research context is public or private. However, there is no simple answer when considering social network sites and other online contexts with this dichotomy in mind. For example, much has been written (e.g. Light & McGrath, 2010; Zimmer, 2010) on ethical considerations for research on individual users' Facebook profiles, which, although they are within the same website as Lenihan's (2011, 2013, 2014) study, constitute completely different contexts from that of the community space of, say, the Translations app. While there are complex ethical issues involved in using virtual ethnography to investigate interaction and online communities, the use of this adapted model for examining multilingualism on the monologic web (i.e. where the interaction is primarily one-directional, see Kelly-Holmes, 2006a, 2013)

176   *A. Lenihan and H. Kelly Holmes*

fortunately raises few concerns. Lurking and observing are much easier in cyberspace than in physical space, since access to online corporate and institutional sites does not need to be negotiated in the same way as when a researcher wants access to an offline institutional or corporate site in order to examine multilingualism. Another major advantage of virtual ethnography is that the 'field' can be accessed whenever the researcher has time, not just when participants have time and are available.

A major challenge of this approach, however, is the sheer quantity of data that can be accumulated and the issue of archiving it. As part of a virtual ethnography, the following types of secondary and primary data can be gathered: the field notes recording the researcher's observations about finding sites, changes on sites, etc.; screenshots documenting multilingual provision and practices; statistics about site traffic and, in the case of social networking sites, data about response rates, participation numbers, etc. (see Herring, 2004), secondary texts, and links and trajectories. Decisions about when to stop following links, which are potentially limitless, and establishing a cut-off point beyond which one will not observe the site are problematic. Another challenge is the constant change which is inherent in the study of online environments. This is something all virtual researchers have to deal with and overcome. Sites can disappear and can change completely in a very short space of time. The virtual ethnographer therefore needs to accept that "understandings of the Internet are, at most, only locally [and temporally] stable phenomena" (Hine, 2000: 147).

Having outlined the basis of virtual ethnography for investigating multilingualism online, we will now look at two specific studies. The first involves research into multilingualism on corporate websites on what can best be termed the monologic web, with corporations using an online presence to market products and project a global image. The second involves looking at how the social network Facebook promotes multilingualism on the dialogic web among its users and members. On dialogic websites, communication and interaction are two way and interaction is usually between members.

Researching multilingualism on the corporate web

Virtual ethnography works very well with a linguistic landscape analysis of corporate sites designed to investigate corporate multilingualism on the dialogic web. Since it was introduced by Landry and Bourhis (1997), a linguistic landscape approach has been advanced by many scholars as a methodology for investigating multilingualism (e.g. Shohamy & Gorter, 2009). The concept of linguistic landscape represents an attempt to account for the visual presence of particular languages in the public space as a reflection of and contribution to ethnolinguistic vitality, i.e. the relative strength of these languages in terms of their status and functions as 'living languages' within their immediate speech communities and beyond, particularly in minority language spaces and sites of complex multilingualism. The technique involves documenting visual multilingualism (and also monolingualism) by systematically counting the presence and frequency of languages on public signs in various domains, including signs which are and are not subject to language policy and planning directives.

The idea behind the linguistic landscape approach is that the visibility of particular languages could reflect their relative position in the sociolinguistic hierarchy, and that a greater visibility of one particular language could send the message that this is the dominant language. Thus, the visibility and visual positioning of particular languages could be used as a way of revealing common-sense ideologies about language(s) that are prevalent in a particular society. As Heller (2008: 518) tells us, "our ideas about language are not neutral; we believe what we believe for reasons which have to do with the many other ways in which we make sense of our world and make our way in it". The languages we see around us every day are considered to be part of this, whether or not we speak them, understand them or recognise them, or whether we are only just able to acknowledge that they are not 'our' language.

Linguistic landscape analysis informs the process of language status planning and investigates the effectiveness of such planning initiatives in minority language spaces. Language planners working in such spaces have both responded to and initiated linguistic landscape studies by reversing what is seen to be an imbalance in visual multilingualism and/or monolingualism and by introducing legislation which requires that the minority language is printed on public signs in addition to the relevant dominant language (e.g. Wales, Ireland) or that it appears on its own (e.g. Quebec). Linguistic landscape studies have not just concerned themselves with the presence and frequency of languages on public signs, but they have also focused on the visual positioning of different languages on the signs. Again, this notion that the positioning of languages is important has also been taken up by language planners, who now often require that the existing visual hierarchy is reversed by placing the minority language on the top of the sign above the dominant language (e.g. in Ireland, where Irish is placed above English) (see Shohamy & Gorter, 2009; Gorter et al., 2011, for examples of studies). Clearly, then, such approaches represent a concern with the material properties of the printed language, rather than with what is being communicated by the printed language, since, in many cases, the content is the same (e.g. on road signs, where the same place name is given in parallel versions). More recently, focus in linguistic landscape studies has moved to the web (e.g. Kelly-Holmes, 2006a, 2006b; Ivkovic & Lotherington, 2009).

In combination with the virtual ethnographic approach outlined above, linguistic landscape analysis has been applied in the study of multilingualism in gateway sites on the web. Gateway sites are portals run by organisations, search engines, corporations, etc., which, as the name suggests, offer access through a gateway, to the web or to other sites. Typically, such sites filter users – often on the basis of language and/or location – and guide them in different directions towards localised content. Thus, the

178   *A. Lenihan and H. Kelly Holmes*

ways in which they carry out this filtering and organisation are not just a way of looking at current levels of linguistic diversity on the web, but also impact on the future development of multilingualism on the web. For example, a researcher interested in multilingualism on corporate sites could start by looking at a site like the McDonald's international gateway site, which asks users to select the region (Asia Pacific, Latin America, North America, Europe, Middle East & Africa) they are visiting from. Each of these regional versions of the site has different language options, content and information according to the geographical location they correspond to. As discussed above, the researcher would go through the various steps outlined earlier (auditing and describing the site, following links to and from the site, researching the background to the site and secondary material about the corporation). Using screenshots and fieldwork notes, the researcher would observe the site over a defined period of time, asking the following questions:

1. How many different languages appear on the site? This is an absolute number, so it includes token uses of a language (linguistic fetish and language display). It is also important to document both written and aural incidences.

2. Which languages are present and which languages are not present? Are there any languages present that were not anticipated? Are there any languages absent that were actually anticipated?

   Hindi is a very obvious absence on the McDonald's site – it is one of the languages in the world with the largest number of speakers. It is considered by De Swaan (2001) to be a 'supercentral' language. Whereas, in contrast, some European languages (e.g. Estonian) with relatively small numbers of speakers are present.

3. Roughly how much space is devoted to the use of each language? Is it equal for all languages? How far can the user go in a particular language?

   The level of localisation on the individual sites is fairly comparable. This has improved massively over the last ten years since we have been looking at sites like McDonald's. For example, in 2005, there were no sites in Arabic for McDonald's. By 2006, limited Arabic was available on MENA (Middle East and North African sites) and this has evolved from having Arabic on the surface only to having all content and hyperlinks fully localised into Arabic in the last few years. This sort of insight is, of course, only possible with long-term observation.

4. How are language options indicated? Are they indicated by flags, maps, words? Do they appear in the language itself or in English?

   In the case of McDonald's, the language options are indicated in English. By clicking on the country link, the user arrives at localised

Virtual ethnographic approaches 179

language content, for example in Chinese, but they need English in order to navigate to this point.

5. Do different languages have different functions?

> As we can see with the McDonald's site, English is increasingly playing the role of global lingua franca. It is constructed as the 'neutral', 'commonsensical' option for managing and guiding traffic to and through the gateway site. Also, English is generally available as an option on sites, even where it is not the official language of the country, and it is used tokenistically, almost in visual ways on many of the sites.

6. What are the differences between the official or *de facto* language policy in certain countries and actual language provision on the gateway site?

> There are considerable differences between national, official language policy and the use of languages on the McDonald's gateway for a particular country. Take, for example, the case of Singapore. Despite Singapore's official multilingual policy, the McDonald's Singapore site is entirely in English with no other language options.

Researching multilingualism in social network sites

Virtual ethnography is traditionally used to consider new interactive media domains such as social network sites in order to investigate the sociolinguistic realities and new media language practices of minority language users, communities and stakeholders. Facebook is a particularly rich site for investigating these realities and practices. One especially interesting dimension to multilingualism on Facebook is how it comes about – namely through the crowdsourcing Translations app. This allows us to look into multilingualism on the Facebook social network site in two ways. We will illustrate this with reference to the case of the Irish language. On the one hand, we have Facebook's 'top-down' language policy and, on the other, we have the language policy developed by the Irish Facebook Translations community in a 'bottom-up' manner. We can then examine two particular aspects of the site, using virtual ethnographic methods: first, the discourse of Facebook as an entity and that of the community of translators as they developed the Irish language version, and second, the design of the Translations app itself to examine how this has affected multilingualism on the site.

Some researchers are prescriptive: for example, both Abdelnour Nocera (2002) and Mann (2006) outline four- and five-stage frameworks, respectively, for carrying out virtual ethnographic studies. The approach to virtual ethnography outlined here, however, is grounded in the particulars of the study, and so it developed, was adapted and 'unfolded' (Gajjala, 2006) as the research progressed. Rather than setting out a number of steps to be followed in a linear pattern, we outline here the approach taken, the decisions taken, the choices made and the lessons learnt.

180 *A. Lenihan and H. Kelly Holmes*

Virtual ethnographers have their own version of an arrival story, discussing how they negotiated access, observed online interactions, communicated with internet users, etc. (Hine, 2000). The arrival story of this ethnography is twofold: Lenihan (the researcher on this project in Ireland) first encountered the Translations app when she read an email newsletter *Cogar* from Gaelport, an Irish language organisation (Gaelport, 2009). This immediately sparked Lenihan's interest, leading her to log in to Facebook and add the Translations app to her personal Facebook profile. After a brief look at the app and the Irish community of translators, its possibilities for study and investigation became apparent. Second, the ethnographic work began in January 2009. Lenihan's timing was fortunate in that observation began when the Irish Translations app was at stage two and had an active and growing community of translators. Also, this was a time when Facebook was working on and developing both the app and its approach to multilingualism. This ethnographic timeliness allowed Lenihan to watch as Facebook, the app itself, and the Irish translation progressed in real time. She was in the same time zone and country of the majority of the Irish language translators, and as discussions on the Discussions board were asynchronous, she was able to experience their communications as the translators did themselves. As time went on, the pace of change and development of the app slowed down and it seemed to lose its popularity with users, with the number of active Irish and other language translators decreasing, and indeed it seemed to become less important to Facebook itself, with queries from translators/users going unanswered and no developments for long periods. This demonstrates the benefit of long-term virtual ethnographic engagement, affording the possibility of observing such changes.

Lenihan's fieldwork diary comprised two elements: a diary with handwritten notes and the screenshots taken of the Facebook social network site, the Translations app and other data sources encountered. Data were also recorded by printing and downloading in the case of audio/video. At an early stage, her field notes outlined the various aspects of the app itself and how it worked, and Lenihan noted down further questions to follow up on as they came to mind, e.g. "How are languages added to the app?" As time progressed, her field notes became shorter and almost patterned. The main activities involved looking for changes in the app and noting the stats of the numbers of translators involved, translations submitted, etc. Also, as Kozinets (2010) writes, data collection does not occur independently from data analysis, they are intertwined. In this study, Lenihan's notes reflected this with potential lines of analysis being noted as data was being gathered.

To ascertain what information Facebook made available on its website regarding the Translations app and to learn as much as possible about it, Lenihan carried out a Google search of the Facebook domain using the advanced search option on a number of occasions. The first search of this kind generated 3,550 results, which she searched through for relevant information and data. Lenihan also carried out wider Google searches looking for information and perspectives on the app outside of the Facebook domain as

Virtual ethnographic approaches 181

she saw necessary. Referring to her own case study, Hine (1998) emphasises how the heart of the ethnography must always be on what one has identified as 'the field' and the interactions within it, although the ethnography may need to follow different connections, as discussed previously. In this study, a thematic analysis was undertaken of Facebook's publications, the text of the app itself and the Discussions board of the Irish Translations app. This was done to identify common language ideologies in relation to multilingualism, to glean as much information as possible about the Translations app and about the design and workings behind it.

Approximately six months into this ethnography, it became clear that some level of online participation was needed to give a true insight into how the app worked and how it worked from the perspective of the translators. Participation was necessary to ascertain what information was available to translators as they translated and voted and to ascertain how much they knew about how the app actually worked, i.e. questions such as: when does a vote become a winning translation? Could they see who voted for their translations? Could they see the number of votes they received? Were they notified of other translations being submitted? Could they vote on their own translations? Participating at this point also allowed Lenihan to test theories as to how the app worked and further her understanding. She does acknowledge that this was not a fully naturalistic ethnography, however, as Markham (1998) points out, an ethnographer inevitably has an impact on a study. Recalling experience in the field, Markham writes as follows:

> Every action I made that influenced the project became a text that engaged and interacted with a multiplicity of other texts. In the process of organizing and doing this study, I was taking part in the organization of that which was to be the study.
>
> (1998: 18)

To participate in the Translations app, Lenihan created a second Facebook profile as a researcher, which contained information about her academic background, interests, the current research, its aims, theoretical framework, the nature of the research, and arrangements regarding confidentiality, etc. This profile allowed her to ascertain and record the level of knowledge and information the translators had about how the app worked. She was in the privileged position of knowing more about the app than the translators involved but she could also experience the app as a translator. Her profile, as ethnographer, also allowed her to receive emails and updates from Facebook in relation to the Translations app and other Facebook issues in various languages.

Discussion and conclusion

In this chapter, we hope to have shown the manifold possibilities for studying multilingualism online and we hope to have demonstrated why

182   A. Lenihan and H. Kelly Holmes

virtual ethnographic approaches are particularly suited to this purpose. Some especially fruitful areas for future research, building on work done to date, would be to investigate the 'filter bubble' (Pariser, 2012) effect on multilingualism caused by new technologies. In effect, what this means is that individuals would be assigned to a linguistic bubble – on the basis of linguistic and geographic data gathered about them, following their web history – and this would be carried through the web, thus filtering out multilingual 'noise' and effectively making their travel through the web as monolingual, localised and personalised as possible. Another highly significant area for virtual ethnographic research would be the long-term impact of crowdsourcing on the multilingualism of the web, particularly in relation to small and previously unwritten languages, as well as the evolution of technologies such as Google Translate, which render the web a multilingual machine that is fed by speakers (to paraphrase Tim Berners-Lee). As the web grows and becomes increasingly normalised in people's lives across the globe, according to current trends, multilingualism seems set to increase, and virtual ethnographic methods will need to develop in line with these changes.

References

Abedelnour Nocera, J.L. (2002) 'Ethnography and hermeneutics in cybercultural research: accessing IRC virtual communities'. *Journal of Computer-Mediated Communication* 7(2). Online journal, available: http://onlinelibrary.wiley.com/.

Anderson, C. (2004) 'The long tail', *Wired*, 10 October, available: www.wired.com/wired/archive/12.10/tail.html?pg=2&topic=tail&topic_set=.

Androutsopoulos, J. (2006) 'Multilingualism, diaspora and the internet: codes and identities on German-based diaspora websites', *Journal of Sociolinguistics* 10(4), 520–547.

Androutsopoulos, J. (2009) 'Policing practices in heteroglossic mediascapes: a commentary on interfaces', *Language Policy* 8, 285–290.

Androutsopoulos, J. (2010) 'Localizing the global on the participatory Web', in N. Coupland (ed.) *The Handbook of Language and Globalization*. Oxford: Wiley-Blackwell, 203–231.

Androutsopoulos, J. (2011) 'From variation to heteroglossia in the study of computer-mediated discourse', in C. Thurlow & K. Mroczek (eds) *Digital Discourse: Language in the New Media*. Oxford: Oxford University Press, 277–298.

Cavanagh, A. (1999) 'Behavior in public: ethics in online ethnography'. *Cybersociology* 6. Available at: www.socio.demon.co.uk/magazine/6/cavanagh.html.

Coupland, N. (2010) 'Introduction: sociolinguistics in the global era' in N. Coupland (ed.) *The Handbook of Language and Globalization*. Oxford: Wiley-Blackwell, 1–27.

Cunliffe, D. (2007) 'Minority languages and the internet: new threats, new opportunities', in M. Cormack & N. Hourigan (eds) *Minority Language Media: Concepts, Critiques and Case Studies*. Clevedon, UK: Multilingual Matters, 133–150.

Crystal, D. (2011) *Internet Linguistics*. Abingdon, Oxon: Routledge.

De Swaan, A. (2001) *Words of the World: The Global Language System*. Cambridge: Polity Press.

Virtual ethnographic approaches 183

Domínguez, D., Beaulieu, A., Estalella, A., Gómez, E., Schnettler, B. & Read, R. (2007) 'Virtual ethnography'. *Qualitative Social Research* 8(3). Special issue of an online journal. Available at: www.qualitative-research.net/

Fay, M. (2007) 'Mobile subjects, mobile methods: doing virtual ethnography in a feminist online network'. *Forum: Qualitative Social Research* 8(3), Article 14. Online journal, available at: www.qualitative-research.net/.

Flicker, S., Haans, D. and Skinner, H. (2004) 'Ethical dilemmas in research on internet communities'. *Qualitative Health Research* 14(1), 124–134.

Gaelport (2009) 'Déan cairdeas le ... .feidhmchlár (Facebook as Gaeilge!)/Make friends with ... .feidhmchláir'. *Cogar*, Eagrán 21, 20 January, available: www. gaelport.com/uploads/documents/edition21.html [accessed 15 May 2012].

Gajjala, R. (2006) 'Cyberethnography: reading South Asian digital diasporas', in K. Landzelius (ed.) *Native on the Net: Indigenous and Diasporic Peoples in the Virtual Age*. London: Routledge, 272–291.

Giddens, A. (2003) *Runaway World: How Globalisation Is Reshaping our Lives*. London: Taylor & Francis.

Gorter, D., Marten, H.F. & van Mensel, L. (eds) (2011) *Minority Languages in the Linguistic Landscape*. Basingstoke: Palgrave Macmillan.

Greenhow, C.M. (2011) 'Research methods unique to digital contexts: an introduction to virtual ethnography', in N.K. Duke and M.H. Mallette (eds) *Literacy Research Methodologies*. New York: The Guilford Press, 70–86.

Heller, M. (2008) 'Language and the nation-state: challenges to sociolinguistic theory and practice'. *Journal of Sociolinguistics* 12, 504–524.

Herring, S.C. (2004) 'Computer mediated discourse analysis' in S.A. Barab, R. Kling & J.H. Gray (eds) *Designing for Virtual Communities in the Service of Learning*. Cambridge: Cambridge University Press, 338–376.

Hine, C. (1998) 'Virtual ethnography', paper presented at *Internet Research and Information for Social Scientists '98*, Bristol, UK, 25–27 March.

Hine, C. (2000) *Virtual Ethnography*. London: Sage.

Hine, C. (2008) 'Virtual ethnography: modes, varieties, affordances', in N.G. Fielding, R.M. Lee & G. Blank (eds) *The Sage Handbook of Online Research Methods*. London: Sage, 257–270.

Howe, J. (2006) 'Crowdsourcing: a definition', *Crowdsourcing* [online], 2 June, available: http://crowdsourcing.typepad.com/cs/2006/06/crowdsourcing_a.html.

Internet Corporation for Assigned Names and Numbers (2011) 'About', *ICANN* [online], available: www.icann.org/en/about/ [accessed 16 November 2011].

Internet World Stats (2016) 'Internet world users by language', *Internet World Stats* [online], 30 June, available: www.internetworldstats.com/stats7.htm [accessed 9 September 2016].

Ivkovic, D. & Lotherington, H. (2009) 'Multilingualism in cyberspace: conceptualising the virtual linguistic landscape'. *International Journal of Multilingualism* 6(1), 17–36.

Kelly-Holmes, H. (2006a) 'Multilingualism and commercial language practices on the Internet'. *Journal of Sociolinguistics* (Special issue on The Sociolinguistics of Computer-Mediated Communication), 10(5), 507–519.

Kelly-Holmes, H. (2006b) 'Irish on the World Wide Web: searches and sites'. *Journal of Language and Politics* (Special issue on the Multilingual Internet) 5(1), 217–238.

Kelly-Holmes, H. (2013) '"Choose your language!" Categorisation and control in cyberspace', *Sociolinguistica* 27, 132–145.

184   A. Lenihan and H. Kelly Holmes

Kelly-Holmes, H. & Milani, T.M. (2011) 'Thematising multilingualism in the media'. *Journal of Language and Politics* 10(4), 467–489.

Kozinets, R.V. (2010) *Netnography: Doing Ethnographic Research Online*. London:Sage.

Landry, R. & Bourhis, R. (1997) Linguistic landscape and ethnolinguistic vitality. *Journal of Language and Social Psychology* 16 (1), 23–49.

Lemke, J. (2002) 'Travels in hypermodality'. *Visual Communication* 1(3), 299–325.

Lenihan, A. (2011) ' "Join our community of translators": language ideologies and Facebook', in C. Thurlow & K. Mroczek (eds) *Digital Discourse: Language in the New Media*. Oxford: Oxford University Press, 48–64.

Lenihan, A. (2013) *The Interaction of Language Policy, Minority Languages and New Media: A Study of the Facebook Translations Application*. Unpublished PhD thesis, University of Limerick, Ireland.

Lenihan, A. (2014) 'Investigating language policy in social media: translation practices on Facebook', in P. Seargeant & C. Tagg (eds) *The Language of Social Media: Community and Identity on the Internet*. London: Palgrave Macmillan, 208–227.

Light, B. & McGrath, K. (2010) 'Ethics and social networking sites: a disclosive analysis of Facebook'. *Information Technology and People* 23(4), 290–311.

Mann, B.L. (2006) 'Virtual ethnography and discourse analysis', in B.L. Mann (ed.) *Selected Styles in Web-Based Educational Research*. Hershey, PA: Information Science Publishing, 439–456.

Markham, A.N. (1998) *Life Online: Researching Real Experience in Virtual Space*, Walnut Creek, CA: AltaMira Press.

O'Keeffe, I.R. (2009) 'Music localisation: active music content for web pages'. *Localisation Focus* 8(1), 67–80.

Paccagnella, L. (1997) 'Getting the seat of your pants dirty: strategies for ethnographic research on virtual communities'. *Journal of Computer Mediated Communication* 3(1). Online Journal, available: http://onlinelibrary.wiley.com/.

Pariser, E. (2012) *The Filter Bubble: How the New Personalized Web Is Changing What We Read and How we Think*. New York: Penguin.

Phillipson, R. (2009) *Linguistic Imperialism Continued*. New York: Routledge.

Shohamy, E. & Gorter, D. (2009) *Linguistic Landscape: Expanding the Scenery*. New York: Routledge.

Sveningsson, M. (2005) 'Ungdomars köns- och identitetsarbete på Internet' [Young people's gender and identity work on the internet], in B. Axelsson & J. Fornäs (eds) *Kulturstudier i Sverige. Nationell forskarkonferens* [Cultural Studies in Sweden: a National Research Conference]. Norrköping, Sweden: Linköping University Electronic Press.

Sveningsson Elm, M. (2009) 'Question three: how do various notions of privacy influence decisions in qualitative internet research?', in A.N. Markham & N.K. Baym (eds) *Internet Inquiry: Conversations about Method*. Los Angeles, CA: Sage, 69–87.

Thurlow, C. & Mroczek, K. (2011) 'Introduction: fresh perspectives on new media sociolinguistics', in C. Thurlow & K. Mroczek (eds) *Digital Discourse: Language in the New Media*. Oxford: Oxford University Press, xix–xliv.

Unicode Consortium (2012) 'The Unicode Consortium', *Unicode Consortium* [online], available: www.unicode.org/consortium/consort.html [accessed 4 November 2012].

Van Dijk, Z. (2009) 'Wikipedia and lesser-resources languages'. *Language Problems and Language Planning* 33(3), 234–250.

Wagner, M. (2011) 'Luxembourgish on Facebook: language ideologies and discourse types on group pages', in R. Sánchez Prieto (ed.) *Minority Languages and the Social Web*. Berlin: Peter Lang, 39–52.

Wilhelm, A. (2010) 'Chinese – the new dominant language of the internet', [online], 21 December, available: http://thenextweb.com/asia/2010/12/21/chinese-the-new-dominant-language-of-the-internet-infographic/.

Wright, S. (2006) 'Regional or minority languages on the World Wide Web', *Journal of Language and Politics* 5(2), 189–216.

Zimmer, M. (2010) '"But the data is already public": on the ethics of research in Facebook'. *Ethics and Information Technology* 12(4), 313–325.

Part 4

Multilingualism in research practice

Voices, identities and researcher reflexivity

12 Reflexive ethnographic research practice in multilingual contexts

Marilyn Martin-Jones, Jane Andrews and Deirdre Martin

Introduction

Ever since the first sociolinguistic and ethnographic studies of multilingualism were undertaken, in the mid twentieth century, researchers have been drawing on multilingual resources in the conduct of their research. Some have drawn on the resources within their own communicative repertoires. Others have worked in multilingual research teams or with interpreters and translators. For decades, multilingual research practice was a taken-for-granted, unremarkable aspect of the research process in the fields of sociolinguistics and the ethnography of communication, until the advent, from the mid 1980s onwards, of feminist, post-colonial and post-modern critiques of ethnography (e.g. Clifford & Marcus, 1986; Harding, 1987; Bhabha, 1994) and the turn to reflexivity across the social sciences. The ripple effect of this epistemological shift began to be felt in research on multilingualism in the 1990s.

Now, two decades later, there is a significant body of work on the nature and scope of research practice in multilingual contexts (e.g. Andrews, 2013; Chimbutane, 2012; Giampapa, 2011, 2013; Gregory & Ruby, 2011; Holmes & Martin, 2012; Holmes et al., 2013; Jones et al., 2000; Jonsson, 2012a, 2012b; Ndayipfukamiye, 1993), and there has been considerable innovation in and reflection on the conduct of fieldwork in linguistically and culturally diverse research teams (e.g. Blackledge & Creese, 2010; Creese et al., 2008, 2015a, 2015b; Gregory & Lytra, 2012; Jones et al., 2000; Martin, 2012). In this chapter, we will take stock of what we have learned thus far from this recent period of critical reflection. We will do this by organising our account around different aspects of fieldwork and, wherever possible, we will provide illustration with reference to qualitative and ethnographic research in different institutional and life-world settings.[1]

Before we move on to the main body of the chapter, we should briefly explain our use of terms such as 'linguistic and semiotic resources'. We have chosen these terms to distance ourselves from the widely held view of languages as fixed and countable entities – a view indexed in certain uses of the term 'multilingualism'. Instead, we wish to foreground the plural and complex nature of individual and group repertoires and focus attention on the

190   *M. Martin-Jones, J. Andrews and D. Martin*

range of communicative resources employed by speakers as they act and interact in different life-world and institutional contexts. Linguistic resources include accents, styles, genres, registers, different forms of spoken and written language and different writing systems. Semiotic resources include gestures, facial expressions, eye gaze direction, and other non-verbal modes of meaning-making. They also include the artefacts, images, photographs, diagrams and textual resources that are produced and used in communication on paper and on screen.

Linguistic and semiotic resources in fieldwork

Building relationships in the field and negotiating identities

In recent research in multilingual settings, there has been a move towards reflection on the way in which communicative resources are bound up with the negotiation of identities and with the building of researcher–researched relationships. These accounts have enabled us to unpack the 'identity' categories of 'outsider' and 'insider' and move away from representing the identities of researcher and research participants (and the relationship between them) in fixed and binary terms.

Here, we show how this reflexive work, with specific reference to language resources and forms of cultural knowledge, has furthered our understanding of some of the dynamics of researcher–researched relations and the ways in which language mediates these relations. We draw on examples of research that has been carried out in different social, cultural and historical contexts, so as to highlight the situated nature of multilingual research practice.

We turn first to an article in which Gregory and Ruby (2011) provide a candid retrospective account of several studies they carried out with families of Bangladeshi origin in East London, United Kingdom (UK). The studies focused on children's learning in and out of school, taking account of the role of parents, siblings and grandparents in this learning. Mahera Ruby was the Bengali-speaking researcher who was involved in these studies. She shared language resources and forms of cultural knowledge with the participating families. In their account of this research experience, Gregory and Ruby (2011: 168) remark that the process of gaining access to the home settings of the children had been "more difficult that we had anticipated". They note that their assumptions about what was shared, in terms of linguistic resources and cultural orientations, were not always well founded. Ruby's own contribution to the article reveals the complex processes of identification and relationship-building involved in doing fieldwork. It also reveals that, despite having some shared funds of linguistic and cultural knowledge, 'insiderness' always had to be negotiated *in situ* and it was often a matter of degree rather than unproblematic membership of a particular social category.

Our second example comes from a different urban context – in Toronto, Canada, and from post-fieldwork reflections by Giampapa (2011, 2013)

Reflexive ethnographic research practice 191

about the challenges involved in gaining access and building relations in the field. Giampapa (2011) writes about her experiences of conducting critical, ethnographic research with eight young Italian Canadians who were living and working in this context. As a researcher, her focus was on the ways in which these young people negotiated their identities in different urban spaces, particularly with respect to different Italian Canadian worlds and to diverse discursive representations of Italian-ness (*italianitá*). The initial challenges faced by Giampapa related partly to her own background as an Australian Italian and partly to the difference between the communicative repertoires of the participants and her own. Giampapa spoke standard Italian and English with a slight Australian accent, whereas the participants spoke different 'dialects' of Italian and had had varying degrees of access to standard Italian.

As the research progressed, Giampapa saw that the young people in her sample moved in and out of intersecting identities, related to class, gender and sexuality, and drew on different linguistic resources, in different domains of their lives – at home, at work, in their local church and in their worlds of sport and recreation. This posed a challenge for Giampapa as she followed their trajectories through the city. It turned out that there were some domain boundaries that she was not able to cross. For example, in one domain frequented by one male participant – a domain of football supporters – the dominant culture and associated language practices were almost exclusively masculine in nature. Giampapa (2013) describes her research practice in this urban context using the metaphor of a 'dance'. As she was conducting her fieldwork she was constantly negotiating her positionality as a researcher and negotiating her relationship with the research participants using different communicative resources. As time went on, she indicates that she became more accustomed to the steps and the rhythm of the dance, the relationships developed and her insights became richer.[2]

Our third example comes from research in Sweden, from a study carried out by Jonsson (2012a, 2012b) in a bilingual (Swedish–Spanish) school in Stockholm. Jonsson herself is a fluent speaker of Spanish, who has heritage links with Peru on the maternal side of her family. The focus of her study was on the vernacular varieties of Swedish and Spanish employed by students in the school in their interactions with each other. The research participants included a sample of students, their parents and their Spanish-speaking teachers. Jonsson reports that, in the early stages of the study, her relationship with the parents and the teachers was cordial and relatively formal. However, over time, the relationship began to change. This change was clearly indexed by a move towards greetings involving a kiss on either cheek – a shared Latino resource for signalling friendliness and closeness.

The key thing to note here with regard to all three studies, is that the fieldwork involved extended engagement – a key dimension of ethnographic work – leaving ample space for the nature of the researcher–researcher relationship to be negotiated and to evolve over time. So we see that the building of researcher–researched relations in the field involves much more than a one-off decision about language use with research participants. Rather, it is a matter of ongoing negotiation and possible shifts in the nature of the relationship over time. This process can also involve fluid and nuanced use of communicative resources, including verbal and non-verbal resources, to index different degrees of insiderness, solidarity or empathy.

Working with interpreters and planning the use of different linguistic resources

Thus far, we have considered examples of research in multilingual settings, where the researchers shared some language resources and forms of cultural knowledge with the research participants. In settings where researchers work in collaboration with interpreters and translators, the negotiation of identities and the building of relationships in the field becomes yet more complex and fluid. There is ongoing discussion in the research literature of the challenges of working in this way (e.g. Andrews, 2013; Temple & Edwards, 2002).

For example, Andrews (2013) writes about the issues arising from her research collaboration with an interpreter, as part of a wider educational research project on out-of-school learning amongst multilingual families in the UK. During the fieldwork for this project, she found that, in mediating the interactions at different moments during research encounters, the interpreter shaped the interaction in significant ways.[3] This finding echoed the observations of Temple and Edwards (2002).

In Andrews' part of the wider study, a fieldwork strategy for the conduct of the interviews had been planned in advance with the interpreter. It was agreed that the interpreter would pose the questions in the language preferred by the research participants, and would then convey the responses to Andrews in English. During the actual research encounters, the interpreter also began by engaging in explicit negotiation of language choice with the participants. These initial moves allowed for the building of a rapport before the more formal, scripted phase of the interview.

Drawing on these and other experiences in the field, Andrews argues that interpreters should be considered to be an integral part of a research team and they should be involved in detailed discussion of the roles and responsibilities taken on by different members of the team when engaging in multilingual research encounters of this kind. She also argues that account needs to be taken of the time and resource implications of working in this way with interpreters. In addition, she notes that ethnographic research lends itself particularly well to detailed research design, planning and innovation which anticipates the need for different linguistic and semiotic resources. We return to this important point in the final section of the chapter.

Developing reflexive practice around the production and use of fieldwork texts

The importance assigned to writing in the field, and to the production of fieldwork texts, is indexed by the presence of the morpheme 'graph' in the word 'ethnography'. Clifford (1990: 51) noted that ethnographers have conventionally been represented as writing three broad kinds of texts during their fieldwork: field notes, transcripts and descriptions. The writing of field notes has been seen as a process of "inscription" and the jotting down of notes to "fix an observation". The process of transcription has been depicted as the writing down of the words of research participants (including those captured in audio-recordings of interactions or of ethnographic interviews). The process of description has been characterised as "the making of a more or less coherent representation of an observed cultural reality. While still piecemeal and rough, such field descriptions ... serve as a database for later writing and interpretation" (1990: 51–52). Clifford also indicated that this latter type of writing in the field is what Geertz (1973) called "thick description".

Having sketched this conventional picture of the texts produced by ethnographers in the field, Clifford (1990) also points out that, in actual ethnographic practice, the distinction between these different kinds of texts often gets blurred. The practices of text production and use in the field are actually much more complex. Moreover, in the decades since Clifford published this article, there has been considerable diversification of textual practices in ethnographic fieldwork. The design of research projects varies but, nowadays, a wide range of texts are produced by both researchers and research participants, on paper and on screen, depending on the aims of the research. The genres of textual material gathered in the field vary from initial jottings, to fuller field-note records, to vignettes, researcher diaries, participant diaries, transcripts of interviews based on participant diaries, transcripts of ethnographic interviews and transcripts of follow-up interviews with participants about audio- or video-recordings of interactions in different settings. In multilingual contexts, different language resources traverse the production of such texts, as well as the talk that is exchanged around the texts. Close attention to the translingual practices involved in text production and in talk about texts can contribute to greater reflexivity in research practice.

In the section that follows, we illustrate these points with reference to ethnographic research carried out by individual researchers. Then, in the next section, we turn to collaborative ethnography developed by research teams which included researchers with different linguistic and cultural backgrounds.

Individual researchers revisiting multilingual field notes and interview transcripts

Revisiting multilingual field notes

One of the earliest reflections on the use and significance of different kinds of field notes in ethnographic research in multilingual settings appeared in a

194 *M. Martin-Jones, J. Andrews and D. Martin*

study conducted by Ndayipfukamiye (1993). This was a study of bilingual classroom discourse in primary schools in Burundi focusing, in particular, on Grade 5 classes where students make the transition from Kirundi-medium education to French-medium education. He made audio-recordings of classroom talk and created field notes of two kinds based on his classroom observations: first, initial handwritten notes and jottings; and second, a fuller set of field-note records. He describes his use of field notes as follows: "I took the field notes ... fairly quickly during lessons. Afterwards, I would go through them and add more comments" (1993: 59). As he scrutinised his hasty in-class notes, he became aware that he had been drawing on resources from three languages, Kirundi, French and English. His use of written resources from Kirundi and French mirrored quite closely the interweaving of Kirundi and French in talk around textbooks in the classes he had been observing, with Kirundi being used to talk about lesson content and about classroom texts that were all in French. He was not surprised to see himself using French since that was the main language of academic research and teaching in Burundi and its use was bound up with his own educational history. Reflecting on his use of English and on his own translingual practices, he wrote, as follows, in his thesis:

> The presence of English in my notes must be due to the [doctoral] training I have received in an Anglophone environment and, maybe, more significantly, to the future audience that I had in mind ... What my field notes indicate is that I draw freely from a multilingual repertoire but the languages within that repertoire have specialised functions and they are symbolic of different dimensions of my identity: as a Murundi, as a former [English] language teacher and as a researcher.
>
> (Ndayipfukamiye, 1993: 60)

Rereading and reviewing early field notes and jottings made while working in multilingual contexts like this serves as a means of taking stock of the nature and significance of different jottings and engaging in reflexive practice, as the researcher moves towards building an interpretive frame. As Blommaert and Dong Jie (2010: 37) put it:

> [field notes] tell us a story about an *epistemic process:* the way in which we tried to make new information understandable for ourselves, using our own interpretive frames, concepts and categories, and gradually shifting into new frames, making connections between earlier and current events, finding our way in the local order of things.
>
> (2010: 37)

As we see from Ndayipfukamiye's work, field notes taken multilingually make this epistemic process more visible.

Reflexive ethnographic research practice   195

Revisiting transcripts of interviews in a multilingual setting

In revisiting the transcripts of interviews conducted multilingually, during several months of linguistic ethnographic fieldwork, Chimbutane (2012) reveals the complex ways in which social meanings were exchanged between him, as researcher, and three research participants. His research was carried out in two villages in Mozambique where bilingual education provision was being developed, and where local African languages (Changana and Chope) were being used for the first three years of schooling, prior to the introduction of Portuguese in Grade 4. The research included the observation and audio-recording of multilingual classroom interaction, the writing of field notes, and interviews with teachers in the bilingual programme and with parents. Chimbutane explains that he had had a particularly long acquaintance with the teachers in the programme before embarking on this research, because he had been working in the field of bilingual education in Mozambique since 2003. He had worked in different capacities: "as a teacher trainer, researcher and advisor" (2012: 290). He had also been providing orientation to the teachers on the use of newly developed orthographies for African languages.

Once he had transcribed the teacher interviews, he took a close, retro-spective look at three of them: two interviews conducted primarily in Portuguese and one conducted primarily in Changana. He showed how the teachers drew on the knowledge they had built up about him over the years, positioning him in different ways as their conversations unfolded – "as a representative of the state education authorities, as a teacher trainer or as their messenger or advocate" (2012: 302). These positionings were indexed through the use of different linguistic resources, from Portuguese and from Changana, such as the use of particular terms of address. He also showed how the teachers took different stances and positioned themselves in dif-ferent ways – again, using different communicative resources – depending on the topic being addressed, e.g. expressing concern about the lack of teaching materials and articulating the views of parents about classroom conditions.

The kind of reflexive practice demonstrated by Chimbutane (2012), in revisiting these interview transcripts, reminds us of the important observa-tion made by Charles Briggs (1986) – in his landmark volume *Learning How to Ask* – about the potential of "speech, whether contained in interviews, myths, or 'natural conversations'" to provide "an ongoing interpretation of its own significance" (Briggs, 1986: 106). As we see from Chimbutane's (2012) account, close attention to the linguistic resources and sociolinguis-tic repertoires that speakers draw upon, in particular multilingual encoun-ters, in stance-taking, in self-positioning or in positioning others, gives us a useful lens on the ways in which situated multilingual practices index wider social meanings and relationships.

196   *M. Martin-Jones, J. Andrews and D. Martin*

Linguistic and cultural diversity in research teams: developing polyphonic ethnography and researcher reflexivity

Increasingly, social research in linguistically and culturally diverse settings is being carried out by teams of researchers yet, as Creese et al. (2008: 199) point out: "Little has been written generally about the process of working in research teams in the social sciences and in ethnography in particular". So, in this three-part section of the chapter, we consider different examples of studies (Creese et al., 2008, 2015a, 2015b; Gregory & Lytra, 2012; Jones et al., 2000) where there has been explicit discussion of: (1) the nature and scope of collaboration between research team members who have different sociolinguistic and cultural backgrounds; and (2) the opportunities for achieving researcher reflexivity opened up through collaborative research practice of this kind. We focus in particular on collaborative, reflexive practice that has been developed around the production of different kinds of texts during visits to the field.

Researching multilingual literacy practices, developing polyphonic research practice

An early strand of work in multilingual settings highlighted the advantages of linguistic and cultural diversity in the makeup of research teams (e.g. Jones et al., 2000). This was research that developed a new approach to the ethnography of multilingual literacy practices. This approach led to the production and use of two different kinds of fieldwork texts which were closely imbricated. The texts were participant diary notes and the transcripts of diary-based interviews. As Jones et al. (2000) explain, the development of this approach to data gathering was motivated by the need to move away from interview strategies which imposed the researchers' agenda, and by the need to create more dialogic means of engaging with research participants, bringing their voices more fully into the knowledge-building process, so as to create what Clifford (1990: 57) called a "polyphonic ethnography".

Arvind Bhatt and Marilyn Martin-Jones employed this approach in a research project focusing on multilingual workplace literacies, enti-tled: *Literacies at Work in a Multilingual City*.[4] All the research participants were Gujarati[5] speakers whose communicative repertoires included spoken and written varieties of Gujarati, and who made active use of these lan-guage and literacy resources during the course of their working lives, e.g. as employees of the City's Translation Unit or as public librarians overseeing a collection of multilingual reading resources for bilingual children. Those participating in this project were asked to keep a record of their daily work routines over the course of a week. They were also asked to provide brief notes about what they read and wrote in Gujarati, in English and/or in other languages. Following a principle of flexible, multilingual research practice, participants were encouraged to write their diary notes by hand, using what-ever literacy resources and scripts they felt comfortable with. Arvind Bhatt

Reflexive ethnographic research practice 197

was the researcher in the team whose communicative repertoire included both spoken and written Gujarati, so when he and Marilyn Martin-Jones met to discuss each of the literacy diary entries, Arvind Bhatt translated for her the sections of the diary entries that had been written in Gujarati. They then discussed the diary entries of each research participant, making links with the field notes from their observations in different workplaces. Their jointly constructed interpretation of the diary entries then formed the basis of the preparations for the diary-based interviews.

The knowledge-building process taking place during the discussions based on these initial texts from the field was described as follows (Jones et al., 2000: 337): "The research involved a complex, three-way dialogue: between us as co-researchers with different linguistic and cultural backgrounds and a dialogue between us and the participants". This three-way, translingual dialogue was taken further through the transcription of the diary-based interviews and subsequent discussion of the transcripts. In a retrospective comment on the discussions they had had about the texts produced at each stage of their research (Jones et al., 2000: 337), Bhatt and Martin-Jones remark on how useful it would have been to have audio-recorded them, with a view to capturing: (1) the ways in which they developed a shared interpretation of the diary notes and the transcripts of the diary-based interviews; and (2) the ways in which their different histories, values and forms of cultural knowledge had been brought into play in the research process.

Linguistic ethnographic research in multilingual teams: extending and refining reflexive practice

In a series of research projects carried out over more than a decade, Angela Creese and Adrian Blackledge have engaged in extensive exploration of the use of different types of field notes in team ethnography. The main research sites for this linguistic ethnographic research have been complementary schools[6] in urban settings in the UK and in other urban contexts in Europe. In an early account of their innovative work, Creese et al. (2008) describe as follows the steps taken by members of their research team, as they moved in and out of the field: (1) initial handwritten jottings and note-taking during school and classroom-based observations; (2) the development of a fuller word-processed version of these initial field notes. They saw this as "an opportunity to extend, delete, reinstate and clarify points" (Creese et al., 2008: 207); and (3) weekly exchanges of field notes prior to discussion at research team meetings. They also point out that participant observation was generally carried out by at least two team members who were paired because they had different language resources, forms of cultural knowledge and different backgrounds.

The discussions at team meetings were all audio-recorded and provided a means of engaging with linguistic and cultural difference within the research team and reflecting on the process of knowledge building. Creese et al. (2008: 200) note that "because of our different backgrounds, we saw different aspects of the context and chose to inscribe these in our field notes". The diverse nature of the inscriptions by members of the research team revealed the differences in their interests, values and histories. Engaging with these differences through ongoing discussions among team members made it possible to provide a fuller, more nuanced interpretation of the language education practices being observed. This approach to the use of field notes in team ethnography was particularly fruitful because, as Creese et al. (2008: 213) indicate, "field notes were the earliest data sets produced" and because the process was iterative, it "served a purpose in team development".

In later studies, Angela Creese and Adrian Blackledge explored the use of research vignettes (Erickson, 1990) as a means of making more visible the *emic* perspectives of researchers and as a means of addressing issues around researcher positionality (see, for example, their chapter in this volume). In this part of their work, individual researchers wrote brief, reflective narrative accounts of their research journey on a specific research project. Creese and Blackledge (2015a) describe the rationale for this way of working as follows: "we think it is important to reveal how our interpretive practices are shaped by our individual histories, values and beliefs, and how these are reproduced in team processes of analysis and text production".

More recently, Creese and Blackledge have focused on the different language values of team members and their beliefs about language by employing the notion of metacommentary (Rymes, 2014). In this part of their work, the focus has been on the field notes and vignettes of different team members and on their metacommentary on the linguistic and semiotic resources employed by research participants in different communicative events, in different complementary school settings (Creese et al., 2015b).

Achieving reflexivity through field narratives in a multilingual research team

The final example in this three-part section comes from ethnographic work on multilingual literacy, multimodality and Early Years socialisation in different faith settings (Gregory & Lytra, 2012). These researchers carried out, with a number of colleagues in a linguistically diverse team, a study of literacy socialisation in four different faith settings in London, UK: Bangladeshi Muslim, Tamil Hindu/Saiva, Ghanaian Pentecostal and Polish Catholic. The background of the members of the research team differed in terms of their linguistic resources, their funds of cultural knowledge and, in particular, their affiliation to different faiths. Some members followed a particular faith tradition, and had done so for many years, and others did not.

A central feature of the design of this study was the use of field narratives. This genre of fieldwork texts is described by Gregory and Lytra (2012: 209) as follows: "A piece of well-formed prose, rather like a longer vignette which might start or finish with a poem or a prayer". The production of these longer fieldwork texts served three main purposes for the research team. One purpose was to share knowledge and to engage in dialogue with other team members about the specific cultural practices and literacy practices associated with the observance of particular faith rituals, and to collaborate in the development of "a polyphonic gaze" (Gregory & Lytra, 2012: 196). A second purpose was to provide a space for individual researchers in the team, who had been involved in religious observance since childhood, to engage in personal reflection on their past and present beliefs and practices and to make comparisons with other faith traditions represented in the research team. The third purpose was to build an account of the wider social and historical context for the situated practices being observed in different places of worship and in different religious classes.

Gregory and Lytra (2012: 201) describe the design and conduct of this part of the project as follows (each of the researchers carrying out the fieldwork was a woman): "Each researcher wrote up approximately ten longer narratives when visiting her own faith setting and three other narratives when visiting the other faith settings". All of these narratives were posted on an online platform and so team members were able to comment on each other's contributions. The narratives were also discussed every two weeks during the meetings of the research team.

One particular insight from the collaborative ethnography of this particular research team related to the prominence of references to emotions in the field narratives. The references appeared in the narratives of those who were visiting faith settings other than their own, e.g. when responding to the moving music or colour in a particular place of worship that they had never entered before, or when seeing particular bodily postures adopted for praying. Reference to emotions also appeared in the personal reflections of team members who had had long-standing faith affiliations. They were making explicit for themselves forms of knowledge that had hitherto been implicit or taken for granted. Commenting on this, Gregory and Lytra (2012: 197) point out that "researching one's own place of worship is different from work undertaken in other settings ... faith has always been a very private part of life". They also acknowledge the challenge of bridging the "emotional distance" between those with a particular faith and those without, and the challenge of finding ways of expressing empathy and showing sensitivity to the beliefs and values of other team members.

Reviewing the methodological and epistemological shifts now taking place in team ethnography, in studies such as those discussed in this section, Martin (2012) argues that such innovations are long overdue. As she puts it: "Multilingual researchers already act, on a regular basis, as mediators and 'resources' for research teams" (2012: 308). Acknowledging their role in knowledge construction, making it more visible and aiming to create a polyphonic ethnographic account not only ensures that greater rigour is achieved but also that research collaboration between researchers with different backgrounds takes place on an equitable basis.

200 M. Martin-Jones, J. Andrews and D. Martin

Concluding comments

As we have endeavoured to show in this chapter, critical reflection on the nature and significance of the linguistic, semiotic and textual resources that traverse our research practice, and on ways of engaging with difference in linguistically and culturally diverse research teams, serves as key means of deepening our understanding of the process of knowledge building. It enables us to take account of the ways in which our perceptions and interpretations of the actions and discursive practices of research participants are shaped by our own histories, values and beliefs. It also enables us to gauge the nature of the relationships we are building in the field and to track the ways in which those relationships are developing over time. In addition, dialogic approaches to the production and use of fieldwork texts, which bring different voices from the field into our research narratives – whether they be those of research participants or those of different members of a research team – help us to create the conditions for building fuller, polyphonic ethnographies.

Given the advantages accruing from reflexive ethnographic practice of the kind described in this chapter, our research projects clearly need to be designed and planned in ways that foster such practice. They also need to be designed and planned with a view to making space for dialogue with research participants and/or with team members around the production and use of different kinds of fieldwork texts. Moreover, the writing of the final ethnographic report needs to make fully visible the complex, translingual processes involved in the building of our research narratives.

Notes

1 This chapter draws on our experience of involvement in multilingual research teams, on our own experience of doctoral supervision in the field of multilingualism and on two recently funded projects: (1) *Researching Multilingualism, Multilingualism in Research Practice*, funded from 2010–2103 by the Economic and Social Research Council (ESRC) under its 'Researcher Development Initiative' (RDI) programme (Round 4). This project was based at the MOSAIC Centre for Research on Multilingualism at the University of Birmingham. The members of the research team were: Deirdre Martin (PI), Marilyn Martin-Jones, Adrian Blackledge and Angela Creese. (2) *Researching Multilingually*, funded from 2011–2012 by the Arts and Humanities Research Council under its 'Translating Cultures' programme. The project team was based in different universities as follows: Jane Andrews (University of the West of England), Richard Fay (University of Manchester), Mariam Attia and Prue Holmes (PI) (Durham University).
2 Giampapa's paper was presented at the final conference of the first project mentioned above – *Researching Multilingualism, Multilingualism in Research Practice*, funded from 2010–2103 by the Economic and Social Research Council (ESRC) under its 'Researcher Development Initiative' (RDI) programme.
3 This research was funded by the UK's Economic and Social Research Council (ESRC) with the title: *The Home-School Knowledge Exchange Project* (part of the Teaching and Learning research programme), ref. no. L139251078.

Reflexive ethnographic research practice 201

4 This research project was funded by the Economic and Social Research Council (ESRC) from March 1995 to February 1996 and it was based in the city of Leicester, UK. Arvind Bhatt and Marilyn Martin-Jones were the two members of the research team.
5 The name of this language is written in English in two ways: Gujerati and Gujarati. We have chosen the latter since, when it is read aloud, the pronunciation is closer to the way it is pronounced by those who grow up speaking the language.
6 These schools are organised by local groups and parents outside the state education system and are known as heritage language schools or classes in other national contexts.

References

Andrews, J. (2013) '"It's a difficult question, isn't it?" Researcher, interpreter and research participant negotiating meanings in an education research interview'. *International Journal of Applied Linguistics* 23(3), 316–328.
Bhabha, H. (1994) *The Location of Culture*. London: Routledge.
Blackledge. A. & Creese, A. (2010) *Multilingualism: A Critical Approach*. London: Continuum.
Blommaert, J. & Dong Jie (2010) *Ethnographic Fieldwork*. Bristol: Multilingual Matters.
Briggs, C. (1986) *Learning How to Ask: A Sociolinguistic Appraisal of the Role of the Interview in Social Science Research*. Cambridge, UK: Cambridge University Press.
Chimbutane, F. (2012) 'The advantages of research in familiar locales, viewed from the perspectives of researcher and researched: reflections on ethnographic fieldwork in Mozambique', in S. Gardner & M. Martin-Jones (eds) *Multilingualism, Discourse and Ethnography*. New York: Routledge, 288–304.
Clifford, J. (1990) 'Notes on (field) notes', in R. Sanjek (ed.) *Fieldnotes: The Making of Anthropology*. New York: Cornell University Press, 45–70.
Clifford, J. & Marcus, G. (eds) 1986 *Writing Culture: The Poetics and Politics of Ethnography*. Berkeley, CA: University of California Press.
Creese, A., Bhatt, A., Bhojani, N. & Martin, P.W. (2008) Fieldnotes in team ethnography: researching complementary schools. *Qualitative Research* 8(2), 197–215.
Creese, A. & Blackledge, A., with Bhatt, A., Jonsson, C., Juffermans, K., Li, J., Martin, P., Muhonen, A. & Takhi, J.K. (2015a) 'Researching bilingual and multilingual education multilingually: a linguistic ethnography', in W.E. Wright, S. Boun & O. García (eds) *Handbook of Bilingual and Multilingual education*. Malden, MA: Wiley/Blackwell, 127–144.
Creese, A., Takhi, J. & Blackledge, A. (2105b) 'Metacommentary in linguistic ethnography', in J. Snell, S. Shaw & F. Copland (eds) *Linguistic Ethnography: Interdisciplinary Explorations*. Basingstoke, UK: Palgrave Macmillan, 266–285.
Erickson. F. (1990) 'Qualitative methods', in R.L. Linn & F. Erickson (eds) *Research in Teaching and Learning*, Vol. 2. New York: Macmillan, 71–194.
Geertz, C. (1973) *The Interpretation of Cultures*. New York: Basic Books.
Giampapa, F. (2011) 'The politics of "being and becoming" a researcher: identity, power and negotiating the field'. *Journal of Language, Identity and Education*

10(3), 132–144. (Special issue on 'Voices in the field: identity, language, power in multilingual research settings', edited by F. Giampapa & S. Lamoureux).

Giampapa, F. (2013) 'Researching identities and researcher identities: the politics of negotiating the field'. Paper presented at a conference on 'Responding to contemporary multilingual realities, recasting research methodologies', University of Birmingham, March 2013.

Gregory, E. & Ruby, M. (2011) 'The outsider/insider dilemma of ethnography: working with young children and their families'. *Journal of Early Childhood Research* 9(2), 162–174.

Gregory, E. & Lytra, V., with Ilankuberan, A., Choudhury, H. & Woodham, M. (2012) 'Translating faith: field narratives as a means of dialogue in collaborative ethnographic research'. *International Journal of Qualitative Methods* 11(3), 196–213.

Harding, S. (ed.) (1987) *Feminism and Methodology*. Bloomington, IN: Indiana University Press.

Holmes, P., Fay, R., Andrews, J. & Attia, M. (2013) 'Researching multilingually: new theoretical and methodological directions'. *International Journal of Applied Linguistics* 23(3), 285–299.

Holmes, P. & Martin, D. (2012) 'Mapping multilingualism in research practice: the view from two research networks'. Colloquium organised at the Annual General Meeting of the British Association for Applied Linguistics, University of Southampton, September 6–8, 2012.

Jones, K., Martin-Jones, M. & Bhatt, A. (2000) 'Constructing a critical, dialogic approach to research on multilingual literacy: participant diaries and diary interviews', in M. Martin-Jones & K. Jones (eds) *Multilingual Literacies: Reading and Writing Different Worlds*. Amsterdam: John Benjamins, 319–351.

Jonsson, C. (2012a) 'Doing ethnography in multilingual schools: shifting research positioning in response to dialogic method', in S. Gardner & M. Martin-Jones (eds) *Multilingualism, Discourse and Ethnography*. New York: Routledge, 256–268.

Jonsson, C. (2012b) 'Doing ethnography in a bilingual and multilingual context'. Paper presented at the third seminar of the *Researching multilingually* project (funded by the Arts and Humanities Research Council, 2011–2012), University of Manchester, May 2012.

Martin, D. (2012) 'A critical linguistic approach to language disabilities in multilingual families', in S. Gardner & M. Martin-Jones (eds) *Multilingualism, Discourse and Ethnography*. New York: Routledge, 305–318.

Ndayipfukamiye, L. (1993) *Teaching/Learning Bilingually: The Case of Grade Five Classrooms in Burundi Primary Schools*. Unpublished PhD thesis, Lancaster University.

Rymes, B. (2014) 'Marking communicative repertoire through metacommentary', in A. Blackledge & A. Creese (eds) *Heteroglossia as Practice and Pedagogy*. Dordrecht: Springer, 301–316.

Temple, B. & Edwards, R. (2002) 'Interpreters/translators and cross-language research: reflexivity and border crossings'. *International Journal of Qualitative Methods* 1(2), 1–22.

13 Reflexivity in team ethnography

Using researcher vignettes

Angela Creese, Jaspreet Kaur Takhi and Adrian Blackledge

Introduction

We conduct our ethnographic research in multilingual teams, using a multi-sited and contrasting case-study approach in which pairs of researchers conduct observations and engage in research in the same context at the same time. We have found that working in an ethnographic team has enabled us to move beyond the unitary point of view of the lone researcher, working instead with coexisting, and sometimes competing, points of view. Reflexivity is a crucial dimension of team ethnography, and we have argued that collective critical reflexivity leads to a rich interpretive process (Creese & Blackledge, 2012). According to Eisenhart, collaborative approaches involve "more different kinds of people" (2001: 219) in designing the research process and creating the final product, and require researchers to disclose more about their own views, commitments, and social positions. Such approaches make clearer "the social position, cultural perspective and political stance" (Eisenhart, 2001: 219) of the researcher and how these influence subsequent actions. A further dimension of ethnographic team research is its affordance of multi-site ethnographic investigation, which enables us to examine mobilities and linkages and helps get at the nature of contemporary social, economic, and political processes (Heller, 2011). Bourdieu argued that in working in ethnographic teams we must "relinquish the single, central, dominant, in a word, quasi-divine, point of view that is all too easily adopted by observers ... we must work instead with the multiple perspectives that correspond to the multiplicity of coexisting, and sometimes directly competing, points of view" (1999: 3).

Ethnographies are typically full of rich descriptions which document the researcher's account of "being there" (Geertz, 1988). These accounts take many different forms, including field notes, diary extracts, vignettes, interview transcripts and participants' oral and written stories. Reporting in ethnography involves many different narrative formats. Rampton, Maybin, and Roberts suggest that "Ethnographies involve rhetorical forms, such as vignettes and narratives (Hymes, 1996: 12–13), that are designed to provide the reader with some apprehension of the fullness and irreducibility of the 'lived stuff' from which the analyst has abstracted structure" (2015: 266).

204   *A. Creese, J.K. Takhi and A. Blackledge*

As the quote points out, vignettes and narratives are fundamental to ethnography because they document "some slice of experience" (Heller, 2008: 250). Indeed, without such narratives, we are probably no longer in the realm of ethnography. In this chapter we will focus on one kind of narrative we have used regularly in our team research processes: the researcher vignette.

Researcher vignettes are written by individual researchers working in a team of ethnographers. We view them as a valuable methodological and analytical exercise because they fulfil several purposes. First, they produce critical accounts of our relationships in the field, and therefore serve as an important data source; second, they make explicit researcher histories, beliefs and values which can be linked to ongoing and future analysis; and third, they extend the number of researcher voices in our final published ethnographic accounts. Vignettes are one way of retaining the complexity of the research process because they recall the contrasting interpretive configurations which are present during any data-collection and analysis phase.

Researcher narratives and reflexivity

A vignette is an ethnographic account providing "a focused description of a series of events taken to be representative, typical, or emblematic" (Miles & Huberman, 1994: 81). Erickson (1990) describes vignettes as rich descriptive narrative accounts, while Fludernik (2009) points out that vignettes do much more than recap events and also communicate human experience. Broadly, we might describe researcher vignettes as examples of "personal experience stories" (De Fina & Georgakopoulou, 2012), or "autobiographical narratives" (Wortham, 2001), because they provide accounts of researchers' perspectives about themselves and others while collecting data in the field. Researcher vignettes are also an example of reflexivity in action as researchers interrogate themselves on the role that context plays in the structuring of their own texts (Baynham & De Fina, 2005). In the team ethnography that we have developed on different research projects, we have written vignettes at strategic points to produce personal accounts which could later be interrogated to reflect on how individuals engaged in the presentation of 'self' in the research process, and to understand interactional positioning within the team. Vignettes have become important reflexive ethnographic tools for considering the power processes at work in different teams.

Reflexivity is not without its problems and faces several criticisms as a methodological approach. Patai (1994) argues that reflexivity is self-indulgent and does not lead to better research or help us to "escape the consequences of our positions by talking about them endlessly" (p. 70, cited in Pillow, 2003: 177). Pillow describes reflexivity as a means to evaluate the quality and validity of qualitative research but suggests that we have become too 'comfortable' with reflexivity, applying it almost mechanically. Through revealing our subjectivities, prejudices, cultural affiliations, and beliefs, ethnographers

Researcher vignettes in team ethnography 205

may make the mistake of assuming that we create validity, truthfulness and familiarity (Berger, 2015). Pillow believes we should not

> situate reflexivity as a confessional act, a cure for what ails us, or a practice that renders familiarity, but rather [should] situate practices of reflexivity as critical to exposing the difficult and often uncomfortable task of leaving what is unfamiliar, unfamiliar.
>
> (2003: 177)

Pillow's central argument is that ethnographers must be content to live with uncertainty, in both their understandings and in their representations of what is 'going on' (see Copland & Creese, 2015)

However, because reflexivity in research is not a singular or one-off process, but rather an approach which "saturates every stage" (Guillemin & Gilliam, 2004: 274), reflexivity might be conceptualized as a 'methodologized ethics' which stresses the 'politics of work' and a commitment to construct knowledge in a fair way (Blommaert, 2010: 5). As Guillemin and Gilliam argue,

> Adopting a reflexive research process means a continuous process of critical scrutiny and interpretation, not just in relation to the research methods and the data but also to the researcher, participants, and the research context ... In being reflexive in this sense, a researcher would be alert not only to issues related to knowledge creation but also ethical issues in research.
>
> (2004: 275)

A reflexive research process includes not only our interpretations and analyses but how we represent ourselves and our participants, and attends to issues of accessibility, engagement, style, and voice in the accounts we write up. Researcher vignettes serve this reflexive process because they document relationships in the field, consider how histories shape what researchers see, and produce published accounts of teams of researchers all of whom are relationally situated in institutional structures of power and agency within the academy.

Researching multilingualism in multilingual teams

For the last twelve years we have been researching language practices in community-run language schools. These are known in the UK as 'complementary' or 'supplementary' schools, and in the US as 'heritage language' schools. Complementary schools are grassroots institutions which have developed with very little government funding. In many ways financially vulnerable, and surviving from hand to mouth, they are nonetheless sites which have a political role in countering the monolingual orientation of mainstream schooling, providing young people with an opportunity to open up ethnic categories and social stereotypes associated with static identity

206 *A. Creese, J.K. Takhi and A. Blackledge*

markers. These non-statutory and voluntary schools provide a community resource for young people, parents, and teachers to network, and to support positive student learner identities. They also create spaces where young people and their teachers are able to negotiate identities through the performance of diverse linguistic repertoires.

We have conducted ethnographies in eleven British complementary schools, spending between ten weeks and one academic year in each site collecting data for projects which have lasted approximately eighteen months to two years each (for more information see Blackledge & Creese, 2010).We have also worked in teams to investigate multilingual practices in teaching and learning in schools in Denmark, Sweden, and the Netherlands (Blackledge et al., 2015). In the UK we have observed the teaching of Bengali, Cantonese, Gujarati, Mandarin, Panjabi, and Turkish to mainly British-born young people. We negotiated access to the schools through contacts made by researchers who, for the most part, were already involved in strong community networks. We then observed, recorded, interviewed, and collected field documents, typically with more than one researcher on site at the same time.

Funding from the UK and European funding councils has allowed us to work in multilingual, multi-site, and increasingly multidisciplinary research teams, and this has become our default approach to conducting linguistic ethnography. We will refer to one research project in this chapter, called the 'European' project, which spanned four contexts in Denmark, Sweden, the Netherlands, and the UK. The UK case study of the project investigated multilingualism in and around a Panjabi complementary school in Birmingham. The school met on Saturdays in two sites. The case-study team comprised three researchers, Jaspreet Kaur Takhi (JKT), Adrian Blackledge (AB), who was also project leader for the wider European team of fourteen researchers, and Angela Creese (AC). As field researchers, Jaspreet and Angela visited the Panjabi school most Saturdays for an academic year, where they observed classes, wrote field notes and set up audio recordings both during class time and at home and elsewhere. The researchers separately visited all classes over the initial four months of the project, before deciding as a team on two focal classrooms for more detailed observation and recording over a further four months. Data sets include field notes, interviews, audio and video recordings, and other field documents. In this chapter we refer mainly to field notes.

Researcher vignettes

In the European project, we wrote vignettes to address researcher positionality, and to make visible field and team relationships. Despite the multilingual nature of the team, it was agreed that English would be the medium of these vignettes. Consent to cite and refer to the vignettes in future publications was negotiated at the point of writing the first draft. The anonymity offered to research participants in the project was not available to researchers in the team, and they were aware of this when they wrote their accounts. In this and other research projects, vignettes have proved to be a valuable reflexive resource.

In recent papers, we explored researchers' different perspectives on the language resources they were bringing to the research (Blackledge et al., 2015; Creese & Blackledge, 2015). We considered how our different ideological positions shaped our construction of multilingualism as the object of research. We argued that researchers' language biographies informed the representation of voice, as our different histories shaped the ways in which we were able to speak on behalf of, and advocate for, research participants. We also looked at how we negotiated insider and outsider perspectives in the field. The researchers in the team viewed insider and outsider positionality as extremely fluid. However, there were marked differences between bilingual and non-bilingual researchers. We found that bilingual researchers' relationships with participants were long term and had involved considerable investment. Some of the bilingual researchers also described their advocacy role while researching the complementary school sites. Three earlier papers investigated researchers' shifting allegiances in the field, and looked at how social capital was brought into play by researchers at critical moments in the research process (Creese & Blackledge, 2012; Creese, 2010, 2011).

In the European project, researchers in the four national settings wrote vignettes during the data-collection period. In this chapter we focus on the UK case study, and consider Angela and Jaspreet's vignettes to illustrate how the autobiographical nature of the genre can be used strategically as a reflexive strategy within teams. We take each researcher vignette in turn, offer a brief summary and then make analytical comments about both.

Jaspreet Takhi

When I first learnt about the research project I would be taking part in I was very excited; complementary schools were a big part of my life until my early teens, when I stopped attending them. I suppose reflecting on it I felt a mixture of excitement and nerves because I didn't want anyone at the school to think that our research was a critical evaluation of the school. Yes we were looking at pedagogy and methods in the classroom, but more about the linguistics behind the pedagogy and how the children learn. This anxiety came as a result of me positioning myself as an 'insider' right away. Testing loyalties. Were my loyalties in making the school shine, or to collect the most honest and open data to be true to our research? What I did know was that I saw it as a personal opportunity to highlight the excellent work that complementary schools do in their local communities, and how they help the young people of today to acquire proficiency in their mother tongue.

My relationship with the research site has been an interesting one. Although the school runs on a Saturday afternoon like most of the complementary schools, I know their actual physical environment and space that surrounds it is very different to what I remember. The school is indeed unique – a building devoted solely to teaching the Panjabi language teaching is such an achievement, and one that I am extremely proud of. I was taught Panjabi at my old primary school. About ten students huddled in a primary school classroom, where our teachers never used to put the heating on nor allow us to move the tables around, because it wasn't 'our space'. There was very much an 'us and them' paradigm which ceases to exist at this school. I think the school building itself is a metaphor for how far the Panjabi community has come, and their commitment to Panjabi teaching for future generations. The sister site that the school has is a lot more like the traditional complementary school structure because it borrows a local secondary school for some Saturday classes. The plan is for all the classes to be moved to the main Panjabi school site eventually.

My relationship with the participants has been something that I have had to work on a lot, especially during the first few months where it would be crucial to build trust with them before we asked them to start recording. I think I have to look at myself before I can try to assess the relationship(s); I think I am somebody who can relate to both sides of the spectrum. I can speak fluent Panjabi with the administrators and teachers and understand their dreams and visions for the school, as well as being able to relate to them on a cultural and social level. I think one of the ways this is manifested is through my relationship with the Panjabi coordinator, GG. Whenever we meet he always speaks to me in Panjabi rather than English. I think this says a lot about how he trusts me and believes in our research. I am glad I have that link there because GG has been supportive of whatever we have wanted to do, and always makes sure that he can help as much as possible in our research. I use my linguistic and cultural knowledge to the maximum when establishing relationships with the key participants. I can relate to parents, teachers, including the teachers from India as my mother has had similar experiences to them.

I also knew it was even more important to form a good relationship with the key participant children as ultimately it's their linguistic repertoires and multilingualisms that we are looking at. A lot of these children are at the point in their lives where they are thinking of what to study and career paths for the future. Working at a university, and being a recent graduate, has formed the basis of a lot of our discussions. Luckily enough, I also share a lot of common interests with the children: similar music, films and television tastes. However sometimes this has proven a bit tricky with some of the children opening up to me about their family lives in interviews. As a researcher I must remember that although I get on with them, I am not their friend, but someone who is there to do a job. This has proved difficult for me sometimes, but eventually I have become comfortable with the lines that I am to keep within.

In her vignette Jaspreet describes her long-term connection with Panjabi language education, and the loyalty she feels to this kind of schooling. She points to the competing positions which doing community-based research of this kind produces. Navigating the role of cool detached scientist on the one hand, and community advocate on the other, presents a dilemma for her. She describes a sense of pride in being part of the Panjabi community and a speaker of Panjabi as a 'mother tongue'. She comments extensively on her own bilingualism, and how this allows her to form relationships across the

Researcher vignettes in team ethnography   209

spectrum. 'Bridging the spectrum' is important to Jaspreet and involves having a good relationship with all participants across the age continuum. She remarks on her own family experiences as a way to make connections with teachers and parents. Her family history is highlighted as a valuable asset. Her insider status is an important identity marker and she uses it to build trust with key stakeholders. But she also points to her own history of growing up in the UK. Her own relative youth in relation to the young people is described as an asset which helps her to make connections. Linguistic and cultural knowledge is central to the relationships she forms in the field, as is her ability to draw on popular culture and recent educational experiences in university. However, the closeness Jaspreet forges with young people is also a challenge. She realizes her youth potentially allows an intimacy in her relationships with research participants, but as the vignette indicates, she is aware of the need to retain some professional distance.

Angela Creese

For this project, I was delighted to be back in the field as a researcher and ethnographer. On the last project I was principal investigator which meant I visited all eight schools but had a limited relationship with the teachers, young people and parents in the case study schools. So, when this third study gave me the opportunity to be a field researcher again, this time with Jaspreet Kaur Takhi in the Panjabi complementary school, I was very happy. I should add a caveat about this happiness, as it came with some drawbacks. For around eight months, the majority of my Saturdays were taken up collecting data, and this meant that I lost time with my thirteen-year-old daughter, and domestic duties were squeezed.

With several 'complementary school' projects under my belt as well as experience as a researcher on at least three other projects in mainstream schools, I am a seasoned ethnographer. I am aware of feeling fairly relaxed about visiting classrooms, approaching teachers and students, and participating to differing degrees in classroom life. Having said that, the hard work of access into this School site happened prior to my classroom visits. It was Jaspreet who developed and negotiated careful and respectful relationships with key gatekeepers. So by the time I got to the classroom I knew we had been through many rounds of negotiation for approval to observe the classes.

My willingness to return to the researcher role is captured in my first set of fieldnotes for the project. They also illustrate one of the identity positions I drew upon in the field.

> Here we go! Roads are quiet and Jas and I arrive together about 9.50. We are one of the first cars in the car park. We walk towards the school and Jas introduces me to one of the teachers, HL, who is with her two children. I think she says they are 8 and 15. I ask some questions to her daughter, who is smiling warmly like her mum. Her son looks like he can do without an over-enthusiastic woman chatting to him so early on a Saturday morning.

> I chat to HL about how everything is starting up again, and explain that I've just dropped my daughter off at her drama group – which isn't quite true, but I wanted to mention that I also have a young teenage daughter starting Saturday classes.

In these fieldnotes I am aware that I am trying to relate to one of the teachers in the school through a shared experience of mothering, of highlighting hectic lives and juggling the professional and personal. Mothering is one of the identities I draw on regularly while in the Panjabi school. In fact, it is the primary identity I use to counter other identities that I am positioned into by our research participants. Although I am welcomed very warmly and generously by teachers whose classes I enter each week, I am never able to shed an identity as a university professor. Despite my efforts to get to know the participants in ways other than via their own institutional roles as teacher and student, I am not successful at this. I try talking about my travels and about weddings, families, holidays, teenagers and family life but I cannot say I am successful in building up a rapport with any of the participants. During the eight months in the field, I am one-dimensional. I never get beyond researcher and professional. Despite reassuring teachers that we are not there to comment on their teaching, I am not sure the majority of teachers ever believe this. Occasionally, teachers construct me as a fellow teacher or responsible adult who would step in to discipline students. But I do my upmost, unsuccessfully, to distance myself from this role. Again my fieldnotes capture this.

> HL [the teacher] gives the rest of the class a stern speaking to about her leaving and showing respect to 'Miss' (NJ) [classroom assistant] when she's gone. HL implicates me in this discussion to whole class saying, 'I am leaving you with two adults'. I start to feel worried that I will be involved in disciplining the kids and I don't want to have to do that.

During this project, my enthusiasm for fieldwork was maintained. The collection of ethnographic data continues to be one of the most fulfilling stages of ethnographic research for me. However, I recognized that my positioning as a middle-aged female professional meant I had little room for negotiation. Throughout the research period I was an outsider. This is OK – I don't need to be everyone's best friend. I am confident about what I can bring to the project. But I acknowledge my social resources are limited as I position myself and am positioned in the field. With the teachers, administrators and young people, there are few asides, thoughtful narratives and personal stories. The participants view me as trustworthy, reliable and professional. I often gaze at the young vibrant Jaspreet with her bilingualism, social and cultural background and youth and remember myself in a different era. As a 'senior' researcher, I know how lucky we are to have her. I am reminded of the importance of different perspectives which a team brings.

Like Jaspreet, Angela uses her vignette to position herself as experienced in relation to complementary education but as researcher rather than a student.

Researcher vignettes in team ethnography 211

Her vignette highlights her authority as somebody with a long-term investment in doing research in complementary schools over a number of projects.
Her researcher identity comes through strongly. However, what is also apparent is her frustration at not being able to escape the grand narratives imposed
by participants. She is keenly aware that her social capital is limited and that
her ability to become an insider of any kind will not bear fruit. She is unable
to escape her age, female, and professional status. Her relationships with participants are distant and the rapport cool.

In Jaspreet's and Angela's vignettes we can see traces of the social, political, and historical forces which have shaped them as researchers. Both insider
and outsider orientations created possibilities to observe and interact with
participants, and the vignettes describe frustrations and opportunities in the
field. 'Generation' is a theme given prominence by both researchers as they
talk about family, relationships, and age. Bilingualism is constructed as an
important identity marker which brings access and participation rights. Both
vignettes also give voice to a number of other actors in addition to their own.
In the vignettes we hear the voices of young people, teachers and parents but
we are also introduced to people beyond the research site, including Angela's
daughter and Jaspreet's mother. These voices from other worlds are brought
into the research site as a mechanism to expand the researchers' identity positions and shape access to data.

Conclusion

Researcher narratives can be said to provide the reader with evidence of
the lived stuff of the research process. They remind us that doing linguistic
ethnography is about making observations and authoring the texts we
produce. In our analysis of two researcher vignettes we have argued that
these personal experience narratives can be used to open up our ethnographic
accounts to a greater number of voices. However, we have also demonstrated
that these are authored texts shaped by wider agendas, not least by research
questions driving the agenda within the team, and by the constant identity
work which goes on when people work and produce knowledge together.
We believe that in linguistic ethnography such narratives should be made
available to readers for the following reasons. First, they produce varied
and protean accounts to alleviate a tendency in ethnography to produce
'squeaky-clean' realist accounts of truth. Instead, they reveal contrast,
difference, and diversity. In publishing these accounts we can "reveal
experiences, struggles, and histories" (Foley, 2002: 486) which have gone
into authoring them. Second, like any data set, they can be subjected to
thematic and linguistic analysis to show how researchers use language to
construct the social world they are observing. Vignettes are primary data
sets, and like other kinds of data, should be rigorously analysed alongside
all other kinds of evidence collected in the field. Third, allowing the reader
access to researcher narratives provides a picture of the social context, its

212   *A. Creese, J.K. Takhi and A. Blackledge*

participants, interactions, rituals, routines, systems, and structures that give them immediacy.

Reflexivity in teams therefore becomes an ethical issue as we consider whose voices are heard in our research accounts (Copland & Creese, 2015). Rather than viewing reflexivity in researcher narratives as a 'confessional act' (Pillow, 2003), we seek to use the narratives we author to highlight the dilemmas and debates which go into knowledge construction in team ethnography. They can be used to reveal the struggles researchers face with their own and others' assumptions. Researcher vignettes are narratives which explicitly locate the author in the text (Tierney, 2002) and are intended to achieve a more dynamic, accessible, and public representational account of both ourselves and those we observe.

Vignettes are only one example of strategic reflexivity in the multilingual team approach we take to researching multilingualism. Other strategies include the sharing of field notes, the pairing up of researchers for observations, and the recording of team meetings (see Creese et al., 2008; Copland & Creese, 2015). These are important strategies for those taking a team approach because they increase the number of narrative accounts available. We see this as an advantage of working in teams because it complicates the research plot by disrupting the proclivity in ethnography to produce overly simplistic realist storylines. In team ethnography there are various and sometimes contradictory stories to be told. We believe that ambiguities and contradictions present rich opportunities for reflection and creativity. In our team orientation, researchers often observe the same site together, interacting with the same participants while writing up their field notes individually. This produces overlapping and sometimes also opposing accounts of events, actions, and emotions from the field. As we analyse data in teams we are therefore presented with paradoxes which require another level of reflexivity as we construct knowledge.

References

Baynham, M. & De Fina, A. (eds) (2005) *Dislocations/Relocations: Narratives of Displacement*. Manchester: St. Jerome Publishing.

Berger, R. (2015) 'Now I see it, now I don't: researcher's position and reflexivity in qualitative research.' *Qualitative Research* 15(2), 219–234.

Blackledge, A. & Creese, A. (2010) *Multilingualism: A Critical Perspective*. London: Continuum.

Blackledge, A., Creese, A. & Takhi, J.K. (2015) 'Emblems of identities in four European urban settings', in J. Nortier & B.A. Svendsen (eds) *Language, Youth and Identity in the 21st century: Linguistic Practices across Urban Spaces*. Cambridge: Cambridge University Press, 167–182.

Blommaert, J. (2010) 'Policy, policing and the ecology of social norms: ethnographic monitoring revisited'. Working Papers in Urban Language & Literacies, Paper 63. Available online, from the Centre for Language, Discourse and Communication,

Researcher vignettes in team ethnography 213

Kings College London, UK, at: www.kcl.ac.uk/sspp/departments/education/research/ldc/publications/workingpapers/search.aspx.

Bourdieu, P. (1999) *The Weight of the World: Social Suffering in Contemporary Society.* Cambridge: Polity.

Copland, F. & Creese, A. (2015) *Linguistic Ethnography: Collecting, Analysing and Presenting Data.* London: Sage.

Creese, A. (2010) 'Linguistic ethnography', in E. Litosseliti (ed.) *Research Methods in Linguistics.* London: Continuum, 138–154.

Creese, A. (2011) 'Making local practices globally relevant in researching multilingual education', in F. Hult & K. King (eds) *Educational Linguistics in Practice.* Bristol: Multilingual Matters, 41–55.

Creese, A., Bhatt, A., Bhojani, N. & Martin, P.W. (2008) 'Fieldnotes in team ethnography: researching complementary schools'. *Qualitative Research* 8(2), 197–215.

Creese, A. & Blackledge, A. (2012) 'Voice and meaning-making in team ethnography'. *Anthropology & Education Quarterly* 43(3), 306–324.

Creese, A. & Blackledge, A., with Bhatt, A., Jonsson, C., Juffermans, K., Li, J., Martin, P. Muhonen, A. & Takhi, J.K. (2015) 'Researching bilingual and multilingual education multilingually: a linguistic ethnography', in W.E. Wright, S. Boun & O. García (eds) *Handbook of Bilingual and Multilingual Education.* Malden, MA: Wiley-Blackwell., 127–144.

De Fina, A. and Georgakopoulou, A. (2012) *Analyzing Narrative: Discourses and Sociolinguistic Perspectives.* Cambridge: Cambridge University Press.

Eisenhart, M. (2001) 'Changing conceptions of culture and ethnographic methodology: recent thematic shifts and their implications for research on teaching', in V. Richardson (ed.) *Handbook of Research on Teaching,* 4th edn. Washington, DC: American Educational Research Association, 209–225.

Erickson, F. (1990) 'Qualitative methods', in R.L. Linn & F. Erickson (eds) *Research in Teaching and Learning,* Vol. 2. New York: Macmillan, 77–194.

Fludernik. M. (2009) *An Introduction to Narratology.* London: Routledge.

Foley, D. (2002) 'Critical ethnography: the reflexive turn'. *International Journal of Qualitative Studies in Education* 15, 469–490.

Geertz, C. (1988) *Works and Lives: The Anthropologist as Author.* Cambridge: Polity Press.

Guillemin, M. & Gillam, L. (2004) 'Ethics, reflexivity, and "ethically important moments" in research'. *Qualitative Inquiry* 10, 261–280.

Heller, M. (2008) 'Doing ethnography', in L. Wei & M.G. Moyer (eds) *The Blackwell Guide to Research Methods in Bilingualism and Multilingualism.* Malden, MA: Blackwell, 249–262.

Heller, M. (2011) *Paths to Post-Nationalism: A Critical Ethnography of Language and Identity.* New York: Oxford University Press.

Hymes, D. (1996) *Ethnography, Linguistics, Narrative Inequality: Toward an Understanding of Voice.* London: Taylor & Francis.

Miles, M.B. and Huberman, A.M. (1994) *Qualitative Data Analysis,* 2nd edn. London: Sage.

Patai, D. (1994) 'When method becomes power (response)', in A.D. Giltin (ed.) *Power and Method: Political Activism and Educational Research.* London: Routledge, 161–176.

Pillow, W. (2003) 'Confession, catharsis or cure? Rethinking the uses of reflexivity as methodological power in qualitative research'. *Qualitative Studies in Education* 16(2), 175–196.

214   A. Creese, J.K. Takhi and A. Blackledge

Rampton, B., Maybin, J. & Roberts, C. (2015) 'Theory and method in linguistic ethnography', in J. Snell, S. Shaw & F. Copland (eds) *Linguistic Ethnography: Interdisciplinary Explorations*. Basingstoke, UK: Palgrave Macmillan, 14–50.

Tierney, W. (2002) 'Get real: representing reality'. *Qualitative Studies in Education* 15(15), 385–398.

Wortham, S. (2001) *Narratives in Action*. New York: Teachers College Press.

14 Researching children's literacy practices and identities in faith settings

Multimodal text-making and talk about text as resources for knowledge building

Vally Lytra, Eve Gregory and Arani Ilankuberan

Introduction

A number of epistemological and methodological challenges have been encountered in ethnographic research related to children's literacy practices and identities in faith settings. These include issues related to researcher positionality, knowledge building and representation. Although ethnographic inquiry takes an emic perspective to data collection, interpretation and analysis, privileging the participants' perspectives, it is now widely acknowledged that researchers bring to the field their own biographies and identities. These biographies and identities are embedded in broader social, historical and political contexts and they have a bearing on their understandings, interpretations and representations of the participants' practices, beliefs and identities. Central to these challenges are issues of power and agency, particularly the important imbalance between adult researchers and child participants. When conducting research with children, therefore, the following questions become pertinent: How can researchers ensure that they hear children's voices and include them in their research narratives? How can children represent their experiences, stories and interpretations in ways that are meaningful to them?

Issues of representation and voice become all the more significant when researching literacy practices associated with faith. Religion is considered to be a very private matter. Moreover, it is commonly held by members of some faith communities that it is only through membership that one can come to fully understand and interpret the practices, rituals, texts and symbols of a given religion (see Fader, 2009; Sarroub, 2005). As we have already noted in Gregory and Lytra (2012: 198–199), the "uniqueness and exclusiveness" of faith literacy practices have additional implications for the process of knowledge building. How can researchers, both those who are members of the faith community and, crucially, those who are not, avoid mis- or over-interpretation of children's literacy practices and identities?

216 *V. Lytra, E. Gregory and A. Ilankuberan*

In this chapter we consider how we sought to address these epistemological and methodological challenges in the context of a three-year collaborative team ethnography of children's faith literacies in four transnational communities in London, UK: Bangladeshi Muslim, Tamil Hindu/Saiva, Ghanaian Pentecostal and Polish Catholic (Gregory et al., 2009). We describe how we took a multi-method approach to data collection where the primary concern was making the children's experiences, perspectives and understandings visible and audible. We encouraged children to use visual as well as verbal ways of sharing and representing their experiences of becoming literate through faith and what this meant for the performance of their personal and collective identities. Nested within this multi-method approach was the use of scrapbooks authored by the children at home during their free time with limited guidance on the part of the researchers. We focus here on the advantages accruing from adopting this particular method of data collection, interpretation and analysis. In particular, we discuss examples from one scrapbook created by two siblings from the Tamil Hindu/Saiva faith community and from their interview with the researcher, Arani Ilankuberan, after the scrapbook was completed. We argue that scrapbooks as text-making practices, along with the conversations around them, provided children with "an alternative way of communicating" (Pietikäinen, 2012: 168), a discursive space where they could select, record, reflect upon and share with researchers aspects of their language and literacy learning experiences, their faith experiences and aspects of the identities that mattered to them, over the course of a calendar year. As we shall illustrate, the children's faith-inspired text-making practices and the conversations around them served as a key resource for documenting the rich and complex multilingual, multiscriptal and other semiotic resources associated with faith (e.g. images, symbols, narratives) that the children were able to draw upon and syncretise to exhibit their knowledge and creativity and represent the faith experiences in their lives. The text-making was also a process in which the children had opportunities to express their sense of being a particular kind of person, as well as co-constructing knowledge with the researcher about literacy learning in the context of the Hindu/Saiva faith community. In addition, the use of scrapbooks contributed to our building of collaborative relations with the children and their families during the team ethnography and to the development of a child-friendly methodology.

Children's literacy practices and identities in faith settings

Faith as a social and cultural practice and as object of study in its own right has received limited attention. Indeed, literacy activities associated with faith tend to be viewed as marginal to children's language and literacy development and identity formation by mainstream, secular societies and their educational institutions (Lytra et al., 2016). Nevertheless, a growing number of recent studies of children's language and literacy practices and identities in faith settings have demonstrated the intertwining of religion with children's

Text and talk in researching faith with children 217

everyday lives, particularly children growing up in transnational contexts where faith provides both community and individual support (Baquedano-López, 2008; Sarroub, 2005). Taking an ethnographic approach, these studies have documented that through their religious socialisation at home, in faith schools, in religious education classes and in places of worship children acquire rich and complex language and literacy repertoires, spanning two or more languages and scripts, including vernacular and standardised languages and liturgical languages (Auleear Owodally & Unjore, 2013; Moore, 2008; Gregory et al., 2013a). Moreover, this line of research has shown how faith mediates children's interactions with sacred texts and other print and digital texts and technologies (Fader, 2009; Rosowsky, 2008; Poveda et al., 2005). The sharing of a common faith, its beliefs and values, along with the literacy practices associated with it, creates ties of memory, social affiliation and belonging across time and space (Gregory et al., 2015; Peele-Eady, 2011).

Our research in four transnational faith communities in London complemented and extended the work in this area. Our focus on children's faith literacies was connected with our understanding of literacy as situated practice embedded within wider social, political, cultural, economic and historical contexts and mediated through different texts that shape ways of meaning-making and the development of interpersonal relations (Barton & Hamilton, 2000). Although we recognised the key role of language and children's multilingual repertoires in their literacy development through faith, we went beyond an exclusive focus on language to examine the broader relationships between language and other communicative modalities, including gesture, body posture and image, as well as the materiality and technological dimensions of multimodal practices. Our focus on the interplay between language and other communicative modalities provides us with the analytical lens to examine the linguistic, embodied, textual, cultural and interactional resources children used in their faith literacy practices in general, as well as in their faith-inspired text-making and in their conversations around these texts in particular. Concurring with Pahl and Rowsell (2006: 8), we understand texts as material objects that include words and images and that are tied to personal and collective identities, and to local and global contexts and concerns.

An important starting point for our investigation of children's literacy practices and identities in faith settings was our understanding of children as knowledgeable, active and creative agents and meaning makers in their own right. Building on work on Syncretic Literacy Studies (Duranti et al., 1995; Duranti & Ochs, 1997), and also on the collections of papers in Gregory et al. (2004, 2013b), we take syncretism to mean "the active creation of new practices – not just blended ones – as people live in multiple worlds, drawing on resources of these worlds without obliterating them, making sense and creating cohesion while crossing borders" (Gregory et al., 2013b: 311). This conceptualisation of syncretism and syncretic literacies foregrounds children's creativity, intentionality and expertise, as they exercise agency over how they construct knowledge, negotiate individual and collective identities

218   *V. Lytra, E. Gregory and A. Ilankuberan*

and make sense of the role of faith in their lives. Moreover, it provides a window on the role of religion in processes of language and literacy learning in faith settings and cultural reproduction and change in transnational communities. Although we are mindful of the fact that "no data speaks for itself" (Bragg & Buckingham, 2008: 12), our understanding of children as active and agentive meaning makers is contingent on a commitment to making their voices visible and audible during the different stages of the research process and "working *with* [emphasis in the original] rather than in parallel to our participants" (Gregory & Ruby, 2011: 171). In the following sections, we turn to the different stages of the research process and to the ways in which we designed the research with the aim of "working with" our research participants.

The study

To our knowledge, the broader study described in this chapter is the first team ethnography of children's literacy practices and identities to be carried out in faith settings. Working in multilingual and multicultural teams is becoming increasingly common in social research in general and in researching multilingualism in particular (Jones et al., 2000; Blackledge & Creese, 2010). Our study "Becoming Literate in Faith Settings: Language and Literacy Learning in the Lives of New Londoners" (Gregory et al., 2009) was a three-year collaborative team ethnography whose aim was to examine how sixteen children aged between four and twelve from Bangladeshi Muslim, Ghanaian Pentecostal, Polish Catholic and Tamil Hindu communities were becoming literate through faith activities in London. The faith communities were chosen because they represented recent migration to London (from 1950 onwards).

From 2009 to 2013, a team of eleven researchers sharing different linguistic, cultural and ethnic backgrounds, age, gender, professional and educational circumstances, religious and no religious beliefs worked with four families from each of the faith communities, their faith leaders and faith teachers, as well as older members of the communities, to investigate the following questions: (1) What is the scope and nature of literacy practices in each faith setting? (2) How do teaching and learning take place during faith literacy activities across different settings? (3) In what ways have faith literacy activities changed over time, in the London setting and across generations? and (4) How does participation in faith literacies contribute to individual and collective identities? We took a case-study approach and worked in four research pairs, where a new researcher who was a member of the ethnolinguistic community (and in three out of the four case studies, of the faith community) was paired with a more senior research partner who was not (in three out of the four case studies). The purpose of these pairings was to bring together researchers with different yet complementary linguistic and cultural knowledge and research experiences.

Making children's voices visible and audible

While collaboration is central to ethnographic research, it often remains implicit. Following Campbell and Lassiter's (2010: 377) call, we attempted to make collaboration between the members of the research team and between the researchers and participants both "deliberate" and "explicit" during the research process.

We endeavoured to develop collaborative relations with the children and the families we worked with through the use of child-friendly methodologies and specifically through the use of scrapbooks created by the key participant children and, where possible, by their older or younger sibling(s). The scrapbooks were part of a multi-method approach to data collection, which we developed in collaboration with the children and their families, the faith leaders and faith teachers and older members of the communities.[1] During the first year of the ethnography, we sought to understand the nature and scope of language and literacy practices associated with faith. We collected demographic and historical data about the faith and the area where the site of worship was located. We also recorded field narratives based on our ethnographic observations in the sites of worship, religious education classes and other faith-related and cultural activities as well as our visits to each other's sites of worship. In collaboration with faith leaders and faith teachers, we identified the sixteen families we were to work with for the next two years.

In the second and third year of the project, each research pair worked closely with the four children and their families in each faith community. Building on research methodologies our team had developed while studying family literacy practices and children's learning in Bangladeshi British and Anglo families in East London (Gregory, 1998; Kenner et al., 2004), we gave each family a digital tape-recorder, a camera and a lightweight easy-to-use Flip video camera and asked the children and the other family members to record for us daily faith literacy practices and routines and special religious celebrations and to take photographs of religious and other artefacts at home and in the place of worship. We also shadowed and recorded the children at their religious education classes. In addition, we interviewed the children, the parents, the faith leaders and faith teachers. For our interviews with the children, we adapted the "draw and talk" method (Coates & Coates, 2006) where the children made drawings, including mind maps, as they were talking with the researcher about their language use and literacy practices associated with faith. In the third year of the team ethnography, we passed on the role of the researcher to the children. The researchers worked with the children to prepare a list of questions the children were to ask either a grandparent or an older member of the community about the faith "then and now".

We had been inspired by the successful use of scrapbooks in a previous project (Kenner at al., 2004), in which several members of the team had participated. The aim of the previous project had been to document learning activities involving children and their grandparents. So, at the beginning of

220   *V. Lytra, E. Gregory and A. Ilankuberan*

the second year of the project, we gave each participating child an A4 size scrapbook with multicoloured pages and asked children to write, draw and stick in it what they considered important about their faith that they wanted to share with the researchers. From the outset we rejected the idea of giving the children a limited and limiting set of questions that we, the researchers, had devised. Instead, we conceived the scrapbooks as a discursive space where the children could select and present aspects of the faith that mattered to them, using writing as well as other as other semiotic resources. They did this with limited researcher guidance or other adult intervention. Moreover, we believed that creative text-making could foster identity work and critical reflection by the children. Finally, as Pietikäinen (2012), Tay-Lim and Lim (2013) and Literat (2013) have argued, using visual modes of representation, such as photography or drawing in researching children's languages, literacies and life experiences is particularly valuable when working with younger children who may be in the early stages of literacy development, as some of the children in our study were.

During home visits, researchers leafed through the scrapbooks, discussed their content and shared their reactions with the children and the other family members who were present. After their completion, the researchers went through the scrapbooks page by page with the children and with siblings who had co-authored them. The children were encouraged to talk about why they had chosen to include a particular faith story or design and what a particular symbol, ritual or practice meant to them and how it might be interconnected with other aspects of their everyday lives, such as their mainstream school. Rather than relying solely on the researchers' understandings and interpretations of the children's faith-inspired text production, the purpose of these conversations was to give children control over how they understood and interpreted the texts they had created and to share this knowledge with the researchers. In the Tamil Hindu/Saiva case study, these conversations were also video-recorded.

Sunthiru and Chanthia's scrapbook

Sunthiru (one of the key participant children in the Tamil Hindu/Saiva case study, who was twelve when we started the ethnography) and his sister Chanthia (nine years old) were born in London.[2] Sri Lanka is their parents' country of origin, which they occasionally visit. Both children go to the local mainstream school during the week and attend the Naalvar Tamil Academy (Tamil school) on Sunday mornings. The Tamil school is located across the road from the Sri Murugan Temple (the site of worship for our study). In addition, on Saturdays, the siblings attend another faith class organised by the Sai Spiritual Education School (Balavi class). Because children attending Balavi class come from different linguistic and cultural backgrounds, the class is taught in English and the children also learn prayers in Sanskrit. Sunthiru and Chanthia reported praying together daily in the morning and at night in front of the family prayer

Text and talk in researching faith with children   221

altar. They sing Tamil hymns and chant in unison, but they also pray privately in Sanskrit, Tamil and English. Both children keep a spiritual diary in English, which has been given to them in the Balavi class. The diary consists of a list of prayers and other rituals for the children to observe daily.

As with their daily prayers, Sunthiru and Chanthia worked together on their scrapbook. Each child designed, researched, wrote, drew and adorned his and her scrapbook entry individually. In their scrapbooks, Sunthiru and Chanthia wrote about religious festivals, their significance, their own participation, religious artefacts and their use for devotional purposes, Hindu beliefs, symbols and rituals and faith stories. Most of the information on Hinduism came from a reference book in English the children had at home and from internet sources which they then adapted and personalised to create their own faith-inspired texts. In addition, they cut, pasted and commented on photographs of their younger selves, which illustrated important moments of their religious socialisation. Their entries were complemented by magazine cuttings, colourful drawings and images of God.

In the next section, we present a scrapbook entry and the conversation between the children and Arani Ilankuberan that took place around it, after the scrapbook had been completed. At the time, Sunthiru was fifteen and Chanthia twelve years old. Arani Ilankuberan is a young woman in her late twenties. She is a native of London with family ties to Sri Lanka and she also grew up in the Tamil Hindu/Saiva faith community under study. Saivaism is a branch of Hinduism. Saivaites believe that Lord Siva is the ultimate deity and all other deities are avatars of Him, an incarnation or manifestation of God.

The scrapbook entry was created by Chanthia and it was entitled "Why do Hindus consider 'Om' sacred?". Chanthia had created a two-page spread about the sacred chant, the single syllable mantra 'Om'. On the first page, she created the 'Tamil Om'. She designed a large 'Om' in Tamil, which took up the entire page and was adorned with minute, glittering stars in different colours (Figure 14.1).

On the top of the second page, Chanthia had written the title of her entry followed by a short explanatory text where she discussed the significance of 'Om' for Hindus and the meaning of the sounds. She wrote:

> 'Om' is the source of all religions and religious scriptures. The syllable 'a' carries mankind like a horse. The syllable 'u' is a pointer to the condition and location. The syllable 'm' is indicative of the rhythm and melody of life.
>
> 'Om' is sacred due to all these qualities. Therefore, chanting 'Om' is a purifying experience for all Hindus. It is said to be a great source of happiness. Nowadays it is also written as 'Aum'. Here are the qualities of 'Aum'.

Below this text, in the middle of the page, she had written the sounds 'Om' in Sanskrit and traced them with a red marker. Emanating from the

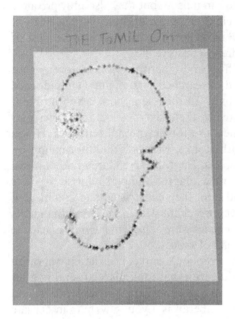

Figure 14.1 The Tamil 'Om'.

sounds like rays of sun were the qualities of 'Om': (clockwise) sacred, happiness, auspicious, solemn, mystical, melodic, powerful and pure. She had also adorned the page with delicate red spirals, hearts and stars (Figure 14.2).

In her faith-inspired text-making, Chanthia was drawing on the rich visual imagery of Hinduism to juxtapose and combine different linguistic, scriptal and aesthetic resources, genres and cultural threads from diverse sources. The crafting of the explanatory text alluded to the 'school genre' of explanatory writing whose purpose is to convey information clearly and accurately. Many of Chanthia and Sunthiru's entries adopted and adapted this writing genre where the aim of the text seemed to be to explain knowledge of Hinduism to a less informed audience and combine this information with their own faith knowledge and experiences. Chanthia personalised this entry in two ways. First, she designed a pictorial representation of the qualities of 'Om', which was reminiscent of the sun and its rays, and she decorated the page with tiny red spirals, hearts and stars. Second, she designed a full-page colourful Tamil 'Om'. In so doing, she was drawing on and combining her knowledge of different languages and scripts: English, Tamil, and Sanskrit. English was undeniably her strongest language. She used it to convey information and express her experiences and feelings about her faith. Tamil was very much a living language for her, which, according to Sunthiru, she spoke far better than he did. She used it to communicate with her parents and grandparents. She was

Text and talk in researching faith with children 223

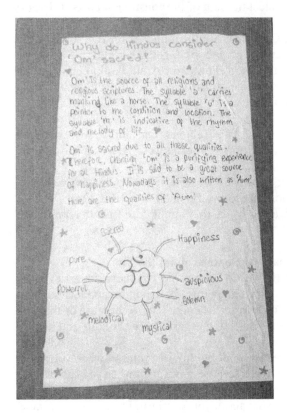

Figure 14.2 Why do Hindus consider 'Om' sacred?

also learning to read and write it in Tamil school and in the religious education classes afterwards. Tamil is also the devotional language of Tamils and it was used almost exclusively in the Temple for worship. Chanthia's knowledge of Sanskrit, the liturgical language of Hinduism, was restricted to the prayers she had learned to recite in Balavi class. Throughout their scrapbook entries both children strategically used Tamil and a few instances of Sanskrit to refer to religious celebrations, religious and cultural concepts, names of God and titles of faith stories. In most cases, they transliterated the words into English, but occasionally used Tamil and Sanskrit scripts, as in the examples here. To these linguistic and scriptal resources, Chanthia added her knowledge of the cultural and religious traditions, practices, rituals and beliefs from her family's Hindu/Saiva faith. She had probably seen the sacred sounds 'Om' in both Tamil and Sanskrit adorn religious images and works of religious art in homes and temples in London and Sri Lanka and had chanted the sounds in her individual and collective prayers. Seen through the theoretical lens of syncretism, her text-making united these different elements to "create

224   *V. Lytra, E. Gregory and A. Ilankuberan*

something that is greater than just the sum of the constituent parts" (Gregory et al., 2013a: 323).

In the following excerpt, Chanthia, Sunthiru and Arani Ilankuberan, the researcher, were going through the scrapbook together and talking about the 'Om' entry in English. The discussion shows how Arani Ilankuberan and the children exchanged meanings and co-constructed shared membership in the Tamil Hindu/Saiva faith community.

 1 *Arani:*   So now you've drawn a lovely glittery 'Om' and you've explained
 2 about 'Om'. Did you get this from the book as well? That same book yeah?
 3 *Chanthia:*   Yeah
 4 *Arani:*   So explain to me … why do we have a Tamil 'Om'? Why do we
 5 have a different 'Om' (pointing to the Tamil 'Om') to this 'Om'
 6 *Chanthia:*   Mmm it's like to say like to mmm it's our [like to represent
 7 *Arani:*   [ours
 8 *Chanthia:*   Tamil people
 9 *Arani:*   OK and what have you learned about the 'Om'?
10 *Chanthia:*   (glancing at the text in front of her) its the 'a' it carries
11 mankind like a horse and 'u' is a pointer to the condition and location and
12 the 'm' is the rhythm and melody of life and it's sacred because of that and
13 if you chant 'Om' it's like it's purifying experience for Hindus and it's
14 a great source of happiness
15 *Arani:*   OK, OK that's really good, but how do you feel when you say
16 'Om'? Do you agree like? Do you feel the same things when you chant 'Om'?
17 *Chanthia:*   Yeah, it's like it sends vibrations
18 *Arani:*   yeah it's like that what about you Sunthiru? Do you feel the same?
19 *Sunthiru:*   It has a calming relaxing kind of sound relaxes the mind
20 *Arani:*   relaxing and so mmm
21 *Sunthiru:*   yeah (nodding his head)
…
31 *Arani:*   How important is 'Om'? Do you think? Personally?
32 *Chanthia:*   Ummm I think it's important cause some people say like it's
33 the sound that started up the world
34 *Arani:*   uum
35 *Chanthia:*   it's really simple but really important
36 *Arani:*   Wow that's really good. What about you Sunthiru?
37 *Sunthiru:*   Just like the effectiveness uum and quite I think just useful and
38 different something that is a bit different to most. It's not really
39 something to describe so much about 'Om' but a different aspect of
40 Hinduism I think
41 *Arani:*   than other religions ok interesting … good … let's turn the page

(Chanthia turns the page)

As in other conversations around the children's faith-inspired texts, Arani used the scrapbook entry as a prompt to ask for further details about the artwork and to elicit the children's personal meanings, understandings and interpretations of their text-making. On their part, the children seemed engaged and keen to elaborate on their personal understandings and experiences with the researcher. First, Arani asked Chanthia about the significance of the drawing of the Tamil 'Om'. Chanthia replied, saying that she drew it "to represent our like Tamil people" (lines 6, 8). The use of the possessive pronoun 'our', which is echoed by Arani in agreement (line 7), shows Chanthia's awareness of the close link between Saivaism, the Tamil language, and the culture, history and identity of Tamils and suggests that she perceived her religious identity to be intertwined with the development of her sense of what it meant to be Tamil. During our observations in different domains of the children's lives, we noted that the link between language, literacy and identity was being fostered through the children's engagement with a range of faith literacy practices in the religious education classes, such as praying, narrating faith stories and discussing the religious and personal meanings of key religious concepts, and through their participation in religious rituals and celebrations at home and in the Temple. All of these activities were mediated primarily through Tamil.

During her conversation with the two children about the scrapbook, Arani also asked about how they felt when they chanted 'Om' (lines 15–16) and then went on to ask about the significance of 'Om' in their own lives (line 31). At this point, she initiated a process of recontextualisation with the purpose of exploring how the children made sense of a highly symbolic and metaphysical concept and related it to their own lives. Each recontextualisation was unique in the sense that each of the children drew on their own experiences. For instance, Chanthia talked about 'Om' as sending vibrations (line 17), while Sunthiru focused on the calming and relaxing effect of the sounds (line 19). At the same time, these recontextualisations were highly scripted: they revealed how, through their religious socialisation, both children had learned how to talk about their personal interpretations of the meanings of the sacred sounds in ways that were appropriate to the faith. It is therefore not surprising that their responses elicited positive back-channelling and enthusiastic feedback (see line 36) on the part of Arani, who is also a member of the faith. These recontextualisations allowed the children to experience their faith as an integral part of their everyday lives, guiding them in the navigation of earthly and spiritual worlds as they were learning to become members of the faith community.

Conclusion

Our collaborative team ethnography of children's literacies and identities in faith settings drew on a multi-method approach that sought to make

226 V. Lytra, E. Gregory and A. Ilankuberan

the children's experiences, understandings and interpretations visible and audible. Situated within this ethnographic approach to multilingualism, the use of scrapbooks and the conversations around them provided a window on the ways in which the children were representing their experiences of becoming members of their faith communities, and on the range of multilingual and multiscriptal resources they were drawing on. Indeed, the scrapbook entry discussed in this chapter illustrates the ways in which the children syncretised linguistic and scriptal resources from English, Tamil and Sanskrit, intertwining them with cultural and aesthetic threads from Hinduism and the 'school genre' of explanatory writing in their faith-inspired text-making. It also revealed how they articulated their personal interpretations of their individual and collective identities in ways that were appropriate to the faith.

Moreover, the use of scrapbooks contributes to current methodological debates on researching multilingualism in two ways. First of all, it highlights the affordances of using visual methods in researching children's literacies and identities across contexts. It complements recent studies of children's multilingual and multiliterate practices which advocate the use of visual methods as a means of providing children with additional possibilities for constructing knowledge, representing their experiences and making sense of their worlds (Pietikäinen, 2012; Kenner, 2004). As a result, through such text-making practices, children come to develop their own voice and agency and become active and creative knowledge producers (Bragg & Buckingham, 2008). Linked to this, the use of scrapbooks provides a way to develop relations of collaboration and trust between the researchers and the research participants. The development of such relationships with children and families is crucial when researching faith settings since religion is considered to be a very private matter. It is equally important in researching other sensitive settings, as the work by Kendrick and Kakuru (2012) in child-headed households in Uganda has shown. Finally, the use of scrapbooks further supports recent research on children's experiences in the social sciences, which stresses the importance of listening to their voices and the different ways they produce knowledge (e.g. see collection of papers in Christensen & James, 2008; Greene & Hogan, 2005).

Notes

1 All scrapbooks can be viewed on the project website: www.belifs.co.uk.
2 The children chose to use their real names.

References

Auleear Owodally, M. & Unjore, S. (2013) 'Kreol at school: a case study of Mauritian Muslim's language and literacy ideologies'. *Journal of Multilingual and Multicultural Development* 34(3), 213–230.

Baquedano-López, P. (2008) 'The pragmatics of reading prayers: learning the act of contrition in Spanish-based religious education classes (Doctrina)'. *Text & Talk* 28(5), 581–602.

Barton, D. & Hamilton, S. (2000) 'Literacy practices', in D. Barton, M. Hamilton & R. Ivanic (eds) *Situated Literacies*. London: Routledge, 7–15.

Blackledge, A. & Creese, A. (2010) *Multilingualism: A Critical Perspective.* London: Continuum.

Bragg, S. & Buckingham, D. (2008) '"Scrapbooks" as a resource in media research with young people', in P. Thomson (ed.) *Doing Visual Research with Children and Young People*. London: Routledge, 114–131.

Campbell, E. & Lassiter, L.E. (2010) 'From collaborative ethnography to collaborative pedagogy: reflections on the other side of Middletown project and community-university research partnerships'. *Anthropology & Education Quarterly* 41(4), 370–385.

Christensen, P. & James, A. (eds) (2008) *Research with Children: Perspectives and Practices*, 2nd edn. London: Routledge.

Coates, E. & Coates, A. (2006) 'Young children talking and drawing'. *International Journal of Early Years Education* 14(3), 221–241.

Duranti, A. & Ochs, E. (1997) 'Syncretic literacy in a Samoan American family', in L.B. Resnick, R. Säljö, C. Pontecorvo & B. Burge (eds) *Discourse, Tools, and Reasoning: Essays on Situated Cognition*. Berlin: Springer-Verlag, 169–202.

Duranti, A., Ochs, E. & Ta'ase, E.K. (1995) Change and tradition in literacy instruction in a Samoan American community. *Educational Foundation* 9(4), 57–74.

Fader, A. (2009) *The Mitzvah Girls*. Princeton, NJ: Princeton University Press.

Greene, S. & Hogan, D. (eds) (2005) *Researching Children's Experience: Methods and Approaches*. London: Sage.

Gregory, E. (1998) 'Siblings as mediators of literacy in linguistic minority families'. *Language and Education* 12(1), 33–55.

Gregory, E., Jessel, J., Kenner, C., Lytra, V. & Ruby, M. (2009) *Becoming Literate through Faith: Language and Literacy Learning in the Lives of New Londoners*. Final Report to the Economic and Social Research Council, UK: RES-062-23-1613.

Gregory, E., Long, S. & Volk, D. (eds) (2004) *Many Pathways to Literacy: Young Children Learning with Siblings, Grandparents, Peers and Communities*. London: Routledge.

Gregory, E., Lytra, V., Choudhury, H., Ilankuberan, A., Kwapong, A. & Woodham, M. (2013a) 'Syncretism as a creative act of mind: the narratives of children from four faith communities in London'. *Journal of Early Childhood Literacy* 13(3), 322–347.

Gregory, E., Lytra, V. & Ilankuberan, A. (2015) 'Divine games and rituals: how Tamil Saiva/Hindu siblings learn faith practices through play'. *International Journal of Play* 4(1), 69–83.

Gregory, E. & Lytra, V., with Ilankuberan, A., Choudhury, H. & Woodham, M. (2012) 'Translating faith: field narratives as a means of dialogue in collaborative ethnographic research'. *International Journal of Qualitative Methods* 11(3), 196–213.

Gregory, E. & Ruby, M. (2011) 'The 'insider/outsider' dilemma of ethnography: working with young children and their families'. *Journal of Early Childhood Research* 9(2), 162–174.

Gregory, E., Volk, D. & Long, S. (2013b) 'Introduction: syncretism and syncretic literacies'. *Journal of Early Childhood Literacy* 13(3), 309–321.

Jones, K., Martin-Jones, M. & Bhatt, A. (2000) 'Constructing a critical, dialogic approach to research on multilingual literacy: participant diaries and diary interviews', in M. Martin-Jones & K. Jones (eds) *Multilingual Literacies: Reading and Writing Different Worlds*. Amsterdam: John Benjamins, 319–351.

Kendrick, M. & Kakuru, D. (2012) 'Funds of knowledge in child-headed households: a Ugandan case study'. *Childhood* 19, 397–413.

Kenner, C. (2004) *Becoming Biliterate: Young Children Learning Different Writing Systems*. Stoke-on-Trent: Trentham.

Kenner, C., Gregory, E., Jessel, J., Ruby, M. & Arju, T. (2004) *Intergenerational Learning between Children and Grandparents in East London*. Final Report to the Economic and Social Research Council, UK.

Literat, I. (2013) '"A pencil for your thoughts": participatory drawing as a visual research method with children and youth'. *International Journal of Qualitative Methods* 12, 84–98.

Lytra, V., Volk, D. & Gregory, E. (eds) (2016) *Navigating Languages, Literacies and Identities: Religion in Young Lives*. New York: Routledge.

Moore, L.C. 2008. 'Body, text and talk in Maroua Fulbe Qur'anic schooling'. *Text & Talk* 28(5), 643–665.

Pahl, K. & Rowsell, J. (2006) 'Introduction', in K. Pahl & J. Rowsell (eds) *Travel Notes from the New Literacy Studies. Instances of Practice*. Clevedon, UK: Multilingual Matters, 1–15.

Peele-Eady, T. (2011) 'Constructing membership identity through language and social interaction: the case of African American children at Faith Missionary Baptist Church'. *Anthropology & Education Quarterly* 42(1), 54–75.

Pietikäinen, S. (2012) 'Experiences and expressions of multilingualism: visual ethnography and discourse analysis in research with Sámi children', in S. Gardner & M. Martin-Jones (eds) *Multilingualism, Discourse, and Ethnography*. New York: Routledge, 163–178.

Poveda, D., Cano, A. & Palomares-Valera, M. (2005) 'Religious genres, entextualisation and literacy among Gitano children'. *Language in Society* 34, 87–115.

Rosowsky, A. (2008) *Heavenly Readings. Liturgical Literacy in a Multilingual Context*. Bristol: Multilingual Matters.

Sarroub, L. (2005) *All American Yemeni Girls: Being Muslim in a Public School*. Philadelphia, PA: University of Pennsylvania Press.

Tay-Lim, J. & Lim, S. (2013) 'Privileging younger children's voices in research: use of drawings and a co-construction process'. *International Journal of Qualitative Methods* 12, 65–83.

15 Multilingual dynamics in the research process

Transcribing and interpreting interactional data

Sabina Vakser

Introduction

One of the most cumbersome tasks many researchers face is the process of transcribing, often met with resounding sighs as hours of speech can translate into weeks of transcription work. It therefore comes as no surprise that some scholars choose to outsource this stage of the process, one which nevertheless remains underexplored as a social practice in its own right. Indeed, as this chapter aims to demonstrate, the practices involved in the transfer between modalities – in this case spoken to written – beckon further critical engagement (see Davidson, 2009 for an excellent overview of the transcription literature). Moreover, the multilingual dimensions involved in transcribing and interpreting interactional data have received little attention in sociolinguistic research. This chapter outlines several key issues central to multilingual data representation and analysis, adopting a critical and reflexive approach to these questions. The examples provided are drawn from my research among three families in Melbourne, Australia (Vakser, 2014), which explores experiences of Russianness in multilingual domestic settings.

Russianness in Melbourne

Adopting an ethnographically informed case-study approach, my research investigates the negotiation of language and identity among three families in Melbourne with very different migrant/expatriate trajectories. Though each family identifies with 'Russian' as a linguistic and social category, these associations span multiple locations and traditions, and thus bear different indexical value. Combining Bakhtinian heteroglossia (Bakhtin, 1981) with the recent lens of 'superdiversity' (Vertovec, 2007), my research contributes to an emerging sociolinguistics of globalization (Blommaert, 2010), exploring polycentric social alignments and the nature of heritage maintenance in transcultural family life, and questioning pervasive monolingual ideologies vis-à-vis evolving semiotic repertoires.

230   *S. Vakser*

The examples in this chapter are drawn from two sets of audio recordings obtained from each family: self-recorded conversations at home, and follow-up interviews elaborating on the themes observed in the self-recordings. The chapter will focus on one of these case studies, a couple named Eva and Dmitri,[1] whose linguistic repertoires include Russian, English, German, and Yiddish, and whose diverse histories with Russian in particular invoke some interesting debate.

Dmitri's family migrated to Australia from Odessa, Ukraine, in the 1970s, when Dmitri was an infant, while Eva, who grew up between St. Petersburg and Berlin, moved to Australia just a few years ago. Both are in their thirties and share Russian as a 'heritage' language. Despite sharing similar linguistic repertoires, however, comprising what we may objectively call 'Russian' and 'English,' Eva and Dmitri's diverse trajectories contribute to ongoing negotiations of, in their words, "what Russia stands for me."

Positioning themselves at "opposite ends of the Russian spectrum," the couple exemplifies the ways in which a single language can become a site of ideological struggle, as individuals navigate the multiple "regimes of meaning" (Weedon, 1987: 34) offered by the "centres of authority" (Blommaert, 2010: 39) involved. In this case, Eva's "Russian-Orthodox-St. Petersburg" history meets Dmitri's experience of "Russian-Odessa-Jew," as the couple has described it, offering a glimpse into the complexity driving observed communication.

The transcription of such interactions leads to similar negotiations as researchers engage with the voices informing their research. As a second-generation Russian speaker who grew up in the United States, with Belarusian and Ukrainian roots, my discussions with participants contributed not only to the eventual transcripts but also to my (re)interpretation of that data in light of a shifting multilingual subjectivity. By illustrating some of these dynamics through Eva and Dmitri's case study, I aim to emphasize the importance of reflexivity and transparency in multilingual transcription, particularly among researchers working within their own language communities.

Main issues related to transcription

Bucholtz (2000) outlines two main processes involved in transcribing: *interpretive* and *representative*. Though each implicates the other, Bucholtz notes that the interpretive process deals with choices pertaining to content, while the representative process deals with choices of form. The technical, or representative, level refers to the actual symbols with which verbal and non-verbal elements are conveyed, such as using a ° symbol to indicate quieter speech.[2] The interpretive level includes analysts' perceptions of linguistic and paralinguistic cues that index the meanings of an exchange, such as the decision to mark off one segment of speech as quieter than the rest. As such, this dimension is much less standardized and vastly open to debate, depending

Multilingual dynamics in transcription   231

on the sociocultural profiles of the interpreter(s), their familiarity with the relevant social context(s), and the reasons motivating their transcription choices.

Take, for instance, the following example from my case study with Eva and Dmitri, drawn from our first interview at their home over dinner. This interview followed my analysis of their self-recordings, and the observed use of English vs. Russian – as well as flexible vs. separate bilingual styles (see Creese & Blackledge, 2011) – became points of extensive discussion:

Example 1

1 *Dmitri*   And I, from analysing my talk, how I sort of jump from one to another, I think that I speak Russian when it's topics or conversations that I'd, uh, that I would have had with my parents, that I'd had, that I have with my parents, so sort of like the first you know 20 years, but I spoke only Russian to my parents, for, for whatever, 25 –

2 *Eva*   You still speak only –

3 *Dmitri*   Yea I only speak Russian to –

4 *Sabina*   **Only Russian? [No English at all?**

5 *Dmitri*   **[So, if it's – yea. °Well...°**
((lots of overlapping speech, laughter, some hesitation))

6 *Eva*   And the hilarious thing is, that's the most funny thing. When he speaks in, um, for example Dmitri talks to his dad a lot about the computer.

7 *Sabina*   Mhm.

8 *Eva*   Or to his mum about booking, um, flights.

9 *Dmitri*   Mhm.

10 *Eva*   **And he pronounces the English words as Russian ((surprised tone)).** So he would say for example not, um, let's book the flights, but he would say, *"Давай мы забукуем флайты."* [3] (*'Let's book the flights'*). ((more pronounced))

11 *Sabina*   Mhm, mhm.

12 *Dmitri*   Yea.

13 *Eva*   And I find that – to me that was just such a novelty.

14 *Sabina*   So you don't, you don't do that at all.

15 *E, D, S*   No. ((in unison))

16 *Sabina*   But, and you hadn't heard that before?

17 *Eva*   Never. No. Never.

In turn 5 of this excerpt, the transcript highlights Dmitri's °Well°, framing it with the ° symbols to suggest metalinguistic hesitation by virtue of the hushed tone. This is further emphasized with my comments, as transcriber, of the ensuing banter from both – ((lots of overlapping speech, laughter,

232   S. Vakser

some hesitation)). These comments also form part of the segments in bold font, which immediately draw in the reader's attention. Overlapping speech is marked with an open bracket ([), and interruptions are symbolized by a long dash (–), likewise magnifying these particular segments, and inviting a particular interpretation of the speech.

Further distinctions are made between English and Russian use. Russian is transcribed in Cyrillic script, italicized, and translated in the same line given its occurrence within a conversational turn (turn 10). This differs from my translation of monolingual utterances, which were provided directly beneath the conversational turn, in parentheses, without single quotes.

The dynamics of this exchange will be explored in greater depth towards the end of the chapter; however, this short excerpt serves to illustrate the simultaneity of both interpretive and representative processes at work: the question of linguistic style, notably Dmitri's linguistic hybridity (turn 10), can be downplayed or intensified depending on the transcriber's notation choices, thereby reinforcing particular ideological stances. Indeed, these notation choices were altered over time with better acquaintance with the couple and changing analytic approaches to the data.

Transcription as social practice

Many scholars have recognized the intersubjective nature of transcription, stressing the ideological foundations and implications of data construction (Ochs, 1979; Duff & Roberts, 1997; Green et al., 1997; Bucholtz, 2000; Vigouroux, 2007; Jaffe et al., 2012). Bucholtz (2000: 1439) describes transcription as "a practice inherently embedded in relations of power," guided by decisions that often remain implicit, and Duff and Roberts (1997: 169) note that in representing speech, "every decision about how to transcribe tells a story." Vigouroux (2007: 63) likewise draws attention to the *trans* dimension of transcription, focusing on the many interpretive choices transcribers face but which rarely leave "the secrecy of one's study room." Yet since transcripts serve to put social life "on dramatic display" (Jaffe, 2012: 204), the transparency of these choices becomes paramount to our understanding of final data sets.

Following Bauman and Briggs (1990), Jaffe (2012: 203) notes that "the act of transcribing is a process of 'entextualization' ... which is by nature selective, interpretive, and shaped by the interests and focuses of the transcriber." This entextualization process marks the inherent challenge of transcription, multiplying its inevitable discrepancies, and making it more vulnerable to intertextual (mis)representation.

For example, issues of accuracy and readability can be exacerbated with the representation of nonstandard varieties of language (see Bucholtz, 2000 on 'naturalized' vs. 'denaturalized' transcription). Recent work on the social meanings of orthography (Jaffe et al., 2012) also highlights some of the tensions involved in spelling choices. Sebba (2012: 13) notes that

Multilingual dynamics in transcription 233

nonstandard orthographies may "covertly attribute sociolinguistic stigma" and Jaffe's (2012) analysis of respellings in the media illustrates the ways in which individuals are ascribed social identities, such as 'rural Southerner', through nonstandard orthography. Such choices are necessarily strategic, and sometimes have the aim of aligning or disaligning with the speaker(s) in question.

Furthermore, Green et al. (1997) argue that transcription conventions reflect the conceptual paradigms of a discipline, including its prevailing beliefs about language (more on this point below), just as the excerpts selected for use in transcripts may reinforce the theoretical underpinnings of a research tradition (see Ochs, 1979).

Scholars thus call for greater reflexivity during the transcription process in order to bring such decisions to light, positing transcripts as "creative and politicized documents in which the researcher as author is fully implicated" (Bucholtz, 2000: 1439).

Transcribing multilingual data

As a methodological issue, multilingual transcription seems to fall under the theoretical radar. While the merits and drawbacks of specific qualitative methodologies have long been discussed, little research to date has explored the influence of multilingual dynamics on the research process itself (for exceptions, see the chapters by Creese, Takhi and Blackledge and by Martin-Jones, Andrews and Martin in this volume). With the added dimension of multilingualism, the decisions inherent in interpretation and written representation – from the most intriguing (was that literal or ironic?) to the most mundane (colon or no colon?) – can quickly multiply.

In addition to 'translating' spoken discourse into textual form, multilingual transcribers are faced with the challenge of representing a much greater range of linguistic and cultural diversity. As Slembrouck (2007: 825) has pointed out, "previously monolingual ... socio-cultural contexts are increasingly characterized by the emergence of multilingual practice under conditions of globalized locality." He thus anticipates that issues of "translation-of/in-transcription" will become much more pressing in years to come.

Indeed, as with the decision to <u>emphasize</u> or *emphasise* a word, the process of multilingual transcription is a process replete with ideological alignments, rendered all the more salient through the rigidity of the written mode. As such, the likelihood of social distinctions and evaluations increases, as a greater range of times and spaces converge in isolated speech events.

In the following section, I consider several key issues pertaining specifically to multilingual transcription. Following Bucholtz (2000), I consider the representational process as a matter of *voice to text*, and the interpretive process a question of *voice to voice*. For multilingual transcription in particular, the following list of points should be considered during both representational

234   S. Vakser

and interpretive processes. The remainder of the chapter elaborates on each of these points in greater detail:

Key issues in multilingual transcription

- formatting and readability
- diverse scripts vs. transliteration
- translation (validity of)
- demarcating 'languages'
- transcriber comments (purpose of)
- textual emphases (implications of)
- resignifying what Kramsch (2009) calls 'symbolic II dimensions' of language.

Formatting, scripts, and translation

The unique need for translation, and capacity for representation in multiple scripts, amplifies general issues of transcript formatting and layout of multilingual data. In his work on code-switching and social identity among Japanese teens, Greer (2003) notes some of the challenges involved in managing Japanese and English bilingual data. Greer's reflections on the transcription process provide an important contribution to theoretical developments in this area.

For instance, Greer chooses *romaji* over *kana* script for his Japanese data in order to reach a wider audience. His translations occur mid script rather than at the end of the exchange to "allow the reader to follow the conversation closer to its source" (Greer, 2003: 48). Japanese and English are distinguished as separate languages through italicized Japanese and non-italicized English (see Example 2 below). When language alternation between Japanese and English occurs within the same turn (e.g. turn 42), Greer only translates the Japanese (rather than the full turn) under the original sentence, in single quotes, without italics (see Greer, 2003 for alternative approaches). He also discusses his choice of font as relevant to conversation analytic transcription conventions.

In my own work, I have chosen to transcribe Russian in the Cyrillic script to retain its historical distinctiveness and to reflect the participants' own orientations. However, the decision to do so has by no means been an easy task given my relatively limited Russian writing skills. Greer (2003) notes that 'native speakers' (to use a currently contentious term) are a vital resource in accurate transcription and translation, and despite my general proficiency in Russian, this has indeed proven true. However, it should be noted that 'native speakers' may not necessarily be able to assist with issues of nonstandard orthography or meanings, as discussed above.

In terms of translation, I also chose to translate only the Russian segments of talk so as to avoid redundancy. Brief turn-internal instances of language alternation were translated in the same line to avoid a cluttered transcript, such as in Example 1, turn 10 above. However, I chose to maintain consistency of italics in my translation of Russian speech, unlike Greer (2003).

Multilingual dynamics in transcription 235

Example 2

TRANSCRIPT 2: (Greer, 2003)

The participants have been discussing racial epithets that have been ascribed to them as multi-ethnic Japanese people.

```
40 Peter:    ore zasshu to iwaretchatta
             'I was called mongrel'
41 Others:   ((loud laughter)) ooh ha ha HUH
             ((jocular hand clap))
             that's (a good one)
42 Eli:      (laughing) Zasshuk That's like you're a dog or something
             'Mongrel?'
43 Peter:    mm((casts gaze down at desk))
44 Eli:      ((Sees it is perhaps not a laughing matter and changes her tone of voice))
             Zasshuk (.6) ° Zasshuk °
             'Mongrel?'   ° 'Mongrel?' °
45 Erika:    Nanim Kodomo ni&
             'What? By some kid?'
46 Peter:    Un
             'Yeah'
47 Eli:      How could someone say that&
48 Peter:    ((smiling again)) hee ha hidokunai&
             'Don't you think that's terrible?'
49 Eli:      ((somewhat subdued laughter)) ° ha ha ha m °
```

Furthermore, I have used bold lettering, as in Example 1, to cue the reader to key segments of the transcript for which more in-depth analysis was provided. Such decisions, though seemingly minor, do not just constitute the "visual gestalt" of the transcript (Jaffe, 2012: 218) but provide "broader semiotic significance" (ibid.) that can reinforce theoretical alignments.

Validity of translation

Achieving accurate translations of the data positioned me in a somewhat ambiguous multilingual space. As mentioned above, I was able to translate most segments but sought help with many others. This revealed a 'less than full' proficiency in a supposed 'mother tongue', raising issues related to multilingual 'competence' and 'authentic' group membership, concepts which are increasingly questioned within a sociolinguistics of globalization. Such dilemmas are crucial not only to adequate representation of speech, but also pose challenges to hegemonic discourses of native-speakerism (Lin, 2013) and draw attention to the shifting links between language and place (see Makoni & Pennycook, 2007; Pennycook, 2010).

Although multilingual repertoires are now recognized as dynamic, integrated, and more than the sum of separate monolingual parts, formerly linked to separate nation-states or centers of authority, such flexibility does not seem to work as well with the relative conservatism guiding the written mode. That is, in issues of translation, the ever-elusive 'native speakers' continue to serve as benchmarks of authority in regulating form, which may signal the need for joint transcription/interpretation when possible. This could

236   *S. Vakser*

involve colleagues in a multilingual team with different language resources, or researchers working together with their participants.

Demarcating 'languages'

One of the most significant shifts in recent critical sociolinguistic theory has been the (re)conceptualization of traditional notions of 'language' or 'code.' The view of 'languages' as bounded, countable, and discrete entities – linked to the nation-building agendas of nineteenth-century Europe – have now given way to more nuanced views of linguistic practice (Heller, 2007). Jørgensen (2008: 161), for instance, differentiates between "*a* language and language," an "ideological construct" versus "observable everyday behaviour," in order to background language as a system and focus on the indexical associations of speakers' variable use of semiotic resources.

'Language,' therefore, is now posited as one of many resources through which individuals negotiate local meanings, thus suspending analytic predictability. Scholars adopting notions such as communicative repertoires (Rymes, 2010), polylingual languaging (Jørgensen, 2008), translanguaging (García & Wei, 2013), and heteroglossia (Bakhtin, 1981; Bailey, 2012; Busch, 2012; Blackledge & Creese, 2014), among others, all aim to transcend enumerative and territorially defined concepts of 'languages' as such.

The question of demarcating 'English' from 'Russian' through bold or italic script is thus not only an aesthetic decision, but also an ideological one. Blackledge and Creese (2010: ix), for instance, in their work in complementary schools in the UK, have preferred not to demarcate the 'languages' in question. They explain that:

> In keeping with the theoretical approach to linguistic practice which emerged from this work, we make no distinction between different "languages" in the transcribed data. We use romanized transliteration for all languages other than Cantonese and Mandarin, where we retain Chinese orthography.

My decision to separate Russian from English by italicizing Russian, as noted above, in addition to using the Cyrillic script, follows the metadiscursive distinctions made by participants in associating language with place of 'origin'. While it is impossible to make such neat separations, the fact that they exist (and bear historical distinction) motivated this decision. Moreover, this separation acknowledges a potential emotional 'shift' in the switch to Russian features, and the subjective resonances (linked to people, places, and events) that these may invoke (see the section on resignifying subjective dimensions below).

Transcriber comments and textual emphases

Transcriber comments and textual emphases may disclose researcher subjectivity more directly, as was evident in Example 1 above. These can

Multilingual dynamics in transcription 237

become opportunities for elaboration of context or meaning, as well as direct evaluation of speech.

However, as we listen repeatedly to the same recordings, our perceptions of paralinguistic cues often change over time. The following two versions of the same self-recorded audio excerpt illustrate some changes made in transcription choices over time, as well as the ambiguities encountered in this particular exchange:

Example 3 Transcript version 1

((♫ ... *Я знаю пароль...* ♫))
((♫ ... *'I know the password'...* ♫))

205	D:	**Это потому, что все в России <u>onli::ne</u>** ((Russ pronunciation)). **И все видят кого <u>status</u>** ((Russ pronunciation)). **Status** ((Russ pronunciation)) **светится.** (*'That's because everyone in Russia is online. And everyone sees whose status. Status is shining.'*)
206	E:	((chuckles)) **Высвечивается.** (*'Is appearing/coming up'*)
207	D:	**Не, светится.** (Tim-Timati) **всегда говорит светится status** ((Russ pronunciation)). (*'No, is shining.* (Tim-Timati) *always says [that the] status is shining.'*)
208	E:	No::. *'Светится'* is to do- to <u>light</u>.
209	D:	Mm.
210	E:	А *'высвечивается'* is to come up.
211	D:	**Ну—** (*'But—'*)
212	E:	But then he probably doesn't know Russian either.
213	D:	((disgruntled tone)) °Mm.° ↓

Example 4 Transcript version 2

((♫ ... *Я знаю пароль...* ♫))
((♫ ... *I know the password ...* ♫))

286	Dmitri	*Это потому, что все в России онлайн. И все видят кого статус... статус светится.* (*That's because everyone in Russia is online. And everyone can see whose status... status is lit up.*)
287	Eva	((chuckles, offers different verb)) *'Высвечивается'.* (*'Appears/comes up'.*)
288	Dmitri	*Не, 'светится'. Тим- Тимати всегда говорит 'светится' статус.* (*No, 'lit up'. Tim-Timati always says [that the] status is 'lit up'.*)
289	Eva	No:: *'Светится'* is to do- to light. (*'Lit up'...*)
290	Dmitri	Mm.
291	Eva	*А 'высвечивается'* is to come up. (*And 'appears/comes up'...*)
(...)		
293	Eva	But then he probably doesn't know Russian either.
294	Dmitri	Mm.

238　*S. Vakser*

The above excerpts clearly illustrate the intersubjective nature of transcription. Not only are evaluations being made in the discussion about types of speakers and types of speech across various Russian-speaking spaces, but the transcripts further emphasize these distinctions through their own evaluative moves.

Version 1, influenced by the conversation analytic tradition (see Jefferson, 2004), displays much more emphasis and detail than Version 2. An ambiguity arose from the words 'online' and 'status' (turn 205), which I first transcribed as English words, emphasizing (indeed, overemphasizing) their Russian pronunciation in Version 1. In the second version, however, I decided to simply write the words in Russian, though they do not 'originally belong' to the Russian lexicon. The ubiquity of their use among Russian speakers, however, as evident in online forums and confirmed with Russian friends, encouraged this simplification. Consequently, this move downplayed the 'otherness' of these words (and by extension, their authors), as implied by overemphasis in the first version. The bold and italics of Cyrillic script were traded for italics only, likewise reducing but not completely eliminating the otherness of the script. Eva and Dmitri's names were also spelled out to better identify the speakers.

The ((disgruntled tone)) and falling intonation (↓) noted in the first version (turn 213) were omitted in the second version due to a lesser-perceived 'disgruntledness' through repeated listening. It was unclear from the recording whether the 'mm' (turn 213) was taken as a personal affront, though it seemed so at first, as I initially approached the interaction with the idea of very strict evaluations of Russianness between the couple. Indeed, as mentioned earlier, Eva and Dmitri's self-positioning at "opposite ends of the Russian spectrum" sometimes framed Dmitri's Russian as less 'proper' by virtue of a more flexible bilingual style, as well as his use of Odessan and Yiddish repertoire elements, as noted in a subsequent interview:

Example 5

Dmitri	But I've got a lot of um **bad Russian words** that are more Odessa slang, or Ukrainian, even Yiddish type of things, and I didn't know that they're the Yiddish or Ru – I just think it's all Russian because I, because I grew up, my parents were Russian Jews here in Bondi which is all Russian Jews so, and I've con-conversed with um – that's –
Sabina	So it's all coming from your [childhood.
Dmitri	[I, I just, yea, so I've always assumed that that's Russian.

Example 6

Dmitri	I'm feeling more, more Odessa. Because I … before I'd say I'm more Russian …

Eva	What do you mean by before?
Dmitri	Before I met you and sort of, really spent close time with, close, closely with someone who's, who's more, like, proper Russian.
Eva	Mhm.

Such explicit self- and other-positioning by Eva and Dmitri throughout the study may have therefore influenced certain transcript emphases in order to reflect these perceptions. Returning to Example 1, for instance, it was retrospectively clear that such interpersonal distinctions contributed to the addition of transcriber comments such as ((surprised tone)) and ((more pronounced)), whose omission may have invited a different interpretation:

Example 1, revisited

10 Eva **And he pronounces the English words as Russian ((surprised tone)).** So he would say for example not, um, let's book the flights, but he would say, *"Давай мы за-букуем флайты."* (*'Let's book the flights'*) ((more pronounced))

Though my interpretation was technically justified by the audio data, I later realized that the reported distinctions may have been (a) motivated by my priming for this awareness through the questions asked, and (b) not as strict and consistent as I wanted to believe them to be over the course of the research. The topic of hybridity seemed to be a sensitive one for Eva and Dmitri, whether or not it was perceived as such prior to my introducing it. The possibility that my presence as a presumed 'authority' on language may have influenced reported 'beliefs' about language mixing cannot be dismissed.

Indeed, the very act of bringing up these observations in interview sessions somehow seemed to invite a view of deficiency, despite my best efforts to share anecdotes that illustrated my Russianness to be as 'mixed' as Dmitri's. At times, it was almost as if I was priming the turn towards ambivalence (Only English? No Russian at all?). I was aware of the improbability of speaking 'only Russian' to one's migrant parents in that context, and in efforts to capture the nature of the 'mixing,' so to speak (with the intent of critiquing monolingual ideology), I was also, unintentionally, creating a space for meta-discursive doubt towards practices not normally exposed to "panoptical view" (Erickson, 2004: 174).

The anecdote presented in Example 1, for instance, thus achieves contradictory purposes: (1) it confirms my knowledge of linguistic adaptation in migrant lexicon; (2) it reifies this adaptation through the interview and the transcript; and (3) it inadvertently positions speakers against a yardstick of standard usage, presupposed by researcher presence and focus on form. It is only through further discussion that my participants and I were able to acknowledge the full complexities and contingencies of migrant repertoires. Further reflection also made me realize that drawing attention to so-called

240 *S. Vakser*

'hybrid' forms – in the presence of greater authorities on standard language (Eva's Russian; institutional standards) – may have served the unintended role of stigmatizing their occurrence.

Resignifying the subjective dimensions of language

To further elucidate the transcription process, it is useful to draw on Kramsch's (2009) discussion of the symbolism of language. As Kramsch argues, language can be considered as doubly symbolic. In the first sense, symbols serve "as signs shared by a social community ... [and] derive their meaning from the force of social convention" (2009: 6). In the second sense, "the use of these symbols triggers subjective resonances," and "constructs ... perceptions, emotions, attitudes, and values" (2009: 7).

In my own experience, typing Cyrillic characters initially proved unnatural and invoked a certain guilt, as these characters indexed not just the voices of my participants but also a family migration history long surpassed in the transition to American life. Thus data collection and transcription, engagement with 'real speakers,' 'real music,' and the Cyrillic script, all triggered in me a sense of 'backwardness' or 'imposture' (Kramsch, 2012), often ringing of extremes (how could I take Russian so seriously?). In its neglect of familiar migrant realities and hybridities, monolingual Russian felt *too Russian*, almost naïve, and had to be resignified as I learned to neutralize an inherited consciousness and enact a new kind of Russian, one that felt utterly foreign in its minimal mixing and irony. Russian as Heritage became decisively objectified as Russian L2.

Likewise, for Dmitri, Russian language use – once distanced from established associations – perhaps becomes a similar type of L2 endeavor: in order to 'succeed' in his efforts, he must 'neutralize' the language, 'objectify' it, attribute new meanings to and resignify its role. Encountering a different type of Russianness in the context of his relationship has meant superseding – indeed, adding greater complexity to – the multilingual realities of his upbringing. In the process, both Eva and Dmitri have expanded their stylistic repertoires to encompass the histories of each, embodying a 'superdiversity' of Russianness in the context of their home (see Vertovec, 2007).

Thus the 'symbolic II dimensions' of transcribing multilingual discourse, which deal with the subjective resonances evoked by symbolic systems (Kramsch, 2009) through transnational migration, must also be considered. Resignifying forms, as described above, often blurs the distinction between heritage and second language, involving an 'othering' of mother tongues. As such, different versions of 'heritage' are created in the process, linked to disparate indexical norms across many times and spaces.

Concluding remarks

In sum, the data-collection and transcription process in my research proved to be far from straightforward. From meeting with participants and negotiating

Multilingual dynamics in transcription 241

linguistic choices (some Russian speakers positioned me as 'Russian,' others did not); to noting the subtleties accompanying speech styles (such as shame arising from language alternation, communicated through tone and gaze); to interpreting the recordings and their ideological implications; and to rendering these as 'final text', became an exercise of reflection that spoke to the nature of multilingualism just as much as the data itself. The research process was, therefore, perpetually dialogic, always in response to both present and absent others (Bakhtin, 1981). Participants, non-participants, and the researcher co-constructed the data each step of the way.

It is my hope that these experiences have highlighted the importance of reflexivity and transparency with regard to language dynamics in the shaping and representation of one's work (see Creese & Blackledge, 2012). The process of transcription is indeed replete with decision-making at every step, and in representing our participants we must stay highly attuned to what is said, how it is conveyed, and how perceptions change as the process unfolds.

Notes

1 Pseudonyms were adopted in this study to preserve confidentiality.
2 The transcription conventions used were adapted from Greer (2003) and Jefferson (2004). The symbols used are listed below.

Transcription conventions

[	point of overlapping speech
=	latched speech; no break between turns
(...)	skipped segment of speech
(word)	imperceptible; approximation of what was heard
(())	transcribers' comments
(xx) / (xxx)	unintelligible speech
> <	rushed speech
°	marked softness in tone
?	rising intonation (or question)
↓	falling intonation
__	emphasis of word or sound (underlined)
::	prolonged vowel or consonant (preceding symbol)

3 '*Забукуем*' is a hybrid construction of the English verb 'to book' merged with Russian affixes '*за*' and '*ем*' to form the translingual 'we will book'; '*флайты*' uses the English 'flight' with the Russian plural marker '*ы*'.

References

Bailey, B. (2012) 'Heteroglossia', in M. Martin-Jones, A. Blackledge & A. Creese. (eds) *The Routledge Handbook of Multilingualism*. Abingdon, Oxon: Routledge, 499–507.

Bakhtin, M.M. (1981) *The Dialogic Imagination: Four Essays*, M. Holquist, ed. and C. Emerson & M. Holquist, trans. Austin, TX: University of Texas Press.

242   S. Vakser

Bauman, R. & Briggs, C.L. (1990) 'Poetics and performance as critical perspectives on language and social life'. *Annual Review of Anthropology* 19, 59–88.

Blackledge, A. & Creese, A. (2010) *Multilingualism: A Critical Perspective*. London: Continuum.

Blackledge, A. & Creese, A. (eds) (2014) *Heteroglossia as Practice and Pedagogy*. New York: Springer.

Blommaert, J. (2010) *The Sociolinguistics of Globalization*. Cambridge: Cambridge University Press.

Bucholtz, M. (2000) 'The politics of transcription'. *Journal of Pragmatics* 32(10), 1439–1465.

Busch, B. (2012) 'The linguistic repertoire revisited'. *Applied Linguistics* 33(5), 503–523.

Creese, A. & Blackledge, A. (2011) Separate and flexible bilingualism in complementary schools: multiple language practices in interrelationship'. *Journal of Pragmatics* 43(5), 1196–1208.

Creese, A. & Blackledge, A. (2012) 'Voice and meaning-making in team ethnography'. *Anthropology & Education Quarterly* 43(3), 306–324.

Davidson, C.R. (2009) 'Transcription: imperatives for qualitative research'. *International Journal of Qualitative Methods* 8(2), 35–52.

Duff, P. & Roberts, C. (1997) 'The politics of transcription; transcribing talk: issues of representation'. *TESOL Quarterly* 31(1), 167–172.

Erickson, F. (2004) *Talk and Social Theory: Ecologies of Speaking and Listening in Everyday Life*. Cambridge: Polity Press.

García, O. & Wei, L. (2013) *Translanguaging: Language, Bilingualism and Education*. Basingstoke, UK: Palgrave Macmillan.

Green, J., Franquiz, M. & Dixon, C. (1997) 'The myth of the objective transcript: transcribing as a situated act'. *TESOL Quarterly* 31(1), 172–176.

Greer, T. (2003) 'Transcription approaches to multilingual discourse analysis'. *Conference Proceedings of the 1997 Symposium JALT Pan-SIG conference, Kyoto, Japan*. Online: www.jalt.org/pansig/2003/HTML/Greer.htm.

Heller, M. (ed.) (2007) *Bilingualism: A Social Approach*. New York: Palgrave Macmillan.

Jaffe, A. (2012) 'Transcription in practice: nonstandard orthography', in A. Jaffe, J. Androutsopoulos, M. Sebba & S. Johnson (eds) *Orthography as Social Action: Scripts, Spelling, Identity and Power*. Berlin: Walter de Gruyter, 203–224.

Jaffe, A., Androutsopoulos, J., Sebba, M. & Johnson, S. (eds) (2012) *Orthography as Social Action: Scripts, Spelling, Identity and Power*. Berlin: Walter de Gruyter.

Jefferson, G. (2004) 'Glossary of transcript symbols with an introduction'. *Pragmatics and Beyond New Series* 125, 13–34.

Jørgensen, J.N. (2008) 'Polylingual languaging around and among children and adolescents'. *International Journal of Multilingualism* 5(3), 161–176.

Kramsch, C. (2009) *The Multilingual Subject: What Foreign Language Learners Say about Their Experience and Why It Matters*. Oxford: Oxford University Press.

Kramsch, C. (2012) 'Imposture: a late modern notion in poststructuralist SLA research'. *Applied Linguistics* 33(5), 483–502.

Lin, A. (2013) 'Toward paradigmatic change in TESOL methodologies: building plurilingual pedagogies from the ground up'. *TESOL Quarterly* 47(3), 521–545.

Makoni, S. & Pennycook, A. (2007) *Disinventing and Reconstituting Languages*. Clevedon, UK: Multilingual Matters.

Multilingual dynamics in transcription 243

Ochs, E. (1979) 'Transcription as theory', in E. Ochs & B. Schieffelin (eds) *Developmental Pragmatics*. New York: Academic Press, 43–72.

Pennycook, A. (2010) *Language as a Local Practice*. Abingdon, Oxon: Routledge.

Rymes, B. (2010) 'Classroom discourse analysis: a focus on communicative repertoires', in N. Hornberger & S. McKay (eds) *Sociolinguistics and Language Education*. Bristol: Multilingual Matters, 528–548.

Sebba, M. (2012) 'Orthography as social action: scripts, spelling, identity and power', in A. Jaffe, J. Androutsopoulos, M. Sebba & S. Johnson (eds) *Orthography as Social Action: Scripts, Spelling, Identity and Power*. Berlin: Walter de Gruyter, 1–20.

Slembrouck, S. (2007) 'Transcription – the extended directions of data histories: a response to M. Bucholtz's "Variation in transcription"'. *Discourse Studies* 9(6), 822–827.

Vakser, S. (2014) *"Как мы codeswitchaeм" [How we codeswitch]: The Range of Russianness in Melbourne*. Unpublished PhD thesis, University of Melbourne.

Vertovec, S. (2007) 'Super-diversity and its implications'. *Ethnic and Racial Studies* 30(6), 1024–1054.

Vigouroux, C.B. (2007) 'Trans-scription as a social activity: an ethnographic approach'. *Ethnography* 8(1), 61–97.

Weedon, C. (1987) *Feminist Practice and Poststructuralist Theory*. Cambridge, MA: Blackwell.

Part 5

Ethnographic monitoring and critical collaborative analysis for social change

16 Countering unequal multilingualism through ethnographic monitoring

Haley De Korne and Nancy H. Hornberger

> … [O]ne can hardly avoid the thought that a latent function of schools has been to define a certain proportion of people as inferior, even to convince them that they are so, and to do this *on the seemingly neutral ground of language.*
>
> (Hymes, 1980: 110, italics original)

Hymes' (1968, 1972, 1980, 1992, 1996) concern with unequal norms of language in schooling, and with values of equality and social inclusion are shared by many researchers today. Ethnographers of multilingualism are frequently in the position to observe effects of prescriptive and hierarchical language norms imposed by top-down policies or elitist systems, but they are less often believed to be in the position to challenge either the norms or their negative effects. In proposing ethnographic monitoring, Hymes countered this perception, laying out ways that ethnographers are especially capable of responding to the contexts that they observe (Blommaert, 2009; Hornberger, 2009, 2014; Hymes, 1980; Van der Aa & Blommaert, 2011). Ethnographic monitoring is a paradigm for researching multilingualism in support of social justice, based on understandings of the researcher as a social actor and of social change as a collective process that emerges from ground-level realities and aspirations. In this chapter we illustrate ethnographic monitoring in practice and discuss how it is particularly appropriate to Indigenous education contexts marked by socio-economic fragility and post-colonial hierarchies. We draw from our experiences conducting ethnographic research in solidarity with efforts to counter language inequalities in Indigenous communities in several parts of the world, including the T'boli of the Philippines, the Isthmus Zapotec of Mexico, the multilingual South African state, and the Sámi of Scandinavia.[1] Our discussion is structured around three fundamental tasks: observation and description, analysis and interpretation, and evaluation oriented towards social change. These tasks build upon each other, may occur in overlapping cycles and/or in collaboration with stakeholders, and may be achieved through a variety of methods. In pursuit of positive social change, Hymes argues that ethnography "must be conscious of values and goals. It must relate description to analysis and objectivity to critical evaluation" (1980: 104). Ethnographers

248   H. De Korne and N.H. Hornberger

are not limited to describing social reality through participant observation but may attempt to monitor positive and negative changes and contribute to evaluation and improvement in relation to local goals.

Monitoring unequal multilingualism

Linguistic differences are often valued unequally in social interactions, institutional practices and policies, with ideologies about some languages being *superior* or *correct* used to create social hierarchies (Fairclough, 1989; Hymes, 1980). Discrimination against ways of speaking consequently creates or removes opportunities for certain speakers. Linguistic discrimination is often bound up in other forms of inequality, and its effects may be difficult to distinguish from among the various setbacks experienced by speakers of lesser-valued languages or dialects. Ethnography, often longitudinal and always attentive to contextual detail, is especially apt for noticing the day-to-day effects of discriminatory language ideologies, practices and policies. Ethnographic monitors can begin to counter unequal or exclusionary multilingual practices in a simple and immediate way through taking the time to notice and draw attention to them – and their opposite, inclusive multilingual practices – in the day-to-day moments in which they occur. As illustrated in the following vignette, noticing inequalities and possible ways to shift them emerges from interacting with and listening to the concerns and aspirations of local stakeholders.

De Korne, August 2011

Having been asked to evaluate a "mother tongue" education programme run by an NGO in the southern Philippines, I begin by learning about the local language ecology. Numerous local Indigenous languages and a regional lingua franca are what I hear around me each day, yet formal education has traditionally been conducted in English and Filipino. Teachers tell me about the pressure they feel from national standardised English and Filipino reading tests, which discourage their efforts to use local languages. A teacher in a remote T'boli village invites me to watch as she administers an English reading test to a 5th grade boy. He reads the short English passage aloud with few mistakes. She then asks him the first comprehension question and he looks at her, saying nothing. She asks another question, and he continues to look at her with wide eyes. "You see," she tells me, "we give them the tests, they can read, but can't understand." She feels it is not fair to evaluate with these measures that are not suited to what students know; the results will show that the students fail, but will not explain why. To prove her point she hands him a text written in T'boli, prepared by the NGO that is promoting mother tongue education. She says this will probably be the first time he reads a text in his home language. He reads it with initial hesitation, but he does not hesitate when she asks the comprehension questions in T'boli, answering correctly. She beams. "In their own language it's different, if only

> we could test them this way." I agree and encourage her to continue promoting mother tongue testing within her district.
>
> As an NGO-affiliated researcher I have no power to influence these testing practices, but in a report for the NGO and government officials (De Korne et al., 2011) I note the barriers that existing tests represent for multilingual students.

Many minority students' language abilities are made invisible by top-down testing regimes, as in the case of the T'boli boy. A 2009 national law allowing mother-tongue-based multilingual education throughout the Philippines and actors like the NGO have the potential to change this, although they must contend with lack of resources and a systemic bias towards English and Filipino (Nolasco et al., 2010).

In contexts where discrimination has become the norm, ethnographers also provide important recognition of practices that are creating equitable opportunities for diverse speaker populations. A nascent positive social change may develop faster with the help of some attention, as evidenced by an example of ethnographic monitoring in South Africa, another country where multilingual education is struggling to gain respect in a previously exclusionary education system.

Hornberger, August 2008

I spent several weeks in 2008 at the University of Limpopo at an undergraduate program taught through the medium of both English and seSotho sa Leboa (Northern seSotho), commonly referred to by the name of its major variety, Sepedi. SeSotho sa Leboa is one of South Africa's nine officially recognized African languages and the highly innovative program in Contemporary English and Multilingual Studies (CEMS) is to date South Africa's only bilingual university-level program in English and an African language, founded in 2003 in direct and creative response to the openings afforded by South Africa's multilingual language policy (Granville et al., 1998; Joseph & Ramani, 2004, 2012). In developing the program, Michael Joseph and Esther Ramani sought to apply research literature including my continua of biliteracy (Hornberger, 1989, 2002, 2003); and at this point, several years into the program, they invited me to consult and collaborate with them to document, analyze, evaluate and strategize on their curriculum and potential ways to improve or extend it. This included sitting in on classes and interviewing undergraduate and postgraduate students and alumni; meeting with university officials about the program; contributing to a developing research culture in the program by offering university-wide lectures and program seminars on my research and advising postgraduate students on their theses; reviewing their curricular modules; developing a proposed Honors degree and Master's degree; and strategizing on ways to extend the program to include other major languages of the province – xiTsonga and tshiVenda – along with Sepedi.

The insights from this ethnographic monitoring of the CEMS program, conveyed as they emerged during my visit and written up in reports and papers in consultation and collaboration with Joseph and Ramani (Hornberger, 2010a, 2010b; Joseph & Ramani 2012), helped to inform the ongoing development, expansion, and recognition of the program while I was there and subsequently. Our collaborative ethnographic monitoring also contributed to CEMS' gaining approval for the new Honors program and to growing appreciation for CEMS within the University, South Africa, and internationally (Joseph and Ramani, personal communications).

This success can only be truly appreciated through an understanding of the context of vast inequity and asymmetry of power in which it has occurred. South African scholars Bloch and Alexander (2003) have described the hierarchical ecology of languages in South Africa, where English is dominant and hegemonic because of its global status and as the mythical language of national liberation during the anti-apartheid struggle, Afrikaans is regarded by black South Africans as 'the language of the oppressor' while remaining necessary for economic reasons, and the nine Indigenous languages lie clustered together at the bottom of the hierarchy on a steep gradient of meagre resource allocation. In this context, CEMS is a project which, like Bloch and Alexander's own efforts through the Project for the Study of Alternative Education in South Africa (PRAESA), is "demonstrating as well as reclaiming the power of the powerless" (Bloch & Alexander, 2003: 93), in the quest to "shift the balance of power in favour of those for whom ostensibly the democratic transition was initiated" (ibid: 117). Shifting power balances, or gaining recognition for attempts to do so, is no easy feat. In this context, an ethnographic monitor can help to heighten awareness of others, and especially official others, so that they notice the accomplishments and vision of successful programs in their midst working hard to counter longstanding and deeply entrenched unequal multilingualisms.

Analyzing and interpreting

What do language practices mean for specific people, places, and times? What constitute positive and negative outcomes of language education through an emic worldview? Beyond the invested time it takes to observe language practices, ethnographic monitoring charts a course for supporting positive change based on a context-specific understanding of what constitutes a positive or negative outcome of language practices. As Hymes (1980: 11) notes, "to achieve equality within a given language it would never be enough to change the way that people speak. One would have to change what the way people speak is taken to mean." Promoting Indigenous languages in post-colonial contexts such as South Africa or the Philippines is thus not simply about allowing the presence of these languages in education but must also involve addressing the persistent hierarchies and ideologies mentioned above. Interpreting what language practices *mean* is indispensable in multilingual contexts, where inequalities and power struggles are often intertwined through

Ethnographic monitoring, principles, practice 251

long histories, as illustrated in this vignette of Indigenous language education in Mexico.

De Korne, December 2013

While researching a fledgling Isthmus Zapotec class in a public university in southern Oaxaca, I notice that there is a hierarchy of Isthmus Zapotec dialects. The dialect of a neighboring town (A) is generally understood as more socially dominant, and by some people is considered more correct than the dialect of the town where the class is being taught (B), and there is an old history of political tension between the towns. The majority of available written materials are in dialect A. The university coordinator who initiated the Isthmus Zapotec class is not from the region, was not aware of the dialects, and hired a speaker of dialect A to teach the class. Based on interviews with a range of participants and observations across 3 semesters, my analysis shows that choosing to teach the class in dialect A is viewed as desirable and more accessible by some participants, but simultaneously alienates a greater number of would-be learners of other regional dialects. One such learner, a young woman who entered the class very motivated, tells me in an interview that she is frustrated that dialect B is excluded, since it is spoken in closest geographic proximity to the university and is the dialect of her family. Although she has more background knowledge of the language than anyone else in the class, she does poorly on the exam and does not re-enroll the following semester. I discuss these observations with the coordinator and other participants, who decide to try including multiple dialects.

Analyzing what it means to speak different dialects (and how meanings may differ among social actors) gives important insights into the dynamics that impact the outcomes of this Isthmus Zapotec education initiative. For many participants, the mere inclusion of an Isthmus Zapotec class means a positive change in the university, community, and national language ecologies, which traditionally privileged European languages (López Gopar, 2007). However, teaching Isthmus Zapotec as though it were a standardized language can mean losing the participation of diverse learners. Including multiple dialects raises potential complications for teaching and obtaining materials; however, here it emerged as a way to increase program success, as understood by participants.

Tensions in the local ecology of languages inevitably attend initiatives to open ideological and implementational spaces for languages previously excluded from formal education, as demonstrated in Hornberger's ethnographic study of the introduction of Quechua into schools of highland Peru in the 1980s, where, despite evident benefits for learners, the program had an uphill battle to fight in a local ideological space where schooling was equated with Spanish (Hornberger, 1987, 2005). Isthmus Zapotec classes in Mexico, the CEMS program in South Africa, "mother tongue" education in the Philippines, and countless other Indigenous language initiatives are all subject to what Fishman memorably characterized as perennial "problems

252   *H. De Korne and N.H. Hornberger*

in the socio-educational legitimization of vernacular languages" (1982: 4). Although there are often similarities in the kinds of tensions observed among different programs – such as dialect hierarchies, debated orthographies, and competing ideologies – each context represents a unique constellation of factors to be understood and analyzed. For example, varietal diversity is a source of tension in the promotion of Sámi language education in Scandinavia, where nine Sámi language varieties with varying numbers of speakers, from a handful to several thousand, are all in need of support through education at K-12 and university levels, but are sometimes positioned as competing for resources.

Hornberger, May 2013

As I sit with faculty key to the development of Umeå University's proposal for the Sámi language teacher education program they hope to mount, we review the myriad curricular dimensions to be taken into account in designing the program, among them the specific Sámi varieties to be included (North, South, and Lule) and the feasibility of contemplating a common Sámi pedagogy across all of them; the need to accommodate both students learning the language and students learning to teach the language in the same courses; the dispersion of speakers and prospective teachers across hundreds of square miles in Sápmi with different varieties geographically concentrated in different areas; and the scarce human resources and competing institutions of language teacher training in Kautokeino Norway and Oulu Finland. Indeed, the tensions and challenges are daunting and as I try to share successful experiences I know of in other Indigenous contexts of the world, I empathize with the discouragements and congratulate the faculty on their perseverance and creativity in confronting them.

Ethnographic analysis typically combines "an accumulative comparative understanding" with case-specific factors in this way (Hymes, 1980: 105), resulting in insights that may not solve perennial problems but do allow participants to frame their concerns in a broader perspective and deliberate what approach to dialect diversity, resource allocation, and the like, seems appropriate in their context.

Evaluation oriented towards social change

Relativism and neutrality are important elements of ethnography; as such, it may seem strange to advocate for ethnography as a key tool in the service of critical evaluation. However, the meanings and comparisons made visible by ethnographic description and interpretation can inform evaluations and decisions in processes of change. In the ethnographic monitoring paradigm, evaluation oriented towards social change is not understood as an individual expert judgment but rather a systematic search for changes that may be tenable relative to contextual priorities. Noticing and amplifying positive

Ethnographic monitoring, principles, practice   253

changes that are already underway is therefore a good point of departure, as well as engaging stakeholders in ongoing monitoring activities. As Hymes (1980: 108) states:

> The temptation of descriptive ethnography is to let understanding imply acceptance, but ethnography can be used critically. In a given case, a community may not have been conscious of some aspects of its patterns of language use, and it might wish to reject some part when brought to its attention. [...] Or it may decide to accept and value a pattern previously little noted. Whatever the case, the goals of bilingual [or Indigenous language] education should be informed by ethnography but set by those affected. (bracketed addition ours)

Evaluating for positive social change requires adapting disciplinary knowledge to local contextual nuance, arriving at what Berryman et al. (2010) call culturally responsive methodology. This is especially appropriate to research with marginalized populations, such as Indigenous people, who have often been voiceless objects of research under colonial and post-colonial systems (Smith, 1999). Ethnographic monitoring is one of the paradigms with potential to shift from research *on*, to research *for*, *with*, and *by* participants, thus creating more equitable forms of knowledge creation (Cameron et al., 1992; Czaykowska-Higgins, 2009). Hymes (1980: 105) argues that "of all forms of scientific knowledge, ethnography is the most open, the most compatible with a democratic way of life, the least likely to produce a world in which experts control knowledge at the expense of those who are studied."

The ethnographic monitoring paradigm does not prescribe methods but suggests principles by which to select from a repertoire of methods. In some cases, the researcher has an acknowledged insider role from the outset, while in others, collaborations may emerge over time, or the researcher's contribution may consist of providing a description from the outside. Where collaborative research is possible it may be pursued through the use of a variety of methods that have been explored and modeled in the literature, including participatory, action, and inquiry methods (e.g. McIntyre, 2008; Cochran-Smith & Lytle, 2009). Researchers must choose methods that are appropriate to the case in hand and remain alert to emergent forms of cooperation throughout the study.

In many regions of the world, economic under-development, under-resourced programs, corruption and even extreme weather create challenges in the provision of quality education. Indigenous communities in particular are often in positions of economic instability and at the bottom of post-colonial social hierarchies. Educational projects that attempt to shift language norms in favor of Indigenous languages must understand and cope with these perennial problems as well. The contextually embedded nature of ethnographic monitoring allows for flexibility in negotiating such factors, enabling the researcher to respond in small or large ways to the opportunities that arise.

254   H. De Korne and N.H. Hornberger

Typical ecological tensions, such as lack of teachers, materials, and language corpus surround the introduction of isiZulu as medium of instruction at the University of KwaZulu-Natal (UKZN) in South Africa. In keeping with the South African multilingual language policy of 1996 and increasing attention to implementing it at higher education levels (Hibbert & Van der Walt, 2014), elevation of the status and use of isiZulu at UKZN is a major aim of the university's language policy, in recognition that 80 percent of KwaZulu-Natal's population speaks isiZulu (Kamwendo et al., 2013; Mgqwashu, 2014; Ndimande, 2004; Ndimande-Hlongwa & Wildsmith-Cromarty, 2010). Achieving this aim is not straightforward, however, and involves understanding the tensions around use of isiZulu, including parents' and teachers' attitudes, as well as a lack of institutional resources, as disclosed through ethnographic monitoring in and around UKZN.

Hornberger, August 2010

At the invitation of the UKZN Deputy Vice Chancellor for Teaching and Learning, charged with implementation of the language policy, I observe and engage in dialogue with faculty, administrators, and postgraduate students of different faculties, as well as at public schools and with the local English Language Education Trust NGO, to analyze and interpret what specific language practices mean to the different social actors in these spaces, and how to move forward with policy goals.

In local school visits, I observe a first-grade lesson on animals skillfully taught through the medium of English with code-switching to isiZulu to clarify meanings and encourage participation; and meet with a group of principals concerned about what they called the gap in Black students' language from "spoken isiZulu at home to written English at school." In a UKZN graduate language planning seminar taught through the medium of isiZulu, the master's students, who are all also teachers, talk about school learners writing Zulu-ized English words rather than pure isiZulu in their isiZulu-medium classes, the negative reaction of parents to new school policies of teaching isiZulu-medium rather than English in the primary grades, and the need for mother-tongue-based multilingual education in the schools and at UKZN to counter the hegemony of English – not to replace English with isiZulu, but in an additive model. In conversations with schoolteachers and university faculty the seemingly irreconcilable tension between parents' demand for English as the language of power and students' biliteracy development needs surfaces repeatedly, as do the challenges of negotiating multilingualism in classroom and curriculum. It is clear that there are numerous ecological tensions beyond the direct control of the university that have a strong impact on the success of the language policy.

Tensions within the university also emerge around the special role of isiZulu and the School of isiZulu Studies in implementing the language policy. There are concerns lest isiZulu become the sole rather than primary focus of UKZN language policy: What about other South African languages? What about languages spoken by immigrants or foreign students, such as French, Portuguese or Kiswahili? And there are concerns as to the appropriate role for the School

Ethnographic monitoring, principles, practice 255

> of isiZulu Studies in the implementation of isiZulu-medium teaching across the university; isiZulu faculty expertise is clearly central to the undertaking, but they are neither enough in number nor do they necessarily cover all the areas of expertise required to meet the need.

Here, the ethnographic monitoring role consisted of hearing and helping to formulate collaboratively with participants strategies for moving forward in the implementation of the policy, bringing together the researcher's comparative perspective with the concerns of participants. The way forward involved attempts to open and reinforce implementational spaces, as well as a need for disseminating and developing further research on the policy within the university. As collaborative consultant, the researcher was able to highlight and advocate for an ethnographic monitoring cycle to be undertaken by participants, providing continuous evaluation towards policy implementation. Locally produced evaluation can help to address the lack of resources among faculty and teachers, provide information to concerned parents, and keep a close eye on policy outcomes. While evaluation may greatly improve education initiatives, it can also be a threat if undertaken with inappropriate measurements, imposed norms, or lack of stakeholder input, as Hymes (1980: 115) discusses:

> The greatest value of cooperative ethnographic monitoring is that the participants of the program will have the firmest grasp possible of the working of the program, of its successes and failures, strengths and weaknesses, in relation to their hopes for it. They will not be in the position of being confronted by an outside evaluator's charts and tables, and told a rating for their program, with nothing to say. [... I]f measures are to mean anything, especially in relation to bilingual education as a process of social change, the ethnography is essential.

Conclusion

Language inequalities are not static – although they may be persistent and rooted in long histories. Recognition of the researcher as a social actor with the capacity to engage and influence language inequalities in the environment in which they work is a key element of the ethnographic monitoring paradigm, and also of a critical paradigm of research on multilingualism. Whether it is simply drawing attention to existing inequalities and/or positive practices, or engaging in more active forms of analysis, collaboration, and planning, there is much that ethnographers can do to counter linguistic and other forms of exclusion in the contexts in which we work. This is most readily put in practice at the level of program implementation, as discussed by Hymes (1980) and exemplified in the cases shown here. However, we believe that the commitment to observing and combating inequalities is applicable to ethnographic research

256   *H. De Korne and N.H. Hornberger*

endeavors across social domains. Researchers engaging in ethnographic monitoring will not have a pre-determined agenda or recipe for social change, but through observation and interpretation may arrive at evaluations of the successes and failures of the context in question and help to identify appropriate ways to respond to them. The ethnographic monitoring paradigm provides an important rationale and useful guidelines for researchers to join with local stakeholders in bringing to light and countering language inequalities.

Note

1   Hornberger is grateful to colleagues who graciously invited and hosted her visits and to the programs that supported them: at University of Limpopo – Esther Ramani, Michael Joseph and the Fulbright Senior Specialist program; at Umeå University – Görel Sandström, Hanna Outakoski, Mikael Vinka, and the University's Visiting Professor program; at University of KwaZulu-Natal – Renuka Vithal, Rubby Dhunpath, Nobuhle Ndimande-Hlongwa, and the UKZN Teaching and Learning Office. De Korne gratefully acknowledges the support of the Autonomous Benito Juarez University of Oaxaca, Faculty of Languages, in particular Ximena Guiomar Léon Fernandez, Mario López Gopar, and participants in the Zapotec program. Thanks also to the staff and affiliates of Save the Children in Koronadal, the Philippines, in particular Bonna Duron, and to the Save the Children-University Partnership for Research, which made her visit there possible.

References

Berryman, M., Glynn, T., Woller, P. & Reweti, M. (2010) 'Maori language policy and practice in New Zealand schools: community challenges and community solutions', in K. Menken & O. García (eds) *Negotiating Language Policies in Schools: Educators as Policymakers*. New York: Routledge, 146–161.

Bloch, C. & Alexander, N. (2003) 'A luta continua! The relevance of the continua of biliteracy to South African multilingual schools', in N.H. Hornberger (ed.) *Continua of Biliteracy: An Ecological Framework for Educational Policy, Research, and Practice in Multilingual Settings*. Clevedon, UK: Multilingual Matters, 91–121.

Blommaert, J. (2009) 'Ethnography and democracy: Hymes's political theory of language'. *Text & Talk* 29(3), 257–276.

Cameron, D., Frazer, E., Harvey, P., Rampton, B. & Richardson, K. (1992) *Researching Language: Issues of Power and Method*. New York: Routledge.

Cochran-Smith, M. & Lytle, S. (2009) *Inquiry as Stance: Practitioner Research for the Next Generation*. New York: Teachers College Press.

Czaykowska-Higgins, E. (2009) 'Research models, community engagement, and linguistic fieldwork: reflections on working within Canadian Indigenous communities'. *Language Documentation & Conservation* 3(1),15–50.

De Korne, H., Duron, B. & Dowd, A. (2011) *Guidelines for Context-Embedded Assessment of Mother Tongue-Based Multilingual Education Programs*. Save the Children International.

Fairclough, N. (1989) *Language and Power*. London: Longman.

Fishman, J.A. (1982) 'Sociolinguistic foundations of bilingual education'. *The Bilingual Review/ La Revista Bilingüe* 9(1), 1–35.

Granville, S., Janks, H., Mphahlele, M., Reed, Y., Watson, P., Joseph, M. & Ramani, E. (1998) 'English with or without g(u)ilt: a position paper on language in education policy for South Africa'. *Language and Education* 12(4), 254–272.

Hibbert, L. & van der Walt, C. (eds) (2014) *Multilingual Universities in South Africa: Reflecting Society in Higher Education*. Bristol, UK: Multilingual Matters.

Hornberger, N.H. (1987) 'Bilingual education success, but policy failure'. *Language in Society* 16(2), 205–226.

Hornberger, N.H. (1989) 'Continua of biliteracy'. *Review of Educational Research* 59(3), 271–296.

Hornberger, N.H. (2002) 'Multilingual language policies and the continua of biliteracy: an ecological approach'. *Language Policy* 1(1), 27–51.

Hornberger, N.H. (ed.) (2003) *Continua of Biliteracy: An Ecological Framework for Educational Policy, Research and Practice in Multilingual Settings*. Clevedon, UK: Multilingual Matters.

Hornberger, N.H. (2005) 'Opening and filling up implementational and ideological spaces in heritage language education'. *Modern Language Journal* 89(4), 605–609.

Hornberger, N.H. (2009) 'Hymes's linguistics and ethnography in education'. *Text & Talk* 29(3), 347–358.

Hornberger, N.H. (2010a) 'Foreword', in K. Menken & O. García (eds) *Negotiating Language Policies in Schools: Educators as Policymakers*. New York: Routledge, xi–xiii.

Hornberger, N.H. (2010b) 'Language and education: a Limpopo lens', in N.H. Hornberger & S.L. McKay (eds) *Sociolinguistics and Language Education*. Bristol, UK: Multilingual Matters, 549–564.

Hornberger, N.H. (2014) 'On not taking language inequality for granted: Hymesian traces in ethnographic monitoring of South Africa's multilingual language policy'. *Multilingua* 33(5/6), 623–645.

Hymes, D.H. (1968) 'The ethnography of speaking', in J.A. Fishman (ed.) *Readings in the Sociology of Language*. The Hague: Mouton, 99–138.

Hymes, D.H. (1972) 'On communicative competence', in J.B. Pride & J. Holmes (eds) *Sociolinguistics: Selected Readings*. Harmondsworth: Penguin Books, 269–293.

Hymes, D.H. (1980) 'Ethnographic monitoring', in *Language in Education: Ethnolinguistic Essays*. Washington DC: Center for Applied Linguistics, 104–118.

Hymes, D.H. (1992) 'Inequality in language: taking for granted'. *Penn Working Papers in Educational Linguistics* 8(1), 1–30.

Hymes, D.H. (1996) *Ethnography, Linguistics, Narrative Inequality: Toward an Understanding of Voice*. London: Taylor & Francis.

Joseph, M. & Ramani, E. (2004) 'Cummins' four quadrants: a pedagogic framework for developing academic excellence in the new bilingual degree at the University of the North'. *Paper presented at the international Conference of the Southern African Applied Linguistics Association (SAALA), University of Limpopo.*

Joseph, M. & Ramani, E. (2012) '"Glocalization": going beyond the dichotomy of global versus local through additive multilingualism'. *International Multilingual Research Journal* 6(1), 22–34.

Kamwendo, G., Hlongwa, N. & Mkhize, N. (2013) 'On medium of instruction and African scholarship: the case of IsiZulu at the University of KwaZulu-Natal in South Africa'. *Current Issues in Language Planning* 15(1), 75–89.

258   H. De Korne and N.H. Hornberger

López Gopar, M.E. (2007) 'El alfabeto marginante en la educación indígena: el potencial de las multilectoescrituras'.[The marginalised orthography in Indigenous education: the potential of multilectal writing systems]. *Lectura y Vida* 28(3), 48–57.

McIntyre, A. (2008) *Participatory Action Research*. Thousand Oaks, CA: Sage.

Mgqwashu, E.M. (2014) 'On developing academic literacy in the mother tongue for epistemological access: the role of isiZulu as the LoLT in a South African university'. *Current Issues in Language Planning* 15(1), 90–103.

Ndimande, N. (2004) 'Language and identity: the case of African languages in S.A. higher education'. *Alternation* 11(2), 62–84.

Ndimande-Hlongwa, N. & Wildsmith-Cromarty, R. (eds) (2010) 'Multilingualism for access, language development and language intellectualization'. *Alternation* 17(1). [Entire issue].

Nolasco, R., Datar, F. & Azurin, A. (2010) *Starting Where the Children Are: A Collection of Essays on Mother Tongue-Based Multilingual Education and Language Issues in the Philippines*. Quezon City, Manila: 170+ Talyatayan MLE Inc.

Smith, L.T. (1999) *Decolonising Methodologies: Research and Indigenous People*. London: Zed Books.

Van der Aa, J. & Blommaert, J. (2011) 'Ethnographic monitoring: Hymes's unfinished business in educational research'. *Anthropology and Education Quarterly* 42(4), 319–334.

17 Ethnographic monitoring and the study of complexity

Jef Van der Aa and Jan Blommaert

The context: increased complexity

In this chapter, we explore the value of long-term fieldwork in the context of ever-increasing complexity in social life. This complexity stems from the phenomenon of 'superdiversity' (Vertovec, 2007) and the effects of globalization. These effects are visible in the contact between languages and cultures, which has spawned a range of new language-cultural phenomena. Sociolinguists and ethnographers concerned with superdiversity argue that the concepts of language and culture themselves, as separate, bounded entities, have become highly problematic and now invite new methodological approaches (Blommaert & Rampton, 2011). Linguistic and cultural change is the rule and not the exception.

Dealing with this diversification of diversity, and concretely with extremely complex migration patterns and the birth of the 'network society' (Castells, 1996), in which the networks of individuals and groups have become immensely intense and diverse, is a real challenge for both civil and civic society in key areas such as healthcare, social work, education, union work. It calls for new frames, concepts, and actions through which it should become possible to deal with the very diverse needs of increasing numbers of people who fall outside the mainstream: for example, within the European Union, newcomers from non-European Union countries, newcomers from other EU countries but also many EU citizens that have become victims of the ever tightening economy and job market.

The particular social conditions of superdiversity also demand a change in our own academic approaches, including our theoretical apparatus as well as our fieldwork. For instance, a homogeneous or unified program to deal with 'problematic youth' can no longer exist because it starts from a specific group of people who are prone to develop particular behavior, and completely ignores the superdiverse background, including the very complex (migration) trajectories which people have experienced before coming into contact with a particular institutional context, e.g. the employment agency. Academically, superdiversity also signals the end of certainty with regard to questions like "Who is the other?" and "Who am I?" Many disciplines, including much of

260   J. Van der Aa and J. Blommaert

linguistic ethnography, are still struggling with the remnants of structuralism concerning their research objects, methods and knowledge frames. These
are inadequate to address society's rapid and permanent change, its instability, unpredictability and complexity. We do not only need more interdisciplinarity, but also a change in the concept of 'science' itself: from an ontology
grounded in synchronic and observable units to a science that has 'change' as
its object of analysis, and 'dynamic details' as its units of study.

To achieve this purpose, we propose an investment in longer-term fieldwork projects that allow for the development of a more social action-oriented
linguistic ethnography in which feedback, valorization, 'theory from below'
and 'slow science' are key concepts. We first outline our understanding of
the contemporary relevance of Hymes' concept of 'ethnographic monitoring' (Hymes, 1980; Hymes et al., 1981); we then illustrate this approach by
presenting an example from an ongoing project in Antwerp with children and
adolescents in 'family care'; and we reflect on the implications of this methodology for 'theory', illustrating the quasi-inseparability in (linguistic) ethnography between theory and method. Finally, we argue that it is only possible
to achieve a turnover in which complex issues are not reduced if we massively
ground our research in the social fields that need it most. If we realize an in-
depth cooperation with and within those social fields, we will be subject to
their 'ethnographic inspection' of our proposed analysis.

Ethnographic monitoring

In *Reinventing Anthropology* (1972) Dell Hymes argued for anthropological
studies that aim at a theoretical and methodological "reintegration within
complex units" of phenomena indexing change (1972: 32–33). To achieve
this reintegration of rapid social changes, we need to study these changes
appropriately, and in order to do so we need to rely heavily on the social
actors we work with. The role of the ethnographer has thus changed from
being a mere 'observer' who describes what he or she sees to an 'active
participant' who makes explicit the changes for which there is no vocabulary
yet. In this spirit, Hymes subsequently developed a research program called
'ethnographic monitoring.'

When Hymes passed away in 2009, his work (after a long period of relative
silence) started to attract the attention of a new generation of scholars (e.g.
Hornberger, 2009; Rampton, 2009 – see also Rampton, 2007 for a survey of
the recent impact of Hymes' work). One of the lesser-used concepts of his
work is what he referred to as 'ethnographic monitoring.' He commented on
this as follows:

> The greatest value of cooperative ethnographic monitoring is that the
> participants in [a] programme will have the firmest grasp possible of
> the working of the programme, of its successes and failures, strengths
> and weaknesses, in relation to their hopes for it. They will not be in the

Ethnographic monitoring, epistemic solidarity 261

position of being confronted by an outside evaluator's charts and tables, and told a rating for their programme, with nothing to say, or nothing, at least, that such an evaluator feels required to heed. The participants will not have been bystanders. They will ... be able to address the processes that have produced whatever statistics and graphs a formal evaluation process may yield.

(Hymes, 1980:115)

Some, like Jørgensen, have organized projects very similar to ethnographic monitoring, having been involved in the same school for decades (see e.g. Jørgensen, 2009, and see Madsen et al., 2013 for a detailed description of this particular project). Let us now take a look at what this program involves (see Van der Aa & Blommaert, 2011 for a more detailed discussion). Hymes proposes the following steps as being part of 'ethnographic monitoring' (Hymes, 1980; Hymes et al., 1981). In parentheses you will find our interpretation of these different steps, which we return to later on.

1. First, ethnographers consult social actors to identify what issues concern them most (the other's position).
2. A second step is to observe behavior relevant to that issue in a series of contexts, in and out of the center (contrasted with observer's position).
3. The third step is to share our findings with the center personnel, and the clients as far as is possible (instant feedback and uptake).
4. Take stock (evaluating 'effect').

We believe, with Hymes, that by following these steps, there is a guarantee that research plans and programs are developed organically and in close consultation with all social actors involved. In other words: static solutions are being replaced by complex dynamics, because understanding the world involves changing it. Therefore, when deploying ethnographic monitoring, one can speak of aiming to achieve "epistemic solidarity" (Van der Aa, 2012) and adopting the positioning of "the ethnographer as pupil" (Velghe, 2011). Researchers and the social actors in the field build shareable knowledge together, showing a long-term commitment. Researchers work together with social actors to introduce and operationalize particular academic concepts relevant to them. We now attempt to make this process more tangible by introducing the idea of the 'researcher in residence', thereby emphasizing the importance of 'long-term relationships' within the field.

Researcher in residence

Increasingly, academic institutions are asked to cooperate with social actors in areas such as education and social work, in an institutional agenda of knowledge transfer/exchange. From an academic point of view, it can be very useful to see how particular academic concepts are deemed

262   J. Van der Aa and J. Blommaert

relevant by social actors and are operationalized. Such a commitment needs to be long term and qualitative: long term because there should be enough time to develop particular networks and strategies and to get used to one another coming from entirely different environments; and qualitative in order to counterbalance the need for educational and social institutions to report evidence-based material by offering a very practical alternative.

The 'researcher in residence' approach can make changing dynamics (which are, of course, responses to these new realities) within institutions visible, explicit and reportable. He or she helps to draw attention to useful dynamics, ideas and routines, strengthens them and makes them work better. The researcher in residence is a long-term academic consultant who can offer help with academic ventures relating to institutional personnel, qualitative reporting, tapping into a wide network of academic colleagues to discuss particular issues, and so on. In some cases, it is also possible for MA or PhD students to work together with the researchers in residence. In our case study in a family care center in Antwerp (see below), particular issues arose with regards to the intake procedure, and an MA student has conducted a project observing and transcribing these procedures in one of the center's branches (Mensaert, 2013).

Social institutions as 'academic workshops'

Concretely, we are working within two field sites, each having a 'researcher in residence'. In Berchem (Antwerp), Jef Van der Aa has developed several lines of research relating to the organizational structure of a non-profit organization consisting of three branches: a 'home supervision' counseling service for families who have problems with one or more children; several day centers catering to the free time and homework needs of young people aged 6–18 of very diverse backgrounds; and finally a service catering to adolescents aged 16–21 who want to live on their own because of problems at home or due to not having a home at all.

In all three branches, there is an intake procedure, a waiting list, and an 'action plan' drawn up after six–eight weeks. After that, families or children are usually under the supervision of the counselors at the center, for between one and two years. In West Flanders we have started a research project with an asylum center, in which Massimiliano Spotti is researcher in residence (Spotti, 2013).

In both places, there are research and participation activities within the centers, such as participant observation, collecting documents, interviews with care providers/counseling personnel as well as clients, the organization of discussion sessions (both in-group and one-on-one sessions), educational sessions, helping out in general, e.g. moving a couch. Most productive has been the organization of an 'office hour,' in which particular issues or problems can be brought to the attention of the academic consultant.

In both cases, one of the significant issues is the importance of the center within the neighborhood and the links that have been established with the neighborhood. In the case of Antwerp, the center is located in an historical neighborhood which bears traces of more than fifty years of migration; and the center in West Flanders is located very close to the French border. In both places there is a good deal of interaction with the local environment, which shows in its infrastructure: telephone and internet shops, shops offering food and products from all over the world.

To achieve an accurate descriptive analysis of the place of the centers in their social environment we have made use of some ethnographic linguistic landscaping "in an attempt to arrive at a detailed and accurate synchronic description of the neighborhood, oriented towards questions of demographic and social presence in the area" (Blommaert, 2013: 60). Centers also work together with other organizations, sometimes offering additional loci for research. Currently there are exploratory talks planned in Antwerp with a low-profile organization offering job guidance to people dealing with structural issues in their lives that prevent them from doing 'regular work.' In all, we propose a longitudinal mix of research and participation in institutions.

The emerging research program

In order to address the complexity of these issues, it is no longer possible to engage with this kind of research from a pre-defined research plan with predicted outcomes and clear-cut pre-defined means of method and analysis. Following the different phases of ethnographic monitoring as described above, one quickly discovers the shortcomings of these plans (such shortcomings are also described in Blommaert & Dong Jie, 2010). Contrasting observers' and others' positions, one almost naturally becomes a 'participant.' As one works through different knowledge trajectories, an emerging research program takes shape slowly and incrementally. Often, instant and long-term feedback changes the course of events and deals with particular issues and problems in the emerging plan. Some of the research questions that we have developed in this way have to do with processes of 'digital citizenship' and questions concerning framing, epistemology and narrativity in the Berchem neighborhood of Antwerp.

In the Antwerp center, for example, the topics of intake procedures are entirely unpredictable, as the causes for seeking assistance often result from instability in a family system – an escalating category in a context of superdiversity. Therefore it is not possible to develop plans that would be targeted at particular populations, the Roma, say, or non-native Belgians, or even, 'problematic' youth. The enormous mobility of people who stay for shorter or longer periods of time in Belgium, in Antwerp, in care, varies greatly. Rather one finds oneself defining research interests and programs along with generically formulated core issues such as learning problems, issues of domestic violence, poverty, housing and so on. In any particular case, one never observes

264   *J. Van der Aa and J. Blommaert*

just one problem, but rather always complex combinations of issues. Working through many months of intense participation in the center, it became possible to formulate 'research questions' that were grounded in and supported by the care providers, the coaches and the direction of the center:

> What do people know about poverty? What other issues does it involve? How do they talk about it? And, what are they allowed to say under what conditions? And, finally, what can we do to improve those conditions?

The formulation of these research questions was the result of an interplay of ethnographic actions: during the 'consultation hour' we organized in the center, important issues came to the table, as well as during participation in intra-center working groups on topics such as 'intercultural management' and 'superdiversity.' Specific case studies were selected for us to participate in over the course of several months, which were then fed back into the working groups. After thorough discussion on different levels within the center (clients, care providers, coaches and management), the research questions were slowly shaped and refined.

We could not have arrived at this point with the old tool of participant observation alone, in which the tension between 'knowledge from below' or 'theory from below' is never really resolved. On the one hand, there is a fear of 'not being objective,' on the other hand, a fear of 'not getting close enough.' We will return to this below. For now, it suffices to say that to formulate fully developed and meaningful research questions which are supported by social actors, one needs to engage in what we call 'full participation.' In the Antwerp case, this included, among other things, hanging around, cooking, doing arts & crafts with youngsters, engaging in professional activities, recording, carrying out analysis, bringing back the patterns noticed, developing training (feedback, workshops, offering social actors access to training facilities at the university). We now illustrate this way of working with a concrete case study from the Antwerp project.

Complexity and the 'total social fact': Nabijah's case

Nabijah[1] ("Brave one") is a 37-year-old Belgian-Iraqi woman living in Antwerp North. She lives with four children in a very small apartment where irregular heating and electricity depend on the values left on the budget meter (a sort of prepaid gas/electricity system). One of the children has a severe learning disability and the oldest child is not hers, but the child of her sister in Germany. Having recently gone through a very rough divorce from her Iraqi husband, Nabijah has a lot on her plate.

Nabijah and her children were being monitored by Lucy, one of the care providers at the center. Lucy had weekly meetings with Nabijah in her home, often together with various people, such as translators, social workers, lawyers (to take care of the debt that remained after the divorce), teachers, and

Ethnographic monitoring, epistemic solidarity 265

the care provider(s) for her mentally disabled son (who lived in a residential center during the week).

During recent fieldwork at the center, Jef Van der Aa came across Nabijah's case and he was invited by Lucy to come along and offer a pair of anthropological eyes, in order to make more sense of the entire situation. Nabijah's story, in the professional vision of the social worker, had been pre-configured, and only particular elements that fitted the professional scheme had been accepted as meaningful. Inevitably, there was also a reduction of complexity because of this pre-configuration (and this was reinforced by the pre-configured nature of the official forms that needed to be filled out). For the ethnographer, everything is potentially meaningful. Latent objects can become manifest at the blink of an eye. In Nabijah's case, her brother in Iraq often listened in and participated in the conversations through Skype. The co-presence of on- and off-line interaction added further complexity to the existing linguistic and generic diversity, and there were other overt and covert influences as well, sometimes manifestly present, sometimes latently lurking. An example of this was Nabijah's headscarf, which suddenly became relevant in a conversation between Lucy and Nabijah regarding her inability to find work. With the best intentions, Lucy said "in Belgium, you'll have to take it [the headscarf] off when the employer wants you to". She explained this to Jef later in the car, saying: "I had to say that for Nabijah's own best interests. I am personally also against the headscarf ban[2] you know. It's ridiculous."

We will now illustrate the complexity of the interactions that occurred during Lucy's home visits to Nabijah's apartment by means of two vignettes. The first vignette recounts an interaction between Nabijah and several social care providers, including Lucy. All the interlocutors are trying to hold their own in the conversation in order to prioritize particular needs. The second vignette presents an example of how the conversations during these visits reached outward to family networks abroad, in this case Nabijah's brother in Iraq. Both of the conversations captured in these vignettes were tape-recorded and conducted in Dutch, and mediated by an Arabic translator (sometimes this was someone who spoke Iraqi Arabic). We complemented the audio recordings with the taking of detailed field notes. (The field notes on which the vignettes below were based were taken by Jef Van der Aa.)

Vignette 1

During one of the visits to Nabijah's house, Lucy was looking at Nabijah while explaining an interactive leaflet which indicated the daily routine for each of the four children. Also present were a translator and two other social workers, who were responsible for the healthcare and education of Abdul, Nabijah's oldest son, the one with learning difficulties. They had just explained how important it is that the 12-year-old Abdul took his medication on time. Every other weekend Abdul went home to Nabijah's house. The intention of the leaflet would be that,

266   J. Van der Aa and J. Blommaert

for each part of the day, Nabijah would engage with Abdul and her two oldest children and together decide whether they would fill out a happy or a sad face on the leaflet. A happy face meant that things went well during breakfast e.g., a sad face meant that it wasn't going as planned for one reason or the other. Following this, Lucy asked for a translation. Nabijah replied by nodding but did not wait for the explanation of the leaflet to be translated. She suddenly broke into another topic and asked the social workers not to let Abdul's dad visit the child in the institution, addressing them directly in Dutch by saying: *"Nee, die man niet bij Abdul, slechte man"* ("No, not that man with Abdul, bad man"). The social workers replied by saying they had no power to do this. Nabijah subsequently turned to the translator, saying in Arabic: "I don't want him anywhere near my children. He's bad."

Vignette 2

Another time, Lucy, the translator and I were at Nabijah's apartment for the weekly visit. The translator was of Iraqi descent this time, translating in spoken Iraqi Arabic vernacular. We were discussing issues of paperwork and explaining procedures for obtaining a passport, something which had been a problem for Nabijah because of her former husband's legal troubles. The translator carefully explained all the steps to Nabijah, using the form Lucy had brought. Suddenly a voice shouted something from the computer behind Nabijah. Lucy and I (Jef Van der Aa) were both surprised, and the translator replied to the voice on the computer, telling us that it is Nabijah's brother, listening in on Skype. Nabijah confirmed this and explained that he was reacting to the information regarding the passport. There had been a request from the brother to Nabijah to formally adopt his son, her nephew. Nabijah then showed us the brother, we waved at him, and he disappeared from Skype as swiftly as he came once the conversation took another direction. Lucy then continued talking about other issues, such as the vacation plans for the family. After a few sentences Nabijah intervened, saying, directly in Dutch *"reispas"* (literally "travel passport"), followed by a 'kiss teeth' sound, implying that this is something she wanted to urgently talk about. She did this a couple of times. Later on in the conversation she did something similar (bypassing the translator and addressing Lucy and me directly in Dutch), saying *"Ja, ik wil verhuizen. IK wil het!"* ("Yes, I want to move house. I want it!") and *"Budget meter, NOG nie goe eh!"* ("Budget meter, NOT yet okay eh!"). The first intervention aimed at convincing Lucy to help Nabijah find a better house for her and her children, the second one at helping her out with a very urgent issue with the budget meter (a sort of pre-paid electricity system which had failed her mid-winter). Nabijah repeated both phrases again several times. All three short interventions were part of a patterned prioritization of Nabijah's urgent needs: mobility (passport), housing and electricity.

Let us now return to the complexity of the situation. The problem here was that Lucy, Nabijah and their respective 'co-interlocutors' (the brother in Nabijah's case, and the social workers in Lucy's case) had different purposes.

Where Lucy and the social workers were following a rather strict protocol in order to execute what needed to be done professionally (checking medication for the disabled son, translating official documents, etc.) within a fixed case frame, Nabijah brought a whole range of other, rather urgent key problems to the table. In fact, in one particular case, all other problems and issues were absolutely subordinate to that of solving the electricity problem in the middle of the winter season. This dominant issue was articulated via a range of language and addressee shifts as well as narrative patterns, something we could consider to be 'frame breaks.' Some of those issues were seen as 'noise' by Lucy and the other social workers, both in the thematic as well as the communicational sense. It was also literally very 'noisy' in the apartment, with children playing around and people intervening through phones and computers.

This was an extremely complex interactional situation which cannot be analyzed synchronically. On- and off-line events merged, latent objects suddenly became manifest, and there was a complex interaction of linguistic, generic, cultural and religious resources. Drawing on Silverstein's (1985) concept of the "total linguistic fact," we can easily see how this notion can be expanded to the analysis of superdiverse settings:

> The total linguistic fact, the datum for a science of language, is irreducibly dialectic in nature. It is an unstable mutual interaction of meaningful sign forms, contextualised to situations of interested human use and mediated by the fact of cultural ideology.
>
> (Silverstein, 1985: 220)

The kind of synchronic analysis, so typical of structuralism, can no longer be valid in these kinds of contexts in which each item is potentially meaningful and stretches outwards to people's complex trajectories.

To recap: important issues for Nabijah were expressed to Lucy and to Jef in Dutch, thereby bypassing the translator. These issues include: poverty (budget meter), a new life (house change, divorce), and mobility (issues stemming from the loss of a passport). Issues important to the care providers, such as the medication for the disabled son, his weekend care, and other practical issues, such as a leaflet indicating the structuring of the children's day, were discussed in Arabic through the translator's mediation.

In the spirit of 'ethnographic monitoring', in which knowledge and analysis is brought back to the field, we discussed with Lucy the fact that Nabijah had addressed Lucy and Jef directly in Dutch when speaking about important issues to her, and that when she had spoken about her ex-husband, she changed deictic footing from "he" to "that man." Taking this into account, Lucy decided to go there the next time without the translator, focusing on issues identified by Jef as being important to Nabijah. Thus, by bringing back analysis to the field right away, both ethnographic research and care practice took new directions. Let us now take a look at the kind of knowledge that can be produced through such ethnographic monitoring practices, and to do that we need to address the concept of 'theory' itself.

The status of 'theory'

One of the desired results of ethnographic monitoring has been achieved here: the refusal to take things for granted. Lucy mentioned in one of the after-visit feedback sessions which Jef had with her over lunch: "You know, this is just such a solitary job you know. Yes, there's a translator there, and many people, but no one to really talk to afterwards. And you saw things that I could not. And now I see those things too. I notice them."

Another small illustration of this happened when we organized a walk through the superdiverse shopping street adjacent to the center. During this walk, we asked social workers of the Antwerp center to pay attention to actual signs, inscriptions, products on sale and so on. Most people's reactions were of the same nature as Lucy's remark. Afterwards, Linda, one of the social workers at the center, told us, "I have been walking through this street for two years, and I never really noticed any of those things."

So what happens, then, when ethnographers make things explicit? What sort of knowledge do we see emerging? To us, this is a question of rethinking the concept of 'theory'.

In this context, we would like to argue that 'theory' here is the *sens pratique* (practical sense) of Bourdieu (1980), or the 'good practice' of the social workers being put into a broader ethnographic context that can be made explicit by the ethnographer. Social workers can understand their *sens pratique* as 'routine' and habituated professional practice: "we've always done it like this." On engaging in dialogue with the ethnographer, they are able to become aware of and reflect on this habituated practice. In this way, social workers or other professionals can become more conscious of the way/s in which they work. It is from this consciousness that it becomes possible to understand particular problems, to formulate (together) relevant research questions related to the problems, and to set up programs of investigation to explore, understand and potentially challenge or change such practices.

In this way, we moved with social workers from experience to expertise and from belief to knowledge. The ethnographic presence turned people's ideas, routines and beliefs about 'good practice' into an epistemic tool that generated 'theory'. Knowledge was shaped by finding and co-constructing a logic for knowledge that was already there. One can think of social actors as 'organic intellectuals' (in the Gramscian sense) whom the ethnographer can assist in formulating counterhegemonic knowledges aimed at achieving lasting social change, a change process in which the ethnographer participates.

Going over Nabijah's case during an informally held 'office hour' at the center, moving from observing, interacting, recording and note-taking to analysis, three kinds of feedback became possible: (1) immediate feedback which allowed the social actors involved to intervene urgently, e.g. in Nabijah's case, occasionally bypassing the translator in certain ways; (2) intermediate feedback which allowed the broader group of colleagues among the participants to understand, rethink and co-analyze a particular case. We led a

Ethnographic monitoring, epistemic solidarity 269

'superdiversity' working group at the center in which Nabijah's issues were discussed and analyzed; (3) long-term feedback which aimed at institutional change. An expert group was set up at managerial level in order to take stock of translation practices in the center, in the light of a tightening budget for translation services at city level. These three types of feedback have led to meaningful interventions and changes in particular practices in the center: for example, there will be more 'duo work' among social workers, building on the strategy of the anthropologist accompanying the social worker. And, as already noted, a 'superdiversity' working group has been set up and will continue using case work as its basis; and an expert group has been set up to look at translation practices.

Towards a program for studying social change

Finally, we would like to distill from the above a few points regarding doing ethnographic monitoring in complex, superdiverse, and rapidly changing societal institutions.

1. We have suggested that we move from participant observation to participation, a process in which ethnographers become an integral part of the fieldwork situations in which they find themselves. The program of Hymesian monitoring gives us an excellent starting point for doing research that is interesting for our collaborators in the field and that allows us to achieve social change. Good ethnography is 'making explicit' what we do anyway: we change situations we observe. Unmediated data do not exist.
2. Our presence in the field can be turned into an epistemic resource: researchers co-create the historical processes they document. In fact, this epistemic grounding can be turned into an advantage for all in a form of: 'epistemic solidarity.' This concept allows researchers to intervene in institutional settings by providing immediate feedback in which superdiversity can be operationalized, can be 'lived.' Creation of knowledge always takes place through a communicative process, and this knowledge is much needed in the fields dealing with superdiversity. Therefore we need to work in our respective fields with both immediate and long-term feedback. The knowledge trajectory then becomes entirely transparent through constant feedback/valorization, and this brings knowledge "under democratic control," as Hymes (1980) put it. In this way, we do not keep theory away from the field but create epistemological circles of activity.
3. There is a false distinction between researcher and object, induced by ideas of replicability in experimental science. There are few things more artificial and subjective than experiments. We have to overcome our fear of "losing" our habitus by grounding it epistemologically in the field, knowing that, even though habitus is never static, it is durable and constitutive of the knowledge we co-create (Blommaert, 2005: 222). Ethnographic

270   *J. Van der Aa and J. Blommaert*

monitoring proceeds by bringing together two situated knowledges and carves out a space for incorporating both forms of knowledge during analysis, followed by intensive multi-leveled feedback and evaluation.

4. Linguistic ethnography enables us to become aware of the importance of language in societal institutions which often put linguistic regimes into place that require subjects to talk, write and behave in ways that are alien to them. One thing linguistic ethnography is well equipped to do is precisely to bring to the surface those voices that are otherwise obscured by these regimes. To 'make those voices heard' is part of the program of social change that is encapsulated by ethnographic monitoring: proposing, doing and reporting analysis on participants' own terms. Some of those voices are subdued and can be extremely precarious, which raises several ethical concerns with regard to privacy, the documented status of refugees, gender issues, and so on. However, long-term relations create precisely the kind of confidence and emancipatory growth which is needed in order to give precarious participants 'voice,' a voice only particular people in particular circumstances can 'give.' We like to think that ethnographers are among those who can work in this way.

In *Reinventing Anthropology*, Hymes reveals the ultimate purpose of anthropological work, in which ethnographic monitoring is firmly grounded: "The analysis of anthropology is radical at least in this, that it accepts the contingency of anthropology and can envision a world in which it has no separate identity" (1972: 54). We interpret Hymes' statement here as meaning that the possible consequence of anthropological work would be to achieve such a profound change in society that all of the above can be taken as a given in ethnography.

Notes

1 We have adopted pseudonyms to maintain confidentiality.
2 In 2007, the City of Antwerp banned religious symbols for city staff.

References

Blommaert, J. (2005) 'Bourdieu the ethnographer: the ethnographic grounding of habitus and voice'. *The Translator* 11(2), 219–236.
Blommaert, J. (2013) *Chronicles of Complexity: Ethnography, Superdiversity, and Linguistic Landscapes*. Bristol: Multilingual Matters.
Blommaert, J. & Dong Jie (2010) *Ethnographic Fieldwork*. Bristol: Multilingual Matters
Blommaert, J. & Rampton, B. (2011) 'Language and superdiversity'. *Diversities* 13(2), 1–22.
Bourdieu, P. (1980) *Le Sens Pratique*. Paris: Minuit.
Castells, M. (1996) *The Rise of the Network Society – The Information Age: Economy, Society and Culture*, Vol. I. Cambridge, MA: Blackwell.

Hornberger, N.H. (2009) 'Hymes's linguistics and ethnography in education'. *Text & Talk:* 29(3), 347–358.

Hymes, D. (1972) 'The use of anthropology: critical, political, personal', in D. Hymes (ed.) *Reinventing Anthropology.* New York: Pantheon Books, 3–79.

Hymes, D. (1980) *Language in Education: Ethnolinguistic Essays.* Washington, DC: Center for Applied Linguistics.

Hymes, D. et al. (1981) *Ethnographic Monitoring of Children's Acquisition of Reading/ Language Arts Skills In and Out of the Classroom,* Vols. I, II and III. Final Report. Graduate School of Education. Philadelphia, PA: University of Pennsylvania.

Jørgensen, J.N. (2009) *Languaging: Nine Years of Poly-Lingual Development among Young Turkish-Danish Grade School Students.* Copenhagen: Danish University of Education.

Madsen, L., Karrebæk, M.S. & Møller, J.S. (2013) 'The Amager project: a study of language and social life of minority children and youth'. *Tilburg Papers in Culture Studies* 52. www.tilburguniversity.edu/research/institutes-and-research-groups/ babylon/tpcs.

Mensaert, R. (2013) *Building and Breaking Frames in Welfare Work.* MA Thesis, Ghent University.

Rampton, B. (2007) 'Neo-Hymesian linguistic ethnography in the UK'. *Journal of Sociolinguistics* 11(5),584–608.

Rampton, B. (2009) 'Dell Hymes' visions of enquiry'. *Text & Talk* 29(3), 359–369. [Theme issue, "On Hymes"].

Silverstein, M. (1985) 'Language and the culture of gender', in E. Mertz and R. Parmentier (eds) *Semiotic Mediation.* New York: Academic Press, 219–259.

Spotti, M. (2013) 'The making of the superdiverse: an exploration of being/doing an asylum seeker'. Paper presented at the Language and Superdiversity conference, University of Jyväskylä, Finland, June 5, 2013.

Van der Aa, J. (2012) *Ethnographic Monitoring: Language, Narrative and Voice in a Caribbean Classroom.* PhD dissertation, Tilburg University.

Van der Aa, J. & Blommaert, J. (2011) 'Ethnographic monitoring: Hymes' unfinished business in education'. *Anthropology and Education Quarterly* 42(4), 319–344.

Velghe, F. (2011) 'Lessons in textspeak from Sexy Chick: supervernacular literacy in South African – Instant and Text Messaging'. *Tilburg Papers in Culture Studies* 1. www.tilburguniversity.edu/research/institutes-and-research-groups/babylon/tpcs.

Vertovec, S. (2007) 'Super-diversity and its implications'. *Ethnic and Racial Studies* 29(6), 1024–1054.

Name Index

Abdelnour Nocera, J.L. 179
Agar, M. 98, 108, 109, 116
Alexander, N. 250
Althusser, L. 50
Andrews, J. 192
Androutsopoulos, J. 11, 145, 152, 157, 160
Appadurai, A. 7
Aronin, L. 122
Atherton, C. 112
Atkinson, P. 62, 64, 109
Auer, P. 143

Bakhtin, M. 49, 53, 56, 229
Bamberg, M. 38
Baynham, M. 9, 33, 36, 37
Benwell, B. 41
Berryman, M. 253
Bhatt, A. 196–7
Blackledge, A. 61, 197–8, 236
Bloch, C. 250
Blommaert, J. 8, 9, 62, 64, 69, 90, 91, 92, 97, 100, 101n, 112–13, 114, 194, 230, 263, 269
Bourdieu, P. 37–8, 51, 81, 203, 268
Bourhis, R. 176
Briggs, C. 195
Brown, K.D. 122, 124
Bucholtz, M. 2–3, 101n, 230, 232, 233
Busch, B. 53, 55
Butler, J. 50

Cameron, L. 90, 100
Campbell, E. 219
Campbell, S. 34
Canagarajah, S. 108
Candea, M. 74
Carranza, I. 33
Cavanagh, A. 175
Cenoz, J. 122–3

Chimbutane, F. 195
Clifford, J. 193
Clifford, M. 5, 196
Cohen, L. 62
Cohen, Y.A. 121
Compton, S. 95
Creese, A. 197–8, 209–11, 236
Cresswell, J.W. 62

Dagenais, D. 126
Dailey-O'Cain, J. 39, 41
Danet, B. 143
da Silva, E. 6–7
De Costa, P.I. 107
De Fina, A. 33, 34–5, 36
Deleuze, G. 168n
Derrida, J. 48, 51
Dixon, J. 37
Dong Jie 62, 64, 69, 194
Dressler, R.A.H. 97
Du Bois, J. 40–1
Duchêne, A. 6, 9, 77
Duff, P. 232
Duranti, A. 217
Durrheim, K. 37

Eisenhart, M. 203
Erickson, F. 63, 204, 239

Falzon, M. 74, 75
Farmer, D. 55
Finder, S. 115–16
Fischer, M.J. 5
Fischer-Rosenthal, W. 47
Fishman, J.A. 251–2
Fitzgerald, D. 75
Flyvbjerg, B. 65
Foley, D. 211
Foucault, M. 51, 52, 60, 67–8, 70, 106, 111

Name Index 273

Gal, S. 3–4
Galasinska, A. 33
Garfinkel, H. 49
Garvin, R. 126
Gee, J.P. 96, 101n
Geertz, C. 109, 110, 193, 203
Georgakopoulou, A. 38
Giampapa, F. 190–1
Giddens, A. 37, 106
Gilliam, L. 205
Goffman, E. 49, 95, 118
Gorter, D. 122–3
Gramsci, A. 51, 268
Green, J. 233
Greer, T. 234
Gregory, E. 190, 198–9
Guattari, F. 168n
Guillemin, M. 205
Gumperz, J. 1, 2, 3, 46, 52

Habermas, J. 106
Hage, G. 75
Hakim, C. 64
Hall, K. 2–3, 101n
Hammersley, M. 62, 64, 109
Hancké, B. 64
Hannerz, U. 73, 74
Haraway, D. 82
Harris, S. 55
Heller, M. 3–4, 6, 9, 63, 74, 76, 77, 177, 204, 236
Herring, S.C. 143, 149
Hine, C. 151, 173, 174, 176, 181
Hornberger, N.H. 98, 100, 251
Horolets, A. 33
Husserl, E. 50
Hymes, D. 1, 2, 3, 5, 11, 13, 50, 63, 69, 92, 203, 247, 250, 252, 253, 255, 260–1, 269, 270

Ilankuberan, A. 216, 221, 224
Irvine, J. 4

Jaffe, A. 232, 235
Jakobson, R. 49, 50
Johnson, N.B. 122, 123, 127
Jones, K. 48, 196, 197
Jonsson, C. 191
Joppke, C. 61
Jørgensen, J.N. 236, 261

Kakuru, D. 226
Källkvist, M. 96, 99
Kendrick, M. 226

Kennedy, H. 149
Khan, K. 60
Khan, M.A. 124–5
Kinginger, C. 65–6, 66–7, 70
Kozinets, R.V. 150, 180
Kramsch, C. 48, 234, 240
Krashen, S. 114
Kresova, N. 33
Kress, G. 122, 135
Kytölä, S. 157, 160–1

Labov, W. 35, 42
Lam, E. 144
Lamarre, P. 74
Lamarre, S. 74
Landry, R. 176
Lane, P. 95
Larsen-Freeman, D. 90, 100
Lassiter, L.E. 219
Lather, P. 111, 112
Lee, C. 143, 148
Lemke, J. 91, 93
Leopold, W.F. 47
Leppänen, S. 143
Lexander, K.V. 145
Liebscher, G. 39, 41
Lin, A. 107
Literat, I. 220
Lyotard, J-F. 46
Lytra, V. 198–9

Madison, D.S. 110–11, 116
Makoni, S. 5
Mann, B.L. 179
Maranhão, T. 39
Marcus, G.E. 5, 73, 74, 81
Markham, A.N. 181
Martin, D. 199
Martin-Jones, M. 8, 125, 196–7
Maryns, K. 34
Mason, J. 76
Merleau-Ponty, M. 50, 52
Merriam, S.B. 64
Mpendukana, S. 6
Muir, S. 81–2
Murchison, J.M. 14, 69
Murphy, M. 36, 37–8, 38
Myers-Scotton, C. 143

Ndayipfukamiye, L. 194
Nikula, T. 126
Nishida (Japanese philosopher) 94
Norton, B. 48
Nussbaum, M. 112

274 *Name Index*

Ó Laiore, M. 122

Pahl, K. 217
Paolillo, J.C. 142
Pariser, E. 182
Patai, D. 204
Pennycook, A. 5, 123
Pietikäinen, S. 97, 100, 125, 216, 220
Piller, I. 40
Pillow, W. 204
Pitkänen- Huhta, A. 126

Ramanathan, V. 105, 107–8
Rampton, B. 10, 203
Relaño Pastor, A.M. 33, 36, 38
Ricento, T. 108
Roberts, C. 34, 232
Roman, L.G. 109
Ronjat, J. 47
Rosenthal, G. 50
Rowsell, J. 217
Ruby, M. 190
Ruiz, R. 106

Sacks, H. 41
Sanchez, L. 113–15
Sapir, E. 111
Scollon, R. 89, 91, 92–8, 97, 99,
    101n, 122, 127, 135
Sebba, M. 232–3
Sheller, M. 82
Siebenhaar, B. 143
Silverstein, M. 267
Singer, R. 55
Slembrouck, S. 233
Spotti, M. 262
Stanley, P. 108
Stokoe, E. 41

Stroud, D. 6
Sveningsson, M. 175

Takahashi, K. 40
Takhi, J. 207–8
Tay-Lim, J. 220
Temple, B. 192
Teutsch- Dwyer, M. 65–6, 66–7, 70
Thomas, G. 64, 67, 69
Thomas, J. 110
Thomas, W.I. 46–7
Tódor, E.-M. 131–4
Tollefson, J.W. 106–7
Tracy, S.J. 66, 67, 70

Urry, J. 82

Vakser, S. 12
Van Leeuwen, T. 122, 135
Vertovec, S. 8, 151, 167, 229,
    240, 259
Vigouroux, C.B. 232
Vološinov, V.N. 49

Waldinger, R.D. 75
Warschauer, M. 143
Weedon, C. 230
Whorf, B. 111
Wong Scollon, S. 89, 91, 92–8, 97, 99,
    101n, 122, 127, 135
Woolard, K.A. 3–4
Wortham, S. 35

Xiang, B. 75

Yin, R. 64, 65, 67, 68

Znaniecki, F. 46–7

Subject Index

academic writing genre 108, 111
action research 56, 117–18, 253
advertising 6
affordances: case study methods 15; classroom layouts 96–7; narrative 36, 41; online communication 19, 145, 150, 157, 161, 163, 167–8; team ethnography 203, 226
African American Vernacular English (AAVE) 161
Afrikaans 250
agency: children's 217–18, 226; and determinism 111; and the historical body 94–5; life story research 38; and migration 36–7; of minority communities 108; policy implementation 117–18; right to speak 128; semiotic construction 101; social media 168; system versus individual 117; visual methods of data collection 125–6
anthropology 2–3, 99, 270
applied linguistics 48, 90–1
Arabic 66, 178, 265–7
arrival stories 180
asylum seekers 34; see also migration
audio-recording 12, 99, 125, 127, 132, 193, 195, 197, 230, 265; see also transcription
Australia 229–41
'authentic' group membership 235
autobiographical narratives 33, 204
auto-ethnography 111, 148, 150

Basque 122–3
Belgium 262–70
belonging 15, 33, 46–7, 217
bias, researcher 109, 116–18; see also researcher positionality; subjectivity

bilingual education 113–16, 205–6
billboard advertising 6
biographical approaches to research 46–59
biographical narrative 33; see also autobiographical narratives; life stories
blogging 156, 163
bottom-up multilingualism 173, 179–81
boundaries of languages 5, 46, 53, 123, 173, 189–90, 236
British citizenship 60, 61
buffalaxing 165
Burundi 194

Canada 9, 39, 48, 55, 74, 190–1
Cantonese 142, 143–4, 149–50, 236; see also Chinese
Cape Town 55
capitalism 6–7, 78–9
case study methods (ethnographically-informed) 11–12, 60–70, 144–50, 218, 229
children's literacy practices 215–26
Chinese 66, 143–4, 148, 149–50, 172, 236
citizenship case study 60–5, 68–9
classroom layouts 96–7, 127
co-construction: of knowledge 38, 107, 108, 110–11, 216, 217–18, 241, 268, 269; of narratives 33, 34, 127
code switching 51, 143–4
codification of languages online 142, 172, 173
collaborative working 14, 69, 196–9, 203, 216, 219, 226, 241, 253–4, 261
colloquial language 160–2
competence, multilingual 53, 168, 235; see also linguistic repertoires
competition, ideologies of 80

276   Subject Index

complementary/heritage schools 4, 201n, 205–6
complexity 90, 100–1, 259, 261, 266–7
computer-mediated communication (CMC) 142, 157
computer-mediated discourse (CMD) 155, 157
conative functions of language 50–1
confessional tales 105
connective ethnography 151
consumption, globalised discourses of 6
contextualisation 2, 33, 61, 66, 68, 69; *see also* sociocultural contexts
Conversation Analysis (CA) 50, 144, 238
conversationalist approaches 109, 143
corporate websites 176–9
counter-cultures 128
'counter-discourses' 111
'critical,' use of the term 105–13
critical discourse analysis (CDA) 13, 91, 98, 112–13, 122
critical ethnography 3–4, 10, 12, 105–20, 191, 252–5
critical language awareness 126, 136
critical language policy research 105–8
critical perspectives, development of 3–5, 13
critical reflexivity 107
critical social theory 106
crowdsourcing 173, 179, 180, 182
cultural capital 81
cultural studies 159

data analysis methods: intertwined with data collection 180; online communication 146, 150; photographic data 132–3; of vignettes 211
deconstruction 51
deficit-oriented beliefs about multilingualism 113, 115, 116, 117
dialects 76–7, 191, 248, 251
dialogic research processes 47–8, 49, 196, 200, 241
diary studies 47–8, 125, 147, 180, 193, 196–7
digital technologies 6–7, 10; *see also* online communication; social media
diglossia 77
discourse: classroom discourse 4, 194; discourse-in-interaction 3; discourse in place 96–8, 99–101; discursive flows 97–9, 100

discourse analysis 4, 6, 11–12, 33, 92–4, 100
discourse-centered online ethnography (DCOE) 11, 145, 157–8
dominant discourses 108, 111, 113, 116, 177
'draw and talk' method 219
drawings 125, 219, 220, 221–2
Dutch 265–7

eclecticism, principled 92
ecology, language 90, 173, 248–50, 251, search
Educational Language Policy Engagement and Action Research (ELPEAR) 117–18
educational linguistics 89–104, 121–38
email communication 143–4
emancipatory perspectives 107, 110
emic perspectives 48, 91, 124, 125, 126–34, 198; *see also* participatory methods; researcher positionality
emoticons 150, 162
emotional language 36–7, 199
English: British varieties 129–31; in field notes 194; on Flickr 147, 151; footballer's use of Twitter 160–3; on gateway sites 178–9; Hungarian schoolscapes 128–30; ideologies of 79, 177; as lingua franca 179; new vernacular forms 8; online communication 143, 149–50, 157, 172; in the Philippines 248–9; as prestige language 125; religious activities 221, 222–3; Russianness in Melbourne case study 230, 231; shredding 165–6; in South Africa 249–50, 254; in team ethnographies 206; transcriptions 234, 236
entextualization processes 34, 155, 158, 160–3, 232
epistemology; biographical research 49–51; epistemic solidarity 22, 117, 261, 269; epistemological shift 1, 17, 73, 189, 199; and field notes 194; and language planning research 107; refocusing of 'object' and 'site' 73–4; *see also* researcher positionality
erasure practices 127
ESOL (English for Speakers of Other Languages) 60
Estonian 124, 178

Subject Index 277

ethics: and critical ethnography 110;
ethnographic monitoring 13,
247–56, 259–70; and language
planning research 107; questioning
105; team ethnography 212; virtual
ethnography 175–6
ethnographic monitoring 13,
247–56, 259–70
ethnographic research: biographical
research 47–8; confessional tales
105; convergence with discourse
studies 157; ethnographically-
informed case studies 11–12, 60–70,
144–50, 218, 229; foundations of
2–3, 10; innovative methodologies
11–12; multi-sited ethnographic
research 11, 73–86; narrative analysis
32–4; naturally occurring data 34;
nexus analysis methods 91–8; and
poststructuralist perspectives 5; and
social action 12–14, 247–56, 259–70;
text production methods 193–9;
virtual ethnography 172–85
ethnography of communication 2,
3, 10, 99
ethnography of speaking 2
ethnomethodology 49
eventualization 67–8
everyday practices 15, 32, 34–5,
46, 69
expressive functions of language 50
extended observations 123, 124, 191–2

Facebook 150, 157, 172, 174–5,
179–81
faith settings 198–9, 215–26
feminist research 46, 48, 51, 112, 189
field descriptions 193
field narratives 198–9, 219
field notes 12, 99, 132, 174, 180, 193–9,
212, 265
Filipino 248–9
'filter bubble' 182
Finland 97–8, 125, 160–3, 164–7, 252
Finnish 126, 143, 160–3
first-person perspectives 50, 52–3
Flickr 145, 147–8, 150–1
'fly on the wall' perspectives 109
footballers' use of Twitter (case
study) 160–3
'footing' 118
formal versus informal learning 126
French 9, 48, 65, 74, 78–9, 194, 254

gateway websites 177–8
gaze, researchers' 11; *see also* researcher
positionality
gender 33
generalizability 67
genre 35, 36, 108, 111
geosemiotics 122
German (language) 16, 39–41, 75–80
German sociological tradition
47, 48, 50
globalisation: critical sociolinguistics
157; development of sociolinguistic
research 6–12; digital media 6–7;
and increased complexity 259; of the
internet 141; narrative analysis 32;
political economy 6–7
Google 172, 180–1, 182
graffiti 128
Gujarati 196–7

heritage maintenance 4, 21, 132–3,
229–30, 240
heritage schools/complementary schools
4, 201n, 205–6
heteroglossia 46–7, 49, 53, 56, 122, 157,
229, 236
high-involvement genres 35
Hindi 178
Hinduism 220–6
historical body discourse in social action
93, 94–5, 96, 98, 100–1
historical dimensions of research 4–5
historicity 91
homogenization 127
Hong Kong 18, 143–4, 146–7, 148–50
Hungarian schoolscapes 126–34
hybridity 5, 32, 166, 173, 232, 239–40

identity: children's literacy practices
216–18, 220, 225; insider identities
190–1; late modern identities 32; life
stories 38; markers of 77; membership
categorization 39–41, 42, 215, 224,
235; migrant and transnational
contexts 32–3; and narrative analysis
35–6, 40–1; negotiating identities
in the field 190–2; as performance
41; performativity 41; polyphonic
identities 32; positioning 39–41, 42;
researcher's own 150–1; Russianness
in Melbourne 229–30; virtual
identities 10; *see also* researcher
positionality

278   *Subject Index*

ideologies, language; biological
  approaches 52–3; critical discourse
  analysis (CDA) 112–13; discourses of
  ideological space 100; discriminatory
  248–50; language ideology work 4;
  and linguistic border-crossing 78–9,
  83; linguistic landscape approaches
  177; researcher's own 77, 107–8;
  and schoolscapes 121–38; and
  social action 97; as social
  practices 108; *see also* language
  policies; languages, boundaries of;
  monolingual paradigms
'in-between' spaces and migration 33;
Indigenous communities 247–56; *see also*
  heritage maintenance
inequality 1, 13, 107, 117, 156, 173, 247–56
innovative methodologies
  (overview) 11–12
insider identities 190–1
Instagram 157
instant messaging (IM) 145, 146–7, 150
institutions 34–5, 107
'intellectual tourism' 109
interaction orders 95–6, 99, 100–1, 122
interactional approaches: biographical
  research 49–50, 52; interactional
  sociolinguistics 2–3, 98, 99, 141;
  narratives as interactional 33; and
  nexus analysis 91
interdisciplinary work: biographical
  research 55; educational linguistics
  89–90, 98; investigating change
  and complexity 260; multi-sited
  ethnographic research 82–3; new
  conceptual compasses 9; visual
  dimensions of communication 10
'internationalisation programmes' 7–8
internet 6; *see also* online
  communication; social media
interpreters 192, 265–7, 269
interpretive research approaches
  12, 49, 64
intersectionality 8, 191
intersubjectivity 50, 95–6, 232–3
intertextuality 100, 174
interviews (research method):
  biographical research 48–9, 51;
  with children 219; conducted online
  147, 148; as 'inauthentic' data 39;
  language of 132; narrative analysis
  34; as narrative elicitation devices
  35–41; online communication 146–7,
  149–50, 151; open-ended interviews

35–6; as part of case studies 66; with
  photographs 125, 132; role of the
  interviewer 38; technobiographies
  149–50; tourist guide technique 126–7;
  transcripts 193, 195
intralinguistic variety 160
introspective data 99
Irish 19, 177, 179–81
isiZulu 254–5
Isthmus Zapotec 251
Italian 16, 35, 75–80, 191

Japanese 40, 234

Kiruundi 194
knowledge: and academic writing
  111–12; co-construction 38, 107,
  108, 110–11, 216, 217–18, 241,
  268, 269; holding knowledge
  versus making knowledge 81; new
  conceptual compasses 8–11; online
  communication 155; polyphonic
  ethnography 5, 196–7

language crossing 51
language ideologies *see* ideologies,
  language
language industries, rise of 6–7
language policies 97, 105–20, 177, 179,
  248–50, 254–5
language portraits 49, 54–6
language of researcher: biographical
  research 51; reflexivity 194; student
  mobility in Switzerland project 77, 82;
  team ethnography 198, 205–6, 207,
  208–9, 211; transcriptions 230, 235, 239
language revitalization 124, 125, 177
languages, boundaries of 5, 46, 53, 123,
  173, 189–90, 236
late modernity 1, 6, 32, 73, 156, 165, 167;
  see also superdiversity
layered simultaneity 91, 98
Life in the UK (LUK) test 60
life stories 38; *see also* biographical
  approaches to research
lingua francas 8, 179
Linguistic Anthropology 50, 91, 98
linguistic capital 78, 81
linguistic landscape approaches 10, 100,
  121–38, 176–9, 263, 268
linguistic repertoires: biographical
  research 46, 52–6; and concepts
  of multilingualism 2, 5, 189–90;
  heteroglossia 49, 53, 56; semiotic

Subject Index 279

repertoires 190; and speech communities 52; transcriptions 230, 235–6
literacy 10
lived experience of multilingualism 48, 49, 50, 52–3, 61, 94–5, 220
localisation 173, 177–8
lurking (online) 174, 176

Mandarin 143, 236; *see also* Chinese
markedness models 143
marketing surveys 142
meaning-making practices; multimodality 7; multisemioticity 158; online communication 158–9; participatory convergence 159; schoolscapes 124; semiotization 91; social actions 92; social media 168; storytelling as 32; unequal multilingualisms 250–1; visual semiotics 122; *see also* knowledge
memory 50–1
metacommentary 12, 198
meta-methodologies 89, 98–100
metapragmatics 162
methodological innovations (overview) 11–12
metrolingualism 151
Mexico 251
micro-meso-macro distinction 101
migration: diaspora 7, 8, 10; as emerging research area 7–8; narrative analysis 31–42; Russianness in Melbourne case study 229–41; single participant case study 60–70; superdiversity 259; transcultural flows 156, 159, 160, 163, 229
minority languages 177
mixed/multi-method approaches 20, 89, 132, 145, 149, 152, 157–8, 173, 216, 219, 226
mobile resources, sociolinguistics of 9
mobile technologies 7
mobility/mobilities: and emergent research methods 263–4; multi-sited ethnographic research 74–83; and narrative analysis techniques 32–3; as recurrent theme 9; social media 156, 163; spatial/ temporal orientation in narrative 37–8; and virtual ethnography 174
mocking 162–3, 164
monolingual paradigms 46, 47, 115, 132–3, 182, 229

monologic web 175–6
mother-tongue-based education 248–9
Mozambique 195
multidimensionality 66, 90, 91–8, 155, 156, 166, 167
multidisciplinary teams 206; *see also* interdisciplinary work
'multilingual internet' 142
multilingual repertoires *see* linguistic repertoires
multi-method studies 20, 89, 132, 145, 149, 152, 157–8, 173, 216, 219, 226
multimodality: biographical research 49, 53–6; children's literacy practices 217; computer-mediated discourse (CMD) 157; innovative methodologies 12; instant messaging (IM) 146–7; interplay between multimodality and multilingualism 10; meaning-making practices increasingly multimodal 7; online communication 158; scrapbooks 219–20; visual dimensions of communication 122, 125, 135–6
multiscriptal practices 145, 146–8, 216, 226, 232–3, 234–5, 236
multisemioticity 10, 158, 159–67, 216, 220
multi-sited ethnographic research 11, 73–86, 99, 124–5, 133, 167, 174, 203, 206
multivocality 66
music videos 163–7

narrative: biographical research 48–9; co-construction of 33, 34, 127; history of narrative analysis 31; migrant and transnational contexts 31–42; narrative analysis 12, 31–45; naturally occurring data 34; as social practices 33; technobiographies 149; time in the study of language practices 9; vignettes 193, 198, 203–12
nation states and languages 4, 97, 123, 124, 127, 128–9, 131–4, 235–6
'native speakers' 234–5
naturalistic ethnographic research 108–9, 181
naturally occurring data 34
negative portrayals of research subjects 116, 117
neo-classical approaches 106
neo-liberalism 80
neo-Marxism 106
'network society' 259
New Literacy Studies 122

280　*Subject Index*

nexus analysis methods 11, 91–104, 167
non-standard varieties 149, 160, 162, 232–3
normativity 52–3
norms 95–6, 99, 247

objectivist epistemologies 108, 109, 110, 264
observation 99, 123, 124, 146, 149, 174, 176, 191–2; *see also* participant observation
online communication: communities of practice 10–11; connecting with offline 157; discourse-centered online ethnography (DCOE) 11–12, 145, 157–8; ethics 175–6; innovative methodologies 11; linguistic landscape approaches 123; longitudinal studies 151; methodologies for researching 141–54; migrant and transnational contexts 33; multisemioticity 155–71; narrative analysis 33; not simply a carry-over of face-to-face practices 141; social media 141, 145–50, 155–71, 172–6, 179–81; texts versus practices 141; 'too much data' problem 148; virtual ethnography 172–85; visual dimensions of communication 10, 135
open-ended discourse 162, 163, 167, 168
open-ended interviews 35–6
orthography 232–3
Other, the 37–8, 107, 259

Pakistan 124–5
Panjabi 20, 206, 207–8
panopticon classrooms 127, 128
para-linguistic features 99, 230–2, 237–40
participant observation: ethnographically informed case studies 144; ethnographic monitoring 263, 264, 269; ethnography not limited to 12, 248; multi-sited ethnographic research 81–2; narrative analysis 34; online communication 174, 181; in team ethnographies 197
participant profiles 147
participation frameworks 118
participatory methods 51, 253, 260, 269; *see also* action research; ethnographic monitoring
Peru 251
phatic functions 49

phenomenological tradition 47, 50, 52–3
Philippines 22, 247, 248–9
photographs 55, 124, 125–6, 132, 148, 219, 220
policies, language 97, 105–20, 177, 179, 248–50, 254–5
polycentric normativities 168
polyhedron of intelligibility 60, 67–70
polylingualism 151, 236
polymorphism 32, 68, 69
polyphonic ethnography 196–9
polyphonic identities 32
portraits, language 49, 54–6
positionality *see* researcher positionality
positivism 108, 109
postcolonialism 5, 32, 46, 48, 51, 189, 247, 250, 253
post-critical ethnography 110
post-Freudian thinking 50
post-Marxist thinking 50
postmodernism 106, 111–13, 116, 189
post-positivism 109
poststructuralist perspectives 3–5, 9, 13, 32, 48, 50–1, 52, 106, 111–13
power: biographical research 46, 48, 50, 51–2, 56; and critical research 109, 110, 111, 112, 116–17; and discourse 111; focus on sociocultural contexts of language 106; language policy discourses 106, 107, 116, 117; and linguistic determinism 111; and narrative 32, 34; and participant voices 69; and researcher objectivity 109, 110; research subjects in the context of 116; and transcription 232; unequal multilingualisms 247–56
practice-oriented research 31–2
pragmatics 36, 217
prestige languages 80, 124, 125
presuppositions 33, 34, 38
problem-centered inquiry 98
prosumers 155, 159, 164, 168
public surveys 142

quantitative methods 122–3, 142
Quechua 251
questionnaires 132, 148, 149

race and ethnicity 34
radicalism 112
reconstruction, understanding through 49, 50
recontextualisation 225

Subject Index 281

reflexivity: by children 220; critical reflexivity 107; criticisms of 204–6; innovative methodologies 12; and the poststructural turn 5; reflexive ethnographic research practice 189–200; of researcher 70, 150; researcher vignettes 204–5, 206–11; self-reflection 107; shift towards greater 5, 12; strategic reflexivity 212; team ethnography 203; technobiographies 149; in transcription 233, 241
refugees 7–8
relativism 252
relevancy of discourse, establishing 99–100
religious beliefs 198–9, 215–26
repertoires, linguistic *see* linguistic repertoires
reported speech 36–7
research design, importance of 62–5
Research Group Spracherleben [Lived Experience of Language] 53–4
research 'with' versus research 'on' 218, 253; *see also* collaborative working; participatory methods
researcher in residence 261–3
researcher positionality: boundaries 191; children as researchers 219; and critical ethnography 109–10; detached involvement 109; ethnographic monitoring 261; indexed by different linguistic resources 195; and language planning research 107–8; objectivity 110–11; online communication 181; revealed via vignettes 198; role of the researcher 13, 38; Russianness in Melbourne case study 230; stance 40–1, 42, 49, 150–1; subjectivity in critical ethnography 112, 116–18; team ethnography 204, 206–11, 215–26; third-person perspective (of researcher) 49; and transcription 230, 232–3; and transcriptions 232–3, 236–40
researcher-researched relationships: co-construction 241; co-construction of knowledge 107; false distinction 269–70; negotiating identities 190–2; participation frameworks 118; power asymmetry 51, 69; shifting of 48, 110–11
researcher vignettes *see* vignettes
resemiotization 155, 158, 160–7

responsive methodologies 146, 147, 179–80, 253
rhizomaticity 158, 162, 163
rich points 98, 100
Romanian 132–3
Russian 21, 124, 229–41

Sámi 125, 252
Sanskrit 220–3, 226
scales/scalar ethnography 9, 11, 89–104, 114
scenes/spaces of research versus sites 82
schoolscapes 10, 121–38
scrapbooks 216, 219–26
screen recording 149
screenshotting 174, 175, 178
second language acquisition 47–8
second-person perspectives 50–1
self-reflection 107
semilingualism, critique of 115
semiotics: linguistic landscape approaches 121–38, 176–7; migrant and transnational contexts 33; multisemioticity 10, 158, 159–67, 216, 220; resemiotization 155, 158, 160–7; and scales 91; semiotic repertoires 190; symbolic capital 78; and transcription 240; visual semiotics 122
shredding 159, 163–7
single participant case studies 65–6
situated practices 3, 9, 151, 217; *see also* lived experience of multilingualism
small stories 39–40
snowballing 146
social action: digitally mediated 155; and ethnographic monitoring 248, 252–5, 260; and ethnography generally 12–14; historical body discourse in social action 93, 94–5, 96, 98, 100–1; in nexus analysis 92–8, 100–1; and postmodernism 111–12
social capital 207, 211
social categories 4
social constructionism 2, 90
social geography 90
social justice 107, 108, 110, 247
social media 141, 145–50, 155–71, 172–6, 179–81
social networks 8
social practices 33, 121, 232–3
social scales 89–91
social units 4

282 *Subject Index*

sociocultural contexts: and interaction orders 96; linguistic data divorced from 106; online communication 155–6; research teams 196–9, 203, 208–9, 211, 212, 218; and transcription 231
sociolinguistics, shifting epistemologies of 2–5, 12
sociology 46–7
South Africa 6, 55, 249–50, 254
space: expansion of spatio-temporal horizon in research 9–10; 'in-between' spaces and migration 33; interaction orders in nexus analysis 95–6; multi-sited ethnographic research 73–86; online communication 174; and scales 91, 101; spatial/temporal orientation in narrative 37–8
Spanish 36, 115, 123, 142, 148, 150, 191, 251
speech communities 52, 106, 152
stance 40–1, 42, 49, 150–1
standard varieties 129–31, 160
storytelling 31–4
structuralist approaches 106, 260, 267
subjectivity 50–1, 52, 68, 110, 232–3, 236–40; *see also* researcher positionality
subversiveness 112, 113, 133–4
supercentral languages 174, 178
superdiversity 8, 151, 155, 167–8, 229, 240, 259–60, 264, 267–9
Swedish 97–8, 160–3, 191
Switzerland 75–86
symbolic capital 78
symbolic interactionism 49
syncretic literacy practices 217–18, 223–4

Tamil Hindu/Saiva 198, 216, 218, 220–6
T'boli 248–9
team ethnography 196–9, 203–12, 218–26, 236
technobiographies 148–50
technoscapes, changing 7
tellability 42
text messaging/SMS 145
texts versus practices 141, 142–3, 144, 145
theory, concepts of 268–9
thick description 193, 203
Ticino-dialect 76–7
time: runaway world 175; and scales 91, 101; spatial/temporal orientation in narrative 37–8, 42

top-down multilingualism 173, 179–81
'topic-oriented' research 11
total linguistic fact 267
tourist guide technique 126–7
trajectory, as conceptual compass 9
transcription 12, 193–9, 229–41
transcultural flows 156, 159, 160, 163, 229
transdisciplinary work *see* interdisciplinary work
transferability 66–7, 70
transgressive practices 128, 159, 165
translanguaging 151, 236
translations 192, 197, 233–6, 265
Translations app 174–5, 179, 180–1
translocal practices 155, 156, 158, 166
transnational population flows 7–8, 31–42; *see also* migration
traversal concepts 175
triangulation 5
Twitter 157, 160–3, 168

units of analysis 61, 62, 63, 64, 65, 70
universities as sites of research 75–86
urban neighbourhoods 8, 10
Urdu 124–5
user communities 173

validity practices 111–12
vertical versus horizontal slicing of data 150
video-recording 12, 99, 193, 219
Vienna 12, 53, 55
vignettes 193, 198, 203–12, 248–52, 254–5, 265–7
virtual ethnography 11, 151, 172–85
virtual identities 10
visual dimensions of communication; biographical research 53–6; expansion of sociolinguistic research 10; innovative methodologies 12; linguistic landscape approaches 121–38, 176–7; online communication 158; research with children 220, 222, 226; in transcriptions 235; visual data collection methods 125, 220, 222, 226; visual literacy 122; visual semiotics 122; *see also* drawings; photographs
voice, participants'; children's literacy practices 219–20, 226; versus collaborative critical analysis 69; ethnographic monitoring 270; and transcription 233–40; in vignettes 211, 212; and visual data collection 125–6; *see also* emic perspectives

Subject Index   283

voice, researchers' *see* researcher
    positionality
Võro 124

walking tour methodology 126
ways of thinking 93, 96–7, 100, 101n
Web 2.0 148–50, 156, 157

web forums 162–3
Wikipedia 172
workplace literacies 196
written communication 143;
    see also multiscriptal practices

YouTube 156, 157, 163–7

Taylor & Francis eBooks

Helping you to choose the right eBooks for your Library

Add Routledge titles to your library's digital collection today. Taylor and Francis ebooks contains over 50,000 titles in the Humanities, Social Sciences, Behavioural Sciences, Built Environment and Law.

Choose from a range of subject packages or create your own!

Benefits for you
- Free MARC records
- COUNTER-compliant usage statistics
- Flexible purchase and pricing options
- All titles DRM-free.

Benefits for your user
- Off-site, anytime access via Athens or referring URL
- Print or copy pages or chapters
- Full content search
- Bookmark, highlight and annotate text
- Access to thousands of pages of quality research at the click of a button.

REQUEST YOUR FREE INSTITUTIONAL TRIAL TODAY | **Free Trials Available** We offer free trials to qualifying academic, corporate and government customers.

eCollections – Choose from over 30 subject eCollections, including:

Archaeology	Language Learning
Architecture	Law
Asian Studies	Literature
Business & Management	Media & Communication
Classical Studies	Middle East Studies
Construction	Music
Creative & Media Arts	Philosophy
Criminology & Criminal Justice	Planning
Economics	Politics
Education	Psychology & Mental Health
Energy	Religion
Engineering	Security
English Language & Linguistics	Social Work
Environment & Sustainability	Sociology
Geography	Sport
Health Studies	Theatre & Performance
History	Tourism, Hospitality & Events

For more information, pricing enquiries or to order a free trial, please contact your local sales team: www.tandfebooks.com/page/sales

Routledge Taylor & Francis Group | The home of Routledge books

www.tandfebooks.com